CHEKHOV

ANTON CHEKHOV (1904) WITH HIS TWO DOGS
IN YALTA

CHEKHOV

A Life by

DAVID MAGARSHACK

GREENWOOD PRESS, PUBLISHERS
WESTPORT, CONNECTICUT

CONTENTS

7

ILLUSTRATIONS

Illustrations

NOTE

All the quotations from Russian sources in this
book have been translated by the author. All the
dates, unless otherwise stated, are according to
the Old Style used by Chekhov. The translitera-
tion of Russian names follows the generally
accepted phonetic rules even in the case of names
which have acquired a more or less fixed spelling
taken over from the French or the German, i.e.,
Chaykovsky instead of Tchaikovsky or
Tschaikowsky, Rakhmaninov instead of Rach-
maninov, etc. Names of a non-Russian origin
are spelt in accordance with their original
spelling, i.e., Schechtel, Schwoerer, etc.

Part One

CHILDHOOD AND SCHOOLDAYS

Anton Chekhov is perhaps one of the most baffling figures in Russian literature. His popularity, which was only rivalled in his lifetime by that of Tolstoy, did not bring him closer to his contemporaries; on the contrary, it seemed to widen the gulf between him and his reading public which admired him for the things he himself thought least of all admirable in his writings. As a playwright, he found himself misunderstood and misinterpreted by both his producers and his audiences. He remained a complete enigma even to the members of his own family to whom he was deeply attached but whom he never took into his confidence. His 'I' was the most sacred thing to him, and he did not allow anyone, as he intimated in a letter to his eldest brother Alexander, 'to poke his nose' into things that concerned it. He remained a lonely figure even in the heyday of his fame when his study was crowded with writers and visitors who flocked to pay homage to his genius. Not even his wife, who during the last three years of his life released the deep fount of tenderness and affection in him, was able to break through the impenetrable wall which he had erected between himself and the outside world.

The key to the mystery of Chekhov's personality must be sought not only in his unhappy childhood but also in his attempts to conceal his grave illness, the nature of which became only too clear to him as early as 1884, from his family and friends. The first seeds of his almost unnatural reserve, however, were certainly sown very early in his life. In the many statements about his childhood that can be found scattered in his letters and even in his stories, it is always the 'despotism' of his father that forms the chief cause of unhappiness. 'I ask you to remember that despotism and lies have ruined your mother's youth,' he wrote to Alexander on January 2nd, 1889. 'Despotism and lies so disfigured our childhood that it makes me sick and horrified to think of it. Remember the disgust and horror we felt every time father made a scene at dinner because there was too much salt in the soup or called mother a fool.' And only a few days later he wrote the famous passage in the letter to Alexey Suvorin: 'Could you write a story about a young man, the son of a serf, a one time shop assistant, choir boy, schoolboy and university student, brought up to fawn on rank, kiss the hands of priests, accept without questioning other people's ideas, express his gratitude for every morsel of bread he eats, a young man who has been frequently whipped, who goes to give lessons without goloshes, engages in street fights, tortures animals, loves to go to his rich relations for dinner, behaves hypocritically towards God and man without the slightest excuse but only because he is conscious of his own worthlessness—could you write a story of how this young man squeezes the slave out of himself drop by drop, and how, on waking up one morning, he feels that the blood coursing through his veins is real blood and not the blood of a slave?' Again, in another reference to his childhood on March 7th of the same year to Vladimir Tikhonov, the editor of a Petersburg periodical, he wrote: 'Thank you for your kind word and your warm sympathy. As a little boy, I was treated with so little kindness that now, having grown up, I accept kindness as something unusual, something of which I have had little experience. That is why I should like to be kind to people, but don't know how: I have grown callous and lazy, though I realise very well that people like us cannot possibly carry on without kindness.' Three years later he wrote to Suvorin: 'When, as a child, I was given a religious education and made to read the lesson at church or sing in the church choir, and the whole congregation gazed admiringly at me, I felt like a little convict, and now I have no religion. Generally speaking, so-called religious education can never do without, as it were, a little screen behind which no stranger is allowed to peep. Behind that screen the children are tortured, but in front of it people smile and feel deeply moved. It is not for nothing that many divinity students become atheists.' In another letter the same year to his friend and fellow writer, Ivan Leontyev, he declared: 'When I recall my childhood now, I cannot help thinking of it as something very gloomy. I have no religion now. You know, when my two elder brothers and myself used to stand in the middle of the church and sing a trio . . . the congregation was touched and envied my parents, but at the same time we felt like little convicts.'

In his story *Three Years*, published at the beginning of January 1895, that is to say, when Chekhov was already a grown-up man of thirty-five, there occurs the following autobiographical passage: 'I remember father began to teach me, or, to put it more plainly, whip me, when I was only five years old. He whipped me, boxed my ears, hit me over the head, and the first question I asked myself on awakening every morning was: will I be whipped again today? I was forbidden to play games or romp. I had to attend the morning and evening church

services, kiss the hands of priests and monks, read psalms at home. . . .
When I was eight years old, I had to mind the shop; I worked as an
ordinary errand boy, and that affected my health, for I was beaten
almost every day. Afterwards, when I was sent to a secondary school,
I studied till dinner, but from dinner till the evening I had to sit in the
same shop. . . .'

That is exactly what Chekhov himself had to do and how he was
treated by his father, whose continual whippings left what one of his
friends called 'a scar on his soul'. Nemirovich-Danchenko, an old
friend of his and one of the directors of the Moscow Art Theatre,
records him as having remarked one day: 'Do you know, I can never
forgive my father for having whipped me as a child.'

Chekhov's first references to his unhappy childhood occur only
after he had become a famous writer. In a letter to his cousin Michael,
the manager of a big Moscow wholesale drapery business, written at
the age of seventeen (on July 29th, 1877) while he was finishing his
secondary school in Taganrog, no references to his sufferings as a
child are made and no indication is given of his resentment of his
father's 'despotism'. On the contrary, Chekhov was deeply conscious
at the time, and later, too, for that matter, of the great debt he owed to
his father for having given him a better education than he had had
himself. 'When you see my father,' Chekhov wrote, 'tell him that I
have received his dear letter and that I am very grateful to him. He
and mother are the only people in the world for whom I shall never be
sorry to do anything I can. If I ever achieve a great position in the
world, I shall owe it entirely to them. They are good people and their
great love for their children puts them above all praise, makes good all
the faults they may have acquired in the course of a hard life and
prepares that quiet haven for them in which they believe and on
which they pin their hopes as only few people do.'

The process of Chekhov's spiritual emancipation, gradual though
it was, began very early. The story of Chekhov as a little boy refusing
to believe that a school-friend of his was never birched has been told
many times. It certainly shows how completely Chekhov was 'a
slave' of his harsh environment; but the shock of the discovery of the
existence of a more decent and humaner mode of life must have contributed the first impulse towards the war he so consistently waged
against every manifestation of inhumanity in man. Indeed, what dis-
tinguished Chekhov from his two elder brothers, Alexander and
Nicholas, whose revolt against their father took the grosser form of
drunkenness, was his courage and his sense of independence. Many

years later Alexander recalled in a letter to Chekhov an incident of their childhood which provides a perfect illustration of that. 'I remember', Alexander wrote, 'the first manifestation of your independent character and my first realisation that my influence over you as your older brother had begun to disappear. . . . To make you submit to my authority again, I hit you over the head with a tin. . . . You left the shop and went home to father. I was expecting a good whipping, but a few hours later you walked majestically past our shop on some errand and deliberately did not even glance in my direction. I followed you with my eyes for a long time and—I don't know why myself—burst out crying.'

It was not only his hurt vanity that made Alexander cry; it was the realisation of Chekhov's superiority over him. Chekhov's reaction against the grim realities of his life took more and more the form of a complete withdrawal within himself, and, by falling back upon himself, he slowly evolved that deep-seated respect for the human personality which he later summarised in a letter to his uncle Mitrofan in one phrase: 'People must never be humiliated—that is the main thing.'

2

Chekhov was born on January 16th, 1860 (Chekhov's name-day, that is, his christening, was on January 17th, and as in Russia it is the name-day and not the birthday that is celebrated, a confusion has sometimes arisen about the exact date of his birth, some biographers giving it as January 17th). His grandfather, Yegor Mikhailovich Chekh (the surname of Chekhov the family assumed after they had left their native village of Olkhovatka in the Voronezh province), was a serf of General Chertkhov, a rich landowner and the father of one of Tolstoy's most devoted disciples. Yegor was a very religious man, somewhat of an eccentric, and, as Chekhov characterised him, 'a most rabid upholder of serfdom'. He was also a most able estate manager, and by the time his children had grown up he had saved up enough money to buy his freedom and that of his wife and three sons for 3,500 roubles, an enormous sum in those days. His savings, however, were not enough to buy the freedom of his only daughter and he asked Chertkhov not to sell her until he had saved up another 700 roubles. 'Never mind,' said Chertkhov, 'I'll throw her in.'

Yegor Chekhov fulfilled his ambition of giving his sons a better social position than that of freed serfs by apprenticing his eldest son

PAVEL
CHEKHOV

YEVGENIA
CHEKHOV

Michael to a bookbinder in Kaluga, his second son Pavel, Chekhov's father, to one of the richest shopkeepers in Taganrog, the mayor of the town at the time, and his youngest son Mitrofan to another wealthy shopkeeper in Rostov. Pavel went through the hard and humiliating training which was usual among shop-assistants in those days when shops were open from five o'clock in the morning till eleven o'clock at night, and when beatings, bad meals, doubtful business morals and constant fawning on the customers were the accepted rules among the mercantile community. 'Father', Chekhov recalls in a letter to Alexander on October 13th, 1888, 'used to smile at his customers even when the Swiss cheese in the shop made him feel sick.' He was a badly educated and foolish man; 'a mediocrity, a man of little ability', as Chekhov·described him in a letter to Suvorin. But he made up for it by his quite extraordinary selfishness and vanity which bordered on megalomania. He liked to hear himself talk, and used to deliver himself of such profundities as: 'Why is the snow lying here and not there?' or 'Why do trees grow here and not there?' He loved to read aloud, and he was especially fond of magazine love stories; but he rarely listened to what he was reading and very often he had to stop and ask his wife to pick up the threads of the story for him. He was extremely vain of his appearance and never went out into the street without a top hat and a spotlessly clean starched shirt. But what in a less selfish and more intelligent man would have been a great benefit to his children, namely his undoubted artistic talents, became with him merely an additional means for imposing his will upon them and making their lives miserable. He was an enthusiastic musician, being particularly addicted to church music. He taught himself to play the violin and fancied himself a fine choir master. He also taught himself to paint (an icon of his has been preserved and is now at the Chekhov Museum in Yalta). 'Singing and violin playing', Michael, his youngest son, records, 'he considered his real vocation in life. To satisfy that passion of his, he organised a choir composed of his children and townspeople, and he gave concerts at home and in public, often forgetting to look after his business, and that, it seems, was later the cause of his financial ruin.' His choir, according to Alexander, was a real curse to his sons, and especially to Chekhov. 'Poor Anton,' Alexander writes, 'who was still a small boy with an undeveloped chest, a thin voice and a rather poor ear for music, had an awful time of it. He often cried bitterly during the choir practice which went on till the late hours and which deprived him of the sleep which was so necessary to his health. Father was meticulously punctual, strict and exacting about everything that had to do with church services. If his choir had to sing at morning mass during the high festivals, he would wake his children at two or three o'clock in the morning and go to church with them regardless of the weather. His children had to work hard on Sundays and holidays as well as on weekdays. . . . Father was as hard as flint, and it was quite useless to try to make him change his mind. Besides, he was a passionate lover of church music and could not live without it.' In a letter to Alexander in February 1883 Chekhov used the same expression about his father. 'He is just like an old believer,' he wrote, 'as hard as flint, and you won't be able to make him budge an inch.'

But in addition to the church services, Pavel organised special services at home. 'Every Saturday', Alexander writes, 'the whole family would go to evening mass, and, on returning from church, spend many hours singing sacred music. Incense burnt in the censer, father or one of his sons read the lesson, after which we all sang in chorus a short motet or anthem. In the morning we went to early mass, after which we had some more singing at home.'

'Father', Michael records, 'loved to say his prayers, but he was really interested in the outer forms of religion rather than in its inner content. In church he used to stand from the beginning to the end of the service, and at home he played the part of the priest. [He would actually dress up as a priest and he was displeased when his wife, who stayed behind in Taganrog for some time after his flight from his creditors, sold his chasubles to buy food.] But in everything else he was as much an unbeliever as ourselves and was entirely preoccupied with worldly affairs. . . For many years he took an active part in the local elections, and he never missed a single public dinner or celebration.'

It was Pavel's formalistic approach to religion that caused bad blood between him and Father Pokrovsky, the chief priest of the Taganrog cathedral, where he would regularly sing with his choir. He did not hesitate to prompt Pokrovsky during the services if he thought they were not conducted strictly in accordance with ecclesiastical rules. Pokrovsky, a fine-looking man with a sonorous baritone voice (he had trained as an opera singer in his youth), naturally resented Pavel's interference. He grew to dislike him so much that he could not stand even his children; and as he was the scripture master at the secondary school to which the three elder boys eventually went, he never looked at them as he called them out to say their lessons, but just gave them three out of the five marks, that is, satisfactory instead of good or excellent. One day he had a violent quarrel with Chekhov's mother during which he told her that no good would come of any of her sons, except perhaps the eldest one. Chekhov himself was only a small boy at the time, but it had worried him so much that he still dreamt of it many years afterwards. 'When I feel cold', he wrote to the novelist Grigorovich in February 1887, 'I always dream of a venerable and learned canon of a cathedral who insulted my mother when I was a boy.'

It was Pokrovsky who nicknamed Chekhov Antosha Chekhonte, which nickname Chekhov adopted as his pseudonym when he began publishing his stories in the Moscow and Petersburg humorous magazines.

Pavel married Yevgenia Yakovlevna Morozov on October 28th, 1854. She was only nineteen at the time. Chekhov's mother belonged to the merchant class. She was the daughter of a cloth merchant, who used to travel all over Russia on business, leaving his wife with his son and two daughters in Shuya, a small town in Central Russia. During one of those journeys he died of cholera in Novocherkask, a city which is not very far distant from Taganrog. Yevgenia's first recollection as a child was travelling with her mother and sister across Russia to Novocherkask, a perilous journey in those days which provided the travellers with many hair-raising adventures, which she often used to relate to her children. They settled in Taganrog, while Yevgenia's brother Ivan was apprenticed to the same shopkeeper in Rostov as Pavel's younger brother Mitrofan. When eventually Mitrofan returned to Taganrog, where he married and opened a small shop of his own, Ivan joined him there, and it was in that way that Pavel first met his future wife. (Yevgenia's brother Ivan and her sister Feodossya, incidentally, both died of consumption, and it would seem that the T.B. strain was passed on to Chekhov and his brother Nicholas through his maternal relatives.)

Chekhov used to say that he and his brothers got their talents from their father and their 'soul' from their mother, and, like all generalisations of that kind, it is only partly true. For along with his father's artistic propensities Chekhov also inherited a great deal of his harshness and stubbornness, and it was his mother who said (as quoted by Chekhov in a letter to his cousin Michael in January 1877) that he possessed 'an inborn and inveterate spite'. So far as his mother is concerned, Chekhov seems certainly to have inherited her deeply sensitive nature as well as her horror of any kind of coercion. She was a very gentle creature, barely educated, and given, as so many gentle creatures are, to quiet and persistent nagging. A fierce opponent of serfdom, she used to tell her children of the unspeakable cruelties inflicted on the serfs by their owners and, in Michael's words, 'inspired in us a love and respect for all who were less fortunate than ourselves'.

Chekhov's eldest brother Alexander was born on August 10th, 1855, during the Crimean War, and almost on the first day of the bombardment of Taganrog by the Anglo-French fleet. Two years later Pavel achieved his ambition and opened his first shop for the sale of groceries and all sorts of other articles, including quack medicines and alcoholic drinks. His family lived at the time in a two-storied house on the outskirts of the town. In this house Chekhov's second brother Nicholas was born in May 1858. He was to be Pavel's chief music assistant, becoming quite proficient at the violin and the piano. His real vocation, however, was art, and he later became a very talented painter. By the time Chekhov was born Pavel had risen in the social scale and became a registered merchant of the third guild. Taganrog was then a town of over thirty thousand inhabitants, mostly artisans and stevedores (it had only about five hundred registered 'merchants'). Its chief trade consisted of the export of corn, but its importance as a port was already beginning to decline owing to the silting up of its shallow roadstead. It boasted a fine cathedral, about a dozen churches, a customs house, a boys' and a girls' secondary school, a few banks, a hospital, a courthouse, a prison, a public library and a theatre. Its central streets were paved and lined with trees. It had two large squares, both near the Chekhov house, in one of which a scaffold with a black post for the flogging of prisoners was regularly erected. The flogging could be watched from the windows of the house and it must have been one of the things Chekhov himself watched as a child. Chekhov's mother used to be very sorry for the prisoners and she kept crossing herself while they were receiving their punishment. At night the streets of the town were not safe, especially for young girls, who were never allowed to leave their houses unescorted, as they might be kidnapped and taken across the Black Sea to Turkey and there sold to the harems. Michael recalls one such kidnapping. He had gone out with the nursemaid to meet his mother one night when he saw a young girl walking on the other side of the street. Suddenly a carriage drew up, two men jumped out, caught hold of the screaming girl and dragged her into the carriage which immediately drove off at high speed. Michael was frightened, but his old nurse merely remarked, 'Good gracious, another girl kidnapped!' and took him back home.

Chekhov was born one year before the liberation of the serfs, but he could have remembered very little of the great upsurge of liberalism which the agrarian reforms of Alexander II produced throughout the country. He would, anyhow, have found little sympathy for it in its own patriarchal home. By the time he went to school no vestige of liberal ideas remained in Russian public life, and the Russian government did its utmost to prevent any such ideas from spreading to the schools.

As for the Russian literary scene, the year of Chekhov's birth saw the split among the contributors of Nekrassov's progressive *Contemporary Review*, as a result of which Turgenev, Tolstoy, Goncharov and Grigorovich, the four great novelists of the period, left the journal. The split occurred because Nekrassov refused to accept Turgenev's ultimatum not to publish a review of *On the Eve* by the critic Dubrolyubov who expressed the view that Russian Insarovs would soon appear to fight for the liberation of Russia from the oppressors of the people. A year earlier Goncharov had finished his famous novel *Oblomov*. Tolstoy had just begun working on *War and Peace*, which began appearing five years later. In addition to *On the Eve*, Turgenev had two more novels to his credit, namely *Rudin* and *A Nobleman's Nest*, but he had still to write *Fathers and Sons*, which was published two years later. Dostoevsky had only just been permitted to return to Petersburg after his imprisonment and exile to Siberia, and the novel in which he was to describe his experiences there, *The House of the Dead*, was to be published a year later in 1861, while *Crime and Punishment* was only to appear six years later. The great Russian satirist Saltykov-Shchedrin, who was to influence Chekhov so greatly during the first years of his career as a writer, had only three years before won fame with his first collection of satirical stories, *Provincial Sketches*.

Russian literature, and especially the Russian novel, had therefore still a large number of masterpieces to come at the time Chekhov was born, though by the time he finished school in 1879 most of them had been written.

When Chekhov was five and ready to be subjected to his father's rigorous discipline, he had two more brothers and one sister: Ivan, the only 'steady' and uninspired member of the family, who was to become a schoolmaster, was born in 1861; Mary, who was also to become a schoolteacher as well as an artist, was born in 1863; and lastly, Michael, future civil servant, journalist, writer of children's stories and Chekhov's biographer, was born in 1865. The family was now complete.

3

Nothing perhaps shows up Pavel's quixotic folly as much as his decision to send his three elder sons to the Greek school at the Church of St. Constantine. At the end of August 1888 Chekhov complained to Suvorin of having grown up, studied and begun writing 'in an environment in which money played a disgustingly large part'. He never could, in fact, rid himself of the influence of that early environment, and all his life he pursued, as unsuccessfully as his father, the mirage of sudden riches, investing in state lottery tickets, trying his luck at the roulette table and, at the very end of his life, selling his works for what seemed to him at the time an enormous sum of money only to discover all too soon that it was just another vain dream. In 1867 Pavel had been in business on his own for ten years and yet his chances of becoming a rich man were as remote as ever. He had to think of some way of giving his children a better chance of becoming prosperous business men than he had had himself. As the only prosperous men in Taganrog were the Greek merchants, it seemed only logical to him that by giving his children a Greek education he would set them on the road to wealth. He intended to send them to Athens University later to complete their education, after which they would return to Taganrog as the equals, if not the betters, of the richest Greeks in town. The whole thing was really very simple, and his Greek cronies, with whom he discussed it over a glass of vodka in his shop, could find no fault with it. It was true, his wife, to his amazement, objected to it very strongly, but, then, she obviously did not know what she was talking about.

Chekhov himself left very little material about his experiences at the Greek school. He mentions it twice in two short biographical sketches he sent to correspondents, in one of which (to his Greek translator) he adds the information that he learnt to talk modern Greek there which, however, he soon forgot after leaving school. He also refers to it ironically as one of the 'delights' they shared together as children in the letter he wrote to Nicholas in March 1886. Though only a boy of seven at the time, Chekhov had become so used to beatings at home that the even grosser brutalities of Vuchina, the teacher at the Greek school, did not shock him any more. Besides, the whole incident of the Greek school did not last long. Pavel at last agreed to examine his three sons in the presence of some of his Greek cronies, and the result of the examination convinced him that he would have to give up his dream of Athens and brilliant business careers for his sons and let them go to the local secondary school to prepare themselves for professional careers. Pavel had the true peasant's respect for a uniform, and to see his children in the official garb of a teacher or a civil servant was almost as pleasing to him as to see them wallowing in riches. When Alexander, after obtaining his degree in mathematics at Moscow University, got a job as a customs official in Taganrog, Chekhov wrote to him in May 1883: 'Father tells everybody that you have a wonderful job. When tipsy, he talks of nothing else except your uniform. Please, describe your uniform to him, and add at least one account of how you stood in the cathedral among the great ones of this world.' When three years later Ivan became a teacher, Chekhov wrote to one of his cousins: 'Father is very happy: Ivan has bought himself a cap with a cockade and ordered a schoolmaster's frockcoat with bright brass buttons.' Again, four years later, when Michael, having graduated from the law faculty of Moscow university, became a tax assessor, Chekhov wrote to Suvorin in December 1890: 'Michael has had a civil service uniform of the sixth class made for him and tomorrow he is going to pay visits in it. Father gazes at him with tears of admiration in his eyes.'

Chekhov was admitted to the preparatory class of the Taganrog secondary school in 1868 and passed into the first class on October 2nd, 1869. The classics were in fashion in those days and he had to take both Latin and Greek. The Russian state schools had eight classes in all, but Chekhov spent ten years at his school, having failed in his annual examinations at the end of the third and the fifth forms. Unfortunately, he very early showed quite an exceptional knack for using the calculating frame and that seemed to his father an excellent reason for keeping him at the till in the shop till the late hours, with disastrous results to his progress at school. 'You've been wasting your time long enough,' Pavel, according to Alexander, used to say to Chekhov. 'You'd better go to the shop and keep an eye on things there. Learn the business!' And Alexander adds: 'Anton had tearfully to give up what was appropriate and indeed necessary for a child of his age and go to the shop which he loathed. In it he somehow or other managed to do his homework and in it he froze during the bitterly cold winter nights.'

However, if Chekhov had little time to himself during the school term, he had enough and to spare during the long summer holidays which usually lasted for over three months. During their holidays the boys ran about barefoot and slept in their own 'huts' in the garden. When he was in the fifth form Chekhov used to sleep under a vine he had planted, calling himself 'Job under his fig tree'. He had his own dovecote and pigeons, of which he was a great connoisseur. The boys got up very early, and Chekhov loved to go to the market for his mother, where he spent a long time round the bird cages, appraising the points of the different varieties of pigeons and songbirds, as though in anticipation of the time when, left to fend for himself in Taganrog while finishing his school, he would catch goldfinches himself and take them to the market to sell. One day, Michael records, Chekhov bought a duck in the market and kept pulling at its feathers on the way home to make it quack. 'Let them all know', he said to Ivan and Michael, 'that we're having duck for dinner today!'

Every day the boys went to the sea to bathe. Chekhov had two black dogs which he usually took with him. They bathed on a big stretch of sand, where they had to walk for half a mile before getting to deep water in the tideless Azov Sea. Later in the day they went fishing to another part of the beach near the harbour, where the sea bed was strewn with sharp stones. One day Chekhov dived into the sea from the mole and cut his head just above the forehead. The cut was a deep one and left a scar which was later even noted on his passport as one of his 'special peculiarities'. Only once did the whole family (except the father, who was for once left to mind the shop) leave Taganrog for the country on a visit to Pavel's father, who was manager of the estate of Count Platov, the son of one of the famous Cossack generals in the war against Napoleon. This trip to the country is described in great detail by Michael, and it certainly shows that at the age of thirteen (as he then was) Chekhov was a very happy child, full of fun and mischief.

Chekhov visited his grandfather again after his family had gone to live in Moscow. Describing one of his visits to Suvorin on August 29th, 1888, he wrote: 'As a boy, while living with my grandfather on the estate of Count Platov, I used to sit from sunrise to sunset by the steam threshing machine, writing down the pounds and hundred-weights of threshed corn; the whistles, the hissing and the low droning emitted by the threshing machine when going at full speed, the creaking of the wheels of the oxcarts, the lazy movements of the oxen, the clouds of dust, the black, perspiring faces of the men—all that has become engraved on my memory like "Our Father. . . ." The steam threshing machine, when at work, seems to be alive; it has a cunning, playful expression; it is the people and the oxen who seem to be machines.'

In his story *The Beauties*, published in Suvorin's paper *New Times* in September 1888, Chekhov recounts another incident which occurred while he stayed at his grandfather's. Chekhov and his grandfather, according to the story, paid a visit to an Armenian village near

Rostov. They stopped at the house of an Armenian farmer, where Chekhov for the first time in his life came across a girl of so striking a beauty that he fell instantaneously under its spell. 'I saw', Chekhov writes, 'the ravishing features of one of the most beautiful faces I have ever seen in my life. A real beauty stood before me and I understood it at the first glance as I understand a flash of lightning.' The young Armenian girl was most likely the same girl Chekhov told Suvorin many years later he had fallen in love with at first sight. According to Suvorin, Chekhov had been standing by a well looking at the reflection of his face in the water. This narcissistic contemplation (Chekhov was a very handsome young boy) was interrupted by the sudden arrival of a girl of fifteen who came to fetch some water. Chekhov was so spellbound by her beauty that he put his arm round her and began kissing her. Then the two of them stood for a long time by the well, silently contemplating their faces in the water. He did not want to go away and she seemed to have forgotten all about the pail of water she had come to fetch. . . .

At the time of that meeting by the well Chekhov was far from a novice in love. Indeed, his sexual experience had begun very early. In a short biographical sketch he sent to Vladimir Tikhonov in February 1892 he wrote: 'I was initiated into the secret of love at the age of thirteen.' Michael relates that when Chekhov was in the seventh and eighth forms he had many love affairs, which, in Chekhov's words, 'were always happy and gay'. Michael goes on: 'When he was already a student, he would often nudge me, who was a schoolboy at the time, and, pointing to a girl who happened to be passing in the street, say to me, "Quick, run after her! A girl like that is a real find for a seventh-form schoolboy!" ' It was during one of his visits to the country in the summer that Chekhov caught a chill while bathing in a cold stream which developed into his first serious illness. The exact year when it occurred is difficult to establish. In a letter to the poet Pleshcheyev, written in February 1888, Chekhov states that it took place in 1877; but it could not possibly have taken place then, for by that time his family was already in Moscow and Michael seems to have a most vivid recollection of it while he was still in Taganrog. It probably happened in the summer of 1876 (Michael gives the date as 1875, but that, too, must be wrong, for in that year Chekhov went on a visit to Count Platov's estate with his family). Chekhov had been invited by the brother of Selivanov, a lodger in Chekhov's house, to spend a few weeks at his country estate near Taganrog. It was during his stay there that he caught his chill. Selivanov's brother decided to drive him back home, but Chekhov was so ill that they had to stop for the night at a Jewish wayside inn. 'In 1877', Chekhov wrote to Pleshcheyev, 'I fell ill with peritonitis while travelling in the country and spent a night at the inn of Moissey Moisseyevich. All through the night they were busy with mustard poultices and compresses.' The wayside inn, its Jewish landlord and his wife and brother Solomon Chekhov later immortalised in his story *Steppe*. 'Antosha was brought home dangerously ill,' Michael writes. 'I can still see him looking pale, haggard and thin. Beside him sits our school doctor Schrempf, who starts every sentence in a strong German accent with the words: "Antosha, if you want to get well . . ." Mother, who looks very worried, is heating linseed in a frying-pan for the poultices and grating almonds for a drink, while I keep running to the chemist's for pills. This', Michael concludes, 'was Anton's first serious illness, and he was convinced that it was mainly responsible for the haemorrhoids from which he suffered all his life.'

It was during this illness that Chekhov first thought of taking up medicine as a career. He got very friendly with Dr. Schrempf, who had studied medicine at Dorpat university, and the doctor's stories of Dorpat made him wish to go there, too, to study medicine.

4

If the idea of medicine as his future career occurred to Chekhov while he was still at school, literature was certainly not the career he ever thought of in those early days in Taganrog. He is known to have contributed a few items to two issues of his school magazine, one of them a little satiric poem on the second master Dyakonov, a strict disciplinarian whom Chekhov heartily disliked, and two short sketches *A Scene from Nature* and *From the Life of a Divinity Student*, none of which has been preserved. Of his school essays only one is still extant. Its subject is *Kirghizes*, and it must have been written very early, probably when Chekhov was a boy of only twelve or thirteen. It is remarkable for its concise and matter-of-fact style, and seems to indicate a strong reaction from the high-flown epistolary style affected by his grandfather as well as by his father and his uncle Mitrofan, a style he satirised in his first published story *A Letter to a Learned Neighbour*.

It was the theatre and acting that Chekhov showed a great passion for as a schoolboy. 'A long time ago', Chekhov wrote to Suvorin in April 1893, 'I used to act very well.' He began acting at home in little sketches of his own invention. 'He was a real master at representing or imitating any event he had seen in town, at his school or at a party,' his sister Mary records, 'and when he imitated the comical traits of one of our friends we all split our sides with laughter.' As some of his recorded sketches show, Chekhov used his histrionic gifts, partly at least, to get his own back on his father. One of his sketches, for instance, represented a bishop examining an old village deacon. 'Stretching out his neck till the veins stood out,' Michael writes, 'which made it look uncommonly like the neck of an old man, and changing the expression of his face so that it was hard to recognise him, Anton, who played the deacon, sang all the responses in the traditional "eight voices" before his eldest brother, who played the bishop. His thin, faltering voice of an old decrepit village deacon would grow suddenly breathless with panic, he would make mistakes, but, finally, was deemed worthy of the bishop's phrase: "I proclaim thee a deacon".'

In his other sketches Chekhov represented the Governor of Taganrog attending the celebration of the Czar's birthday, standing in the middle of the cathedral on a rug among the foreign consuls, or an important civil servant dancing the quadrille at a ball, or a monk from the Mount Athos monastery, or a professor giving a lecture on some abstruse subject (he later wrote a one-act monologue on the same theme), or a dentist extracting a tooth. In the last sketch he would arm himself with a pair of coal tongs, extract the 'tooth', usually a cork, from Alexander's mouth after a great deal of 'business', and then display it triumphantly to his audience, which by that time was roaring with laughter. This sketch, too, he later used for one of his most famous early stories—*Surgery*.

But his real talent as an actor Chekhov was to show only after he had become a regular visitor at the Taganrog theatre. His mother first took him to the theatre in 1873 to see Offenbach's operetta *Fair Helen*. His mother had a seat in the stalls, while Chekhov and his two elder brothers went to the gallery. Here again Chekhov could not resist the temptation to get his own back on his father. Instead of shouting for the actors after the last fall of the curtain, he shouted the names of the rich Greek merchants who sat in the stalls near his mother and in that way expressed his contempt for the wealthy Greek citizens of the town on whom Pavel constantly fawned. ('Father', Chekhov wrote to Alexander in October 1888, 'used to write begging letters to Mrs. Alferaki.' Mrs. Alferaki was the wife of one of the wealthiest Greeks in Taganrog, and one of Pavel's letters, couched in the most fulsome terms, has been preserved. In it he begged 'her excellency' to take his second son Nicholas under her personal protection and help him to enter the Petersburg Academy of Arts. He justified his request on the ground that his son had sung 'at the Palace Church when you prayed there with such fervour'. His request, needless to say, was ignored.)

Having tasted the joys of a real stage performance, Chekhov was no longer satisfied with merely acting in short sketches. He soon organised an amateur performance of Gogol's comedy *The Government Inspector*, in which he took the part of the mayor. This performance was given in Chekhov's house, but the subsequent performances of Russian classical plays, including Ostrovsky's *The Forest* and two melodramas, took place in the large drawing-room of the house of one of Chekhov's schoolmates.

It was, however, after his family had left Taganrog and he was freed from the drudgery of his father's shop and church services that the theatre began to play a really important part in his life. He became very friendly with a number of actors, including the comic actor Solovtsov, for whom he later wrote his one-act comedy *The Bear*, and quite often appeared on the stage himself. He became very good at making up (he later claimed that make-up helped him to overcome his stage fright), and, as schoolboys even of the higher forms were not allowed to go to the theatre without special permission, he would some-times disguise himself before venturing to enter the theatre. It was in this way that he gained a first-hand knowledge of the stage. Soon he felt himself sufficiently competent to try his hand at writing plays him-self. From a letter Alexander wrote to him in October 1878 it appears that he had actually written no less than three plays during his last years at school: a full-length drama under the title *Without Fathers*, a comedy *Laugh It Off If You Can*, and a one-act farce *Diamond Cuts Diamond*. Unfortunately, he deferred too much to Alexander's literary judgment at the time and, as a consequence, none of these plays has been preserved.

5

The financial catastrophe which overtook Pavel in 1876 was largely of his own making. Four years earlier his father had presented him with a small plot of land in Taganrog on which to build a house. His shop was still a going concern at the time, in spite of his neglect of it, and he himself had risen in the social scale by becoming a merchant of the second guild. The prospect of becoming a house-owner raised his ambitions, but unfortunately it also awakened his native peasant guile. He thought of a plan of saving a great deal of money on the building of his house by paying a certain sum of money for every thousand bricks used instead of a lump sum for the whole job. But his builder Mironov got the better of him in the end: he built the walls twice the ordinary thickness, which not only took up much of the space of the rooms, but also ran up the price of the house by 500 roubles. Pavel was forced to raise the additional money from a local bank, the loan being guaranteed by a certain Kostenko.

The family moved into the house in 1874. It had four tiny rooms, and a basement which was let to Feodossya Dolzhenko, the widowed sister of Chekhov's mother who had a little boy by the name of Alyosha. There was a tiny cottage in the yard which was let to another widow who had a son, who was to become Chekhov's first pupil, and a daughter Iraida, with whom Chekhov conducted what Michael describes as 'a curious sort of love affair'. The two used to quarrel and exchange insulting remarks. 'One Sunday', Michael records, 'Iraida came out all dressed up for church and wearing a new straw hat. Anton was at the time putting charcoal in the *samovar*. As she passed by, he made some joke about her hat and she pouted and called him a yokel. Anton picked up the empty sack and hit her over the head with it, smothering her in a cloud of coaldust.' It was to Iraida that Chekhov addressed his first four lines of doggerel in reply to some sentimental verses she had chalked on the fence, advising her to go and play with her dolls instead of writing poetry. During his visit to Taganrog twelve years later he met Iraida again. She had by that time buried her mother and her first husband and, as Chekhov put it, was about to marry a second time 'out of grief'.

Meanwhile Pavel's affairs were going from bad to worse. He could no longer pay his dues to the merchant guilds and reverted to the despised 'artisan' class. He had not only failed to repay his loan to the bank, but could no longer afford to pay the interest on it. The bank was forced to demand the money from Kostenko, who took out a writ against Pavel. As defaulters were in those days sent to prison, Pavel decided to run away to Moscow, where his two elder sons had been studying for the past year—Alexander at the physics and mathematics faculty of Moscow University and Nicholas at the Moscow School of Painting, Sculpture and Architecture. To make sure that he was not recognised and arrested on the station, he took the train at the first stop beyond Taganrog.

The disappearance of Pavel did not, of course, pacify his creditors. The problem that now faced Chekhov's mother was how to save something from the general wreck. At that point Selivanov, their old lodger who claimed to be a friend of the family, came on the scene. Selivanov was an official of the county court, who, as Michael writes, 'used to play cards for high stakes at the club and in ten years amassed enough money to keep his own horses and buy a large estate'. But from the way he treated the Chekhovs it is safe to assume that he had other sources of income which were even more lucrative than his gambling gains. Selivanov promised Chekhov's mother to save the house for her family by paying Pavel's debt to Kostenko. 'I shall do it', he told Chekhov, 'for your mother and sister.' What he did, however, was to secure the house for himself by some piece of legal trickery merely by paying five hundred roubles to Kostenko, who immediately took out a court order for the sale of the furniture in payment of the interest on his loan. Thus at one blow the ruin of Chekhov's family was consummated. There was nothing more to keep Chekhov's distracted mother in Taganrog, and, leaving Chekhov and his brother Ivan in occupation of the house till the arrival of its new owner, she left for Moscow at the end of July 1876, with Mary, who was thirteen at the time, and Michael, who was eleven.

Chekhov had to stay in Taganrog for another three years before he could obtain his matriculation certificate. It was then that Selivanov came to his help by proposing that in return for his board and lodging he should coach his nephew, Peter Kravtsov, for his entrance examination to a military school. Chekhov began helping his family almost immediately, both financially by sending them what little money he could spare and morally by his letters which, as Michael puts it, 'were full of humour and comfort'. Not that his family, and least of all his mother, were in a mood to enjoy his jokes. 'We have received two letters from you,' his mother wrote to him shortly after her arrival in Moscow, 'and they were all full of jokes, while we had only four copecks to buy bread and candles, and we were expecting to get some money from you, and we are in a terrible plight here, and you don't believe us, and Mary has no winter coat and I have no warm shoes, and we sit at home. . . .'

The family found shelter in a dark basement in one of the worst slums in Moscow (they changed their quarters twelve times before Chekhov joined them in 1879). They all slept on the floor in one room, covered with blankets and overcoats. In winter they froze because they could not afford to buy logs, and two of Nicholas's friends used to go out at night and steal some planks which they sawed up for fuel. Pavel could not get a job for a long time, but the calamities which had befallen him brought about no perceptible change in his character. One night he pinned a set of rules on the wall in which the duties of each member of the family were carefully enumerated. The first morning these 'Rules and Regulations of the domestic Duties of the Family of Pavel Chekhov, resident in Moscow' appeared, Michael got up later than he should have done and was given a whipping by his father. When he pointed out that he did not know anything about the rules as he was asleep when they were pinned up on the wall, Pavel replied: 'You should have known about them.' After Ivan, who was a boy of seventeen, joined his family in Moscow, he, too, committed some offence. Pavel took him out into the yard and whipped him so mercilessly that the neighbours came running at his cries and the landlord threatened to give them notice.

Chekhov had kept in touch with his two elder brothers ever since they had left for Moscow. He even edited an illustrated, humorous magazine for them under the title of *The Stammerer*, in which he described the latest happenings in Taganrog. In a letter to Alexander on March 9th, 1876, written in a schoolboy's German, Chekhov announced the dispatch of yet another number of *The Stammerer*. '*Ich schicke dir den* 'Stammerer'. *Lese und bewundere dich.*' Later that year Alexander acknowledged the receipt of two more numbers of the magazine, adding that they had produced a sensation in Gavrilov's wholesale warehouse, where their cousin Michael was employed. 'The last number even moved Ivan Gavrilov himself, merchant of the first guild, to pat me on the shoulder and say: "Ah, yes, young man!"'

After their family had gone to live in Moscow, Alexander sent Chekhov regular accounts of their life, mostly occupied with stories of their father's absurd escapades. What he did not tell him was that the little money he earned by journalism and placing stories in the Moscow humorous magazines he spent on drink. For both Alexander and Nicholas, as their mother wrote to Chekhov, were always 'going to parties', a euphemism for getting drunk she used in her letters again and again. It was clear to Chekhov that the money he sent his mother from time to time could not possibly be of any help to them. There was only one way in which they could be helped and that was for his father to obtain a job at Gavrilov's warehouse with the help of their cousin Michael. Chekhov was too young to realise that his cousin belonged to quite a different set of people who, as he wrote to Alexander in August 1888, had 'Chokhov and Mironov souls'. Gavrilov had nicknamed the Chekhovs Chokhovs, and that nickname later became to Chekhov a sort of symbol for a man whose whole life was devoted to the making of money. Between December 1876 and April 1878 Chekhov wrote ten letters to his cousin, all of them couched in the most extravagant terms of friendship. 'I press your hand', he declared in his first letter, 'with a feeling of pride and dignity as the hand of an elder brother.' He told his cousin in another letter that his mother put him on the same footing as his uncle Mitrofan, 'of whom', ·he wrote, 'I shall always speak well because of his kind heart, and his good, pure and cheerful character'. In a letter he wrote him 'exactly at midnight, December 31st, 1876', he told him that his pupil, Peter Kravtsov, had been letting off fireworks while he himself had been firing off his gun. He had just drunk his cousin's health in water instead of champagne, and as he fired his gun again he sent his cousin the following New Year's wishes: 'May all your troubles disperse like smoke with this shot and may happiness and prosperity take their place.' He had decided to go up to Moscow himself to try and see what could be done for his people there. 'I shall be in Moscow next Easter,' he wrote to his cousin in the same letter, 'but I am not sure whether it will be a mistake or not.'

Chekhov did visit Moscow for the first time during Easter week from March 20th to April 3rd, 1877. Moscow made a tremendous impression on him. 'I went to the Taganrog theatre the other day,' Chekhov wrote to his cousin on November 4th, 'and compared it with the Moscow theatre. What a difference! And there is also a great difference between Moscow and Taganrog. If I ever finish school, I shall come flying to Moscow on wings—I liked it so much.' He even liked the employees at Gavrilov's warehouse. For the first time in his life he realised how petty and insignificant the Taganrog shopkeepers and their assistants were in comparison. 'Give my regards to your friends,' he wrote to his cousin a little earlier. 'They are nice people, not at all like our petty Taganrog crowd, I mean the aristocracy among our shop assistants who turn up their noses because they live in a port.' One has only to recall Chekhov's description of the same Gavrilov employees, including his own cousin, in *Three Years* to realise how immature his judgment of men still was. But small as his knowledge of character may have been, his respect for man's dignity had during the six odd months he had lived on his own developed to such an extent that he could not help noticing the difference between him and Alexander, as the following incident which occurred during his Moscow visit shows. 'I remember', Alexander wrote to Chekhov in January 1886, 'how you and I were walking along Znamenka, I think (I am not quite sure). I was wearing a top hat and, being already a student, I did my best to impress you. I wanted to do something that would show you what a fine fellow I was. So I belched straight into the face of an old lady. But I'm afraid this did not produce the sort of impression I expected. My action disgusted you. You said to me with a note of reproach in your voice: "You're still as big an oaf as ever." I did not understand you then, and I took it as a compliment.'

That Alexander, a second-year student, should have considered being called a big oaf a compliment is a good illustration of the sort of environment in which Chekhov grew up. It must have also convinced Chekhov that he could not rely on Alexander to be of any help to their mother in her unequal struggle to keep their home together. 'Every day', she wrote to him on his return to Taganrog, 'I pray to God that you should come, but your father says that when Anton arrives, he, too, will go to parties and do nothing, while Fenichka [her sister Feodossya who had joined her in Moscow] argues with him and says that you are an industrious boy who prefers to sit at home, and I don't know which of them to believe. . . . Please, finish your school in Taganrog as quickly as possible and come at once, I haven't the patience to wait, and let it be the medical faculty, darling, we don't like Alexander's occupation, and send us our icons, and let me tell you again, Anton, my dear, that if you are industrious you will be sure to get something to do in Moscow and earn money. I just can't help feeling that when you come to Moscow things will be much better for me.'

'Alexander's occupation', which his parents did not like, was, of course, his work for the humorous journals which in a very short time were to provide Chekhov with the means of supporting his family. Already during his first visit to Moscow, Chekhov, casting around for something to augment his meagre income from lessons in Taganrog, took a great interest in his brother's work. He decided to try his hand at it himself and during 1877 and the following two years he sent his brother a number of small items of an anecdotal nature. Some of them Alexander was successful in placing in the Moscow magazines, but none of them has been traced. The only existing evidence of them is contained in a letter Alexander wrote to Chekhov on November 23rd, 1877. 'Your anecdotes will appear,' he wrote. 'I am sending by post two of your jokes to *The Alarm-Clock*. . . . The others are weak. Make them as brief and as funny as possible. Long ones are colourless.' It will be seen that Chekhov's entry into literature, unlike his work for

the theatre, was entirely fortuitous. Indeed, for a long time he looked
upon his writing merely as a way of earning a few desperately needed
roubles to support his family.

6

Chekhov did not show any outstanding ability at school. His marks
for Russian were uniformly good but never excellent. But an examination of Chekhov's early stories in their unrevised form reveals a
generally slapdash style which is astonishing when one considers what
a meticulous stylist he became later. Unlike Gorky, Chekhov was not
a born stylist: he had to work very hard before his prose became a
model of good writing.

The two years he had lost at school owing to his failure to pass the
annual examinations must have had a very depressing effect on a boy
who was as sensitive as he, not to mention the rows and beatings it
must have occasioned at home. His father became worried by his
being put down a year in the third form and decided that he ought to
learn some trade. That seems to be the only feasible explanation of his
being sent to a trade school to learn tailoring. But the only article of
clothing Chekhov ever sewed was a pair of grey trousers for Nicholas.
As narrow trousers were in fashion in those days, Nicholas kept
pestering Chekhov to make his trousers as narrow as possible. As a
result the trousers Chekhov produced were so narrow that Nicholas
could only just manage to wriggle into them. Chekhov at once nicknamed them macaroni-trousers, which remained a standing joke in
the family for a long time.

Chekhov is said to have been very reserved at school, but his reserve never made him into an unsociable boy. According to one of his
teachers, he used to amuse his classmates by reading funny stories to
them. 'Chekhov', he relates, 'used to dig up some very funny stories
from somewhere and read them to the whole class. I would often hear
homeric laughter in the classroom. That was Antosha amusing his
schoolmates by his stories, and every time I had to confiscate his book
as a punishment.'

His relations with his teachers were not as bad as one is sometimes
led to believe, though he certainly detested quite a few of them.
Michael records that during his last years at school he made friends
with several of his teachers. It is known, for instance, that Chekhov
took a fancy to the wife of his history master, a lady by the name of

Ariadne, who was as free with her husband's affections as she was with his money. It was she Chekhov had probably in mind in the story *Ariadne*. which he wrote in 1895. But the strict discipline and his constant dread of Latin and Greek made his life at school unhappy. 'I still dream of my school,' he wrote in 1886 to a fellow-writer; 'an unlearnt lesson and fear that the teacher might call me out.' A year later, in a letter to Grigorovich he wrote in February 1887, he complained of nightmares in which some of his teachers figured. 'When my blanket slips off my bed at night', he wrote, 'I usually dream of huge, slippery boulders, cold autumn water, bare banks of a river—all this rather indistinctly, as though through a mist, without a patch of blue sky; depressed and gloomy, as though I had been abandoned by the whole world or lost my way, I keep staring at the stones and I get the curious feeling that I must cross that deep river; at the same time I see tiny tugs hauling enormous barges, floating tree-trunks, rafts, etc. Everything is very grim, depressing and damp.... And when I start running away from the river, I come across crumbling cemetery gates, funeral processions, my former school teachers. ... It is then that I am filled with a peculiar nightmarish chill which is never experienced by people who are awake but only by those who are asleep. ...' The lumping together in his subconscious mind of funeral processions with his former school-teachers is interesting, as it seems to indicate his fear that some of his teachers, at any rate, could, if he got into their bad books, ruin his medical career long before he had embarked on it.

It is generally assumed that for his prototype of Belikov, the hero of his famous story *The Man in a Case*, first published in July 1898, Chekhov took Dyakonov, the second master of his school whose main subject was Russian literature (he also taught geography). It was Michael who first advanced this theory, and he was followed by several other critics and biographers. Chekhov mentions Dyakonov only three times in his correspondence, the longest reference being in a letter home during his visit to Taganrog in April 1887. 'Dyakonov is as thin as ever,' Chekhov wrote, 'thin as a viper, wears calico trousers, and a frying-pan instead of a cap.' Dyakonov, in fact, was as unlike Belikov as could be. According to a schoolfellow of Chekhov's, he was a little man who never seemed to grow old. He was very thin and agile. He took an active part in municipal affairs, being a member of the town council. He was very strict and was fond of lecturing young teachers. He had a dislike of 'liberals'. He was a rich man and left his houses to be converted into elementary schools and seventy thousand roubles as a special benevolent fund for elementary-school teachers. Chekhov must have known all these facts, which certainly do not tally with the character of Belikov.[1]

It is, however, remarkable how long the memory of his schooldays and, particularly, of his teachers lingered with Chekhov. For instance, the headmaster of Kulygin's school in *The Three Sisters*, published three years later than *The Man in a Case*, bears striking resemblance to E. P. Reitlinger, the headmaster of Chekhov's school. Reitlinger, too, liked to organise outings and concerts for teachers and pupils and was a great stickler for form. In a letter to Alexander in March 1876 Chekhov records that Reitlinger gave him a ticket to a concert of the famous violinist, Leopold Auer, which shows that he was on quite friendly terms with his headmaster.

Chekhov could not afford to fail in his examinations again during his last years at school. The very thought of it was so appalling that the month of May, when the annual examinations were usually held, was, as he wrote to his cousin Michael at the beginning of June 1877, 'the hottest time of the year' for him. 'I nearly went off my head because of these wretched exams,' he declared. 'I forgot all my pleasures and all the ties that bound me to this world during those days of constant worry and anxiety.' But he was glad to be able to announce that he had passed his examinations well; 'that is to say', he hastily corrected himself, 'I have passed into the seventh class'.

It was in the summer of 1877 that he was thinking of leaving Russia in two years' time and going to study medicine in Zürich. 'Goodbye,' he wrote in the same letter to his cousin. 'We shall not see each other again for the next seven years. Everything seems to point that way—and I may not have the chance for some time of travelling across Mother Russia to Mother Moscow and to my own darling mother.'

It is very likely that his recent visit to his family in Moscow had convinced him that unless he severed his ties with his family its demands on him would be so great that he would never be able to achieve his ambition of a medical career. Besides, having set his mind on becoming a doctor, he was determined to get the best possible medical training obtainable, and Zürich seemed to him the best possible place to get it in. Alexander, however, soon talked him out of

[1] As an entry in Chekhov's diary on August 18th, 1896, shows, his model for Belikov, the hero of *The Man in a Case*, was most probably the journalist M. O. Menshikov, who visited him at his country house in Melikhovo. Menshikov, Chekhov noted down, "wears goloshes even in dry weather, carries his umbrella as a precaution against sunstroke, is afraid to wash in cold water, and complains of palpitations."

ANTON
CHEKHOV
1875

ANTON CHEKHOV
1879–80

his plan of going abroad to study medicine by pointing out the difficulties he would have to overcome in familiarising himself with German sufficiently to be able to follow his lectures. Chekhov had always found the study of foreign languages an almost impossible task, although he had tried hard several times to learn French and German. His difficulty was mainly psychological: he had grown to hate swotting up Greek and Latin so much that he dreaded the task of learning any language.

With the beginning of the new school term he was again immersed in work—going to school, giving lessons in his spare time and, in the autumn, shooting goldfinches in order to sell those he only winged in the market. It was the sufferings of the little birds that eventually made him into a determined opponent of all bloodsports. These various activities kept him so busy that he could not keep up his correspondence with his cousin. 'I am well,' he wrote to Michael Chekhov in November 1877, 'and that means that I am alive. I have only one secret illness which torments me like an aching tooth—lack of money.'

But neither lack of money nor his dread of failing his examinations could deprive Chekhov of one of the most precious natural assets he possessed—his tremendous vitality and his ability to enjoy life under any circumstances. 'I love every kind of merry-making,' he wrote to his cousin in the same letter, 'and Russian merry-making especially with its folk-dances, its dancing and drinking.' He was very sorry not to have been able to be at the wedding of his cousin's sister, for, he assured Michael, he would most certainly have danced the *gopak* and drunk with him as he had done in Moscow. He had just sent two 'money packets' to his family, he added, and he could not understand why they did not get them. He also sent his regards to Alexander and promised to write him a letter in defence of polygamy. And he could not resist the temptation of playing a practical joke on Nicholas: he asked his cousin to arrange a fake rendezvous for the artist on one of the Moscow boulevards.

Hard as his life in Taganrog was, it had its compensations. His pupil Peter Kravtsov invited him to spend the summer at his father's farm in the Don basin. The country seat of the Kravtsovs consisted of a small thatched cottage and a few stone barns. The cottage had only three rooms with clay floors and crooked ceilings. The walls were hung with rifles, pistols, sabres and horsewhips. The window-sills, chests of drawers and tables were piled high with cartridges, tools for repairing guns, tins with gunpowder and little sacks filled with shot. Chekhov had to sleep on a hard wooden settle. There were no civilised comforts or conveniences of any sort, and in the night, whatever the weather, Chekhov had to rush outside and look for the nearest bush, making sure first there was not a viper under it. The farm was swarming with fierce dogs, most of which seemed to take a keen dislike to Chekhov. The food was plentiful but rough. For breakfast he usually had tea, eggs and ham; for dinner goose soup, resembling (Chekhov declared in a letter) the slops left in a tub after a fat shopkeeper's wife had had a bath in it, roast goose or turkey with pickled sloes, roast chicken, milk pudding, sour milk and coffee, which, 'to judge by its taste', Chekhov wrote, 'must have been made of roasted dung'; at five o'clock he had thick wheat porridge with lard, which was usually cooked over a wood fire in a nearby copse; and, lastly, for the evening meal, tea, ham, and any scraps left over from dinner. His pleasures included hunting, picnics, the making and letting off of fireworks (a favourite pastime of his pupil's), target shooting, etc. The chief occupation of the household, according to Chekhov, was 'wholesale murder'. They shot sparrows, swallows, rooks and every other bird they considered harmful to farming. They also shot their chickens, geese, turkeys, and even pigs. As soon as they got out of bed in the morning, they grabbed their guns, rushed to the open windows and started shooting. It was this early morning firing that woke Chekhov, who left a vivid description of this primitive household in his story *Pecheneg*. It was on that farm that Chekhov learnt to ride wild steppe ponies. The countryside round the farm was very hilly and picturesque. There were coalmines in the vicinity, and occasionally he would hear a mysterious sound that seemed to be coming from the sky: it was the sound of a bucket falling to the bottom of a coalmine, a sound effect Chekhov used in *The Cherry Orchard*. Life on that farm, which he revisited ten years later, provided him, according to Michael, with other material for his stories, such as the railway embankment in *Lights* and the empty goods waggon careering down a railway line in *Fears*. Chekhov recalled his stay in the Donetz steppe twenty years later (in a letter to Pavel Iordanov, medical officer and former mayor of Taganrog, to whom he used to send books for the Taganrog public library) as one of the most delightful memories of his schooldays. 'I love the Donetz steppe,' he wrote, 'and many years ago I felt at home there and knew every little ravine in it.'

Part of his summer holidays Chekhov spent on the estate of his school-friend Vassily Zembulatov, whom he later brought to Moscow with him as a lodger. Life there was, no doubt, much more civilised than at Kravtsov's farm, which is perhaps why Chekhov left no description of it.

Chekhov passed his final examinations in June 1879, having been placed eleventh out of twenty-three in his class. He obtained five (the highest) marks only in the less important subjects of scripture, geography and German. In Russian, history and logic he obtained only four marks, and in Latin, Greek and mathematics only three marks, that is to say, a pass. But though his scholastic attainments were not brilliant, he could claim to have gained something much more valuable during the three years he had been away from home, namely intellectual freedom and a sense of human dignity. In a letter to his fourteen-year-old brother Michael in April 1879 he wrote: 'One thing in your last letter I did not like: why do you refer to your own person as "your worthless and insignificant little brother"? Conscious of your worthlessness, are you? . . . You know before whom you ought to be conscious of your worthlessness? Before God, perhaps, before the human intellect, beauty and nature, but not before people. Among people one must be conscious of one's human dignity. You're not a swindler, are you? You are an honest fellow. Well, then, respect the honest fellow in yourself and remember that no honest man can be insignificant. Do not mistake "humbling oneself" for "being conscious of one's worthlessness".' His upbringing made him mistrust authority of any kind, and the experience of life he had gained while fending for himself in Taganrog made him rely, a little too confidently perhaps, on his own judgment. His mistrust of other people's opinions made him particularly wary of accepting literary judgments. In his letter to Michael he praised him for reading books. 'Try to acquire the habit of reading,' he wrote. 'With time you will learn to appreciate this habit. Mrs. Beecher Stowe has wrung tears from your eyes, has she? I read her a long time ago and I read her again six months ago with a scientific aim, and afterwards I experienced the unpleasant sensation mortals experience after eating too many raisins and currants.' The sentimentality of *Uncle Tom's Cabin*, in fact, proved too much for Chekhov, who was beginning to test literature 'scientifically', that is, by submitting it to the test of his own experience of life. His own reading had been very extensive, and, indeed, all through his life he was a voracious reader of books as well as of newspapers and periodicals. His reading at school included the Russian classics, Shakespeare, Cervantes, the contemporary German novelists, especially Spielhagen, whose novel *Between the Hammer and the Anvil* he seems to have enjoyed greatly, and Victor Hugo. It also included such abstruse works as Humboldt's five-volume *Kosmos*. It was Alexander who, impressed by the German philosopher's compendious work, advised Chekhov to read it, but Chekhov had already read it. 'I am sorry for Alexander,' he wrote to his cousin. 'He failed to achieve his object because I have already read *Kosmos*, and I remain the same even after having read it.'

Before leaving Taganrog Chekhov made sure that his arrival in Moscow would bring an improvement to the financial position of his family. He stayed behind for three months to obtain a scholarship of twenty-five roubles a month from the Taganrog town council (he obtained an advance of 100 roubles) as well as to arrange for two of his school-friends, Vassily Zembulatov and Dmitry Savelyev, who were also leaving for Moscow to study medicine, to stay with his mother as boarders. His father had at last succeeded in getting his job at Gavrilov's warehouse at thirty roubles a month, and, what was even more important, he had to live at the warehouse with the other emplöyees, thus freeing his family from his undesirable presence and ceding to Chekhov the place of the actual head of the family, which he was to keep for the rest of his life. 'Anton', Michael writes, 'has taken the place of father, and father's personality has receded into the background.'

Before Chekhov arrived in Moscow, his family had moved to another basement flat in Grachevka, the slum district in which they had lived for the last three years, known especially for its numerous brothels. All they could see out of the windows of their flat were the feet of the passers-by in the street Chekhov drove up from the station in a cab, and Michael, who was sitting at the gates of the house, did not recognise him. He had grown into a well-built giant of a man (he was just over six feet tall), with light-brown hair, which he wore long and brushed back from his high forehead, dark brown eyes and a full, firm mouth. Chekhov got out of the cab and, seeing his brother, said in a deep baritone voice, 'How are you, Mikhail Pavlovich?'

'It was only then', Michael records, 'that I knew that it was my brother Anton, and with a scream of delight I rushed downstairs to tell mother. A gay young man entered our flat and everybody rushed to embrace him. I was sent off to the post office at once to send a telegram to father about Anton's arrival. Soon Zembulatov and Savelyev came and, after their rooms had been made ready for them, we all went out sightseeing together. I acted as their guide and took them round the Kremlin, showing them everything, and we were pretty tired by the time we returned home. In the evening father came, we had supper in a large company, and we were as happy as never before.'

And they had good reason to be happy: from now on they had someone on whom they could rely to take good care of them all.

Part Two
LITERARY APPRENTICESHIP

Moscow with its cobbled, humpbacked streets, its rich mansions and wooden hovels, its drab churches which filled the air with the sound of bells, its fire-stations with their tall towers on which two look-out men were constantly watching for the first signs of smoke, its theatres and amusement places, its markets and shops, its horse-trams and cabs, its cheap pubs and magnificent restaurants, its hotels and lodging houses, its daily and periodical press, its civil servants, students, writers, actors, artists, wealthy business men, shopkeepers, shop-assistants, errand boys, factory workers, water carriers, house-porters, beggars and prostitutes—that was the human scene, rich in character and incident, which provided Chekhov with his material for the hundreds of stories and articles he was to begin writing even before he had time to familiarise himself with it. Moscow had fascinated him during his first visit in 1877, and it fascinated him even more two years later when he plunged into its life with the zest and enthusiasm of a nineteen-year-old student who believed in seeing and experiencing everything for himself. But Moscow also gave him his first shock that removed the romantic spell the city had cast upon him and made him see it in its true light. It was his visit to the university to fill up the necessary forms for his admission to the medical faculty that brought him down to earth. 'Anton', Michael records, 'did not know Moscow very well and it was I who took him to the university. We entered a small dirty room with a low ceiling, full of tobacco smoke and crowded with young people. Anton apparently expected something grand from a university, and the place in which he found himself produced a far from pleasant impression on him.' Recalling his first impression of Moscow university ten years later, Chekhov wrote in *A Boring Story*: 'And there are the gloomy, battered gates of the university; the bored caretaker in his sheepskin coat, a broom, heaps of snow. . . . On an inexperienced boy who has just arrived from the provinces and who imagines that a temple of learning is a real temple such gates cannot produce a healthy impression. Indeed, the dilapidated condition of the university buildings, the gloomy corridors, grimy walls, bad light, and the depressing stairs, coat-stands and benches have undoubtedly played an important role in the history of Russian pessimism.'

It was the same kind of salutary shock his medical training always administered to him whenever he felt like giving in to the inborn romantic strain in his nature. Towards the end of his life he summed up the influence his medical training had on his writing in these words (in a letter to Professor Rossolimo): 'I do not doubt but that the study of medicine has had a great influence on my literary work; it has considerably widened the field of my observations and enriched my knowledge, the real value of which for me as a writer can only be understood by one who is a medical man himself; it has also exerted a guiding influence upon me, and, I suppose, it is because of my knowledge of medicine that I have succeeded in avoiding making many mistakes. An acquaintance with the natural sciences and the scientific method always kept me on the look out for such mistakes, and wherever possible I tried to take the scientific data into account; and where it was not possible I preferred not to write at all. Let me, by the way, point out that the conditions of creative work do not always permit a complete agreement with scientific facts; it is, for instance, impossible to depict death from poisoning on the stage as it actually occurs in life. But agreement with scientific facts must be felt even in such a stage convention, that is to say, the reader or spectator ought to be conscious of the fact that it is only a stage convention and that he is dealing with a knowledgeable author. I do not belong to those writers who take up a negative attitude towards science; and I should not like to belong to those who depended entirely on their own insight for everything.'

Chekhov had always had a healthy contempt for those writers who had no scientific background of any kind, and he was not averse from pulling their legs occasionally. Tatyana Shchepkina-Kupernik, a well-known poetess, story-writer and translator, who was a great friend of the Chekhov family, tells of the following 'most cruel' joke Chekhov had once played on her: 'In the garden of Chekhov's Melikhovo country house there were a number of white and coffee-coloured, so-called Egyptian, pigeons and a cat which had exactly the same markings. Chekhov assured me one day that the pigeons had originated from a crossing of the cat and the ordinary grey pigeons. In those days we were not taught natural history at school and I was totally ignorant of it. Though the whole thing seemed odd to me, I did not dare to disbelieve such an authority as Chekhov, and on my return to Moscow I told someone about the remarkable pigeons Chekhov had. One can easily imagine the delight the story caused in Moscow literary circles and how much I was ashamed of my ignorance.'

Such a classic example of the ignorance of the facts of life was, no doubt, due to the lady writer's 'Victorian' upbringing, but Chekhov was no less severe on writers of much wider experience. Alexander Kuprin recalls an occasion when Chekhov became greatly incensed with someone for talking 'in a superior way' of medicine and basing his opinion on Zola's novel *Dr. Pascal.*

'Your Zola', Chekhov exclaimed, 'knows nothing and he invents it all in his study. He ought to come and see how our country doctors work and what they are doing for our peasants.'

Chekhov's reverence for medicine was only another expression of his deep-seated sense of realism, from which he was deflected only during his Tolstoyan period in the second half of the 'eighties. He had an extraordinary ability to detect the slightest insincerity in the relationship between people. He could see through the sham senti-ments with which people sought to cover up their acts of cruelty and injustice towards one another, and his hatred of a lie in any shape or form remained with him to the end of his life. As the years passed and his experience of life grew he became more and more tolerant, but at first, when as a boy of nineteen he found himself the head of an impoverished family, he would not put up with anything that went counter to his convictions. By nature, he told his wife many years later, he had a harsh character, he was liable to lose his temper on the slightest provocation, and in former days he was guilty of the most inexcusable actions. 'Anton's will', Michael writes, 'became the dominant one in our family. Harsh and brusque remarks I had never known him use before, began to be heard, such as, "That's not true", or "One must be just", or "One mustn't tell lies", and so on. . . . Anton's views were accepted as law, and who knows what would have happened to our family after Alexander and Nicholas had left it if Anton had not arrived just in the nick of time from Taganrog. The need of earning money at all costs made Anton write stories, and Nicholas, who had returned to the bosom of his family, draw cartoons, for the humorous journals. Ivan soon became an elementary-school teacher, and little Michael began copying students' lectures and dia-grams. Our mother and our sister Mary worked hard, too. It was, indeed, a touching reunion of all the members of the family, who rallied round one person—Anton—and who were bound to each other by ties of sincere and tender affection.'

Michael is rather apt to slur over the less agreeable facts in his famous brother's life, particularly the violent conflicts that arose between him and Alexander and, less acutely, between him and Nicholas. It was not only Chekhov's attempt to wean him from his life of dissipation that roused Alexander's anger; what he resented was that Chekhov should have seen through his literary pretensions and should no longer have accepted him as an authority on literary matters. It was Chekhov's independence of mind that irked him, as it was when Chekhov had walked 'majestically' past the shop after their first violent quarrel as children. How tense the situation between the two brothers became can be gathered from the following letter Chekhov wrote to Alexander at the beginning of 1881.

'Alexander,' Chekhov's letter began, 'I, Anton Chekhov, am writing this letter while entirely self-composed and in the full possession of my faculties. I am resorting to this schoolgirl's expedient in view of your express desire that I should not talk to you again. If I won't allow my mother, sister or any woman to say a wrong word to me, I shall certainly not allow it to a drunken cabby. Even if you were a hundred thousand times dearer to me than you are, I should refuse on principle, and on anything else you like, to put up with any insults from you. If, however, contrary to all expectations, you should like to make your usual excuse and put all the blame on your "irresponsible state", I, for my part, should like you to know that I am perfectly well aware that 'being drunk" does not give you the right to —— on anyone's head. I am quite willing at any time to expunge from my vocabulary the word "brother" with which you tried to frighten me when I left the battlefield, and that not because I have no heart, but because in this world one must be ready for anything. I myself am afraid of nothing, and I should like to advise my brothers to be the same. I am writing this in all probability in order to save myself in the future from all sorts of unpleasant surprises and, perhaps, from being slapped in the face, for I realise very well that on the strength of your most charming "but" (which, let me add parenthetically, does not concern anyone) you are capable of slapping anyone's face anywhere. Today's row showed me for the first time that the delicacy of feeling which you extol so much in your story *Somnambula* would not prevent you from slapping a man's face and that you are a most dissembling fellow, i.e. a fellow who always consults his own interests first, and therefore, I remain your most humble servant, A. Chekhov.'

Perhaps the most noteworthy sentence in this furious and characteristic letter, written in the heat of the moment and hence so free from all attempts to conceal the hidden thoughts in his mind, is: 'I myself am afraid of nothing'. It is a statement of sober and unadorned fact which is typical of Chekhov's attitude to life. It comes out unmistakably in the fearless expression of his eyes, which is such a remarkable feature of his portraits as a schoolboy and as a young man.

The old relationship between Alexander and Chekhov, in which the elder brother was the literary mentor of the younger, came to an end with Chekhov's arrival in Moscow. Very soon it was Chekhov who became the literary mentor of Alexander, and already in 1882 Chekhov was providing Alexander with literary work, and five years later he got him a job on Suvorin's daily. In these few years Chekhov became a famous writer, while Alexander, in Chekhov's own words, remained a 'third-rater'.

But it would be wrong to assume that this spectacular rise in Chekhov's reputation came about without a hard struggle. On his arrival in Moscow Chekhov was faced with an impossible situation. The income of his family consisted of his own scholarship of twenty-five roubles a month, which did not always arrive punctually, the forty roubles paid for their board and lodgings by his two school-friends and fellow-students, and another twenty roubles paid by a third lodger, a medical student by the name of Nicolai Korobov, who had been brought by his father from far-away Vyatka and who was to become a life-long friend of Chekhov's. That made eighty-five roubles a month for nine people. Soon they moved from their dank cellar to a larger and more expensive flat in the same street, Zembulatov and Korobov sharing one room, Savelyev having a smaller room to himself, Chekhov, Nicholas and Michael occupying a third room, Chekhov's mother and sister a fourth, and the fifth room forming a sort of combined dining- and sitting-room and at first presumably also Ivan's bedroom. It is doubtful whether Nicholas's earnings amounted to much. He was the most feckless member of the family, very often disappearing for days and never bothering to carry out his commissions, which Chekhov mostly obtained for him. It was Chekhov, for instance, who arranged an exhibition of Nicholas's paintings in a Moscow art shop, and in a letter he wrote in May 1880, and which he signed characteristically, 'Your stern but just brother', he reminded Nicholas that he had forgotten to sign the authorisation empowering him to conclude an agreement with the owner of the shop. Ivan was too busy working for his teacher's diploma, which he got in 1880, to be able to help the family, but even he had often to walk to the other end of the town to earn a few copecks by copying the manuscripts of a popular novelist.

In this desperate situation Chekhov could only think of one thing: he had to capitalise his gift of improvising humorous stories, which kept his family and friends in fits of laughter. Having made up his mind to write for a living, he did not, however, send his stories to the Moscow humorous magazines, where Alexander had been publishing his stories, but to the Petersburg 'artistic and political' weekly *The Dragonfly*. According to Michael, the first thing Chekhov did on receiving his scholarship money from Taganrog was to buy all the Petersburg and Moscow papers and journals and read carefully through them. Having thus studied his market, he sat down to write his stories.

Michael recalls how on returning from the university one January afternoon in 1880 Chekhov learnt of the acceptance of his first story. He bought a copy of *The Dragonfly* and was turning over its pages with hands that had gone numb with cold to find the 'letter-box' in which editors informed their contributors of the success or failure of their literary efforts. The reply he received was very encouraging. 'Drachevka. A. Che-v,' he read. 'Not at all bad. We shall publish what you have sent us. Accept our good wishes for your future valiant efforts.' A few days later he received the following letter from the editor of the magazine, Ippolit Vassilevsky, better known under the pseudonym of 'Bukva' or 'Letter' with which he signed his weekly Petersburg column in the *Russian Gazette*, one of the most reputable liberal papers in Russia: 'Dear Sir, This journal has the honour of informing you that the story you sent us is not bad and will be published. We shall pay you five copecks a line.' The story was *A Letter from the Don Landowner Stepan Vladimirovich N. to his Learned Neighbour Dr. Friedrich* (Chekhov shortened the title to *A Letter to a Learned Neighbour* for the first collection of short stories, *At Leisure*, which he prepared for publication at his own expense in 1883, but which he could not bring out for lack of funds).

Chekhov began sending stories to *The Dragonfly* almost every week, but between March and December 1880 only eleven of them were published. In fact, his first entry into the world of literature ended in failure. Again and again he read Vassilevsky's uncomplimentary remarks on his contributions in the 'letter-box' of *The Dragonfly*, ending in the most crushing criticism of all on December 21st: 'You are withering away without flowering. It is impossible to write without a critical attitude to one's work.'

The eleven stories published in *The Dragonfly* in 1880 reveal quite clearly the pattern Chekhov was to follow during the next five or so years. With the exception of two of them (*A Letter to a Learned Neighbour*, signed '—v', and *My Jubilee*, a complaint of an unsuccessful author on the receipt of his two thousandth rejection slip, signed 'A

Prosaic Poet'), they are all signed by Chekhov's famous nom-de-plume 'Antosha Chekhonte', which appears in different variations, such as 'Antosha', 'Chekhonte', 'Antosha Chekhonte', 'Antosha Ch.', and so on. They include a parody on Victor Hugo, *One Thousand and One Passions* or *The Terrible Night*, the forerunner of several other literary parodies, some of them the longest stories Chekhov ever wrote, soon to appear in the Moscow periodical and daily press; satires on the upper and middle classes, such as *Daddy*, a father who, at the instigation of his wife, tries to bribe a school-teacher to let his little son pass into a higher form; or *For (Stealing) Apples*, a fierce exposure of an old-fashioned landowner who discovers two young peasant lovers helping themselves to his apples and who punishes them by making the man flog the girl and the girl flog the man; or *Before the Wedding*, a typical lower-middle-class scene, in which the parents of the bride try to cheat their future son-in-law, a fatuous ass with literary pretensions, of his promised dowry; a story in a more broadly humorous vein, *He that runs after two Hares will not catch One*; and a piece of illuminating literary criticism, *What Does one Mostly Find in Novels, Short Stories, etc.?*

It says little for Vassilevsky's literary flair that he should have failed to discover the latent potentialities of Chekhov's stories, but there is also a great deal of justice in his remark that it was impossible to write without a critical attitude to one's work. In his first letter to Grigorovich of March 28th, 1886, Chekhov himself admitted that his attitude to his early literary work was 'thoughtless and negligent' and that he looked upon his stories merely as potboilers. 'I can't remember a single story', he wrote, 'on which I spent more than one day, and I wrote my stories just as newspaper reporters write their notices of a fire, mechanically, half-consciously, with little thought of my readers or myself.' As late as October 1887 the thought of his uncritical attitude towards his work worried him. 'Of all the Russians who are at present successfully engaged in writing', he wrote in his first letter to the writer Vladimir Korolenko, 'I am the most thoughtless and frivolous; in the language of the poets, I loved my chaste Muse but I did not respect her; I was unfaithful to her and took her to places where she had no business to go.' But even in those early years, when he never thought of becoming a professional writer, his stories were remarkable for their criticism of life. His style may have been slipshod, his choice of subjects may have been haphazard, but he always tried to look at life dispassionately and with the critical eye of a true creative writer. As early as February 1883 he warned Alexander against the dangers of subjectivity. 'Subjectivity', he wrote, 'is a dangerous thing. It is bad because it gives the poor author so completely away. But for this subjectivity of yours, you would have been a most useful artist. . . . And yet all you have to do is to be honest with yourself: throw your own personality overboard, don't make yourself into the hero of your own story, renounce yourself for at least half an hour. You have a story in which a newly married couple go on kissing each other all through dinner. They slobber and talk nonsense. Not one sensible word. Just sheer *complacency*. You did not write it for a reader. You wrote it because you like this sort of empty chatter. But if only you had taken the trouble to describe the dinner, to show us how they ate, what they ate, what their cook was like, how vulgar your hero and heroine were, how absurd she was with her love for that well-fed, greedy ass . . . It is true', Chekhov went on, 'that everyone likes to see well-fed and contented people, but to describe them it is not enough to tell us what *they* said to each other or how many times they kissed each other. Something more is wanted: one must renounce the personal impression of the happiness which a honeymooning couple produces on good-natured people.'

It is this quality of digging below the surface of life, of exposing the hidden motives of the actions of his characters and of revealing the influence of social forces upon them that can already be detected, in however rudimentary a form, in the first stories he contributed to *The Dragonfly*, and it was Vassilevsky's failure to perceive it that accounts for his harsh criticism. Chekhov never forgot or forgave his treatment by the editor of *The Dragonfly*, and except for two stories he contributed to it in 1883 and 1884, after Vassilevsky had repeatedly begged him for a story, he did not send any stories to it again. How badly his vanity was hurt can be seen from the fact that for the next six months he stopped writing stories altogether. Instead he turned to the stage again. He wrote a long play (*Platonov*) and took it himself to the Maly Theatre, hoping to hand it personally to the famous actress Maria Yermolova. Whether he saw Yermolova or not is not known, but the play was returned to him by post. For once he betrayed his great disappointment by tearing up the manuscript of the play which his brother Michael had copied out for him. The rough copy of the play, however, has been preserved. It is very long and unwieldy, but it shows Chekhov's first attempt to deal with the new social forces which were just then coming to the fore in Russia and contains many themes which he used in his great plays.

It was thus that Chekhov's first attempts as a short-story writer and as a playwright ended in failure. Greatly as it must have disheartened him at the time, it only spurred him on to further efforts. Indeed, in later years he always warned young writers against the dangers of an early success. He was to experience many more bitter disappointments, but the memory of his first failure always sustained his faith in himself and in the things he believed in as a writer.

2

In June 1880 a great literary event took place in Moscow at which Chekhov was most certainly present. It was the unveiling of the Pushkin Memorial on Tversky Boulevard in the centre of Moscow. It was the only time Chekhov could have seen the two giants of the Russian novel, Turgenev and Dostoevsky, who were the main speakers at the celebrations held in connexion with the unveiling of the memorial. There was no question of his meeting either of them, or indeed any other of the well-known Russian writers who were present on that memorable occasion, for at the time he was just an unknown medical student who had contributed four humorous sketches to an unimportant Petersburg weekly. Dostoevsky's speech created a great impression on those who heard it, and it must have stuck in Chekhov's mind, for eighteen years later, in a letter to Jacob Merpert, lecturer in Russian literature at the Sorbonne, who had asked him his opinion of a lecture on Dostoevsky he intended to deliver and the manuscript of which he had sent him, Chekhov wrote: 'You must not forget that Pushkin had a tremendous influence on him.' Chekhov could have seen Dostoevsky three times: at the unveiling of the memorial, at the meeting when he delivered his famous oration on Pushkin, and at a concert in honour of the poet during which Dostoevsky recited Pushkin's poem *The Prophet*, a poem he was very fond of reciting in public on all sorts of occasions. When reciting the poem, Dostoevsky used to work himself up into a state of terrific excitement. He would come out stooping on the platform, facing the audience sideways. Then he would raise his right arm and utter the first two words of the poem in a shrill, passionate voice: 'Poet, arise!' And he would finish his recitation in the same high-pitched shrill voice: 'And with thy word burn the hearts of men!'

That was certainly not the kind of recitation that would impress Chekhov or increase his rather lukewarm respect for Dostoevsky, whose politics he detested and whose novels he never could bring himself to like.

Dostoevsky died in Petersburg six months later. In 1880 his last novel *The Brothers Karamazov* was being serialised in *The Russian Messenger*, a Moscow monthly edited by the reactionary journalist Mikhail Katkov, who was also the editor of the Moscow conservative daily *Moscow Gazette*. Chekhov must have heard of, if not witnessed, the incident between Katkov and Turgenev at the dinner which followed the unveiling of the Pushkin memorial, when Turgenev deliberately snubbed Katkov by turning away as the latter offered to clink glasses with him.

The beginning of the 'eighties was a time of high political tension in Russia. Reaction was in full swing, and the reactionary journalists were becoming more and more clamorous. Though he took no part in the disturbances in Moscow University between 1881 and 1883, Chekhov did not conceal his detestation of the reactionary regime. He was present at several of the meetings organised by the revolutionary students, but he mistrusted the genuineness of their political opinions. 'While our men and women students are undoubtedly fine and honest people', he wrote to a correspondent as late as February 1899, 'and while it is no less true that they are our hope and Russia's future, it is only necessary for them to grow up and become independent for our hope and the future of Russia to go up in smoke. What remains are doctors, owners of country cottages, hungry civil servants and thieving engineers. Don't forget', Chekhov added, 'that Katkov, Pobedonostsev [the reactionary Procurator of the Holy Synod] and Vyshnegradsky [Finance Minister] are nurslings of our universities, that they are our professors, and not by any means Bourbons, but professors, luminaries. . . .'

In his early writings Chekhov went out of his way to underline his opposition to the conservative press. He was particularly severe on *The Citizen*, owned by Prince Meshchersky, which Dostoevsky edited between January 1873 and February 1874 and in which he began publishing his *Writer's Diary*. He took every opportunity to point the shaft of his satire at the reactionaries, among whom he most certainly included Dostoevsky. Nor did he trust Dostoevsky's psychological insight, which even as late as in 1899 struck him as pretentious. In 1883 he wrote a story, *An Enigmatic Nature*, which certainly reads like a satire against Dostoevsky and his followers. A more transparent skit on Dostoevsky is one of his two parodies on the detective story which was very popular in Russia in those days. The parody *The Phosphorus*

Match was written in 1884. It describes the disappearance of a land-owner in mysterious circumstances which lead the police to suspect foul play. The assistant of the examining magistrate, a great reader of Dostoevsky's novels, forms the theory that the missing man was murdered by his sister, a religious maniac, who regarded her brother as the antichrist. 'Oh,' he tells his chief, 'you don't understand these pious old maids. Read Dostoevsky!' He goes on to develop his theory on Dostoevsky lines, but in the end, of course, the landowner turns up unscathed.

It is Dostoevsky's shrillness that Chekhov found so distasteful. In 1889 Suvorin tried to induce Chekhov to change his mind about Dostoevsky and asked him to read his novels again. 'I have bought Dostoevsky's works in your bookshop,' Chekhov wrote to Suvorin, 'and I am reading him now. They are all right, but much too long and immodest.' But there was undoubtedly also a touch of envy in Chekhov's strictures on Dostoevsky. Ten years after this letter to Suvorin, a woman writer asked him whether she should write a novel based on the murder of a Warsaw actress by her twenty-two-year-old lover. Chekhov advised her against it. 'Perhaps Dostoevsky alone', he wrote, 'could have made some sense out of such a complicated absurdity as the life of that poor woman.'

The writer who did influence Chekhov at the very beginning of his literary career was Saltykov-Shchedrin, author of *The Golovlyov Family* and one of the foremost Russian satirists. Till 1884, when it was suppressed by the Government, Saltykov-Shchedrin was the editor of the progressive *Homeland Notes*, a monthly he had edited together with the poet Nekrassov till the latter's death in 1878. Chekhov was a devoted reader of the *Homeland Notes* and a great admirer of its editor, to whom he refers again and again in his early stories and articles. Saltykov's great satire *A Tale of a Town*, and particularly his *Fairy Tales*, which he began publishing after the suppression of his journal and in which he exposed, in the compact allegorical form of a fairy-tale, the social injustices of his time, figure a great deal in Chekhov's early writings. Indeed, Chekhov himself wrote several 'fairy stories' in direct imitation of Saltykov-Shchedrin. There was a great difference, though, between Saltykov-Shchedrin's bitter and uncompromising satire and Chekhov's sly and mischievous digs at the Government and its minions. Chekhov possessed a great fund of impish mischievousness, which took the form of all sorts of innocent pranks and mystifications which caused much merriment among his family and friends. He never could withstand the temptation to play a practical joke on someone, though with time his practical jokes assumed the much more subtle and disguised form of a leg-pull which he could chuckle over in the privacy of his study, such as his grave assurance to Shchepkina-Kupernik that his marmalade cat had sired his chocolate doves. His political satires may have lost some of their point today, but at the time when they were written their sting went home and sometimes brought about the suppression of his stories. Thus, Chekhov published the following brief note in the Petersburg weekly *Fragments* in April 1883: 'We are informed that the other day one of the contributors of *Kievlyanin* [a conservative Kiev newspaper], having made a thorough study of the Moscow papers, carried out, in a fit of doubt, a search of his own home for illegal literature. Having discovered nothing of a subversive nature, he nevertheless took himself off to the police station.' In a much more deadly vein is the story *The Sign of the Times*, published in *Fragments* in October 1883. In a drawing-room with light-blue wallpaper a good-looking young man is proposing to a girl who is about to accept him, when she is suddenly interrupted by her brother.

'Here a moment, Lily,' he says.

'What's the matter?' asks Lily, going out to her brother.

'Forgive me, my dear,' her brother says, 'but as your brother I think it is my duty to warn you to be careful with that gentleman. Don't talk too much. Take care not to say anything that is not absolutely necessary.'

'But he is proposing to me!'

'That's your affair. Accept him, marry him, if you must, but for goodness' sake be careful. I know him. He's an awful scoundrel. Sure to inform the police if there's anything——'

'Thanks, Max, I didn't know.'

But the real sting of the story is in the last sentence: 'The girl went back to the drawing-room, said "yes" to the young man, kissed him, hugged him, vowed to be true to him, but she was careful: she spoke only of love.'

One of Chekhov's fairy-stories in which he dealt with the same dilemma of whether to talk or not to talk was suppressed by the censor on the ground that in it 'our internal political life is represented in a most unseemly fashion.' But on the whole Chekhov was rather pleased with the 'leniency' of the Petersburg censors as compared with their Moscow colleagues. In one of his letters to Nicolai Laykin, the editor of *Fragments*, he wrote (in February 1884): 'My *Young Man* [a short dramatic sketch in which the falling value of the rouble and the corruption of the high-grade civil servants are referred to in far from flattering terms] arouses surprise here by its frankness. Our Muscovites are so used to the depredations of the censors that they cannot help being astonished. And well they may be: here our censors delete such words as "cockade" and "General of Medicine".'

With time Chekhov became very clever ('crafty' would have been his own word) at avoiding the 'red cross' of the censor, though, as his experience with *The Seagull* shows, the vagaries of the censorship were quite unaccountable; but it was just that cleverness of his in eluding the censor's clutches that gave rise to the opinion (so widely held in and outside Russia) that he was indifferent to the political problems of his day.

The two other writers who strongly influenced Chekhov were Turgenev and Tolstoy. Turgenev, in particular, fascinated Chekhov all through his life both as a writer and as a stylist. He was the other famous writer, beside Dostoevsky, he had seen as a young man and the only one whose ghost he had ever called up. Turgenev died on August 22nd, 1883, and a month later Chekhov wrote his topical story *In the Landau* in connexion with his death. He was at that time very interested in spiritualism and took part in many spiritualist séances. Thus in November 1882 he asked Alexander, who after graduating from Moscow University had got himself a job as customs official in Taganrog, to find out from an acquaintance of theirs the details of a spiritualist séance. 'Let her describe briefly but precisely', he wrote, 'the spiritualistic séance she has seen somewhere in the Tula province, I believe. Let her describe where, how and who, who was called up, did the ghost speak, what time of the night or day and how long, and let her send it to me. I want it badly. I promise to do something for her in return.' It was during one of the séances in Moscow that Chekhov called up Turgenev's ghost. In recalling that occasion in a letter to Suvorin in July 1894 Chekhov wrote: 'Turgenev told me, "Your life is drawing to a close" ', a prophecy he could hardly have expected, but that most likely put an end to his preoccupation with spiritualism.

The longest and profoundest influence on Chekhov was undoubtedly exercised by Tolstoy both as a writer and as a preacher of a new morality. That, however, happened much later in his life.

3

It was Leykin who gave Chekhov his first real chance as a writer. Before the end of 1882, when he became a regular contributor to Leykin's Petersburg weekly *Fragments*, Chekhov placed his stories in the Moscow humorous journals, which paid him irregularly and scantily. Having failed with his play, he sat down to write stories again, the first one, *St. Peter's Day*, a humorous sketch in connexion with the end of the close shooting season, being published in *The Alarm-Clock*, an old-established Moscow humorous weekly, on June 19th, 1881. All his other stories and sketches in that year appeared in the *Onlooker*, an illustrated 'literary, artistic and humorous' magazine, founded in August 1881 by Vsevolod Davydov, the owner of a small printing works who, according to Chekhov, was 'a great dreamer and enthusiast, full of grandiose but unsound ideas'. The *Onlooker* was practically run by Chekhov and his two elder brothers Alexander and Nicholas in 1881. It was to have come out three times a week, but actually appeared very irregularly and entirely stopped publication for one year at the end of 1881. During that year Chekhov contributed eleven stories and articles to it, and between January and March 1883, when it made another sporadic appearance, twenty-one stories. It then ceased publication again, coming out for the last time in 1884 and 1885, when six numbers were published, but Chekhov did not contribute to any of them. It was on November 10th, 1881, that Chekhov, after a short visit with Nicholas to Taganrog where they were present at a wedding of a relative, published in the *Onlooker* his sketch *The Marriage Season* (actually a series of captions to his brother's cartoons), which made his friends and relations so furious that they threatened to give him a beating if he came to Taganrog again. His one-act comedy *The Wedding*, written in October, 1889, was partly based on that early sketch.

Chekhov also contributed three articles to the *Onlooker* in 1881. Two of them were on Sarah Bernhardt, who was appearing at a Moscow theatre with her company in December of that year, and another on a popular Moscow night-club, the *Salon des Variétés*, which he had visited with some of his Shuya relatives and which he found so objectionable that he advised its proprietor to charge people for going out rather than for going in.

Chekhov became a regular contributor to *The Alarm-Clock* a year later. Altogether he published thirty-five stories in it between 1881 and

ANTON
CHEKHOV
1883

ANTON
CHEKHOV
1888

1886, including his long parody on the popular translations of romantic novels, *An Unwanted Victory*, serialised between June and August 1882. The story was written as a result of an argument with the editor of *The Alarm-Clock*, A. Kurepin, Chekhov claiming that he could write a novel which would not be worse than any translation of a romantic novel. *An Unwanted Victory* was, in fact, extremely popular and many of its readers mistook it for a novel by the Hungarian novelist Maurice Jokai. It was later filmed four times, the last time in 1924.

Chekhov disliked *The Alarm-Clock* both because it was one of those journals which never could afford to pay its contributors (its owner, L. Utkina, paid her contributors in kind, mostly in furniture, in 1883, and a clock she gave Nicholas in payment for some of his illustrations can still be seen in the Chekhov Museum in Yalta) and because of the general low level of its humorous stories. 'I cannot stand *The Alarm-Clock*,' he wrote to Alexander in May 1883, 'and if I still go on writing for it, it is with a feeling of pain.' What he found so objectionable about the magazine was the familiar tone it affected towards its contributors and its readers. As late as August 1887, when Chekhov was already a well-known writer and when his contributions to *The Alarm-Clock* had practically ceased, it published an article on the topical subject of the solar eclipse in which Chekhov himself figured. 'A. Chekhonte', the writer of the article declared, 'has ordered the following dinner from his cook (he has a cook, I assure you): sun with trimmings, mayonnaise of stars and moon with horse-radish. "No hot dishes, sir?" asked his cook. "No," replied the witty humorist; "I'm hot-blooded as it is." ' Chekhov referred to this article in a letter to Leykin in October of that year. 'Either because of their third-rateness or because of Moscow's general lack of good manners,' he wrote, 'these gentlemen think it the very essence of wit to be on familiar terms with the public and its contributors. There is not a single issue without some offensive reference to the public, to a contributor, or to an actor. In a circus it is the clowns who are the favourites of the public, and so these absurd and incorrigible fools like to behave in the same way.'

But it was to *The Alarm-Clock* that Chekhov owed his friendship with two men who proved of inestimable value to his literary career. From one of them, Fyodor Popudoglo, he received his only training in the writing of the short story. Writing of Popudoglo's death to Alexander in October 1883 Chekhov declared: 'To me it is an irreparable loss. Popudoglo was not a talented writer, though they are publishing his portrait in *The Alarm-Clock*. He was a literary veteran and possessed a wonderful literary flair, and such people are indispensable to beginners like me. I used to visit him at his home like a thief in the night, and he would open up his heart to me. He liked me, and I knew him inside out. He died of an inflammation of the hard membrane of the brain in spite of being attended by such a famous doctor as myself. He had twenty doctors, but I was the only one who diagnosed his illness correctly while he was alive. May he rest in peace. The real cause of his death was alcohol and his dear friends whose *nomina sunt otiosa*, complete lack of commonsense and his careless attitude towards his own life and the lives of other people—that was why he died at the age of thirty-seven.'

Chekhov's circle of friends included many people of that sort, his two elder brothers among them. Popudoglo left his large library (mostly literary junk) to Chekhov, who, however, refused to accept it as a gift, but paid his widow for it in spite of the fact that he had little money himself. He dedicated one of his earlier realistic stories, *Living Goods*, to Popudoglo. It was published in August 1882 in *World Opinion*, edited by N. Pushkaryov, a poet as well as an inventor (he invented the first gas mantle in Russia), of whom Chekhov wrote many years later: 'I am sorry for Pushkaryov. A long time ago he used to be a very tender and sensitive lyric poet, but now he has apparently grown old and written himself out.'

A friendship which lasted much longer and had a much more decisive, though perhaps less direct, influence on Chekhov's work was that with the poet Iliodor Palmin, who was also a regular contributor to *The Alarm-Clock*. Palmin had been very popular among the Russian progressives of the 'seventies, but by the time Chekhov got to know him poverty and drink had reduced him to a state of senile decrepitude though he was only in his early forties. Chekhov described Palmin as 'a poetic personality in a state of perpetual ecstasy, stuffed full of ideas and themes'. He never got tired of talking to him. 'It is true', he wrote to Leykin, 'that when talking to him you have to drink a lot, but then you can be sure that during the three or four hours you will never hear him utter a single lie or one vulgar phrase, and for that alone it is worth while getting drunk.' Palmin was a tall, spare man with a pockmarked face who walked with a stoop. He was very fond of animals and usually kept five or six stray dogs about him. He was always shabbily dressed. 'His coat', Chekhov described his appearance to Leykin, 'is covered with stains, his trousers are always unbuttoned and his tie is at the back of his neck.' One day Chekhov took two young women to see Palmin. There was a quart of vodka under the table and some pickled cucumbers and white fish on it. Chekhov had three glasses of vodka and Palmin also treated 'the young ladies' to a few glasses. He lived with a fat, slovenly old woman he had picked up in the gutter and, to everybody's surprise, quite unaccountably married. At five o'clock she used to enter his room with the same phrase: 'Liodor Ivanovich, isn't it time you had your beer?' A year after the poet's death, Chekhov used that phrase in his story *Ward No. 6*, where he put it into the mouth of Dr. Ragin's cook.

Palmin was an unrepentant romantic. The gods, as Chekhov expressed it, had entered into his flesh and blood and he regarded all mundane affairs as unworthy of his pen. In his letters Chekhov always referred to him as 'the pagan god', or 'His Inspiration'. But prejudiced against romanticism as Chekhov was, he could not help admiring a man whose head was always in the clouds and who simply ignored the earth. 'I suppose', Chekhov wrote to Leykin, 'he is right from his own point of view and it is a waste of time to try to make him change his mind. Besides, I don't think it is necessary to make a different man out of Palmin. He is an original poet, and, notwithstanding the monotony of his poetry, he is still infinitely superior to the hundreds of little poets who are trying to be topical at all cost.'

Palmin was a regular contributor to *Fragments*, and it was he who introduced Chekhov to Leykin and thus was more than anyone instrumental in shaping Chekhov's literary career. During his visit to Moscow in the autumn of 1882, Leykin took Palmin out to dine at a fashionable restaurant. While driving there in a cab the poet saw Chekhov and his brother Nicholas walking in the street. He pointed them out to Leykin. 'There', he said, 'are two talented young men, one an artist and the other a writer. They are both contributors to our humorous journals.' Leykin immediately stopped the cab and was introduced to Chekhov, whom he invited to contribute to *Fragments*, for which Chekhov was to write about three hundred stories during the next five years.

Chekhov was afterwards rather apt to regard his contributions to *Fragments* with the condescending eye of a famous author who was ashamed of his youthful indiscretions. But it would be a mistake to take Chekhov's own valuation of his work for Leykin, or indeed treat seriously his own attitude to 'the limping devil' (Leykin was a short, thick-set man who walked with a pronounced limp), as he called the editor and the owner of *Fragments* after his first visit to Petersburg at the end of 1885. Chekhov had many good reasons for being angry with Leykin, who could never grasp the real significance of Chekhov's genius nor curb his own greediness in wishing to exploit it. But it was Leykin who forced Chekhov to go through the hard school of literary training and to learn the art of compactness and condensation.

Chekhov began his work for *Fragments* with great enthusiasm. He had been a great admirer of Leykin's stories of merchant life as a schoolboy. 'I lived in the provinces as a boy,' he wrote to Leykin in March 1883, 'and was one of your most enthusiastic readers.' Unlike the Moscow humorous journals, *Fragments* was an old-established journal of good reputation. '*Fragments*, for which I am now writing,' Chekhov wrote to Alexander in December 1882, 'is one of our best magazines.' And three months later in another letter to Alexander he wrote: '*Fragments* is now one of the most fashionable journals. Its stories are being reprinted; it is read everywhere. . . . To work for it is to receive a certificate. Now I have every right to look down on *The Alarm-Clock*, and I don't think I shall agree to work for five copecks a line for anybody.' Leykin had offered Chekhov eight copecks a line, and had gone out of his way to express his delight with Chekhov's first contributions. 'I thank you for your contributions to *Fragments* in 1882,' he wrote to Chekhov on December 31st of that year, 'and I beg you not to leave my journal without your contributions in 1883.' Chekhov was no less polite. 'I am working for *Fragments* with particular pleasure,' he wrote to Leykin in January 1883. 'The general tendency of your journal, its make-up and the efficient way in which it is conducted, will draw to you, as indeed it has done already, many more contributors besides myself.'

But it did not take Chekhov long to discover that Leykin's policy hampered his development as a writer. Leykin specialised in miniature stories, which, though rather of a 'liberal' tendency, did not give a writer of Chekhov's genius sufficient scope to express himself. In reply to Leykin, who wrote on January 12th, 1883, that what he wanted was 'very short stories and sketches—just the sort of thing you have been sending me', Chekhov declared that he was all in favour of 'little' stories and that if he had been the editor of a literary journal he would have cut down everything that was too long. 'I myself', he went on, 'am conducting a campaign against long stories in the Moscow journals (which does not prevent me, however, from occasionally giving them a story that is rather long—you can't kick against the pricks), but at the same time I must confess that an imposed limit "from here to there" does cause me a great deal of trouble. It is not always easy to accept such a limitation. For instance, you do not want any stories of over a hundred lines, and you may have a good reason for it. Now, I get a subject for a story and sit down to write it, but the thought of one hundred lines and no more interferes with my writing from the very start. I condense as much as I can and keep cutting it down, sometimes (as my literary sense warns me) to the detriment of my subject and, (above all) to the story's form. Having strained and compressed it, I begin to count the lines, and having counted 100, 120, 140 (I never wrote more than that for *Fragments*) I begin to get frightened and I don't send it. Very often I have to rewrite the ending of a story in a hurry and send you something I should not ordinarily have liked to send you. As soon as I go over the fourth page of small note-paper I begin to be assailed by doubts. . . . I should therefore like to ask you to increase the length of my stories to 120 lines. I am sure I shall not avail myself of this concession too frequently, but the knowledge that I have been granted it will save me a lot of worry.'

Leykin was only too anxious not to antagonise Chekhov and he readily agreed to grant him that 'concession'. 'While I rely on you not to misuse it,' he wrote, 'I willingly give you my blessing on 120, 140 and even 150 lines, only please send me something without fail for every issue of the magazine.'

For the time being, therefore, this difficulty was got over. But very soon another difficulty arose. Leykin only wanted mildly humorous stories. He strongly objected to anything serious. In April 1883 Chekhov sent him two stories, *The Thief*, dealing with the advantage a 'dishonest' thief had over an 'honest' one even while serving a sentence of transportation, and *The Willow*, exposing the corruption of civil servants who misappropriated the money a murderer had hidden under a tree. In reply to Leykin's complaint that the two stories were 'a little too serious for *Fragments*', Chekhov for the first time formulated the principle that was to underlie all his writings in future. The thing he valued most about a story, he wrote, was its good plot and its *effective protest*. And, indeed, what is so remarkable about Chekhov's juvenilia is that in one form or another they all contain a criticism of life. That at once marked him out as different from the hundreds of other contributors to the Russian popular magazines. In his early twenties, therefore, Chekhov was already deeply conscious of the high purpose of literature, however little he may at the time have respected his own writings. 'A small story', he told Leykin, 'containing a good plot and an effective protest is, so far as I am able to observe, read with pleasure or, in other words, is not dull. Besides,' he added rather ingenuously, 'a good word uttered on behalf of a thief at Easter will not ruin your journal. And, to tell you the truth, it is not so easy to chase after humour. In running after humour you are sometimes liable to write something that will make you sick. So that you just can't help trying to be serious occasionally.' However, he was not yet in a position to disregard Leykin's wishes, and he promised to write serious stories only at Easter and at Christmas.

What Chekhov valued so greatly about *Fragments* was the regularity with which he was paid for his contributions on the first of each month. 'If all magazines were as honest as *Fragments*', he wrote to Alexander in May 1883, 'I should by now have had my own carriage and pair.' And a few months later he could not help expressing his thanks to Leykin himself. 'How punctually you send me my money,' he wrote. 'To us Muscovites this certainly seems like a miracle.' Leykin, on the other hand, did not hesitate to turn Chekhov's financial difficulties to his advantage. He seemed determined to make Chekhov into one of his hacks. In June 1883 he asked Chekhov to write a fortnightly Moscow column for him and he also wanted him to write captions for the cartoons he published in his journal. These captions, especially, became a real nightmare to Chekhov. 'If the writing of captions were as easy as lighting a cigarette', he wrote to Leykin in 1884, 'I should have sent you hundreds of them. But you know very well that it is easier to find a subject for a story than to think of a decent idea for a cartoon. I have even sent out an S O S promising to pay fifty copecks for an idea for a cartoon.' And some time later: 'I try hard to think of an idea for a cartoon, but all I get is a subject for a story or nothing at all.' And, finally, in October 1885: 'Alas, my brain is simply incapable of thinking of any more captions.'

But by that time he had already made up his mind to cut adrift from Leykin. The only thing that stopped him was his fear of insecurity: he could always get an advance from Leykin and he was sure of his monthly cheque. That was more than he could expect from any Moscow journal. Besides, he felt under an obligation to Leykin, however much he may have disliked his bullying and threats. Leykin, too, realised that unless he found a market for Chekhov's longer stories Chekhov would sooner or later find one himself and quite possibly give up writing for *Fragments*. He therefore had a talk to Sergey Khudekov, the owner and editor of the *Petersburg Gazette*, to which he was a regular contributor himself, and arranged with him to publish a weekly story by Chekhov. 'I have had an offer from Khudekov for you,' he wrote to Chekhov on April 24th, 1885. 'Would you be willing to write each Monday a story for the *Petersburg Gazette*? But having agreed to write every Monday, you must not let the paper down and must send your story punctually every Saturday. You will be paid seven copecks a line.'

Chekhov, as was to be expected, was overjoyed at the offer. At last he would be able to escape from Leykin's strait-jacket. 'I shall be glad to write for the *Petersburg Gazette*,' he wrote to Leykin on April 18th, 'and I promise to be as punctual as possible.'

It was characteristic of Leykin, however, that, having got Chekhov this opening on a daily newspaper, he immediately became jealous of the new opportunities it offered to a young writer of undoubted genius. The very first two stories (*The Last Female Mohican* and *The Diplomat*) Chekhov published in the *Petersburg Gazette* on May 6th and May 20th, 1885, provoked an ill-tempered outburst from Leykin. 'I was very angry indeed', he wrote to Chekhov on May 19th, 'about your failure to send me your stories regularly. Two of your stories have been published in the *Petersburg Gazette* and I was half minded to stop their publication and I was sorry I ever recommended you there. I am still sorry I did it, because I am sure that now you will be even less punctual with your contributions because of the *Petersburg Gazette*. I must always have one of your stories in reserve—remember that. It's the only way I can make sure that you won't leave me in the lurch, especially in the summer months when it is so confoundedly difficult to get contributors to send in their stories in time.'

It was Chekhov's first visit to Petersburg in December 1885 that brought about the final rift between him and Leykin. For it was in Petersburg that Chekhov discovered to his own amazement that he had become a famous writer. Indeed, his reception there opened his eyes to his own importance as one of the most influential young writers. 'They gave me such a reception in Petersburg', he wrote to his uncle Mitrofan, 'that two months later my head is still swimming from the praises they heaped upon me. . . . It seems that I am much better known in Petersburg than in Moscow.' And to Alexander he wrote: 'I was amazed at the reception they gave me in Petersburg. Suvorin, Grigorovich, Burenin—they all invited me and sang my praises.' His first reaction to this unexpected reception was a feeling of deep resentment against Leykin, who had gone specially to Moscow to fetch him and whose lavish hospitality he had enjoyed during his fortnight's stay in Petersburg. He blamed Leykin, and not without good reason, for having kept him in ignorance of the great reputation his stories had won him in Petersburg because he wanted him to be tied to his own magazine. How furious he was with Leykin can perhaps be best gathered from the letter he wrote to Alexander shortly after his return to Moscow. After warning his brother not to believe 'the limping devil', he went on: 'If in the scriptures the devil is called the father of lies, then our editor can at least be called their uncle. It was not he who dragged me to Petersburg; I went there of my own free will and against Leykin's wishes, for my presence in Petersburg was in many respects disadvantageous to him. . . . In general, he is a liar, a liar, a liar. Don't pay any attention to him and keep on writing, remembering that you are not writing for limping men but for men who go straight.' And in another letter, after warning Alexander not to permit Leykin to cut down his stories or to rewrite them, Chekhov wrote: 'Living with Leykin I suffered all the tortures about which it is written in the scriptures: "he endureth to the end". He fed me like a king, but—the beast—he nearly choked me with his lies. . . . Do not rely on Leykin. He is doing his best to trip me up in the *Petersburg Gazette*. He will trip you up, too.' And in a letter to Alexander in April 1886 he roundly declared: 'Leykin is no longer popular. I have taken his place. I am enjoying great popularity in Petersburg now, and I shouldn't like you to lag behind.' He summed up his final opinion of Leykin in a letter to Suvorin in November 1888. 'Leykin', he wrote, 'is a good-natured and harmless man, but a bourgeois to the marrow of his bones. If he goes to see someone or says something, there is always something at the back of his mind. . . . A fox is always in fear for his life, and so is he. A subtle diplomatist! . . . In his letters to me he always warns me, frightens me, advises me, reveals all sorts of secrets to me. Poor limping martyr! He could have lived happily for the rest of his life, but some evil genius doesn't let him.'

After his return to Moscow from his first visit to Petersburg, it was Chekhov's firm intention to sever his connexion with *Fragments* as soon as possible. His contributions to the journal, which rose from seventy-five stories in 1883 to eighty-seven stories in 1884, dropped to fifty-nine in 1885 and to forty-eight in 1886. But Leykin hung on to him like grim death and Chekhov did not find it easy to shake him off. 'I should be glad', he wrote to Alexander, 'to stop working for *Fragments* altogether, for I am sick and tired of the trivial stuff. I want to do bigger things, or nothing at all.' He began sending Leykin his stories at longer intervals and recommending all sorts of writers to him to fill the gap left by himself. 'I feel guilty before you,' he wrote to Leykin in May 1886. 'I am working badly for *Fragments*.' A month later he wrote: 'I am still as lazy as ever.' Two months later he thought a longer excuse necessary. 'I haven't sent you a story for the last number,' he wrote, 'because, to be quite frank and honest with you, I could not think of a subject. I thought and thought, but could not think of anything, and I did not want to send you some rubbish, and, besides, it is so boring. But I did make my brother promise to send you a story and to tell you that I would not send you anything for that number.' He then tried to palm off a new acquaintance of his, Maria Kisselev, on him. 'I am sending you a story by a lady I know,' he wrote on October 7th. 'She is a very nice and intelligent woman, who is working mostly for children's magazines. Having read one of her stories, I asked her to write something for *Fragments*. She has now written a story for you which, as you will see for yourself, is not at all bad. It's literary and not without a certain idea behind it. The important thing is that it is so short. (Ladies rarely write short!) It's a little sentimental, but that doesn't matter. She is a very literary lady, a great friend of my family, highly respectable and (not to suggest any wrong ideas to you) middle-aged.'

Leykin wrote back indignantly that Chekhov wanted to shake him off, but he would not admit so ungrateful an action. 'Now', he wrote to him in January 1887, 'I'd like to discuss a rather ticklish matter with you. Money should never be allowed to interfere with friendship, and therefore I make bold to write the following. Since so far as *Fragments* are concerned I am no longer to be relied on as a punctual contributor, I think it would be only fair if you stopped paying me extras. Don't you think so? Please do as I ask, and give the necessary instructions to your office. I shall do my best to go on working for you as before, but I can't guarantee that I shan't again feel too stupid to write anything for *Fragments*. That will be fair all round and I expect to be paid per line in future.' Five days later he wrote to Alexander: 'I am expecting Leykin's visit to Moscow with a sad and contrite heart. I am now engaged in a dispute with this Quasimodo. I have refused to accept any extra payments or to send him any regular contributions, and he sends me lachrymose and hectoring letters, accusing me of treachery, double-dealing, etc. He lies that he is getting letters from subscribers who ask him why Chekhonte is no longer writing for his journal. He is cross with me for not working for him. I shall demand twelve copecks a line.' He got his twelve copecks a line, but that did not alter the situation. He had gone to Taganrog and the Don steppe for six weeks in April and May and on his return he found an angry letter from Leykin for sending stories to the *Petersburg Gazette* and not to *Fragments*. Chekhov apologised, pleading that he had to force himself to write during his travels so as not to let his family starve, and when Leykin pointed out that he could have got the money from him, he replied—this time with his tongue in his cheek: 'You write that I should have got no less money for my stories from *Fragments* and that they would have been just the thing for your journal. Oh, what an awful man you are!' And quite brutally for a change, for Leykin had got him thoroughly roused by this time, he wrote on August 11th: 'Tell me quite frankly, aren't you sick and tired of editing *Fragments*? If I were you, I should have sent everything to the devil, put all the money I had in my pocket and gone on a tour round the world. Singapore, I am told, is a wonderful spot. . . . Life is short, and in Petersburg it is dull and grey—one ought not to miss such a chance.' And in December, in reply to Leykin's last desperate appeal to him not to forsake *Fragments*, he wrote: 'You write that you don't care how bad my story is, but I don't agree with you. *Quod licet Iovi, non licet bovi.* What will be forgiven a man like you who has already done his share of work and who therefore has earned the right to be careless now and then, will never be forgiven to a mere beginner like me.' That was open derision, and to soothe Leykin's pain, Chekhov added: 'For heaven's sake do not think there is some evil purpose in the tardiness with which I work for you or that I am shunning *Fragments*. Not a bit of it. *Fragments* is my font and you are my godfather.' And there could be no fairer admission than that.

Chekhov had contributed only fourteen stories to *Fragments* in 1887, and after that year his work for Leykin stopped.

4

In the five years between 1882 and 1887 Chekhov had not only become a famous writer, but, as his relations with Leykin show, had also acquired the necessary degree of self-confidence in his literary ability to be able to stand on his own feet. He did not achieve it all without a hard struggle. Indeed, the first five years of his literary work were the hardest years of his life. And yet, though he was devoting most of his time to his study of medicine and, in addition, turning out innumerable stories and articles (by the end of 1887 he had written about six hundred short stories), he did not by any means live the life of a recluse. Indeed, his zest for life in his early twenties was so great that nothing could curb it. He had a wide circle of friends, particularly among the bohemian set of his brother Nicholas, whom he used to amuse by his remarkable gift of dramatisation. His sense of observation was so keen and his ability to pick out the comic sides of a man's character so natural that a walk in the street provided him with enough material for the comic improvisations with which he constantly regaled his friends. In telling his stories he would act his characters so convincingly that his voice, face and gestures would change instantaneously as soon as he brought a new character into his story. But it was not only his gaiety that was so infectious. Already in those early days he possessed the strange magnetic power of attracting people and fascinating them by his mere presence. There was an inexhaustible source of sympathy and goodfellowship in him which was irresistible. Women, in particular, found him very attractive, and the fantastic tales of his love affairs which went the rounds of Moscow and Petersburg when he had already become famous as a writer no doubt went back to the time when he was a student. One of his love affairs with a ballerina he recalled in a letter to Suvorin in December 1889. He never liked the ballet, finding it too artificial an art for his taste. 'No one wants the ballet,' he went so far as to declare in one of the Moscow notices he wrote for *Fragments* in 1883, 'and yet it is eating up hundreds of thousands of roubles every year. It keeps going simply because it has become a tradition, and that tradition costs us more than any novelty. The repair of an old watch sometimes costs more than the purchase of a new one.' The reason why he went to the ballet in 1882 was a purely personal one. 'I don't understand anything about the ballet,' he wrote to Suvorin. 'All I know about it is that during the intervals the ballerinas stink like horses. When I was a second-year student I fell in love with a ballerina and used to go to the ballet very often.' The writer Yozhov, who was very friendly with Chekhov in the 'eighties, though after his death he wrote a most venomous attack on him, records another affair of his with a French comédienne at the Hermitage amusement park. There can be no doubt that Chekhov's profound knowledge of women was derived at first hand. The same is true of the Moscow prostitutes. 'As for the tarts,' he wrote to the poet Pleshcheyev in connexion with his story *A Nervous Breakdown* in November 1888, 'I used to be a great expert on them many years ago.'

Chekhov's curiosity was not only insatiable—it was also creative, and, above all, critical. He never accepted anything at its face value. So far as the art of the stage was concerned, it is surely remarkable that at the age of twenty-two he should have come to the same conclusions as those Stanislavsky reached only towards the end of his life after many years of painstaking analysis. This is clearly shown by the two articles on Sarah Bernhardt which he published in 1881 and the article on a performance of *Hamlet* which he published in 1882. At the Russian Empire Exhibition, which took place in Moscow in the summer of 1882, Chekhov had a furious argument with a well-known Petersburg playwright in which he expressed views which were substantially identical with Stanislavsky's views at the time of the foundation of the Moscow Art Theatre. The Russian actor, he claimed, possessed everything except a good education, culture and, generally, 'gentlemanliness in the good sense of that word'. The absence of that 'inner gentlemanliness' was even more characteristic of the Russian actors than their addiction to drink, their reckless neglect of their work, and their love of the limelight. He maintained that good education was a prime necessity of good acting, and, like Stanislavsky, he deplored the prevalence of drinking habits among the actors. The stage, he insisted, was not a pub or a 'Tartar restaurant', and once the 'public house' element was introduced into it, it would never come to anything, 'just as a university which smells of the barracks can never come to any good'.

It was at the same exhibition that Chekhov delivered himself of an incautious remark that might have involved him in serious trouble. A bad train crash had occurred just then and the news of it reached Chekhov while he was standing at the kiosk of one of the smaller magazines to which he was contributing at the time. His comment was that such a terrible accident could only have occurred 'in our swinish Russia'. According to Michael, an army general in a blue peaked cap and with large epaulettes overheard Chekhov's remark and rushed up to him, shouting, 'What did you say, sir? Repeat it, please! Was it "in our swinish Russia"? What's your name, sir? Who are you?' Chekhov expected to be arrested (which would have ended his university career), but, fortunately, the incident passed off harmlessly.

The constant nervous strain under which he lived aggravated by overwork and money worries, soon made itself felt. Michael records that 'the moment he fell asleep, he began "to jerk". He would suddenly wake up terrified, a strange force seemed to throw him up on the bed, something inside him seemed to be torn up "by the root", he would jump out of bed and could not go to sleep for a long time'. Chekhov refers to these convulsions of his in several of his letters. They usually occurred whenever he sat up late writing his stories after a hard day's work at the university. In November 1882, that is, just when he was beginning to work for *Fragments*, he sent the following characteristic account of an evening at home to Alexander in Taganrog (Ivan had by that time got a job as a teacher at an elementary school in Voskressensk,

72

a small town near Moscow, famous for the New Jerusalem monastery in its vicinity): 'Nicholas is in Voskressensk with Mary, it's Michael's name-day, father is asleep, mother is saying her prayers, Aunt Feodossia is thinking about her currants, Anna [their maid] is washing up and will presently bring in the chamber-pot, I am writing and wondering how many times I shall be jerked out of bed in the night because I dare to go on writing. I am also working at my medicine. Operations every day. I read, write, go a-roving in the evenings, drink vodka in moderation, listen to music, singing, etc.' Five months later he again mentioned his convulsions in a letter to Alexander. 'My writing', he wrote, 'brings me nothing but violent nervous convulsions. The hundred roubles a month I get for it is all spent on food and I can't afford to change my shabby jacket for something less old and threadbare. I pay and pay and am left with nothing. The family alone spends more than fifty roubles. I can't even afford my fares to Voskressensk. Nicholas hasn't a penny, either. My only consolation is that I haven't any creditors. I received seventy roubles from Leykin in April and now I can't afford a cab.' He had, in fact, to borrow a morning coat from a friend in order to go to a wedding. The conditions under which he had to work were also quite intolerable. He and his numerous family (their lodgers soon found other accommodation) lived in a small flat for which they paid forty roubles a month and in which Chekhov had no room of his own. 'I am writing under the most disgusting conditions,' he wrote to Leykin at the end of August 1883. 'There is, besides, my non-literary work that has to be done, in the next room the child of a relative of mine [Alexander and his family were just then staying with them] is crying, in the other room father is reading aloud a Leskov story to mother, someone has wound up our music-box and I can hear *Fair Helen*. I wish I could escape into the country, but it is one o'clock in the morning. For a writer there can be nothing worse than such a situation. . . . My bed is occupied by my visiting relative who comes up to me every minute and starts talking about medicine. "I expect baby must have a tummy-ache," he says, "that's why he's crying." I am unfortunate enough to be a medical man and everyone I know thinks it incumbent upon him "to have a chat" about medicine with me. When they get tired of discussing medicine, they discuss literature. It's quite an extraordinary situation. I'm cursing myself for not having run away to the country where I should most certainly have been able to have a good sleep and to write a story for you, and, above all, medicine and literature would have been given a rest. . . . The child is bawling! I have just made a

73

resolution never to have any children. I expect the French have so few children because they are a literary people and write stories for the *Amusant*. I understand their government wants to force them to have more children—a good subject for *Amusant* and *Fragments* in the form of a cartoon: The State of Affairs in France—enter a policeman and demands children.'

More than a year later, in October 1884, Chekhov still complained of living 'abominably'. In a letter to Ivan he wrote: 'I am earning more money than any of your army lieutenants, but I have no money, no decent food, no room of my own where I could do my work. . . . At this moment I haven't a penny and I'm waiting anxiously for the first of the month when I shall receive sixty roubles from Petersburg which I shall spend immediately.' In the same month he wrote to Leykin, who had been appealing to him not to write for any other journal, but send all his stories to *Fragments*: 'Please don't be angry with me. I am a family man, and an impecunious one at that. . . . I simply must earn between one hundred and fifty and one hundred and eighty roubles a month, otherwise I am bankrupt.' And when Leykin tried to persuade him to pay a visit to Petersburg in 1885, his reply was: 'Because I live with a large family, I never have ten roubles at my disposal, and I must have a minimum of fifty roubles for such a journey. I simply don't know how I can possibly squeeze it out of my family. If I reduce their dinners from two courses to one I shall die of remorse.'

Leykin did the next best thing: he came to see Chekhov in Moscow, and in October 1883 he brought Leskov with him. The twenty-three-year-old Chekhov took the fifty-two-year-old Leskov round all the Moscow entertainment places, including the notorious *Salon des Variétés*, and on October 12th Leskov presented Chekhov with an autographed copy of his *Lefthanded Artificer*. One night as they were returning in a cab from some Moscow night-club, Leskov, who was tipsy, turned to Chekhov and uttered a few prophecies.

'Do you know who I am?' he asked.

'I do,' replied Chekhov.

'No, you don't. I am a mystic.'

'I know that, too.'

Leskov glared drunkenly at him.

'You will die before your brother,' he mumbled.

'Possibly,' said Chekhov, thinking of the even more sinister prophecy of Turgenev's 'ghost'.

'I am anointing thee with oil,' Leskov went on in his most Biblical vein, 'as Samuel anointed David. Write.'

'That man', Chekhov wrote to Alexander, after describing this conversation in the cab between himself and Leskov, 'looks like an elegant Frenchman and also like a defrocked priest. He is a big man worthy of attention. When I am in Petersburg I shall call on him. We parted great friends.'

They did meet again several times, and in 1892 Leskov presented Chekhov with a copy of his famous novel *Cathedral Folk*, inscribed: 'To the successful Dr. Antonio from the author.'

Chekhov's brother Ivan indirectly played an important part in the development of Chekhov's talent. For by staying at his flat in Voskressensk, which provided spacious summer quarters for the whole Chekhov family, he was able to make a thorough study of the Moscow countryside which plays so prominent a part in his stories. An artillery battery was stationed in Voskressensk, commanded by a Colonel Mayevsky, whose children supplied Chekhov with the subject for his story *Children*, written in 1886. The artillery battery and its officers provided him with the background of his story *The Kiss*, written in 1887, and many years later of his play *The Three Sisters*. Michael left this description of him during his visits to Voskressensk: 'Tall, in a black cape and a wide-brimmed black hat, Chekhov took part in all our country walks, the Mayevsky children running ahead and the grown-ups walking behind, carrying on "liberal" conversations on the burning topics of the day.' Chekhov made other acquaintances among the doctors of the district, including Dr. Arkhangelsky, who was in charge of the hospital in Chikino, a small town near Voskressensk, where Chekhov began to work as assistant doctor as early as 1881. Some evenings Chekhov would spend at Dr. Arkhangelsky's house, where impromptu parties were held during which the usual amount of vodka was consumed and current literature hotly discussed. 'Saltykov-Shchedrin', Michael records, 'was the constant subject of debate and everybody raved about him. Turgenev, too, was read a lot.'

Some of the most famous of Chekhov's stories of that period, such as *A Daughter of Albion, He Understood, A Dead Body, The Surgery, Sergeant Prishibeyev, A Chameleon, A Malefactor, The Last Female Mohican* (the first story published in the *Petersburg Gazette* in May 1885), were based on his experiences in Voskressensk and its surroundings. 'I shall take you to the hospital (a story of three hundred lines),' Chekhov wrote to Leykin whom he had invited to visit him in the country. 'On July 20th I shall have sixty out-patients and on July 22nd forty.'

'I live in New Jerusalem now,' he described his life in the country in a letter to Leykin on June 25th, 1884, after he had finished his course at the university. 'I am in fine fettle, for I have my medical diploma in my pocket. The countryside all around is magnificent. Plenty of room and no holiday-makers. Mushrooms, fishing, and the district hospital. The monastery is very romantic. Standing in the dim light of the aisle beneath the vaulted roof during an evening service, I am thinking of subjects for my stories. I have plenty of subjects, but I am absolutely incapable of writing anything. I'm too lazy. . . . I am writing this letter—lying down. With a book propped up on my stomach, I can just manage to write it. I'm too lazy to sit up. They have an Easter Service with all its glories every Sunday in this monastery. Leskov probably knows of this peculiarity of our monastery. Every evening I go for country walks in a company that flaunts its men's, women's and children's *modes et robes*. In the evening I usually walk down to the post office to get my letters and newspapers from our local postmaster and rummage among his letters, reading the addresses with the zeal of a curious idler. Our postmaster gave me the subject for my story *A Civil Service Examination*. In the morning one of our local veterans, Grandpa Prokudin, a desperate fisherman, comes to fetch me. I put on my waders and go with him to make an attempt on the lives of perch, tench and chub. Grandpa sits fishing all day long, but I am quite content with five or six hours. I eat a lot and drink in moderation. My family lives with me, cooking, baking and roasting whatever I can afford to buy for the money I earn by my writing. Life isn't too bad. One thing, though, is not so good: I am lazy and not earning enough. . . .'

In his next letter to Leykin of June 27th, 1884, he gave the following detailed description of an autopsy he had to carry out in a field as part of his medical duties, which a year later he incorporated in his story *A Dead Body*:

'I have just come back from a post-mortem which took place eight miles from Voskressensk. I drove there in a *troika* together with an ancient and decrepit examining magistrate who was so old that he was scarcely able to draw his breath and was generally entirely useless—a dear little white-haired old man who had been dreaming of a place on the bench for the last twenty-five years. I carried out the post-mortem assisted by the local district doctor in a field, beneath the green foliage of a young oak-tree, beside a country road. The dead man was not a "local man", and the peasants on whose land the body was found entreated us tearfully not to carry out the post-mortem in their village. At first the examining magistrate, afraid that it might rain, made difficulties, but realising that he could write out a draft of his report in pencil first, and seeing that we were quite ready to cut up the body in the open, he gave in. An anxious village, the witnesses, the village policeman with his tin badge, the widow raising a clamour fifty yards from the place of the post-mortem, and two peasants acting as watchmen near the corpse. . . . Near them a small camp fire dying down. To keep watch over a corpse day and night till the arrival of the authorities is one of the unpaid duties of peasants. The body, in a red shirt and a pair of new boots, is covered with a sheet. On the sheet is a towel with an icon on top of it. We ask the policeman for water. There is plenty of water—a pond a few yards away, but no one offers us a bucket: we shall pollute it. The peasants try to get round it: they steal a bucket from a neighbouring village. Where, how and when they have had the time to steal it remains a mystery. But they are terribly pleased with their heroic feat and are grinning quietly to themselves. The post-mortem reveals twenty fractured ribs, emphysema, and a strong smell of alcohol from the stomach. Death was due to suffocation. The man's chest had been crushed by something heavy, probably by a drunken peasant's knee. The body is covered with abrasions as a result of the artificial respiration. The local peasants who found the body applied artificial respiration so energetically that the future counsel for defence would be quite justified in asking the medical expert whether the fracture of the ribs could have been caused by the attempts to revive the dead man. But I don't somehow think that the question will ever be asked. There won't be any counsel for the defence and there won't be any accused. The examining magistrate is so decrepit that not only a murderer but a sick bedbug would escape his notice. . . . Let me add one more interesting fact and I shall have done. The murdered man was a factory worker. He was coming from a nearby pub with a small barrel of vodka. One of the witnesses who was the first to discover the body deposed that he saw the barrel near the body. But an hour later, passing the same way, he saw that the barrel was no longer there. Ergo: the publican, who has no off-licence, stole the barrel from the dead man to destroy the evidence.'

5

It was at the very start of his career that the dark shadow of tuberculosis fell across Chekhov's life. Even today it is little realised how radically his illness influenced his character, or, indeed, what far-reaching changes it brought about in his private life. It is generally believed that his illness began during the trial of Rykov and his associates, all of them directors of a bank in the small town of Skopin near Moscow, which Chekhov reported for the *Petersburg Gazette*. It was one of the most sensational trials of the time, it being rumoured that many high-placed persons, including members of the Czar's family, received big 'loans' from the Skopin bank, which had attracted thousands of depositors from all over Russia by the offer of an enormous rate of interest. Chekhov was naturally eager to be present at the trial, and on November 4th he asked Leykin to arrange for the publication of his reports of the trial in the *Petersburg Gazette*. 'On the 22nd the trial of Rykov will open,' he wrote. 'I shall be at the district court, for I have a ticket. Would the *Petersburg Gazette* like a series of articles on it? If they would, please recommend me. I shall not ask much: fifty roubles an article. The trial will go on for twelve days. There are sure to be sensational developments.' Leykin replied that he had had a talk with Khudekov, who would like 'short humorous sketches' from the court for which he was willing to pay seven copecks a line. Chekhov agreed, though the sixteen articles he wrote were not exactly the 'humorous sketches' Khudekov wanted, but dramatically written summaries of the court proceedings. The trial lasted from November 22nd to December 8th, and on December 8th Chekhov's first serious haemorrhage occurred.

It is now certain, however, that his illness started long before Rykov's trial. A year earlier, on December 10th, 1883, a passage occurs in one of his letters to Leykin, which, in view of the subsequent development of his illness, shows that it was then that he fell ill with tuberculosis. 'I am dreadfully tired, bad-tempered and ill,' Chekhov wrote. 'Last week I lay ill with a fever for three days. At first I thought that I must have contracted typhus at the hospital, but, thank God, I have been spared that.' The identical kind of fever recurred on November 4th, 1884. 'I have a splitting headache and a fever,' he wrote to Leykin on that day, 'and I am not in a condition to work.' On December 10th he wrote to Leykin: 'For the last three days blood has been flowing from my throat. This haemorrhage is interfering with my writing and will prevent me from going to Petersburg. I must say I hadn't expected this to happen to me. I haven't seen a white spittle for three days, and I do not know whether the medicines my colleagues are stuffing me with will be of any use. My general condition is satisfactory. The cause of it is probably a burst blood vessel. . . . My only consolation is that the chemist is letting me have my medicine at a reduced price. . . . And it would be just not that I would get patients. I ought to go to see them, but I can't.'

Chekhov's first haemorrhage was quite likely precipitated by the excitement of Rykov's trial and the extremely bad conditions under which the reporters had to work in the courtroom. 'The reporters', Chekhov wrote in his first article in the *Petersburg Gazette,* 'are terribly cold. Their tables have been placed between the cold columns of the courtroom and right in front of the windows from which an icy wind is blowing as if from a cellar. Their faces are blue with cold. It would not surprise me if half of them fell ill with rheumatism and fever.' His illness created, in Chekhov's own phrase, 'an upheaval at his home, for an uncle (his mother's brother) and a cousin of his had died of consumption. It was to calm them that he pretended that his blood-spitting was due, as he wrote to Leykin, to a burst blood vessel in his throat and had nothing to do with consumption. He repeated this denial in a letter he wrote on December 17th to his former school-fellow Peter Sergeyenko, who had also been a contributor to the Moscow humorous journals. 'I wanted very much to be in Petersburg for the holidays,' he wrote, 'but I had to postpone my visit because of blood-spitting (not tubercular).' Writing to the wife of his friend Savelyev on January 2nd, 1885, he confessed that his illness had frightened him a little, but added that it had also given him many happy hours, for he had received so many tokens of friendship that he almost imagined himself 'an Arcadian prince surrounded by a crowd of courtiers'. But in a letter to his uncle Mitrofan, with whom he was always more out-spoken than with any other member of his family, he did not hesitate to hint that he had consumption. 'Last December', he wrote on January 31st, 'I fell ill with blood-spitting and made up my mind to raise a loan from the literary fund and go abroad for treatment. Now I am feeling a little better, but I'm afraid I shan't be able to avoid a journey abroad. Wherever I decide to go,' he added, 'whether abroad or to the Crimea or the Caucasus, I shall pay a visit to Taganrog first.' He did not pay his visit to Taganrog nor did he go abroad or to the Crimea till a long time after, but the very fact that he contemplated such a journey shows that he knew perfectly well that he had T.B. That, indeed, was the reason why he always refused to be medically examined. Only once— in the summer of 1887—did he seem to have made up his mind to consult a doctor. In his reminiscences of Chekhov, Dr. Arkhangelsky recalls how one day in July or August of that year Chekhov came to see him. He was looking very tired and, in that roundabout way which was already becoming a habit with him, began to complain that his 'spleen' was aching. Arkhangelsky, who, like many other of Chekhov's friends, must have known what his real trouble was, offered to examine him. At that very moment, however, Chekhov caught sight of the proofs of a medical treatise his friend had written and, as he had been contemplating writing a book on the history of medicine in Russia himself, he began looking through them. 'We began discussing my treatise,' Arkhangelsky writes, 'and our talk about his "spleen" did not take place after all. Chekhov', he adds, 'often complained of a pain in the left side. "My spleen aches," he used to say, but in so jocular a way that he never gave one the chance of insisting on a medical examination.'

Chekhov had no choice but to conceal the true nature of his illness, for the only cure known in those days—a prolonged stay in the Crimea or some recognised resort abroad—was beyond his means and would in any case have meant sacrificing his family and giving up his medical as well as his literary career. But as his illness could not be concealed even from those of his friends who were not doctors, he persistently denied its existence. That, at any rate, made it easier for him to live at home, for he could never have endured his mother's nagging solicitude for the state of his health. Having therefore made up his mind to deny the existence of his illness, he resorted to all sorts of 'logical' explanations of its symptoms. 'First about my blood-spitting,' he wrote, for instance, to Suvorin in October 1888. 'I noticed it for the first time in the district court three years ago: it went on for three or four days and produced an upheaval at home. It was profuse. The blood flowed from my right lung. Since then I have noticed a flow of blood twice a year, either profuse, i.e. thickly colouring the sputum, or not so profuse. The day before yesterday, or a day earlier—I can't remember —I noticed that I was again spitting blood. Yesterday, too, but not today. Every winter, autumn and spring, and on every damp day, I cough. But all this alarms me only when I see blood: there is something sinister about the sight of blood flowing from the mouth, just as sinister as the red glow of a fire. But when there is no blood, I am not in the least worried, and I do not threaten Russian literature with "one more loss". The point to bear in mind is that consumption, or any other serious affection of the lungs, can be recognised only by a combination of symptoms and it is just that combination that does not exist in my case. By itself a discharge of blood from the lungs is not serious: blood sometimes flows from the lungs for a whole day, it simply pours out, the patient and his family are terrified, but it all ends in the patient's recovery—more often than not, at any rate. So you'd better make a note of it, just in case: if someone who is known not to be consumptive should have a discharge of blood from the mouth there is no need to be alarmed. A woman can lose half her blood without any danger to herself, and a man nearly half. If my haemorrhage in the district court had been a symptom of incipient consumption,' Chekhov concluded, 'I should have been dead long ago—that is my reasoning.'

But however curious that kind of reasoning may appear in the light of subsequent events, Chekhov never really believed in it himself, though he certainly did his best to make others believe in it. Thus he would occasionally murmur half-jestingly as he coughed: 'Consumption!' as though wishing to dispel suspicion by uttering the fearful word. Even after his illness could no longer be concealed from anybody but his parents, he would dismiss it lightheartedly, and during the last years of his life the phrase that recurred again and again in his letters and conversations was: 'I am perfectly well.' Professor Rossolimo thought that Chekhov's attitude towards his illness was 'remarkably characteristic'. 'As is well known,' he writes in his reminiscences of Chekhov, 'he suffered for more than ten years [actually for about twenty years] from tuberculosis of the lungs, which afterwards affected his bowels, too. It is also a well-known fact that T.B. patients regard their illness very optimistically, sometimes ignoring its symptoms altogether and sometimes trying to explain them by something other than tuberculosis, and quite often, even a short time before death, they think they are quite well. Chekhov, a doctor of medicine and a man of great sensibility who possessed the ability of analysis and self-analysis, though not denying the existence of his illness, treated it extremely thoughtlessly, to say the least, and tried to provide his own explanation of its symptoms. For instance, in a letter of September 30th, 1900, when the pulmonary process had quite obviously reached an acute stage, he wrote to me: "My health isn't too bad. I had a mild attack of influenza, but I am all right now, except that I am still coughing, but not much." Or on July 17th, 1904, that is, a fortnight before his death, he sent me a postcard on his arrival in Badenweiler, on which he wrote: "I have already recovered, except for my shortness of breath and my great and probably incurable laziness. I've grown very thin. The pain in my arms and legs had ceased even before I got to Warsaw." Even more striking', Rossolimo continues, 'is that passage in his letter in which he expressed the hope that he would be able to return to Russia by way of the Mediterranean and the Black Sea: "I have been running a high temperature these last few days, but today everything is all right. I feel quite well, especially when I do not walk, that is, when I am not troubled by shortness of breath. My

81

breathlessness is so bad that I almost feel like crying for help and even at times lose heart. Altogether I have lost fifteen pounds in weight. It's terribly hot here, which makes me almost feel like crying for help, and I have no summer clothes, just as if I had gone to Sweden. But I am told it is hot everywhere, at least in the south." Here we have shortness of breath and the sensations caused by a high temperature, and debility (handwriting, style, etc.), and yet the diagnosis is wrong, since even while he was departing from life, a fact that could no longer be doubted by those around him, he was still making plans to return to Yalta by a long sea voyage.'

But, as a matter of fact, there is nothing even in Chekhov's last letters to Rossolimo to suggest that he was not aware that he had only a short time to live. No one, not even his doctor, suspected that he would die within three days of his writing his last letter to Rossolimo, and the 'long' sea voyage he was planning would only have taken a few days. Nor was he unaware of the optimism of T.B. patients as can be plainly seen from a passage in his last short story *The Betrothed*, which he had expunged from the printed version no doubt because he feared that it might alarm his wife and family. It describes the last meeting between the heroine of the story and her childhood friend and mentor, Alexander, who, like Chekhov, was dying of consumption.

'They sat down and had a chat, then they drove to a restaurant for lunch; he ate, talked, and coughed all the time. She could not eat; she was looking at him fearfully all the time, afraid lest he should collapse in the restaurant and die.

' "Alexander, my dear," she said, putting her hand on his, "you are ill. You know you are."

' "No," replied Alexander [in the same phrase Chekhov used again and again], "I'm perfectly well."

'. . . He took her to the station, treated her to tea and bought her apples, and when the train began to move out he smiled and waved his handkerchief, but even his thin legs showed that he was very ill and would not last long.'

Chekhov wrote this when his own wasted legs, too, showed clearly that he was very ill and would not last long. Chekhov, in fact, never deceived himself. The great illusion he created round his illness was just another of the mystifications for which he was so famous, with the difference, however, that he had become so proficient in it that at times he almost believed in it himself.

6

In December 1884, his health having improved, Chekhov put up his brass plate and started his medical practice. Neither he nor any member of his family ever thought of his writing as anything but a temporary expedient to tide him over the difficult period before he could earn his living as a doctor. Leykin had 'prophesied' that the time would come when he would devote himself entirely to literature, but Chekhov did not take him seriously. Medicine, he was fond of saying, was his 'lawful wife' and literature only his 'mistress'. His mother, in particular, hoped fervently that he would follow the example of other Moscow doctors and marry the daughter of a rich Moscow merchant (Chekhov's story *Late Flowers* dealt with that particular aspect of a Moscow doctor's career), and his father heartily approved of her plan. They had even chosen his future bride for him—the daughter of Pavel's employer Gavrilov. 'I threatened father', Chekhov, who detested Gavrilov and all he stood for, wrote to Alexander in March 1888, 'that if I ever married Gavrilov's daughter I should make him into an errand-boy.' The intended match must have led to some stormy scenes in the Chekhov household, especially as Chekhov found it almost impossible to make any money by his medicine. 'My medical practice', he wrote to his uncle Mitrofan at the end of January 1885, 'keeps me busy. Every day I spend more than a rouble on cabs. I have many friends and acquaintances and therefore not a few patients. Half of them I have to treat gratis, and the other half pay me three or five roubles for a visit. (In Moscow doctors are never paid less than three roubles a visit. Here every kind of work is paid more highly than in Taganrog.) I haven't made my fortune yet and I don't expect to make one soon, but I live tolerably well and am not in need of anything. If my health continues to be good and I keep alive, the position of my family will be secure. I have bought new furniture, I employ two maids, I have a decent piano and am giving musical parties at which we play music and sing. I have no debts and there is no need for me to incur any. Not so long ago we used to get our provisions (groceries and meat) on credit, but now I have stopped all that and we pay cash for everything. I don't know what is going to happen in the future, but for the time being it would be invidious of me to complain.'

Chekhov's musical parties usually took place on Tuesdays. Mary, who had by then finished at her secondary school and was attending private university courses for women, brought her friends, and a gay company of young men and women would sing, play and read, Chekhov infecting everybody with his high spirits. 'Chekhov', Adolf Levitan, the brother of Chekhov's closest friend, the landscape painter Isaac Levitan, records, 'was the life and soul of those parties. The things he thought of to make us all enjoy ourselves! We nearly died of laughter.'

It was in 1885 that Chekhov and his family spent their first summer on Alexey Kisselev's Babkino estate near Voskressensk. Ivan had been appointed headmaster of an elementary school in Moscow and his flat in Voskressensk was no longer available. Kisselev had met him at a party given by Colonel Mayevsky and his fellow-officers and invited him to be the tutor of his two children. Mary, too, soon became a great friend of Kisselev's wife Maria. On learning of Chekhov's difficulty in finding a suitable country place for the summer, Kisselev offered to let him one of the cottages on his estate.

Chekhov had known of the great Russian country houses and their owners only from literature. His first attempt to deal with them in his rejected play *Platonov* was entirely derivative. Now he got the chance to study them at close quarters. The Kisselevs were the finest representatives of the class that had ruled Russia for centuries. Kisselev himself was the nephew of a former Russian ambassador to France and a Minister of State in the reign of Nicholas I. His wife Maria was the daughter of Vladimir Begichev, a former manager of the imperial theatres and a great friend of the popular novelist and playwright Boleslav Markevich. His latest theatrical venture, which failed for lack of financial support, was the foundation in Moscow of a 'people's theatre'. 'Begichev', Chekhov wrote in the Moscow column he was contributing to *Fragments* from July 1883 to October 1885, 'loves the theatre, but there is in him about as much energy and business acumen as there is truth in Markevich's works.' Markevich had just then turned his successful novel *Abyss* into the even more successful play *The Whirl of Life*. The play created a sensation in Moscow because its author had introduced many of his acquaintances and friends into it, 'a sign', Chekhov wrote, 'of a writer who cannot see further than his nose'. In his Moscow column Chekhov described *The Whirl of Life* as 'a play which was written with a broom and which has a bad smell'. Ten years later he referred to it again in *The Seagull*, Konstantin Treplyov bracketing it with *La dame aux camélias* as the two plays in which his mother scored a great success. He even wrote a parody of it for *Fragments*, but at the last moment decided not to publish it. 'Markevich', he wrote to Leykin, 'has a habit of bursting into tears every time he reads something uncomplimentary about himself. I shall have to quarrel with some of his admirers and friends however much I try to conceal myself behind a pseudonym. And it isn't worth while starting a row because of such rubbish.'

Chekhov certainly looked forward to his life at Babkino. He got an advance of a hundred roubles to cover the expenses of moving his household to the country. 'I shall live in the grounds of a landowner's country house where one can live even in winter,' he wrote to Leykin at the end of April. 'My summer cottage is within two miles of Voskressensk (New Jerusalem) on the estate of Kisselev, the brother of your Petersburg Kisselev-Hofmeister, etc. etc. I shall live in the rooms which were occupied last year by Markevich. His ghost will haunt me at night! I have rented the cottage with its furniture, vegetables, milk, etc. The country house is situated on the steep bank of a river. It is a very picturesque spot. Below is the river, famed for its fish; on the other side of the river is a huge forest; and there are woods also on this side of it. Near the cottage are hot-houses, flower-beds, etc. I love to be in the country at the beginning of May. It is so jolly to watch the buds opening on the trees and to listen to the first songs of the nightingales. There are no houses near the estate and we shall be completely alone. Kisselev and his wife, Begichev, the former opera tenor Vladislavlev, Markevich's ghost, and my family—that is all. The month of May is excellent for fishing, especially crucian carp and tench, that is, pond fish, and there are ponds on the estate.' He took his mother, his sister Mary and their maid Olga to Babkino on May 6th, and in his letter to Michael, who was then a twenty-year-old student of the law faculty of Moscow University, he left a detailed description of their journey and his first days in the country.

'At last', he wrote, 'I have taken off my heavy waders, my hands no longer smell of fish, and I can sit down to write to you. It is six o'clock in the morning now. Our people are asleep. It is extraordinarily quiet all round. Only from time to time is the silence broken by the twittering of the birds and by the scratching of a mouse behind the'wallpaper. I am writing these lines sitting before the large square window of my room. From time to time I glance through it. An extraordinarily enchanting and lovely landscape stretches before my eyes: the little stream, the distant woods, a corner of the Kisselev house. . . .

"We arrived here after a great deal of trouble. At the station we hired two ancient peasants to drive us to Babkino at three roubles each. . . . They drove us at a disgustingly slow pace. . . . The roads were terrible. . . . I had to walk more than half of the way. We crossed the river near Chikino. I was the first to cross over (it was dark by then) and I nearly got drowned and was drenched to the skin. Mother and Mary had to be rowed across in a boat. You can imagine the squeals, railway hissings and other expressions of female terror! In the Kisselev woods the traces of one of the horses got broken. More waiting. So it went on, and by the time we reached Babkino it was already one o'clock in the morning. . . .

'The doors of the cottage were not locked. We went in without having to rouse our landlord, lighted a lamp and beheld something that exceeded all our expectations. The rooms are huge, and there is more furniture than we need. Everything is extremely charming and cosy. Matchboxes, ash-trays, cigarette boxes, two wash-basins and—goodness only knows what the dear people did not put there. Such a country cottage would cost at least five hundred roubles near Moscow. You will see for yourself when you come. Having settled in, I put away our trunks and sat down to have a bite. I had some vodka and some wine and, you know, I experienced a wonderfully pleasant sensation as I looked out of the window at the dark shapes of the river and the trees. I listened to the song of the nightingale and could hardly believe my ears. I still imagined myself to be in Moscow. At daybreak Begichev walked up to our windows and blew a horn, but I did not hear him, for I slept like a drunken cobbler.

'As I was putting in a creel next morning, I heard a voice shouting, "Crocodile!" I looked up and saw Levitan on the other bank. He was taken across on a horse. After coffee I went shooting with him and the huntsman (a very typical one) Ivan Gavrilov. We wandered about for three and a half hours, covered about twelve miles, and shot one hare. The hounds were no good.

'Now about the fish. I have had no luck with my fishing rods. They usually fish for gudgeon and ruff here. I caught one chub, but it was so small that it should really be going to school and not be fried in a pan. It is possible to catch something with a pike-rod. I caught a huge burbot with Ivan's pike-rod. But pike-rods are not much use now because there aren't any small fish we could use for bait. Last night it was too windy for fishing. Bring some trailing hooks of medium size. I haven't a single one left.

'Oh, my creels! I had no trouble at all in bringing them. They were not crushed in the luggage and afterwards we tied them behind the carts. I put one in the river and it has already caught a roach and a gigantic perch. The perch is so big that we have invited Kisselev to lunch. The other creel I put in a pond first, but it caught nothing there. I put it in the stretch of water behind the pond. Yesterday I caught a

ANTON CHEKHOV 1898–99

perch in it and this morning Babakin [a small boy of a poor family Chekhov had befriended in Voskressensk] and I got *twenty-nine* crucian carp out of it. How do you like that? Today we shall be having fish soup, fried fish and jellied fish. So don't forget to bring two or three creels when you come. . . .

'Maria Kisselev is very nice. She gave mother a pot of jam and she supplies me with (old) anecdotes from French magazines. Profit—fifty-fifty. Kisselev spends every day with us. Yesterday he had a pasty with us and three large glassfuls of vodka. Begichev also lunched with us, but he did not drink. He had to be content with gazing longingly at the decanter of vodka.

'I don't drink, but we have no more wine left for all that. The wine is so excellent that Ivan and Nicholas must bring a bottle each when they come (they can carry it in their suitcases as I did). Wine is a god-send here. And what indeed can be more pleasant than a glass of wine on the terrace after lunch! You explain it to them. The wine is first-rate. . . . It's called Ahmet or Mahmet—white.

'Levitan lives near here in the village of Maximovka. He calls all fish crocodiles and has already made friends with Begichev who calls him Leviathan. "I'm bored without Leviathan," sighs Begichev when the crocodile isn't here.

' . . . Today', Chekhov concluded his letter, 'I got up at half-past three in the morning. I am drinking tea now and then going back to bed. I usually sleep till coffee and after coffee go to inspect the creels with Kisselev. Yesterday I wrote a lot and I am sending it off now. . . . On Sunday we shall go shooting again. Vladislavlev will be arriving shortly and he is bringing a sweep-seine with him. We shall have good sport! Give my regards to everybody.'

Maria Kisselev, too, was a passionate fisherwoman, and she and Chekhov spent hours fishing and discussing literature. She was a close friend of the composers Chaykovsky and Dargomiszky, and it was at Babkino that Chekhov first learnt to appreciate classical music. Begichev, whom Chekhov was to use as his model for Count Shabelsky in *Ivanov* three years later, had an inexhaustible fund of stories, some of which, such as the story of the low-grade civil servant who sneezed on the head of a Privy Counsellor at the theatre, Chekhov used for the subjects of his short stories. The beautiful Babkino countryside, too, and its lovely grounds—the 'English' park, the well-tended flower-beds, the hot-houses and the river—left their mark on Chekhov's writings. 'Nature herself', Michael writes, describing

Chekhov's life at Babkino, 'provided Chekhov with innumerable subjects and purely Babkino stories emerged from his pen. The moonlit garden in *Verochka* with the wisps of mist floating through it is the Babkino garden. His story *The Burbot* was actually based on an incident which had taken place during the erection of a bathing pavilion in Babkino. *The Witch* was suggested by the lonely church and its caretaker's lodge near the highway in the big Babkino forest. In almost all his stories of that period some traces of the Babkino landscape or some figure from Babkino itself or from the neighbouring villages can be detected.'

Babkino, too, had a most beneficial effect on Chekhov's health, chiefly owing to the regular life he led there. He usually got up at seven o'clock and immediately sat down at his improvised desk (the bottom part of a big sewing-machine from which the treadle had been removed) and wrote his stories, raising his eyes from time to time to have a look at the magnificent view through the large, square window, as though drawing inspiration from it. His room was sparsely furnished: a small bed covered with a striped blanket, a tall wardrobe at the bottom of the bed by the window, a bedside table with a candle in a cheap candlestick, a washbasin, and on the wall above the head of the bed a pair of chemist's scales in which he weighed out the medicines for the patients who flocked to him from all over the countryside. 'My patients', he wrote to Leykin in September 1885, 'are coming to me in droves and I am getting sick of the sight of them. During the summer I had several hundreds of them and all I earned was one rouble.' His surgery hours were from ten to one o'clock. At one o'clock he usually had lunch and then went for a walk in the woods. After tea he sat down to his writing again. In the afternoon he would fish or have a game of croquet, which would sometimes go on till after nightfall, when they would stick lighted candles near the hoops. At eight o'clock he had dinner, after which they all went to spend the evenings with the Kisselevs. Begichev was usually laying out patience, Vladislavlev would sing the latest songs accompanied on the piano by a friend of the family, an excellent woman pianist who would often play Beethoven and other classical composers (Chekhov's favourite piece of music was Chopin's Nocturne in G major and during his last years in Yalta he would often ask a visiting pianist to play it to him). Chekhov would sit down beside Maria Kisselev and listen to her stories of the great composers she had known or engage in literary discussions. There were also the two Kisselev children, Sasha and Sergey, with whom he loved to romp about and for whom he wrote his children's story *Softboiled Boots*, which he illustrated with pictures cut out from different children's magazines.

A great deal of his free time Chekhov spent with Levitan. One day Levitan's landlady, the wife of the village potter, came to see Chekhov (she was a patient of his) and told him that Levitan had fallen ill. It had been raining for several days and Chekhov surmised that Levitan must be suffering from one of his usual fits of depression. That night he, together with his brothers Ivan and Michael, trudged through the pouring rain across waterlogged fields to Levitan's village. They recognised the potter's cottage by the broken bits of pottery strewn all round it and, wishing to give Levitan a surprise, broke into his room, directing the beam of light from their lantern on his face. Levitan jumped up and snatched up his revolver, which he pointed at them. Then, recognising Chekhov, he muttered morosely: 'What on earth are you up to? Damn fools!' It did not take Chekhov long to cheer his friend up and soon they were all laughing together. Levitan soon left the potter's cottage and went to live in a small cottage on Kisselev's estate. Chekhov hung up a sign-post over his door with the inscription: 'Pawnshop of the Merchant Levitan.' Occasionally he would indulge in his elaborate pranks of mystification and fooling. Michael records one of these rather laborious pieces of play-acting. One evening Chekhov and Levitan put on long Bokhara coats, blackened their faces with soot, wound scarves round their heads to represent turbans, and proceeded to a field to enact an 'oriental' scene. Levitan rode off on a donkey, dismounted in the middle of the field, spread out a rug and began offering up evening prayers to Allah in the true fashion of a Mohammedan pilgrim. Suddenly Chekhov, who was acting a Bedouin tribesman, rushed out from behind some bushes and began firing blank shots at Levitan, who fell 'dead', thus bringing the 'oriental' scene to an end.

That was Chekhov's way of escaping from the constant worries that beset him on all sides. His greatest disappointment on graduating as a doctor was not lack of patients, but the slender chance there was of his being able to earn a living by medicine. He had been offered a job at a district hospital, but he refused it. He next tried to get a job through Leykin at one of the Petersburg hospitals, but that, too, came to nothing. Neither his medicine nor his writing seemed to guarantee a decent living to him, and he had to prolong his stay at Babkino till the end of September because he had not enough money to return to Moscow. Fortunately, the weather had improved by the middle of September and the fishing was good. 'The weather is excellent now,' he wrote to Leykin on the 14th. 'Indian summer. The cranes are flying. All the same, it is high time I returned home. The post has come, but there is still no money from the *Petersburg Gazette*. Without that money I cannot leave, for, counting on getting it, I have lived like a second Lucullus and got into debt. If I do not receive the money by the next post, I shall stay here for the whole of the winter, which will be new and original.'

He got his money at last and was back in Moscow on September 24th. On October 1st he went to the races for the first time in his life and had a flutter on a horse, winning four roubles. He was looking for a more comfortable flat, and on October 12th he moved into one on the other side of the river in the merchants' quarter of Moscow which he found very provincial—clean, quiet, cheap and a little dull. Just then the censorship at last got on Leykin's tracks and an entire issue of *Fragments* was censored and Leykin himself was warned that unless he mended his ways his journal would be closed down. 'The pogrom on *Fragments*', Chekhov wrote to Leykin on October 12th, 'was a terrible blow to me. On the one hand, I am sorry for my wasted labour, and, on the other, I cannot help feeling stifled and scared. . . . We shall have to wait and make the best of the present situation. But I expect that I shall have to cut and cut now . . . for I can foresee the time when even the word "merchant" will become a prohibited article. Literature certainly provides a very uncertain piece of bread, and you did well to be born earlier when it was so much easier to breathe and to write.' And in reply to Leykin's constant requests for more stories, Chekhov added: 'I cannot write more than I am doing now, for medicine is different from law: if you stop work, you are bound to lag behind. It follows, therefore, that my literary earnings must remain as they are. They may diminish, but increase they cannot.' This is Chekhov's first admission of the impossibility of combining a literary with a medical career. The time was near when he would have to choose between them. 'The fact that I write so little', he returned to the same subject in his next letter to Leykin, 'does not mean that I am lazy. I am so busy the whole day that I haven't yet been to a theatre. There is all the difference in the world between keeping up with the latest developments in medicine and working at it.' In the same letter he told Leykin that he was putting up shelves for a library: this is his first mention of his library which in the course of years was to include well over a thousand volumes.

Meanwhile his new flat proved unsatisfactory: it was too cramped and he still had no room of his own, but, above all, it was damp and that drove Chekhov into a panic, for he feared that there might be a recurrence of his illness. 'I am in a proper mess,' he wrote to Leykin in November. 'My new flat is awful: cold and damp. If I don't move out there is sure to be a repetition of my chest trouble: coughing and blood-spitting. There is nothing I dislike more than moving into a new flat. Now I shall again have to waste money on moving and changes of address. There is a vacant flat in the same street and I shall go and inspect it tomorrow. It's such an awful nuisance to live with a family,' he added, as though wishing to minimise the real reason for his decision to change his flat.

He moved into the new flat at the beginning of December, shortly before his first visit to Petersburg. There for the first time he had a room of his own: a study with an open fireplace where he worked and received his patients. The flat was on the ground floor, and that turned out to be a serious disadvantage, for the first floor of the house was occupied by a restaurant which was regularly let out for wakes and wedding parties. 'In the afternoon a wake, in the evening a wedding —death and procreation,' Chekhov wrote to Leykin. It is true that Chekhov, as was his wont, tried to exorcise the incubus by organising mock wedding parties at home and raising a row that sometimes drowned the row upstairs, but that did not stop the noise of the real wedding party which went on till the small hours of the morning and interfered with his sleep. 'Someone', he wrote to Leykin, 'has just rushed over my head, stamping his heels like a horse. The best man probably. The band is making a terrible din. Whatever for, for goodness' sake? What are they so happy about, the fools?'

It was not, however, till the autumn of 1886, that Chekhov at last found a decent two-storied house in Sadovo-Kudrinskaya Street, where he stayed for the next four years.

Part Three
FAME

Chekhov's first visit to Petersburg—he was there between December 10th and 24th, 1885—was the turning point in his career as a writer. For five years he had been contributing stories to various journals, and by the end of 1885 he had published almost three hundred of them, only six of which dealing with stage life he succeeded in bringing out in a separate volume in 1884 under the title of *Tales of Melpomene*. In addition, he published a large number of articles, most of them in the Moscow column of Leykin's journal under the heading of *Fragments of Moscow Life*, in which he dealt with every possible aspect of life in Moscow, such as the position of the shop assistants and factory workers, the high death-rate among the poor, the insanitary condition of the houses and streets, the unsatisfactory state of the cobbled roads, the high-handed behaviour of the water-carriers, the extortions of the undertakers, the uncivilised manners of the merchants, the absurd customs of the middle-classes, the vulgarity of the popular press, the villainy of the professional men who refused to repay their debts to the Society for Aiding Necessitous Students, the craze for champion runners, hypnotists, mediums and thought-readers,[1] the lamentable state of the theatre and the actors,[2] and so on. But he still did not take himself seriously as a writer and did not even suspect that he had made a name for himself in the Petersburg literary circles. In July 1885 he wrote two stories for the *Petersburg Gazette*—*The Burbot* and *The Gamekeeper*—in which he showed himself to be a descriptive writer of

[1] Among the famous thought-readers was an Englishman by the name of Bishop, whom Chekhov used for the following satirical notice:
'Mr. Bishop has been reading our "thoughts". Whether that occupation has made him more intelligent is hard to say, but, somehow, I don't think it has, for, having examined a thousand men, he found that they all had only one thought, namely "I hope to goodness they don't find out what I am thinking about—I am a family man!"
'A police inspector, who was present at one of these experiments in thought-reading, came to the alarming conclusion that every man had certain thoughts. "That's all due to lack of proper supervision," he muttered, frowning. "Mr. Bishop," he turned to the Englishman, "do you really think that people should have thoughts?"
' "Oh, yes, I most certainly do."
' "Well, sir," said the policeman, "all I can say is that you have just made a subversive statement. In England you may be permitted to have thoughts, but in our country all we are permitted to do is to obey our Lord and honour our parents. Move along there!" '
[2] 'The Muscovites', Chekhov wrote, 'are not interested in serious drama. What do they want drama for if they can do without it? The *Folies Bergère* does not put on any serious plays and yet see how packed it is and how the audience there enjoys itself!'

great originality. In Moscow these stories passed almost unnoticed, and Chekhov himself certainly did not realise that he had written anything out of the common. In Petersburg, on the other hand, these and many others of his stories had made him, as he later wrote to his uncle Mitrofan, 'into one of the most fashionable writers'. Dmitry Grigorovich, one of the veterans of the Russian novel, who at the age of sixty-four still lived on the reputation of the two novels of peasant life which he had published in 1846 and 1847 and which had been highly praised by so universally respected a critic as Vissarion Belinsky, was so impressed (as he wrote to Chekhov on March 24th, 1886) 'by the remarkable truthfulness of the delineation of the characters and the descriptions of nature' in *The Gamekeeper* that he went specially to see Suvorin to ask him to invite Chekhov to become a regular contributor to his big Petersburg daily *New Times*. Grigorovich's letter, as Chekhov expressed it in his excited reply to the venerable novelist on March 28th, came 'as a bolt from the blue'. The prestige of the novel as an art form was so great that it never occurred to Chekhov that his short stories had already placed him among the foremost writers in Russia. It seemed almost unbelievable to him that a novelist of such standing as Grigorovich should hail him as such. 'Unexpectedly, suddenly, like a *deus ex machina*,' Chekhov wrote to Victor Bibilin, the humorous writer who was secretary of *Fragments*, on April 14th, 'I received a letter from Grigorovich, followed shortly by another letter with his photograph, each over twenty pages long: handwriting illegible—of an old man. He is convinced that I possess real talent (underlined) and to prove that I am a genuine creative artist he cites passages from my stories. He writes warmly and sincerely. I am, of course, glad, but I cannot help feeling that he is rather overdoing it.' Chekhov, however, was much less reserved in his letter to Mitrofan. 'Russia', he wrote, 'has a great writer, D. V. Grigorovich, whose portrait you will find in *Modern Personalities*. Not so long ago, quite unexpectedly, I received a letter from him of over twenty pages. Grigorovich is so highly respected and popular a man that you can imagine how pleasantly surprised I was. I will quote you the following extract from his letter: " . . . You have *real* talent, which places you far above the present generation of writers. l am already a man of sixty-five, but my love for literature is still so great, I follow its successes with so much enthusiasm and I am so overjoyed to discover something living and talented that, as you see, I could not help writing this letter and I hold out both my arms to you." ' Chekhov then proceeded to quote the following extract from Grigorovich's second letter of

April 2nd: 'I hope to see you when you are in Petersburg again, when I shall embrace you as I am embracing you now in my thoughts.'

Chekhov's reply to Grigorovich, whom he addressed as 'my dear and beloved bringer of glad tidings', shows that his attitude to his literary work was not as 'condescending' as he pretended. It is significant that he should have stressed the importance of Grigorovich's letter to his 'ambition' as a writer and should have put the blame for his 'thoughtless, careless and perfunctory' attitude to his writing on his family which 'never thought much of my work and have kept telling me in a friendly way not to sacrifice my profession to my scribbling', and on his friends who 'neither read anything I have written nor ever regard me as an artist. We have in Moscow a so-called "literary circle",' he went on. 'Writers of talent and mediocrities of every age and colour meet once a week in the private room of a restaurant and wag their tongues. If I were to go there and read even a few lines from your letter to them, they would laugh in my face.' His second 'excuse' for not taking his literary work seriously was that his medicine kept him so busy that 'the proverb of running with the hare and hunting with the hounds never interfered with the sleep of anyone as much as with mine.' The first thing that drove him to self-criticism, he pointed out, was a letter from Suvorin, but he still had no faith in his literary ability till he received Grigorovich's letter which made him vow to get out of the rut in which he was stuck as soon as possible. Grigorovich had advised him to give up his commissioned work which had to be delivered at a certain date, but he felt that he was not yet in a position to do so. 'I don't mind starving as I have starved before,' he declared, 'but it is not a question of myself alone. I usually devote my free time to writing, two or three hours a day and a few hours of the night, that is to say, the time that is only good for unimportant work. In summer, when I shall have more time at my disposal and when my expenses will not be so great, I shall devote myself to serious work. My only hope is in the future. I am only twenty-six. Perhaps I shall be able to accomplish something, though time passes quickly.' And after asking for Grigorovich's photograph, he concluded: 'Your great kindness has thrown me into such a turmoil of excitement that I could write a whole ream to you and not only sixteen pages. May God grant you happiness and good health and believe in the sincerity of your grateful and deeply respectful A. Chekhov.'

But, in spite of all these expressions of admiration and respect, Chekhov and Grigorovich never became friends. There is indeed a great deal of insincerity in all these avowals of sincerity. Chekhov never really regarded Grigorovich as a major writer, and as time passed he got tired of being lectured by him. He certainly never accepted the generally held view that Grigorovich had 'discovered' him. When in January 1894 a dinner to Grigorovich was given in Moscow in honour of the fiftieth anniversary of his literary activities Chekhov refused to be present at it just because he feared that Grigorovich would be boasting of having 'discovered' him. When it was pointed out to him that he ought to be present at that dinner because of the famous letter Grigorovich had sent him, he replied: 'Yes, it is all so plain, isn't it? I was discovered by Grigorovich and therefore I must make a speech. And I mustn't forget to mention that he discovered me, otherwise it wouldn't be polite. Well, I'm not going to deliver any such speech.' And after describing how the various writers at the dinner would all be harping on the same thing, he went on: 'Then Grigorovich will rise, walk up to me, clasp me in his arms and, deeply moved by the solemnity of the occasion, burst into tears. Old writers love to have a good cry. However, that's his business. But, you see, the trouble is that I, too, will be expected to burst into tears, and I just can't do it.'

At the dinner Grigorovich, of course, made a speech in which he told of his discovery of Chekhov and the letters they had exchanged. Chekhov's comment (in a letter to Suvorin) was: 'Those who gave the dinner to Grigorovich are now saying: "What lies we told at that dinner and what lies *he* told!" '

The man who was to become Chekhov's closest friend was Suvorin, whom Chekhov met for the first time during his visit to Petersburg in December. Suvorin was twenty-six years older than Chekhov. Recalling their first meeting many years later after their long friendship had come to an end, Suvorin sadly remarked that when they had first met he was still in the prime of life, to which Chekhov replied with a laugh: 'But even then you were twenty-six years older than I!' And indeed the friendship between these two men who were so different in age and political convictions is one of the most astonishing facts in literary history. It was Suvorin's personality that attracted Chekhov. Suvorin, too, was the son of a serf who had risen to his position by dint of his own unaided efforts. Indeed, he came from the same district as Chekhov's father and grandfather. After promising his uncle Mitrofan to send him Suvorin's edition of Pushkin's works, published 'at a fabulously low price', Chekhov observed that only 'such a great and intelligent man as Suvorin, who does not spare anything for literature' could do such a thing. 'He owns five bookshops,' Chekhov went on, 'a newspaper, a periodical magazine, a huge publishing firm, he is worth millions, and all that he has earned by honest and agreeable work. He is a native of the Voronezh province, where he was once a teacher in a school. Every time we meet, we talk of Olkhovatka. I see him twice a year when I go for a visit to Petersburg. He pays me *one hundred* roubles for a story. As proof I am enclosing an account from his paper which shows that I received one hundred and eleven roubles for my last Christmas story.' But Chekhov's enthusiasm for Suvorin was not reserved for his uncle alone. 'Whatever they are saying about him,' he wrote to Bibilin in February 1886, 'he is a good and honest man.' And two years later he wrote to the writer Ivan Leontyev whom he also met for the first time in Petersburg: 'Suvorin is a great man. In art he represents a setter on a snipe shoot, that is, he works by a sort of devilish scent and is always burning with passion. He is a bad theoretician, he never applied himself to serious study, he doesn't know a lot, he is a self-taught man in everything—hence his purely dog-like soundness and integrity and hence also his independence of mind. Being poor in theory, he had to develop those qualities with which nature had so richly endowed him and he has acquired so infallible an instinct for good literature that it is indistinguishable from great intelligence. He is pleasant to talk to, and once you have grasped his conversational method and his sincerity, which people who are fond of engaging in discussions usually lack, a conversation with him becomes almost a treat.' It was Suvorin's 'devilish literary scent' that perhaps best explains Chekhov's long association with him. 'Suvorin', Chekhov wrote to the poet Pleshcheyev, a 'liberal' like him, but a lifelong opponent of Suvorin's, 'has an uncontrollable passion for every kind of talent, and he regards every man of talent in a magnified light. I assure you it is so. If he had his way, he would build a crystal palace and put all the prose writers, playwrights, poets and actresses there.' And a little later he wrote to another friend: 'If Suvorin sees a bad play, he *hates* the author.'

While Leykin, who, as Chekhov put it, did not recognise anybody 'except himself and Turgenev', merely saw in Chekhov a useful hack who might attract a larger reading public to his journal, Suvorin immediately sensed that he was dealing with a man of genius and it was the humility with which he made Chekhov aware of it that was perhaps the strongest link in their friendship. He described Chekhov in his private diary as 'an eagle' and he knew perfectly well that there could be no question of any rivalry between them. 'Today', he noted down in his diary on February 8th, 1893, 'is the twenty-fifth anniversary of my literary career. I have written an enormous amount, but I have never known life and I have felt it very little.' But he sensed that, though twenty-six years his junior, Chekhov knew life as he himself would never know it and that Chekhov *felt* life even more than he knew it because he had been endowed with perceptive qualities that nature bestows only on a man of genius. Such an unwonted attitude towards him could not have escaped Chekhov, who had not found anyone in his family or among his numerous friends who had been sufficiently sensitive to recognise his genius. It was with Suvorin alone that Chekhov felt he could speak freely and as an equal, unembarrassed by petty professional jealousies or by the difference in their social position. Suvorin's eccentricities, too, appealed to him, who had an inveterate *penchant* for the odd and incongruous. During his second visit to Petersburg, for instance, he went to see Suvorin at the offices of *New Times*. Suvorin received him graciously and, Chekhov added in describing the interview in a letter to Michael on April 25th, 1886, 'even offered me his hand'.

'Do your best, young man,' said Suvorin. 'I'm satisfied with you, only don't forget to go more often to church and don't drink vodka. Let me smell your breath!'

Chekhov let him smell his breath, and, failing to discover the presence of any alcoholic fumes, Suvorin shouted: 'Boy!'

A boy appeared and was ordered to bring a glass of tea and a lump of sugar, after which 'the esteemed Mr. Suvorin' called for Chekhov's account and paid it.

'Don't go wasting your money,' said Suvorin, 'and pull your socks up!'

2

The way his money seemed to vanish into thin air, if Suvorin only knew, had been one of Chekhov's nightmares for a long time. It was largely due to his own inability to live within his income. Once he even tried to run away from Moscow before his birthday, which, he wrote to Leykin on January 22nd, 1884, cost him more than any journey. His family, too, had been through such a dire time before he took charge of it that it seemed to have lost all sense of economy. If Chekhov did suceed in saving up a little money, it was all spent during one of the great festivals—at Christmas or Easter. 'A propos,' he wrote to Bibilin on January 22nd, 1886, 'Christmas has cost me three hundred roubles. Don't you think I'm just crazy? Yes, it certainly is a great misfortune to have a family. . . . Thank goodness Christmas is over. If it had gone on for another week I should have had to go begging in the streets. At the moment I haven't a farthing in my pocket.'

While Chekhov was no doubt pleased with the higher pay he was getting from Suvorin ('When I started work for *New Times*', he confessed to Suvorin 'frankly and in confidence' in August 1888, 'I felt as if I were a gold prospector in California—till then I did not earn more than seven or eight copecks a line—and I vowed to write as often as possible in order to earn more money'), that made no appreciable difference to his income. 'Suvorin has offered to pay me twelve copecks a line,' he wrote to Leykin shortly after his first visit to Petersburg, 'but that won't make any difference to my financial position, for I cannot possibly write more than I am writing now. I have neither the time nor the energy.' And that was true. In fact, the next two years were the worst years of financial worry Chekhov had ever experienced. On his return to Moscow his situation was so desperate that he had to send Michael to the offices of the Moscow journals to collect as much of his debts as possible, having first supplied him with the following authorisation:

January 15th, 1886.

A Medical Certificate

This is given to the student of the Imperial University Michael Chekhov, aged twenty, of the Greek Orthodox faith, to certify that he has been my brother since 1865 and is authorised by me to collect as much money as I may need at the offices of the journals to which I have been contributing, which I confirm by affixing my seal and signature.

Dr. A. Chekhov.

Not so long ago he had boasted that he was no longer taking his groceries and meat on credit, but already at the beginning of February he wrote to Alexander: 'Tomorrow I am taking one hundred and five roubles to the grocer's—that's how much food we got from him in one month.' And at the beginning of March he received a summons from another shopkeeper from whom Alexander and Nicholas had taken goods (presumably drinks) on credit in his name. 'I have nearly forgotten to tell you a pleasant piece of news,' he wrote to Leykin on March 8th. 'I had to appear in court in answer to a summons and was ordered to pay fifty roubles. If you have ever had to pay someone else's debts, you will appreciate what a revolution these absurd and unexpected fifty roubles have made in my small financial world.' And a month later, in reply to Leykin's query as to what he was doing with his money, Chekhov wrote: 'You ask me what I am doing with my money. I don't lead a dissipated life, I don't walk about dressed like a dandy, I have no debts, and I don't even have to keep my mistresses (*Fragments* and love I get gratis), but nevertheless I have only forty roubles left from the three hundred and twelve roubles I received from you and Suvorin before Easter, out of which I shall have to pay twenty tomorrow. Goodness only knows where my money goes.' The phrase that recurred again and again during the next year and a half was—no money! In August he had to beg Leykin for an advance to pay the rent for the new flat into which he was about to move; in September he had to pawn his watch and his only gold coin; in January he had to send out another S O S to Leykin, as he had not a farthing ('literally not a farthing!' he wrote); in March, while on a visit to Petersburg, he had to send a letter to his sister Mary to ask her 'to spend as little as possible'; and, after having, as he phrased it, 'robbed' Suvorin by getting an advance of three hundred roubles to cover the costs of his proposed journey to Taganrog and the Don steppe, he left half of it with his family and returned to Moscow in May 'without a penny' (as he wrote to Leykin). He raised a small loan from Franz Schechtel, one of his closest friends and the future architect of the Moscow Art Theatre, and in August he had again to apply for an advance to Leykin to pay the Kisselevs for his summer cottage. In September (1887) he could not afford to pay his rent and had to tell his landlord that if he did not want to wait he had better sue him for it. In the same month he wrote to Maria Kisselev: 'Yes, indeed it is a great joy to be a famous writer. I have to work from morning till night, but I don't seem to profit from it. I haven't a penny. I don't know how it is with Zola and Shchedrin, but . . . I certainly have much less money than creative talent.' In October, when, after repeated threats not to write any more stories for the *Petersburg Gazette*, Khudekov raised his pay to twelve copecks a line, Chekhov wrote gleefully to Maria Kisselev: 'That's what patience, pertinacity and impudence mean. You won't get anything by meekness.' And, as an anti-climax, he added the now familiar two words: 'No money.' Finally, as a fitting conclusion to this record of financial misery, Chekhov illustrated a letter in which he asked Schechtel for another loan with a hook from which a body was suspended by a rope round its neck. 'The firm of Dr. Anton Chekhov & Co.', he wrote, 'is, as always, going through a financial crisis. If you don't lend me twenty-five or thirty roubles till the first of the month, you are a heartless crocodile.'

His financial worries were aggravated by domestic troubles and bad health. Alexander had given up his job as customs official and he and his family were carrying on a hand-to-mouth existence in Moscow. Nicholas, like Alexander, had become a confirmed drunkard, given up painting, and was leading the life of a tramp, having to be rescued from the gutter and kept at home almost by force. 'Not a day passes', Chekhov complained to Leykin, 'without some unpleasantness. Again and again I come across some vile piece of news so that I am even getting afraid of receiving letters.' Chekhov had now become a disciple of Tolstoy. His Tolstoyan period, as he later confessed to Suvorin, lasted for about six years, but between 1886, the year in which Tolstoy's remarkable treatise *What Then Must We Do?* was published, and 1890, the year of Chekhov's departure for Sakhalin, it assumed its most virulent form. The Chekhovs were generally fond of giving utterance to fine and noble sentiments. Pavel and Mitrofan enjoyed writing what Chekhov called 'manifestos', which he and his two elder brothers delighted in lampooning. When Chekhov took over the care of his family, he, like his father, brooked no opposition and he imposed his will on the members of his family without bothering to consult their views or desires. His intolerance became more pronounced when he embraced Tolstoy's philosophy. The sentiments he expressed were also fine and noble, though perhaps somewhat commonplace, but, unfortunately, they produced no effect whatever on his two elder brothers. The letter Chekhov wrote to Nicholas in March 1886 is full of these admirable platitudes. It is often quoted as representing Chekhov's views on the duties and obligations of an educated man. What is hardly ever mentioned is that when he had grown to maturity Chekhov hated moralising of any kind, having learnt by experience how futile it was. But at the age of twenty-six the fact that it was impossible to reform a man by exposing his faults and talking fine sentiments to him never occurred to him. Certain admissions in his letter to Nicholas, however, are valuable as throwing light on his private life, such as, for instance, his statement that were he to leave his family to fend for itself he would have found a good excuse in his mother's 'impossible character', his blood-spitting, etc.

Another interesting fact that emerges from this letter is the change his Tolstoyan views had brought about in his attitude to women. In 1883 Chekhov had contemplated writing a scientific treatise on

Darwinian lines on the *History of Sex Dominance*, the purpose of which was to provide a scientific background to the 'woman question' which was at the time agitating public opinion in Russia. His main contention was that the bearing of the young was chiefly responsible for the subjugation of the female to the male, and he foresaw the time when nature would evolve a new species of beings in which the superiority of the male over the female would disappear with the disappearance of the long period it took a female to bear children. He thought it quite possible that man might come to the help of nature in shortening that period. 'Nature', Chekhov wrote in the outline of his proposed work, 'does not suffer any inequality between the sexes, and in her attempt to evolve a perfect organism she does not envisage the necessity of any inequality or superiority among them, and indeed the time will come when the existing inequalities will entirely disappear.' On the other hand, he refused to admit that the existing inequalities between men and women were due entirely to the imposition of his authority by the man over the woman. He regarded the greater passivity of women as due to biological causes. He disagreed with Buckle that women possess greater intuitive powers than men. A woman might be a good doctor, a good lawyer, etc., but 'in the sphere of creative art she is a goose. A perfect organism', he maintained, 'is creative, but woman has so far created nothing. George Sand is neither a Newton nor a Shakespeare. She is not a thinker.'

His views of the temporary inferiority of women to men in the creative field had not been coloured by any moral considerations till his Tolstoyan period. When in 1882 Alexander went off with the wife of a Moscow writer and, defying his father's fiat, lived with her as his 'civil' wife (she was refused a divorce by the ecclesiastical courts), Chekhov did not hesitate to condemn Pavel's moral scruples. 'What do you care', he wrote to Alexander, 'what some bigot thinks of your private life? Let him think what he likes. You know that you are right whatever they [i.e. their father and mother] may write and however much they suffer. The whole point of life consists in making a protest without asking for pity. Every man has a right to live with anyone he likes and how he likes.' But under the influence of Tolstoy's teaching his views had undergone a complete change in 1886. In his letter to Nicholas, who had also become involved in an affair with a married woman, Chekhov demanded that his brother should 'curb his sexual instincts'. What an educated man, and especially an artist, expected of a woman, he now maintained, was kindness and the ability to be a mother and not a whore. There was, in fact, no more any question of a man having the right to live with whom he liked and how he liked. It was now the moral implications of the union between man and woman that Chekhov considered to be of paramount importance.

Within a few years Chekhov would find himself in a situation similar to the one in which his two elder brothers had been placed, and that experience of his was to have a profound influence both on his private life and on his development as a writer.

3

A few weeks after writing his letter to Nicholas, Chekhov had another haemorrhage. Again he felt that he ought really to go to the Crimea, but, he wrote to Leykin, he had no money. Nor would he consult a doctor, because he was afraid, as he ingenuously confessed to Leykin in the same letter, that he might discover murmurs in his chest or some tubercular patches on his lungs.

On April 25th he was in Petersburg again. His first three stories published in *New Times* (*Requiem* on February 15th, *The Witch* on March 8th, and *Agafya* on March 15th) produced a sensation in the Petersburg literary world. After the appearance of his first story he sent off a very respectful letter to Suvorin. 'You can judge for yourself', he wrote, 'what a refreshing and even inspiring influence the kind attention of such an experienced and talented man as yourself has had on my writing.' He even thanked Suvorin for cutting out the end of his story, adding (not quite truthfully): 'I have been writing for six years and you are the first to take the trouble to offer me some advice and give a reason for altering my story.' For one thing, though, Chekhov had good reason to be grateful to Suvorin, namely for insisting that he should publish his stories in *New Times* under his own name. Till then he had been using three pseudonyms: 'Antosha Chekhonte' for the stories he considered to be above the average, 'A Man without a Spleen' for those he considered less good, and 'The Brother of my Brother' (a hint at Alexander's mediocre literary efforts) for those he definitely considered to be worthless. 'My pseudonym A. Chekhonte', he wrote to Suvorin, 'is, I admit, perhaps odd and a bit pretentious, but I invented it in the misty dawn of my youth and that is why it does not strike me as being odd.' He was more cautious, however, about his higher remuneration of twelve copecks a line. 'The fee you have fixed for my stories', he told Suvorin, 'is entirely sufficient for the time being.'

Fame

In Petersburg he did not this time stay with Leykin, with whom he was arranging for the publication of his first large volume of short stories, which eventually appeared under the title of *Motley Stories*, but at a guest house. 'I had a good wash,' he described his first day in Petersburg in a letter to Michael, 'put on my new pair of trousers, my new shoes with pointed toes and my new overcoat and took a cab to the offices of *Fragments*. There Leykin's secretary met me as though I were her future husband and poured out her heart to me. She told me that Leykin was a very difficult man to get on with and that I was one of their best contributors. From there I went to see Roman Golike [the owner of the printing works and publisher of *Fragments* who became a great friend of Chekhov's], but he was out. I therefore took a cab to Mr. Bibilin's. The door was opened by his fiancée, who had a sheaf of lectures in her hand (she is a student of *two* faculties!). She was very pleased to see me. I bowed and scraped my new shoes, said how do you do to her, and so on. After a glass of tea, which was as black as pitch, Bibilin and I went for a walk along the Neva. We took a boat and the river made a great impression on me. After that we went to Dominique's, where we had a meat-pie each, a glass of vodka and a cup of coffee. I then went to the *Petersburg Gazette* and from there to *New Times* [where he had his talk with Suvorin]. Miss Leontyev, the clerk who sends me my money, is not at all bad-looking. I pressed her hand, Michael, and tomorrow I shall go to see her again. From *New Times* I went to Volkov's bank and sent you a money order for one hundred (100) roubles. From there I returned to my rooms and went to sleep. Oh, wonder of wonders! What a lot done in five hours! Who would have thought that such a genius would emerge out of a privy?'

Two days later he was present at a party at Suvorin's house, where he met Grigorovich, who welcomed him with open arms. At the beginning of May he was back in Moscow, and by the end of the month he and his family were again installed at their Babkino cottage. It was a bad summer for fishing, but there were plenty of mushrooms. 'Everything is beautiful here,' Chekhov wrote to Schechtel on June 8th. 'The birds are singing, Levitan is acting a Caucasian mountaineer, the grass smells deliciously, Nicholas drinks.' Where Nicholas got his liquor from was a mystery to Chekhov. He suspected Levitan, and one day a mock trial of Levitan was held 'according to all the rules of jurisprudence', Chekhov acting the counsel for the prosecution and the indictment including a clause accusing the painter of 'running an illegal still', since, as Chekhov explained to Schechtel, 'it is quite clear

ANTON CHEKHOV IN HIS STUDY IN YALTA (1900)

that Nicholas is getting drunk at his place, for he does not get a drop of liquor anywhere else.' Levitan, incidentally, was also accused of evading military service, keeping a secret pawnshop and leading an immoral life.

In July Chekhov had to rush off to Moscow to have two teeth extracted, and the operation, performed without an anaesthetic, gave him a terrible headache. On his return to Babkino he was dismayed to discover that he could neither walk nor sit down: he had an attack of haemorrhoids, which plagued him for several weeks. As it happened, he was very busy with his medical practice at the time. In addition to his own patients, he had to replace Dr. Arkhangelsky at the Chikino hospital for a fortnight. The weather, too, was dreadful. It rained all summer, the countryside was flooded and the harvest was ruined.

In September he moved to the house with bay windows in Sadovo-Kudrinskaya Street, for which he paid six hundred and fifty roubles a year. 'My house', he wrote to the poet Leonid Trefolev, 'looks like a chest of drawers. Its colour is "liberal", that is, red.' His own large study and bedroom as well as Michael's bedroom were on the ground floor. The whole wall near the door leading from Chekhov's study to his bedroom was covered with bookshelves. His library was growing steadily, and every time he went to Petersburg he brought back a trunkful of books with him. A fine spiral staircase, with a large landing half-way up covered with a wolf's skin, led to the first floor, which had five rooms: the bedrooms of his mother and sister, the dining-room, the drawing-room, and a spare room with a lantern. The drawing-room had a piano, an aquarium and a large unfinished painting by Nicholas of a sempstress asleep over her work at daybreak. It was that picture Chekhov mentioned in his letter to Alexander on February 20th, 1883. 'Nicholas', he wrote, 'is loafing about, as you know very well; a fine, strong Russian talent is being wasted. Another year or two and our artist is finished. He will be lost in the crowd of pub-crawlers. You know his present work. What does he do now? He does everything that is cheap and vulgar, and yet in our drawing-room we have a remarkable picture of his which he does not want to finish. *The Russian Theatre* has asked him to illustrate Dostoevsky. He promised to do so, but he won't keep his promise, and yet these illustrations would have made his reputation and provided him with a piece of bread. . . .'

When Alexander Lazarev-Gruzinsky, a short-story writer who was one of Chekhov's literary protégés, first visited him at the beginning of 1887, Chekhov said, pointing to the furniture, the aquarium and the piano: 'It's good to be a writer: literature has given me all that!' And seeing how greatly impressed his visitor was, Chekhov laughed and explained that the piano was on hire and that part of the furniture Nicholas had received in payment for his illustrations in *The Alarm-Clock*.

Chekhov was already wearing a beard at the time: a little imperial round the chin, and a small, drooping moustache. He spent most of his time in his study, where he received his patients from ten o'clock in the morning till three o'clock in the afternoon. He worked on his stories mostly in the evenings. In the drawing-room his sister's friends used to gather almost every evening, playing the piano and singing, and Chekhov would occasionally interrupt his work and join them upstairs. He was getting very fond of music, and when he felt depressed he would ask Michael to play something for him while he worked.

His fame had at last spread to Moscow, too. 'I am beginning to get famous,' he wrote to Maria Kisselev in September 1886. 'In restaurants people point me out; they even try to be nice to me and treat me to sandwiches. Korsh got hold of me in his theatre and gave me a season ticket. My tailor bought my book and is reading it aloud. He prophesies a brilliant future for me. My medical colleagues sigh when they meet me, talk to me about literature and assure me that they are sick and tired of medicine.'

At the end of September Nicholas fell seriously ill, and Chekhov nursed him back to health. His brother's ruined life, his own bad health and financial difficulties brought on another fit of depression. 'Everyone', he wrote to Maria Kisselev, 'is having a bad time. When I try to think seriously about life,' he went on, 'I can't help feeling that people who are afraid of death are not logical. So far as I can see, life is composed only of horrors, squabbles and vulgarities, which either come in droves or follow one another.' And to Leykin he wrote at the same time: 'I can't say that I am enjoying life. I am in a bad state myself and I don't see any happy people around me. Alexander now lives in Moscow and can barely make ends meet. Nicholas was seriously ill. . . . It's terrible how much unpleasantness I have experienced during the last few days, and on top of it I have no money. I suppose it will all end by my giving everything up and taking a job as a country doctor.'

After recovering from his illness, Nicholas again disappeared. And to add to Chekhov's worries, his mother and aunt decided that it was just the right moment to restart their campaign for Chekhov's marriage to a rich girl. 'Mother and aunt', Chekhov wrote to Maria Kisselev in October, 'are imploring me to marry the daughter of a merchant.'

Fame

Between November 16th and 19th Leykin paid one of his brief visits to Moscow, and he and Chekhov seem to have spent all their time together, chiefly drinking. In December Chekhov paid another visit to Petersburg. Suvorin was as nice to him as ever and made him a present of books. His popularity, however, was beginning to pall on him. Like a famous comedian who is dying to play Hamlet, he was now determined to write 'serious' stories. 'I am getting as popular as Nana [Zola's latest novel was a best-seller in Petersburg],' he wrote to Maria Kisselev. 'I have to listen to compliments all day long, and my soul does not suffer them any more. At a time when the editors here hardly know the serious Korolenko, the whole of Petersburg is reading my trash. It is, of course, highly flattering, but my literary feeling is offended by it. I feel sorry for the public which pays court to literary lap-dogs only because it has not the sense to notice the elephants, and I am absolutely convinced that when I start writing serious stories not a single dog will ever know me.'

On his return to Moscow at the end of December he found that Nicholas had once again disappeared and he suspected that he had again run off to his 'bergamot', though on his return home Nicholas assured him that he had spent his time with 'a highly respectable old man'.

The Christmas holidays and the New Year of 1887 Chekhov spent 'very noisily'. He had not a single quiet day, he wrote to Leykin; there were hundreds of visitors who 'took his study by storm' and engaged 'in long discussions, etc.' He also attended a medical conference which met in Moscow at the beginning of January. His birthday on January 16th seems also to have been celebrated in great style, and everybody, including Chekhov, was very gay.

The year 1887 was to be a decisive one in his career. He had made up his mind to write a 'serious' story, and as his subject he had chosen the steppe. It was a very ambitious subject, since to be successful he would have to rival no less a writer than Gogol, whose description of the steppe in *Taras Bulba* is rightly considered one of the descriptive masterpieces in Russian literature. It was because of the magnitude of this undertaking that he dared not breathe a word about it to anyone. He did, however, announce his intention to go south in the spring, and more specifically to the Don district.

There was one serious difficulty, though: he had no money for the journey. All the money he had was spent on the holiday festivities and his birthday party, and, as he intended to publish his story in a literary periodical, he could not very well ask any of the editors for whom he worked for an advance. This dilemma, however, was solved in a most unexpected fashion. Early in March Chekhov received a telegram from Alexander, who had by then migrated to Petersburg, that he was dangerously ill. Chekhov immediately hurried off to Petersburg. His train journey was very uncomfortable. Their cat, Mikhail Timofeyich, he wrote to Michael, enjoyed greater comfort when it was out on the tiles than he did during his journey to Petersburg. The train was slow and crowded, he had forgotten to take a pillow with him, and the cigarettes he smoked were so vile that he had a frog not only in his throat but also in his goloshes. 'What an extraordinary thing,' he exclaimed bitterly in his letter home, 'the water in my decanter stinks of the privy, my cigarettes are vile. . . .' He was in a dreadfully overwrought state. He dreamt of coffins, torchbearers, typhus patients, doctors. His only consolation was his 'darling Anna'—Tolstoy's *Anna Karenina*—to whom he devoted himself during the whole of the journey. When he arrived in Petersburg he found that his fears were justified: the city was in the throes of a typhus epidemic of a most virulent kind. 'Petersburg', he wrote to Maria Kisselev, 'made an impression of a city of the dead on me. I arrived there full of all sorts of dreadful premonitions, and on the way from the station I saw two funeral processions, and at my brother's I found typhus. [There was nothing the matter with Alexander; it was his wife who was ill.] From there I went to see Leykin, who told me that his doorkeeper had 'only that minute' died of typhus. From Leykin I went to see Golike, and found his eldest son ill with croup and breathing through a tube in his throat. I then went to the exhibition and, as though on purpose, every woman I came across was in mourning. Next day I attended the mother of the office clerk of *Fragments*, who was dying of consumption.'

That, however, was not all, by any means. He went to see Grigorovich, who received him very affectionately, kissed him on the forehead, and was so excited and touched by Chekhov's visit that he had a violent attack of angina pectoris. 'He was suffering dreadfully,' Chekhov wrote in the same letter to Maria Kisselev, 'tossing about and moaning, while I sat beside him for two and a half hours cursing the impotence of my medicine. Fortunately, Dr. Bertenson arrived and I could run away.'

His nerves were in a dreadful state and his pulse was irregular, but whatever happened, he wrote to Schechtel, he was determined to go south, 'for my nerves will hold out no longer'. But in a letter to Suvorin after his return to Moscow he was much more specific about the real purpose of his journey. 'Not to dry up,' he wrote, 'I shall go south to the Don district at the end of March, where I shall hail the spring and refresh what is already beginning to fade in my memory. I think I shall be able to work much faster then.'

Suvorin, whom he was at first loath to ask for an advance, as he had known him for so short a time, not only gave him three hundred roubles but offered to publish a volume of his stories which would include those that had already appeared in *New Times* and those he would write in repayment of his advance. 'I robbed Suvorin,' he wrote to Maria Kisselev, 'having taken a big advance from him. . . . My success', he added, 'can no longer be denied. In Petersburg they now recognise only one writer—me. You see, I am deceiving even myself. What are my impressions? Well, they are so horrible that I am surprised I haven't taken to drink yet. However, I'm told that everything comes in useful to a writer.'

Chekhov gave half of the money he had received from Suvorin to his family and left Moscow on April 2nd for Taganrog with a trunk he borrowed from Schechtel and a bottle of vodka his mother thoughtfully bought him for the journey.

4

Little is known of Chekhov's painstaking efforts to perfect himself as a writer and, especially, as a good stylist. It was his reception in Petersburg that, as he wrote to Alexander, made him frightened to think how carelessly he had been writing. 'If I had known that I was read like that,' he declared, 'I should never have written anything to order.' And to Bibilin he confessed that 'when I did not know that I was read and discussed, I wrote lightheartedly, as though I were eating pancakes; but now I write and tremble.' Yozhov records that one day he found Chekhov transcribing a story by Tolstoy, and when asked what he was doing it for, he replied, 'I am rewriting it.' Yozhov was greatly shocked by Chekhov's impertinence in daring to 'rewrite' Tolstoy, but Chekhov was doing it as an exercise, for he realised that only by mastering the technique of the great writers would he be able to evolve a style of his own. He did the same with Turgenev's stories, and Grigorovich was right when he pointed out in one of his letters to Chekhov that 'such a masterly way of conveying one's observations [as was to be found in Chekhov's story *Agafya*] can be found only in Turgenev and Tolstoy'.

Fame

There was, however, one invaluable experience Chekhov had gained in his first five years of work for the humorous journals: he learnt to gather the material for his stories straight from life. His journey to the Don steppe in the spring of 1887 was, therefore, entirely in conformity with his firmly established method of work as a writer of fiction. He had to get his impressions direct from life and then allow them to mature in his mind. That, at least, is true of his great stories, such as *The Steppe*, which bears the sub-title of *The History of a Journey* and which he did not start writing till January 1888. Before leaving for Taganrog he arranged with his sister Mary to keep the letters he was going to write home, as he was going to use them as the raw material for his story. These letters provide a most circumstantial account of his journey. There is the description of his fellow-passengers; first the business men, who talked mostly of the price of flour; then an army officer, who helped him to beguile the time till his arrival in Kursk, where he changed trains. From Kursk to Kharkov he had quite a lively time 'solving social problems' with a general, a country police inspector, another army officer and a middle-aged lady who had just undergone an operation in Petersburg. The country policeman interested him. Before speaking, he would open his mouth and growl like a dog: grr ... grr ... grr. ... The middle-aged lady kept giving herself injections of morphia and sending out the men to fetch ice at the stations. After Kharkov, Chekhov, who was left alone with the army officer, curled up on his seat and went to sleep 'without', he wrote to Mary, 'the help of mother's bottle'. When he woke up, the officer had left and he had new company: a landowner and a railway ticket inspector, who told him the story of one Russian railway company which stole three hundred carriages from another and painted them its own colour. He was now entering the steppe region. Through the window of his carriage he could see his 'old friends': the vultures hovering over the steppe. Everything, in fact, was familiar to him: the tumuli in the distance, the water towers, the farm buildings. Everything brought back memories of his childhood—even the greasy cabbage soup at the station buffet which was so tasty. He took a walk on the platform of one railway station. 'Young ladies. At least one pretty girl in a white blouse, looking very romantic as she sat at the window of the second floor of the station building. I look at her and she looks at me. I put on my pince-nez and she does the same. Oh, glorious vision! I get a heart attack and rush back to the train. The weather', Chekhov went on, 'is wonderful, quite disgustingly wonderful. Ukrainian peasants, oxen, vultures, whitewashed cottages, southern streams, branches of the Donetz railway with one telegraph wire, daughters of country squires and farmers, brown dogs, green foliage—all that passes before my eyes like a dream.' Soon the Azov Sea came into view, and as the train moved into the station he caught a glimpse of the streets of Taganrog.

He was met by his cousin Georgy and they drove into town. Taganrog was a great disappointment to him: everything looked so small. It reminded him of Herculaneum and Pompeii: no people and, instead of mummies, sleepy individuals with heads shaped like melons. His uncle Mitrofan was the same as ever: mild, gentle and sincere. His aunt had grown very fat, and Chekhov could not help being struck by her utter stupidity. 'Quite an inconceivable creature,' he wrote to Mary. 'I haven't forgotten my anatomy yet, but looking at her skull I can no longer believe in the existence of the substance called brains.' What struck him most, however, was the extraordinary tenderness of the relationship between his uncle and his five children. It was so unlike anything he could remember of the relationship between the children and their father in his own home. He went to have a look at the house which had ruined his father and in which he had spent five years of his life himself, but it was empty. Selivanov had had it boarded up before leaving for his country estate. 'It made me sick to look at it,' Chekhov wrote to Mary, 'and I shouldn't have consented to live in it for anything in the world.' In the afternoon he went for a walk with his cousin Georgy in the main street of the town. 'The street', he wrote, 'looks very decent and the roadway is much better paved than the roadways in Moscow. It has a European look about it. On the left side the aristocracy takes a walk, on the right side the democracy. An awful lot of young girls: fair-haired, dark-haired, Greek, Russian, Polish. The most fashionable female attire: olive-green dresses and blouses. Not only the aristocracy, that is, the dirty Greeks, but even the girls from the poorest districts wear these olive-green dresses. The bustles aren't too large. Only the Greek girls are brave enough to wear large bustles, the rest have not sufficient courage.'

In the evening Chekhov helped his uncle to put on his church-warden's uniform and the huge medal he had received in recognition of his charitable works and then went with him and his cousins to church (it was Good Friday). 'We arrive at the church,' Chekhov wrote. 'Poor, dull, uninteresting. Little candles burning on the window-sills—that is all the illumination. Uncle's face is wreathed in a beatific smile—a substitute for an electric sun. The interior of the church is very modest. It reminds me of the church in Voskressensk. We are selling candles. Georgy, a dandy and a liberal, is not selling candles, but stands in a corner and gazes at everything with an expression of complete indifference. Young Vladimir (a divinity student), on the other hand, is entirely in his element. The procession. Two fools walk in front of it, waving bengal lights, filling the church with smoke and sending sparks flying all over the congregation. The founders, patrons and chief worshippers with uncle at their head stand by the door of the church, holding icons in their hands and waiting for the return of the procession. Young Vladimir sits on top of a cupboard and throws incense into the censer. The smoke is so thick that it is impossible to breathe. Presently the clergy and the bearers of the crosses and banners return. A solemn silence. Everybody's eyes are turned towards Father Vassily. "Daddy," Vladimir's voice comes suddenly from the top of the cupboard, "shall I throw any more in?" '

The following day Chekhov spent in paying visits to his old friends and aquaintances. 'Passing through the New Market,' he wrote, 'I could see how filthy, empty, lazy, illiterate and uninteresting Taganrog is. I could not see a single signpost on which the words were correctly spelt; the streets are deserted; the stevedores wear satisfied expressions on their faces; the dandies walk about in long overcoats and caps. The girls in their olive-green dresses, their boy-friends, the peeling stucco of the houses, the general laziness and the knack of being satisfied with a few pennies and an uncertain future—all that strikes me as so horrible that Moscow with its dirt and typhus epidemics seems quite attractive to me.'

The 'pious atmosphere' of his uncle's household or, what seems more likely, his aunt's rich food gave him diarrhoea, which forced him to stay indoors for most of the time, and an inflammation of a vein on his left leg made him limp like 'forty thousand Leykins'. 'There is no end to my ailments,' he wrote. 'The biblical saying that in sorrow thou shalt bring forth children is being fulfilled so far as I am concerned, for my children are my stories, and I cannot bear to think of them now. The very idea of writing is repugnant to me.'

His final verdict on his native city was that there were only five things he could really admire in it: the delicious doughnuts, the local wine, the caviare, the excellent cabs, and his uncle's genial disposition. Everything else he found execrable. It was true the girls were not bad-looking, but, Chekhov thought, one had to get used to them. 'They are', he wrote to Mary, 'brusque in their movements, frivolous in their relations with men, amorous and apt to elope with actors; they laugh boisterously, whistle shrilly to their dogs, drink wine, etc. There are even cynics among them. For instance, fair-haired Manya Khodakovskaya, who attacks the dead as well as the living. When I went for a walk in the cemetery with her she laughed all the time at the dead and their epitaphs, at the priests, deacons, etc.'

And to Schechtel he wrote: 'Taganrog is a nice town. If I were as good an architect as you I should demolish it.'

He spent a fortnight in Taganrog and then continued with his journey. He followed the route taken by Yegorushka in *The Steppe*, gathering impressions and first-hand material as he travelled. He stayed at the farm of his former pupil Kravtsov, where he set up his headquarters for some time. Nothing there had changed: there was still the same incessant shooting and indiscriminate slaughter of bird and beast. He was also the best man at a Cossack wedding in a borrowed frockcoat, wide trousers and not a single stud to his shirt. 'I saw many rich girls,' he wrote to Mary, 'and I could have married anyone of them, but I was so drunk all the time that I mistook the bottles for the girls and the girls for the bottles. It was probably because I was drunk that the girls found that I was witty and a "wag". They are just like sheep: if one of them gets up and leaves the room, the others are sure to follow. The most daring and clever one of them, anxious to show that she knew how to behave in good company, kept tapping me on the hand with her fan and saying, "Oh, you naughty man!" with a frightened expression on her face. I taught her to say to her boy-friends: "How naïve you are!"'

'The young married couple (the girl was only sixteen), no doubt in accordance with a local custom, kept kissing every minute; they kissed with such abandon that their lips gave a loud smack from the compressed air, and every time I got a cloying taste of raisins in my mouth and a spasm in my left leg. The inflammation in it grew worse from their kisses.'

He had by that time spent almost all his money and, he wrote, was beginning to look like a Nizhny-Novgorod cardsharper who lived at the expense of others but scintillated with wit.

On leaving his generous hosts, he missed his train and had to sleep in a second-class carriage. Leaving his compartment at night 'on small business', he was amazed at the beauty of the landscape: 'the moon, the endless steppe with its hillocks, looking like a flat desert, the graveyard stillness all around, the railway carriages and the railway line standing out very clearly in the darkness'. It looked as if the whole world were dead. Such a picture, he thought to himself, he would not forget as long as he lived.

'I have been living lately in the Don Switzerland,' he wrote to Leykin on May 5th, 'in the centre of the so-called Donetz mountain range: mountains, valleys, woods, streams and the steppe, the steppe, the steppe. . . . Countless impressions. If Bibilin had spent one day with me here he would either have run away or imagined himself somewhere in Singapore or Brazil. The only thing that worries me is lack of money. It sounds incredible but it's true: when I left Moscow I had one hundred and fifty roubles.'

To his sister he wrote: 'Wonderful views. Excellent weather. Am filled up to the neck with poetry. It will last me for five years.'

But his travels were not over yet. He finished up by spending two days at a big monastery—the Sacred Mountain monastery, packed with fifteen thousand pilgrims, eight of every nine of whom were old women. 'Till now', he wrote to Mary, 'I did not know that there were so many old women in the world, or I should have shot myself long ago.' There were six services a day, from midnight to six o'clock in the afternoon, and before every service a monk rang a bell in the corridors of the monastery inn and shouted 'in the voice of a creditor imploring his debtor to pay him at least five copecks in the rouble: "Lord Jesus Christ, have mercy upon us! Please, come to mass!"' As it was impossible to ignore this request, Chekhov would usually leave his room and go down to the bank of the Donetz, where he sat through all the services.

His visit to the monastery gave him the subject for his story *The Rolling Stone*, published in *New Times* on July 14th, 1887. In a letter to his cousin Georgy in Taganrog on October 17th, 1887, Chekhov wrote: 'I have described the Sacred Mountain in *New Times*. A young man, a nephew of a bishop, told me that he saw a bishop reading it to two other bishops. They liked it. Which means that they also liked it at the Sacred Mountain.'

Another story in which Chekhov used his impressions of the steppe —*Happiness*—was published in *New Times* on June 6th. 'In this story', Chekhov wrote to the poet Polonsky, to whom he subsequently dedicated it, 'I am describing the steppe: a plain, night, pale sunrise, a flock of sheep, and three human figures discussing happiness.' The story created a sensation in Petersburg, and it was in connexion with it that the critics began talking about 'the absence of a theme' in Chekhov's stories, a delusion that has become an accepted cliché in the criticism of his plays. Chekhov disposed of it in his own vigorous fashion. 'My steppe story', he wrote to Alexander on June 21st, 'appeals to me just because of its theme which blockheads like you don't find in it. It's a product of inspiration. A quasi-symphony. Actually a lot of nonsense. It appeals to the reader as a result of an optical illusion. The whole trick consists of the additional ornaments like the sheep and the finish I gave to separate lines. I could write about coffee grounds and astonish the reader with the help of such tricks.'

He was back in Taganrog on May 11th and in Moscow on May 14th, where he had another attack of what he called his 'hereditary' haemorrhoids. 'My sedentary life', he wrote to Leykin, 'is not the only cause of it. There are also my excesses *in Baccho et Veneris*—diseases of the heart and the liver play no small part in ætiology.' His last summer in Babkino was spoilt by bad weather and ill health. It was again not a particularly good year for fishing, but there were plenty of mushrooms, and Chekhov spent days gathering them. 'I have gone mad on mushrooms,' he wrote to Alexander on August 11th. 'I wander in the woods for days, looking under my feet. I shall have to give it up, for this pleasure is interfering with my work.' Another of his amusements was the feeding of a young hare. 'To judge by his ears', he wrote in the same letter, 'he must be a very talented hare: they are longer than a donkey's.' He also discovered a very effective, though perhaps not very original, way of dealing with peasant boys. 'Some boys', he wrote to Leykin, 'have just brought me two woodpeckers; I gave them five copecks and released the birds. The idea appealed to them and they brought me another pair of woodpeckers. I took the birds and gave the boys a good hiding. Here you have a sample of my holiday amusements.'

5

The autumn and the winter of 1887 Chekhov spent in writing his first novel. Suvorin, in his obituary of Chekhov, observed that the greatest tragedy of Chekhov's life was that he could never write a novel. And indeed the prestige which the novel as an art form enjoyed in the second half of the nineteenth century in Russia was so great that Chekhov could not help being distressed by his inability to write one. His first attempt must have caused him great unhappiness which, aggravated by his financial worries and the looming spectre of tuberculosis (his hearing, too, was troubling him at the time and he was afraid of going deaf), brought on a particularly severe fit of depression.

On September 5th he wrote a desperate letter to Alexander in which he complained of hearing and reading nothing but lies. The vulgarity he observed everywhere, he wrote, drove him to a state of 'moral vomiting'. If fate did not become more merciful to him, he added, he would not be able to bear it much longer. 'I should call you the basest of pessimists if I agreed with your phrase: "My youth has been wasted," ' Alexander wrote to Chekhov in reply. To Leykin Chekhov wrote on September 11th: 'For the last three weeks I gave myself up cravenly to a fit of melancholy. I lost all interest in life, my pen dropped out of my hand; in a word, "nerves", which you refuse to recognise. I was so disturbed mentally that I simply could not bring myself to sit down to work. There are all sorts of reasons for it: the bad weather, some family trouble, lack of money, moving into town from the country, etc.' It is characteristic of Chekhov that neither in his letter to his brother nor in his letter to Leykin does he mention the fact that he was just then working upon his first novel. To Maria Kisselev, with whom he did discuss some of the literary problems that were worrying him, he was equally uncommunicative. 'What shall 1 write to you about?' he asked in his letter of September 13th. 'That I haven't any money and that I am going deaf? But you know that already.' His letter contained this indirect hint at his state of mind: 'Our cat Fyodor Timofeyevich comes home occasionally to eat, but the rest of the time he walks about on the roofs looking at the sky. He must have come to the conclusion that life is meaningless.'

Fortunately, two quite unforeseen events brought about a change in his mood. One day a friend of his, Eugene Werner, who edited the literary weekly *The Cricket*, to which Chekhov had contributed seven stories in 1885, asked him to choose a dozen stories for publication in a book. Chekhov selected the stories and then and there received 150 roubles for them. (The stories were published in a volume under the title of *Innocent Speeches* in 1887.) That relieved Chekhov's pressing financial difficulties to some extent. Secondly, Korsh invited him to his theatre and insisted that he should write a play for him. At first Chekhov refused, but as Korsh kept on pestering him he sat down and wrote the first version of *Ivanov* in ten days. He then went back to his novel and he must have finished it at the beginning of October, for on the 10th of that month he asked Alexander to find out from Suvorin whether he would agree to publish his novel as a serial. Alexander replied that he did not think Suvorin would dare to refuse to publish anything Chekhov sent him. But Chekhov did not send the novel to Suvorin. Nothing, in fact, is known of it except that Chekhov did not want to send it to a literary periodical (he had had offers for his stories from *The Northern Herald*, a liberal monthly published in Petersburg, whose literary editor was the venerable poet Pleshcheyev, and from *Russian Thought*, another liberal monthly published in Moscow) because its chief characters were the president and the members of a military tribunal, that is to say, people of conservative views. In spite of the fact that he assured Alexander that his novel was 'not boring', he must have decided to destroy it, a proceeding to which he resorted only in cases of extreme dissatisfaction with his work.

But undismayed by his failure in 1887, Chekhov spent the following two years in another attempt to write a novel. He had a splendid subject for one, he told Pleshcheyev in February 1888. Indeed, he grew quite ecstatic about it. 'Oh,' he wrote, 'if only you knew what a subject for a novel I have in mind! What wonderful women, what funerals, what marriages! I have already written three printed sheets.' These outbursts of ecstasy (a sure sign of his nervous fear of failure) repeated themselves again and again in the course of the two years, followed almost immediately by long periods of disappointment and almost despair. In August 1888 he had to admit sorrowfully to Pleshcheyev that his novel was 'almost at freezing point' and that he would probably finish it only in two or three years. In October he told Grigorovich that he had a wonderful subject for a novel and that at times he felt a passionate desire to sit down and write it, but, he added; 'I have not got the power. I have begun it, but I am afraid to go on. I have decided to write it without hurrying and only when I feel up to it, correcting and polishing; I shall spend a few years on it, for I have not the courage to write it all at once in a year; I am terrified at my own helplessness, and, besides, there is no need to hurry. I have a genius for disliking one year what I wrote the year before, and I can't help feeling that next year I shall be much stronger than now; and that is why I am in no hurry to risk taking a definite step immediately. For if my novel fails, I shall never recover from the blow. The ideas, women and landscapes I have accumulated for my novel will be safe. I promise you not to waste them on trifles.' He then went on to give some particulars about the plot of his novel from which it would appear that he intended to devote a great deal of it to descriptions of nature. 'My novel', he wrote, 'deals with several families and a whole country district with its woods, rivers, ferries and railways. In the centre of the district are two main characters round whom the other pawns are grouped.' Meanwhile, Chekhov concluded his letter, he would continue to write short stories. Later in the same month he seemed to have given up the idea of writing the novel altogether. 'I haven't the power to write a novel,' he told Suvorin. 'The time for it hasn't come yet.' A few days later, however, he again reverted to the subject of his novel in another letter to Suvorin. He had two different plots for novels, he wrote, one of which he had been considering for so long that its characters had already grown old-fashioned. But in spite of all his doubts and difficulties he went on writing his second novel. In November he reported to Suvorin that he had written three hundred lines of his future novel about a fire in a village. 'People in a country house wake up at night and see the glow of a big fire—impressions, conversations, the patter of bare feet on an iron roof, bustle . . . .' This incident he apparently used eight years later in his story *Peasants*.

In January of 1889 Chekhov was still busy with his novel. 'Perhaps something will come of it,' he wrote to Pleshcheyev. 'I don't know, but when l write it I feel as if I were lying after a good dinner in a garden on some grass which has just been mown. Such a lovely sensation of restfulness! Shoot me if I go off my head and try doing something I am not fit for.' Two months later he seemed to have made such good progress with his novel that he promised Pleshcheyev to dedicate it— 'my best work'—to him. He seemed to be so sure about finishing it that on March 10th, 1889, he wrote to Anna Yevreinov, the editor and owner of the liberal monthly *The Northern Herald*, in which a year before he had published *The Steppe, Lights* and *Name-Day* ('a very intelligent and nice old maid who is a doctor of law and whose profile reminds me of a roasted starling', as he described her in a letter to Maria Kisselev), promising to send her his novel for publication in November. 'Oh, what a novel!' he went on ecstatically. 'But for the thrice cursed censorship, I could let you have it in November. There is nothing in my novel that could be interpreted as an incitement to revolution, but the censor will ruin it nevertheless. Half of my characters say, "I don't believe in God," there is a father whose son is serving a life sentence for armed insurrection, there is a country police inspector who is ashamed of his police uniform, there is a marshall of nobility who is hated, etc. Rich material for the censor's blue pencil. I have plenty of money now,' Chekhov went on, 'enough to last me till September, so now is the right time for writing my novel. For if I don't write it now, when shall I write it? That's what I keep on saying to myself, though I am almost sure that in two or three weeks I shall get thoroughly sick of it and put it away again.'

On the following day he dashed off a letter to Suvorin, announcing joyfully (as though he had never mentioned the subject before) that he was engaged in writing a novel and giving many more particulars about its plot, though, knowing Suvorin's conservative views, he was careful not to mention its highly unorthodox character. 'I write and write and there seems to be no end to my writing,' he declared. 'I have begun it, my novel, that is, afresh, greatly condensing and correcting what I have already written. Nine characters are clearly outlined. What a plot! Its title is *Stories from the Life of my Friends*, and I am writing it in the form of separate finished stories which are closely connected by the same characters, idea and plot. Each story has its own title. But don't imagine that my novel will consist of bits and pieces. No, it will be a real novel, an entire body, in which every character will be organically necessary. Grigorovich, whom I told the contents of the first chapter, was afraid that the student, who was going to die and therefore would not figure throughout the whole of the novel, would be superfluous. But this student will be merely one nail in a big boot. He is merely a detail.' Still Chekhov could not honestly say that he was satisfied with his novel. 'There are bound to be long boring passages and stupidities,' he wrote. 'I shall, however, try to avoid unfaithful wives, suicides, close-fisted or virtuous peasants, kind-hearted nannies, country wits, red-nosed army captains, and "new" men, though I do rather tend to become hackneyed in places.'

Writing to Leontyev on the same day, Chekhov confessed that he derived 'a certain voluptuous pleasure' from writing his novel, a curious way of putting it, but which probably merely expressed his feeling of heightened excitement at the progress he had made with it. A month later, during a further lull ('I have run aground again,' he wrote to Pleshcheyev, 'and am waiting for the tide to refloat me'), he gave the following outline of the main idea of its plot. 'Its foundation', he told Pleshcheyev, 'consists of the life of good people, their characters, deeds, words, thoughts and hopes; my aim is to kill two birds with one stone: to paint life truthfully and at the same time to show how this life deviates from the norm. What the norm is I don't know, and none of us knows. We all know what a dishonest action is, but what honour is we don't know. I shall keep within the framework which is dear to my heart and which has already been tried by people who are stronger and more intelligent than I. This framework is the absolute freedom of man, freedom from coercion, prejudices, ignorance, the devil, freedom from passions, etc.'

The idea was certainly too vague to fit into a well-defined plot for a novel. Still, Chekhov was not finished with his novel by any means. A month later, on May 6th, 1889, he wrote to Leontyev that he had 'scribbled something' that was rather 'valuable from the material point of view' which he would bring to Petersburg to sell in the autumn. A week later he said the same thing in a letter to Pleshcheyev, adding that he would not take less than two hundred and fifty roubles for a printed sheet of thirty-two pages of his novel. 'I shall sell it and go abroad,' he declared. He also wrote to Suvorin to the same effect: 'I shall go to Petersburg and sell my novel at a public auction.' When Suvorin wanted to know more about his plans for disposing of his novel, Chekhov replied (on June 9th): 'I think it is still a little too soon to discuss the date of publication of my magnificent novel. I mean, it is too soon to promise anything. When it is finished, I shall send it to you to read and we shall then decide what is to be done. . . . Today I am going to write one chapter. I feel a strong desire to write.' His last reference to his ill-starred novel occurs in a letter he wrote to Plescheyev on June 26th. 'I go on writing my novel slowly, but I am crossing out more than I write.' He never mentioned his novel again, and in the end he must have destroyed it all, for no trace of it has been discovered among his papers. Instead of carrying on with the novel, he wrote one of his most profound short stories—*A Boring Story*—and, of course, his unsuccessful play *The Wood Demon*, about the financial success of which he was, as it turned out, also over-optimistic.

Whether Chekhov made any use of the different stories he had in mind for his novel is difficult to say. Apart from the incident of the fire which bears a strong resemblance to the fire he described in his story *Peasants*, it has been suggested that three of the stories he wrote in 1898, namely *The Man in a Case*, *Gooseberries* and *About Love*, represent some of the stories he had intended to use in his novel. But there is no foundation whatever for this theory. Indeed, Chekhov's notebooks show that the plots of all these stories had occurred to him long after he had finally abandoned his attempt to write a novel.

It can therefore be stated with a fair amount of certainty that Chekhov's work on his two novels as well as the half-hearted attempt he made later on to write a third one were to all intents and purposes wasted. The answer to the question why he had failed as a novelist is supplied by his finding no difficulty at all in writing *Ivanov* even while he was struggling in vain to get on with his first novel. His approach to creative art, in fact, was that of a playwright. This is perhaps best shown by his advice to Alexander to make the emotional state of his characters clear from their *actions*. Chekhov himself realised very well why he could not write a novel. 'Before sitting down to write a novel,'

he wrote to Suvorin in November 1888, 'I must train myself to com-
municate ideas freely in a *narrative* [and not, that is, in a *dramatic*]
form. That is what I am doing now.' But in March 1889 he had to
confess (again in a letter to Suvorin) that the narrative form of the
novel was beyond him. 'I don't think I shall be able to master the
technique of the novel,' he wrote. 'I am still weak so far as that is
concerned and I feel that I am making a great number of big mistakes.'
In the end, unable to master the technique of the novel, he turned, 'out
of boredom', as he put it, to the writing of a play, finishing the first
version of *The Wood Demon* in a few weeks.

6

There was yet another reason Chekhov advanced for his failure as a
novelist. 'I haven't acquired a political, philosophic and religious outlook on life,' he wrote to Grigorovich in October 1888 in explanation
of the difficulties he experienced in writing his second novel. 'I keep
changing it every month, and I have therefore to confine myself to
descriptions of how my characters love, get married, beget children,
talk and die.' And a month later he wrote to Suvorin: 'My brain is
flapping its wings, but where to fly I know not.' It was his friendship
with Suvorin and the passionate intensity with which he embraced
Tolstoy's teachings that caused this painful state of indecision. His
early stories show no such hesitations about his political, philosophic
or religious views. He was a radical and an agnostic, and he remained a
radical and an agnostic all his life. His temporary acceptance of Tolstoy's philosophy did not affect his attitude to religion, for it was not
the religious but the moral views of Tolstoy, and most of all his dogma
of non-resistance to evil, that for a time exercised a powerful influence
on him. As for politics, Chekhov, like Tolstoy, remained a most
confirmed opponent of the autocratic Czarist regime.

It was his faith in the absolute objectivity of a writer that had first
led him astray. One of his last purely 'objective' stories was *Slime*,
published in *New Times* on October 29th, 1886. It provoked a spirited
protest from Maria Kisselev, whom Chekhov had sent a cutting of it.
'I did not like the story you sent me at all,' she wrote. 'It is well
written and I daresay the men who read it will be sorry not to have
come across a similar Susannah who would be able to satisfy their
lower instincts. The women will envy her and the public at large will
read your story with interest and say "What a clever fellow that

Chekhov is!" Perhaps such opinions and the one hundred and fifteen roubles you got for the story satisfy you, but, personally, I feel sorry that a writer of your sort, that is to say, one who has been so richly endowed by God, should only show me the "dunghill". The world is full of filth and scoundrels, and the impressions they produce are not new, but how grateful for that very reason you must be to writers who, having taken you through the stench of the dunghill, suddenly produce a pearl out of it. You, I'm sure, are not so shortsighted as to be incapable of producing that pearl. Why, then, are you satisfied with the dunghill only? Give me the pearl so that I should forget all about its filthy surroundings. I have a right to demand that from you. As for the writers who cannot find a human being among the quadrupeds, I shall not read them. Perhaps I ought to have kept quiet about it, but I just cannot help scolding you and your nasty editors who ruin your talent by their indifference. If I were an editor, I should have refused to publish your disgusting story for your own good.'

Chekhov waited till his first 'Tolstoyan' story, *Excellent People*, was published in *New Times* on November 22nd before answering Maria Kisselev's letter. His long and circumstantial reply (a sure sign that he took his friend's criticism to heart) is partly an admission that he, too, shared her views and partly an angry justification of an author's right to overlook 'the pearl in the dunghill' if he liked. Chekhov protested that his story could not possibly have a depraving influence on his readers, for literature, he maintained, was creative just because it showed life as it was, its purpose being honest and absolute truth. To narrow down its function to the production of 'pearls' was as deadly as 'forcing Levitan to paint a tree without showing its dirty bark or its withered leaves'. A writer was not an entertainer or a cosmetician and he ought not to be afraid 'to soil his imagination with the filth of life'. He admitted, however, that when writing his stories in the past he had not always consulted his conscience, but at the same time he thought it necessary to utter a warning against the dangers of leaving literature at the mercy of personal prejudices. 'There is no police which is competent to deal with literature,' he wrote. 'I admit that it is impossible to do without some sort of restraint or a stick, for all sorts of scoundrels find their way into literature, but however hard you try you will never invent a better police for literature than the critic or the author's own conscience.'

But the very fact that he now embarked on his brief but virulent career as propagandist of Tolstoyan ideas shows that his views on the objectivity of a writer had undergone a radical change. His Tolstoyan phase was his last phase as a writer who was the slave of other people's ideas. When he finally rid himself of the influence of Tolstoy's philosophy, he had 'squeezed out' the last drop of the slave in him and emerged as a mature writer and thinker. But Tolstoy's philosophy certainly left a deep mark on his writings which he was not entirely successful in removing. Some of the most 'Tolstoyan' of his stories, such as *The Meeting, The Cossack,* and *A Misfortune,* as well as his play *The Wood Demon,* in which the principle of non-resistance to evil plays havoc with his dearly held theory that a writer should present life as it is, he refused to include in the complete edition of his works; others like *Excellent People,* his first purely 'Tolstoyan' story in which the arguments for and against non-resistance to evil are formulated, *The Beggar, The Letter, The Bet* and *The Shoemaker and the Devil,* he thoroughly revised before allowing them to be included in the complete edition of his works. But most of his stories written between 1886 and 1889 bear traces of Tolstoy's philosophy, which Chekhov could not remove without ruining them completely. Even in *Uncle Vanya,* which is based on *The Wood Demon,* he was for the same reason forced to leave many 'Tolstoyan' passages from his earlier play. His defence of *Slime* was indeed his last assertion of independence before he embraced a theory of human behaviour that ran counter to his own conception of humanity. The moralist and reformer, baulked in his efforts to convert his elder brothers, for a time submerged the creative artist in him. 'I do not know a single reason', he wrote to Leykin in September 1887, 'why it should be considered useful and proper to represent reality in its worst aspects.' But he himself was not representing reality in its best aspects; he was representing it in a way that was a perversion of the truth which had always been so dear to him. What drove him to do so was his realisation that a story like *Slime* had no 'serious purpose'. But by borrowing from Tolstoy's new and fashionable morality and trying to write stories with a 'serious purpose' he became a preacher and betrayed his own conception of art which was to represent life fearlessly and at the same time arouse the dormant forces of good in the reader.

The tendency to preach was so characteristic of Chekhov at that period that it provoked an attack on him by *Entertainment,* one of the old-established humorous journals in Moscow to which he had contributed seven stories in 1884 and 1885. In its series of 'moral stories for children between the ages of three and eighty' which it was then publishing, there appeared one under the title of *The Tendentious Anton* in which Chekhov's Tolstoyan moralisings were held up to ridicule.

'Anton', the anonymous author of the story wrote, 'was a veterinary surgeon, but that did not satisfy him, so he became a writer. He had little sense but plenty of tendentiousness, and his writings were published in *Splinters* [a hint at *Fragments*]. "Physician, heal thyself," his friends told him, "and stop lecturing others." But Anton did not listen and went on writing and lecturing people and was tendentious. *Splinters* no longer understood him and he began publishing his stories in the *Petersburg Tuckshop* [a hint at the *Petersburg Gazette*], forgetting his duties of a veterinary surgeon, so that in the end he could no longer carry on with his profession.' Chekhov's reaction to this attack was typical of the preacher who takes himself so seriously that he cannot tolerate his leg being pulled even in fun. 'Enemies have appeared in *Entertainment*,' he wrote to Alexander. 'Someone has published a story there under the title of *The Tendentious Anton* in which I am referred to as a veterinary surgeon, though I have never had the honour of being called in to treat its editor.'

His friendship with Suvorin had made Chekhov suspect in the liberal camp, to which most of the literary periodicals traditionally belonged, and that, in turn, forced him to take up a bitter, almost an embittered, attitude towards the liberal circles in Russia. He himself realised very well the risk he was taking by his association with Suvorin's *New Times*. Already in February 1886, when Bibilin urged him to write something 'big', he replied that he would be glad to do it if he were sure that any literary periodical would accept a story of his. 'I am afraid that after my début in *New Times*', he wrote, 'I can hardly expect to be admitted to any important literary periodical. What do you think? Or am I mistaken?' And when two years later Grigorovich hinted to him that his work for *New Times* was damaging his reputation, he replied firmly: 'I shall not leave *New Times* because I am attached to Suvorin.' His friendship with Suvorin, however, did not mean that he had abandoned his radical faith; it merely intensified his feeling of dissatisfaction with the strong party spirit of the literary periodicals. 'A clannish spirit reigns in all our "fat" journals,' he wrote to Pleshcheyev on January 23rd, 1888. 'It's stifling. That's why I dislike the literary periodicals so much and why the prospect of working for them does not tempt me. The party spirit, especially when it is dull and without a spark of talent, hates freedom, daring and initiative'. Chekhov wrote this before *The Steppe* was finished and, as always, his views were strongly coloured by his doubts and fears, doubts whether his story would be accepted by the Petersburg literary periodical *The Northern Herald* and fears whether—if accepted—it would prove sufficiently successful to secure his entry into the larger literary world of the so-called 'fat journals', which enjoyed enormous prestige in Russia. 'We have fewer literary periodicals than theatres and universities,' Chekhov wrote to Pleshcheyev two years later. 'All the reading and thinking public is interested in their future; their progress is closely watched, all sorts of things are expected of them, etc. They must therefore be saved from destruction—that is the bounden duty of us all.' But in January 1888 he felt, as he wrote to the poet Polonsky, that to demand that talented writers should contribute only to literary reviews was petty and smelt of bureaucracy. 'There was some sense in it', he went on, 'when the monthly periodicals were edited by men of well-known views, such as Belinsky, Herzen, and so on, men who not only paid you decently but also attracted, taught and educated you; but now when instead of such men they are edited by nonentities, the preference shown for literary periodicals is beneath contempt . . . and is not worthy of the attention of the creative artist.'

Chekhov reserved his bitterest attacks for *Russian Thought*, whose literary editor he became in the last year of his life, and particularly for its editor Victor Goltsev, who was to become one of his closest friends. In March 1888 he had a talk to Goltsev on behalf of a literary friend of his. He found that the 'grand vizier' of *Russian Thought*, though an exceedingly nice man, did not seem to have any understanding of literature whatever. 'Goltsev', he wrote to his friend, 'conducted himself with dignity, as behoved the vice-director of one of the fattest and most intelligent periodicals in Europe.' Goltsev told him that *Russian Thought* was not anxious to publish long stories because modern fiction writers could not write anything 'big'. (Chekhov took that statement as a direct reflection on himself.) Goltsev further deplor d the fact that young writers, in general, did not possess any 'profundity of thought', which led him to the conclusion that it was a mistake for them to write long stories or novels, for 'our contemporary life provides no themes for a long story or novel and our literature is now going through a transition period'. Which made Chekhov declare in a letter to Leykin a week later that 'our Goltsevs are dry, dull and inept like the bare bones of a crow'. He wrote at greater length to the writer on whose behalf he had been to see Goltsev. 'All these Goltsevs are good and kindhearted people,' he declared, 'but they are extremely uncivil. Whether they are uneducated or slow-witted or whether their trivial success has gone to their heads, I don't know, but you need not expect any sympathy or ordinary attention from them. There is one thing they would be glad to give you and all Russians, and that is a *constitution*, everything less than that they consider to be beneath their calling. . . . I don't want to conceal from you', Chekhov went on, 'that I am indifferent to them as people, and if I do sympathise with them it is because they are without exception failures and have suffered a great deal in their lives. But as editors and men of letters I cannot abide them. I have never published anything in their journals and have not experienced their dreary censorship myself, but I can't help feeling that they are stifling something and that they have sunk deep into a lie somebody else has invented for them. It is my opinion that these literary dachshunds (I can't help feeling that dachshunds with their long bodies, short legs and pointed muzzles are a cross between mongrels and crocodiles; our Moscow editors are a cross between professors, who are civil servants, and dull-witted men of letters), inspired by their successes and the praises they receive from their admirers, will create a whole school or order which will succeed in so perverting the literary tastes and views for which Moscow has become famous that we shall not be able to recognise them.'

In August of the same year Pleshcheyev wrote to Chekhov that he had been told that the head of the Government Press Department had said that *Russian Thought* was not subject to any preliminary censorship because 'it is entirely ours: it writes what we want and it always consults us'. Chekhov pounced on that piece of news gleefully in spite of the doubtful source from which it came. 'You wait,' he wrote to Pleshcheyev with the acute perception of the outcast whose resentment has opened his eyes to the glaring faults of his dearest friends which otherwise he would never have noticed, '*Russian Thought* will play even better tricks! Under the banner of science, art and freedom of thought such toads and crocodiles will reign in Russia as were not known even in Spain under the inquisition. You will see. Narrow-mindedness, large pretensions, inordinate vanity and a complete absence of any literary or social conscience will all play their part. All these Goltsevs and Co. will make the air so stifling that everyone who possesses the least bit of originality will become sick and tired of literature and every charlatan and wolf in sheep's clothing will find a place in which to tell his lies, play the hypocrite and die "with honour".'

There was no doubt a great deal to justify Chekhov's strictures on the radical circles in Russia in the late 'eighties. An interesting light on their narrow-mindedness and lack of humour is thrown by the following advertisement which was published in the liberal *Russian Gazette* and which Chekhov quoted in a letter to Suvorin on March 11th, 1889:

'A middle-aged lady is wanted by a family residing in a country house near Moscow to help with domestic and educational duties. The lady must be acquainted with the views on education and the outlook on life of . . . Victor Goltsev and Leo Tolstoy. Imbued with the views of these writers and conscious of the importance of physical work and the danger of mental fatigue, she must aim at inculcating on the minds of the children a desire for truth and goodness and a love of their fellow-men.' Chekhov's comment was: 'This is what they call freedom of conscience. For her board and lodging the woman must be imbued with the views of Goltsev & Co., while the children, thankful, no doubt, for having such intelligent and liberal parents, must always remember to love their fellow-men and not to be mentally fatigued. It is strange that people should be so much afraid of freedom.'

It was no less strange that Chekhov should have been expressing these sentiments to a man like Suvorin who certainly had no love for freedom. Indeed, his association with Suvorin sometimes led him to express opinions which were entirely out of tune with his deepest convictions. For instance, when Goltsev was arrested in October 1888, because an escaped political prisoner had applied to him for a job, all Chekhov had to say was that he should not have poked his nose into things that were no concern of his. On the other hand, when Suvorin about a year later expressed the opinion that there could be nothing more contemptible than 'our opposition', Chekhov replied: 'Those who do not belong to the opposition are scarcely any better. The mother of all evil is gross ignorance, and it is equally characteristic of all our parties and movements.' Again, commenting on the death of Saltykov-Shchedrin on April 28th, 1889, Chekhov wrote to Pleshcheyev: 'I am sorry for Saltykov. He was a man of great intellect and strong convictions. The petty spirit that dwells in the average Russian intellectual has lost one of its deadliest enemies in him. Every journalist knows how to expose, even Burenin knows how to ridicule, but Saltykov alone knew how to despise openly. Two-thirds of his readers did not like him, but everyone believed him. No one doubted the sincerity of his contempt.'

7

When preparing his edition of collected works in 1899, Chekhov remarked: 'Chekhonte may have written a great deal that Chekhov cannot accept.' This critical attitude to his early works became apparent already at the time of the publication of his volume of stories (*Motley*

Stories) by Leykin in June 1886. He refused Leykin's request to include any of his stories published in *New Times* which he considered
'his most important work'. And in a letter to his uncle Mitrofan in
January 1887 he described the volume as 'a collection of my unimportant trifles which I published not so much for reading as in memory
of the beginning of my literary work. Those stories I like in my book
I shall tick off with a blue pencil. The rest deserve notice only as a
sample of the stuff that one is sometimes forced to write under the
pressure of financial exigency'. These unimportant trifles, however,
included such gems of Chekhov's genius as *Anyuta*, *Misery*, *A
Daughter of Albion*, *A Malefactor* (which Tolstoy included among
the most excellent and profound of Chekhov's stories), *Surgery*, *A
Chameleon*, *Fat and Thin*, *On the Nail*, *A Civil Service Examination*,
The Ninny, *A Retired Slave*, *The Death of a Government Clerk*,
The First-Class Passenger, *A Living Calendar*, *A Work of Art*, and
many others of great social significance, showing a deep understanding
of human nature and sympathy for the underdog, a fine appreciation
of the dignity of man, and above all a humour that arouses both tears
and laughter, as well as stories dealing with 'serious' social problems,
such as *The Willow*, *The Charitable Thief*, *A Publican*, *In the Autumn*,
and *Oysters*, in which, Chekhov declared, he tested himself for the
first time as a 'medicus' (the story—a physiological and pathological
study of hunger—was written in November 1884, about two years
before Chekhov himself had ever tasted oysters, which perhaps accounts
for the ghoulish descriptions of an oyster).

It is unfortunately not unusual for a certain type of academic critic
to accept Chekhov's severe judgment of his early stories too uncritically and dismiss them as 'unimportant'. But Chekhov himself
resented Skabichevsky's criticism of his *Motley Stories* in *The Northern
Herald* and dismissed it as 'most venomous abuse'. And yet Skabichevsky merely gave expression to an opinion that Chekhov seemed
to sanction by his repeated dismissals of these stories as 'mere trifles'.
'Chekhov', Skabichevsky wrote, 'is wasting his talent on trifles,
writing the first thing that enters his head and not bothering to give
much thought to the contents of his stories.' Taking this view, he came
to the conclusion that 'the book presents a very sad and tragic spectacle
of the suicide of a young man of talent', who, like many another newspaper writer, 'will most probably die in a ditch in a state of intoxication'. Chekhov never forgot Skabichevsky's review of his book.
'I have been reading criticisms of my stories for twenty-five years,' he
told Gorky many years later, 'and I can't remember a single valuable

hint, nor a single piece of useful advice. Only Skabichevsky once made an impression on me. He wrote that I would die in a state of intoxication in a ditch.'

What Skabichevsky failed to perceive was that he was not dealing with a writer of talent but with a writer of genius, a cardinal failure in perception that is characteristic of all mediocre critics. As for Chekhov, his attitude towards his early stories was influenced first of all by the fact that as a creative writer he could not stand still but had to go on doing bigger things and, secondly, by his preoccupation with the problem of good and evil and its bearing on literature as a result of the ascendancy of Tolstoy's teaching, which was sweeping Russia just then.

By the time Chekhov began contributing his long stories to *New Times* he had six years of experience as a writer behind him. He was therefore fully able to offer advice to his friends who were just entering on their literary careers. The first thing he insisted on was that a young writer should write as much as possible. 'Write, write, write—till your fingers break,' he told his friend Maria Kisselev in a letter he wrote in September 1886. 'Write as much as you can, bearing in mind not so much your intellectual development as the fact that more than half of your short stories will be returned to you. . . . Don't be disturbed by these rejections. Even if you get half of your stories back, it will still have been worth your while. As for your vanity—well, I don't know how you feel, but I got used to getting my stories back long ago. Write', Chekhov went on, 'on all sorts of subjects, funny and tearful, good and bad. As for adaptations of stories by foreign authors, there is nothing wrong about it legally, provided you do not transgress the eighth commandment. Avoid popular subjects. However stupid our editors may be, you won't find it easy to convict them of ignorance of French literature and especially Maupassant. Write a story at one go . . . and don't forget that brevity is the mother of all virtues especially if you write for the popular press, and the best way to check that is by your notepaper (the same I am writing on now). The moment you come to page 8—10 stop!'

In a letter to Yozhov a year later, Chekhov scolded him for writing too little. 'You are a "beginner" in the full sense of the word,' he wrote, 'and you must not forget that every line you write now constitutes your capital of the future. If you do not train your mind and your hand to discipline and forced marches now, you will find that in three or four years it will be too late. It is my belief that you and Gruzinsky must force yourselves to work for hours every day. You work too little—both of you. If you go on writing so little, you will write yourself out without having written anything. As a warning you can take my brother Alexander, who was very niggardly as a writer and who already feels that he has written himself out.'

Throughout his correspondence of this period one finds here and there a number of interesting observations on what Chekhov considered to be the essential characteristics of creative writing. To begin with, he insisted that a writer must never describe any emotions he had not experienced himself. 'Don't invent sufferings', he wrote to Alexander, 'which you have not experienced and don't paint landscapes you have not seen, for a lie in a story is a hundred times more boring than in a conversation. Don't forget that your pen and your talents will be more useful to you in the future than they are now, so don't profane them now. Write and consider carefully every line you put down to make sure you aren't making a mess of it.' A year later he again drew his brother's attention to his ignorance of life and, particularly, of women. 'You positively don't know women,' he wrote; 'there is not a single human being among the women in your stories, all of them are just quivering jellies who speak the language of absolute ingénues.' In another letter he reminded his brother that it was possible to write 'lightly and playfully' not only about 'young girls, pancakes and pianos', but also about 'tears and privations. An author's originality', he continued, 'finds expression not only in his style, but also in the way he forms his thoughts and his convictions'.

Commenting in a letter to Korolenko on the first chapters of Thoreau's *Walden or Life in the Woods*, a translation of which was being published in serial form in *New Times*, he found that it contained interesting thoughts, freshness and originality, but that in spite of that it was difficult to read. 'The architecture and construction', he wrote, 'are impossible. Beautiful and not so beautiful, light and heavy ideas are piled one on top of the other, they are crowded together, squeeze the sap out of each other and at any moment may begin to squeal in the crush.'

Chekhov had always his reader in mind. What he therefore valued most was an absolute clarity and directness of style, a style of great evocative power. 'In my view,' he wrote to Alexander on May 10th, 1886, 'descriptions of nature must be very brief and have an apropos character. Generalities like "The setting sun, bathing in the waves of the darkening sea, sheds a light of crimson gold" and so on, or "The swallows, skimming the water, chirped merrily," must be done away with. In descriptions of nature one must get hold of the small details,

ANTON CHEKHOV AND LEO
TOLSTOY IN GASPRA (1902)

ANTON CHEKHOV AND MAXIM GORKY IN
YALTA (1901)

arranging them in such a way that, when you shut your eyes, you get a clear picture in your mind. For instance, you will get a picture of a moonlit night if you write that a bit of glass from a broken bottle shone like a tiny star on the dam of the water-mill and the dark shadow of a dog or a wolf flashed by like a ball, and so on. Nature will come to life if you are not afraid to compare its phenomena with human actions. In the emotional sphere, too, it is little details that are important. May the Lord preserve you from generalities. The best thing of all is not to describe the emotional state of your characters; you ought to try to make it clear from their actions. Neither should you have too many characters. The centre of gravity should be two: he and she. . . ."

Both these statements contain important points which have often been misunderstood. Chekhov's statement about the moonlit night, in particular, has been quoted by his critics again and again without paying proper attention to the *time* when Chekhov made it. Chekhov had obviously in mind the description of the moonlit night he gave in his story *Hydrophobia*, later renamed *The Wolf*, published in the *Petersburg Gazette* on March 17th, 1886. The passage in the story runs: 'There was not a shadow to be seen on the dam of the water-mill, which was bathed in moonlight; in the middle of it the neck of a broken bottle gleamed like a pale star.' In Act IV of *The Seagull* Chekhov makes Konstantin Treplyov quote these lines as Trigorin's and hold them up as an example of how a moonlit night ought to be described. But in that play Chekhov had purposely chosen a passage from a story he himself had not thought good enough to indicate that Trigorin was the kind of writer he himself had outgrown. It is the second suggestion in his letter to Alexander regarding the personification of inanimate objects, still rather tentatively thrown out, that was for a short period to become characteristic of Chekhov's stories. In *The Post*, published in the *Petersburg Gazette* on September 14th, 1887, the clouds whisper to one another so as not to be overheard by the moon, the harness bells laugh and cry, and a man's shadow leaves the train with him. It is this type of anthropomorphism that Chekhov later vehemently condemned in Gorky's prose poems. The writer Alexander Tikhonov, who met Chekhov in 1902, recalls the following criticism Chekhov made about Gorky's description of the sea in one of these poems:

'"The sea laughs,"' Chekhov said, twirling nervously the cord of his pince-nez. 'You are, of course, in raptures about it. But it's crude and cheap. You read "the sea laughs" and stop dead. You think you have stopped because it's good and artistic. But it's nothing of the kind. You have stopped simply because you haven't understood how the sea can possibly laugh. The sea doesn't laugh or cry, it roars, plashes, glistens. Just look how Tolstoy does it: the sun rises and sets, the birds sing. No one laughs or sobs. And that's the chief thing—simplicity.'

Chekhov, in fact, soon abandoned this method of describing inanimate objects, replacing it by one in which nature is described through the eyes of his characters. The famous description of lightning in *The Steppe* is of that kind. It is the boy Yegorushka who quite appropriately sees the lightning in the simple terms of a match being struck on the sky. This method obviously lends itself to infinite variations and is much more subtle than that Chekhov used in *The Wolf* and *The Post*. The main thing about it is that the image must be concrete and simple; that is to say, it must express the feelings, moods and thoughts of the character so perfectly that the reader will not only see it instantly but also experience the same mood, feelings and thoughts. 'The simpler the movement,' Chekhov wrote to Maria Kisselev on October 29th, 1887, 'the greater the verisimilitude and the better.' It was this amazing power of evocation that Chekhov went on refining as his sensibility broadened and deepened and that made people even in the late 'eighties refer to him as the most 'sensitive' writer of his time.

8

In the last four months of 1887 Chekhov wrote, in addition to his play *Ivanov*, fifteen stories, including three long stories for *New Times* (*Cold Blood*, *The Kiss* and his famous children's story *Kashtanka*). In October he met the writer Vladimir Korolenko, who left this description of him: 'I saw before me a young man who looked even younger than his actual age. He was just over medium height, with an oblong, regular, clean-cut face which had not yet lost its characteristically youthful contours. His face indeed had something peculiar about it which I could not define at once, but which my wife, who also met Chekhov, afterwards defined as a face which, though undoubtedly that of an educated man, had something which reminded her of a village lad, and that was particularly attractive. Even his eyes, blue, radiant, and deep,[1] were thoughtful and at the time almost childishly artless. The simplicity of his speech and behaviour was the most characteristic part of his personality, as, indeed, it is of his writing, too.

---

[1] Chekhov was over six feet tall and his eyes were brown and not blue.

In general, at my first meeting with him, Chekhov produced the impression of a man who was full of the joy of life. His eyes seemed to irradiate an inexhaustible fund of wit and high spirits, of which his stories were full. But at the same time one also caught in them a glimpse of something more profound that still had to develop.' Korolenko was so charmed with Chekhov's personality that he even forgave him his 'freedom from party prejudices', which he thought was an advantage to a man who was undoubtedly very talented and sincere. Chekhov, on the other hand, felt that the difference between him and Korolenko was very great, since Korolenko was 'serious, strong and true', while he himself was 'the most frivolous of all the contemporary Russian writers'. So convinced was Chekhov of Korolenko's superiority over him that when Alexander wrote to him on October 21st that the Russian Academy of Science had decided to award him the Pushkin Prize of five hundred roubles for his last volume of short stories *In the Twilight* which he dedicated to Grigorovich and which was published by Suvorin in August, he wrote back to say that he would only accept it if it were shared out between him and Korolenko. In any case, he comforted himself, the final decision about the prize would not be taken till October of next year and they would certainly not give it to him if only because he was working for such a reactionary paper as *New Times*.

It would seem from a letter Chekhov wrote to Korolenko on January 9th, 1888, that during their first meeting they discussed the subject of his proposed long story *The Steppe*. When he actually began working on the story it is impossible to say, but it must have been during the last months of 1887. He certainly found it very difficult to write. After the failure of his first novel, the writing of a long story gave him so much trouble that he often gave way to despair. 'I am again suffering from an attack of acute depression,' he wrote to Alexander on October 29th. 'I don't work. I sit for days in my armchair gazing at the ceiling. Still, there is my medical practice.' Soon he was immersed in the production of *Ivanov*, discussing it with Vladimir Davydov, the leading actor in Korsh's company who was to play Ivanov, attending the rehearsals and quarrelling with the actors who did not know their parts and, generally, made a mess of things. 'My play', he wrote to Leykin on November 4th, 'has so tired me out that I have lost count of time, gone off the rails completely and shall probably end up as a lunatic. Korsh', he added, 'is just a business man and what he wants is not the success of my play but a full house.' And asked by Leykin why he wanted to bother about plays at all, the most original, if not the greatest, dramatist of modern times explained ingenuously and illogically that to give up his play meant to give up the hope of making money. At the same time, however, he was planning to write another play with his young friend Lazarev-Gruzinsky (a one-act skit on *Hamlet*).

Ivanov was performed for the first time on November 19th, a most gruelling day for Chekhov, who at long last saw a play of his performed on the stage by professional actors (his fifth play, though he spoke of it as his first). The excitement in the audience and behind the scenes was such that the prompter, who had been working for the theatre for thirty-two years, told Chekhov that he could not remember anything like it. People were shouting, applauding and booing. There was nearly a fight in the bar during one of the intervals; in the gallery the students wanted to throw a man out and the police had to be called in to restore order. Chekhov's sister Mary nearly fainted. One of his friends could not stand the tension and rushed out of the theatre. Kisselev clasped his head and, according to Chekhov, screamed at the top of his voice: 'What am I going to do now?' Chekhov sat behind the scenes in a special cubicle, cursing the actors for not knowing their parts and for inventing their own dialogue. After the performance (he had to take many calls, during one of which some of the audience booed him) he felt dead tired and angry. However, the play at any rate provoked a great deal of discussion, which was nothing compared to the discussions it provoked in Petersburg when Chekhov arrived there on December 1st and showed it to Suvorin and his other friends. The play, Chekhov decided as a result of these interminable discussions, would have to be entirely rewritten on his return to Moscow.

In Petersburg Chekhov stayed with Alexander. He was thoroughly disgusted with his brother's 'Taganrog' background: 'Filth, stench, screams, lies,' he described his brother's household to Michael. 'It is enough to spend one week at his place to go clean off one's head and become as filthy as a kitchen rag.' But the city itself he found wonderful this time. 'I am in the seventh heaven,' he wrote to Michael. 'The streets, the cabbies, the food—everything is excellent, and there are so many intelligent and decent people here that if I were asked whom I liked best I'd find it difficult to decide.'

He spent over a fortnight in Petersburg, thoroughly enjoying himself for once. It was, as Leontyev observed, the 'honeymoon' of Chekhov's fame. For the first and last time of his life he emerged from his shell and spoke to everybody with quite unwonted expansiveness. He even put on weight. 'In three days I've grown fat,' he wrote to

Michael on December 3rd. 'Yesterday I spent the night and had dinner at Leykin's. That's where I had a really good meal, a good sleep and a good rest from the filth. The December number of *The Northern Herald* has a long article about me. What a pity I can't live here always! The thought of returning to Moscow, which swarms with Gavrilovs and Kicheyevs,[1] puts me into a bad humour. I'm getting to know some society women, too. I have received several invitations from them. I shall go, though every sentence of their complimentary speeches reveals the neurotic. I shall bring back many books with me.'

His visit to Petersburg brought about the fulfilment of one of his fondest dreams—his entry into the world of monthly periodicals. He had already received an invitation to contribute to *The Northern Herald*, and now the arrangements for his regular contributions to that monthly were finally clinched at a meeting with its literary editor, Alexey Pleshcheyev. Like Grigorovich, Pleshcheyev belonged to an earlier generation of famous men. He had been a member of the Petrashevsky circle of young disciples of the French school of utopian socialists and had been sentenced in 1849 to be shot together with Dostoevsky. In fact, when taken to the Semyonovsky Square for his execution he found himself standing beside Dostoevsky, and, thinking that their last hour had come, the two men embraced and took leave of each other. Pleshcheyev, too, was sentenced to a term of hard labour in a Siberian convict prison, and in 1887 he was one of the few survivors of that band of young rebels against Czarist autocracy who, unlike Dostoevsky, remained faithful to the liberal ideas of his past.

Chekhov went to see Pleshcheyev in the company of Leontyev, who wrote under the pseudonym of Shcheglov and whom he had also met for the first time during his present visit to Petersburg. According to Leontyev, Chekhov was very excited at the prospect of meeting the old poet. 'Chekhov', Leontyev recalls, 'was always able to keep himself under control and that was the only occasion I can remember seeing him so excited; he seemed to have sensed that his meeting with Pleshcheyev would usher him into the world of great literature.'

Pleshcheyev was also perceptibly touched by Chekhov's visit.

'Ah, at last,' he murmured, 'I'm so glad you've come.'

Chekhov looked a little embarrassed as he exchanged the usual civilities, and to put him at his ease Pleshcheyev inquired after one of their mutual acquaintances in Moscow. Chekhov smiled and made a rather pointed, if good-humoured, remark which made them all laugh. The ice was broken, and within a short time the venerable old poet and

---

[1] Nicolai Kicheyev was the editor of *The Alarm-Clock*.

the young writer who was to outshine him so soon were talking like two old friends.

It was during that Petersburg visit that Chekhov appeared in public on December 12th for the first and last time as a reader of his stories at a literary evening organised by the Writers' and Scientists' Benevolent Society. His usual excuse for turning down the many invitations for public readings he received was that he suffered from stage fright and that his vocal chords went dry after forty or fifty lines. But it seems that he was no less concerned about the injury to his reputation such public readings might cause. When Leykin first broached the subject of a public reading in aid of the Petersburg Writers' Benevolent Fund, Chekhov asked Alexander to find out 'in a roundabout way' and 'without mentioning any names' what reputation those evenings enjoyed and whether it would not be considered undignified for him to participate in them. He must have been reassured on that score, for on the following day he wrote to Maria Kisselev: 'Yesterday I read at the Literary Society and was quite successful.'

On his return to Moscow he summed up the general impression of his Petersburg visit in the biblical phrase: 'Put not your trust in princes, nor in any child of man.' He had met many kind and interesting people, but he did not find anyone among them to whom he could turn for helpful advice. And he wanted advice very badly just then, as he found the last chapters of *The Steppe* particularly difficult. Before sitting down to finish it, he took a few days off for a holiday in the country. He went to Babkino on January 3rd and spent three days there. The country in winter, with the fields and woods covered in dazzlingly white snow, looked charming to him, and he enjoyed his visit, though he did have to perform, in the absence of a veterinary surgeon, an autopsy on a cow that had died suddenly. In Moscow there were the traditional drinking bouts on January 12th, the anniversary of the foundation of Moscow University, at which he had to drink numerous healths to the people who had taught him 'to cut up corpses and write prescriptions' (the occasion, the last one before Tolstoy's fiat put an end to it, struck him as rather meagre and boring), and on his own name-day on January 17th. On the whole, there was little apparent change in his life at first. He was busy with his writing and his medical practice, and occasionally he would leave home, where, as he complained to a friend, he lived like a hermit, to go to a party. 'I write and write,' he described his daily routine to a friend, 'then go to visit a few patients, and from time to time go out to see a few friends I do not particularly enjoy seeing.' Suvorin advised him to give up his medical practice, but he felt more cheerful and contented when he had two occupations instead of one. 'Medicine', he wrote to Suvorin, 'is my lawful wife and literature my mistress. When I get tired of one I spend a night with the other. That may not be quite respectable, but at any rate it isn't boring, and, besides, neither of them loses anything from my unfaithfulness. If I had not had my medical practice, I should not have given my leisure and my superfluous thoughts to literature. I lack discipline.' But it was not discipline that he lacked so much as peace of mind. He no longer suffered from violent convulsions at night. A worse trouble beset him now. In addition to the recurrent symptoms of tuberculosis as well as the constant attacks of haemorrhoids, he was now obsessed by mental terrors, caused chiefly by the suppressed thought of his grave illness. When alone in his study, he felt frightened, and his patients helped him to take him out of himself, apart from providing him with valuable material for a first-hand study of people in surroundings which did not conceal the stark facts of life. It was also those hidden terrors that made Chekhov put up with the countless visitors and friends who from that time on were to become one of the most troublesome plagues of his existence. But though a terrible nuisance, he could not live without them. 'I simply cannot live without visitors,' he wrote to Suvorin in June, 1889. 'When I am alone, I am for some reason terrified, as though I were a castaway in a small boat in the middle of the Pacific Ocean.' At night his terrors increased, and Michael had to light a lamp in his bedroom, for the darkness intensified his terror; and in the daytime, too, he would often ask Michael to play something on the piano for him while he worked because his feeling of loneliness oppressed him. Occasionally his visitors and friends would get on his nerves and he would positively hate them, a feeling, he confessed to Suvorin, he had never experienced before. They would interfere with his work, they would borrow money from him and forget to repay it, they would steal his books, and they would plague him with long and stupid conversations and requests to read their stories and plays. But he put up with it all patiently, for he had to have them as a distraction.

Even on his way to the railway station during his frequent journeys to Petersburg in 1887 and 1888 Chekhov was overcome by what he called 'a horrible feeling of loneliness' and would insist on some friend accompanying him to the station and seeing him into the train. Though deeply attached to his family, he did not share any of his intimate thoughts with them. His family, he wrote to Leontyev, was 'his benignant tumour', and, to make sure that it did not interfere with him, he always carried it about with him. 'It sews my shirts beautifully, cooks me splendid dinners and is always cheerful. In winter it consists of eight people and in summer of five (including two maids). At any rate, I am more often cheerful than sad, though, come to think of it, I am bound hand and foot. You, my dear fellow, have a flat, but I have a whole house, a rotten house, but still a house, and on two floors. You have a *wife* who will forgive you if you don't happen to have any money, but I have an entire *order* which will crash about my ears if I don't earn a certain number of roubles every month; it will crash about my ears and hang like a millstone round my neck.'

He was even more outspoken to Alexander, who after the death of his first 'civil' wife had asked him to look after his children till he got settled again. 'You know', Chekhov wrote, 'that I have a whole multitude of grown-up people living under the same roof with me. Because of some inexplicable set of circumstances we don't find it possible to separate: mother; sister; Michael, who won't leave till he has finished his university course; Nicholas, who is doing nothing and who has been jilted by his lady-love and is always drunk and walking about in rags; auntie and Alexey,[1] who live with us rent free; Ivan, who spends all his time here from three o'clock in the afternoon till late at night, not to mention Sundays and holidays; and father, who usually comes along in the evenings. All of them are exceedingly nice and cheerful people, but vain and full of themselves, always talking, stamping their feet, and with never a penny in their pockets. It makes my head swim. . . . If I had to add two more children's beds and a nurse, I should have to seal up my ears with wax and put on a pair of dark glasses. If I had a wife and children, I'd gladly take another half-dozen children, but with my present family always on top of one another, noisy, moneyless and kept unnaturally together, I cannot undertake to have one more person, and particularly one who has to be brought up and put on his feet.'

Actually Chekhov was pleased to have Kisselev's son Sergey to live with him, as he felt he would 'renew and refresh the air' in his house. He was amused by the boy's high spirits as well as by his appalling laziness, and he loved to watch him walking on his hands and jumping on the backs of his visitors. When the boy fell ill he sent daily bulletins to his mother. 'Fresh news,' he wrote in one of them. 'Ivanov came today to tell Sergey about his homework. Invited upstairs, he went into Sergey's room, looking very embarrassed and making Sergey

[1] Feodossia and her son Alexey Dolzhenko, who stayed with Chekhov in Taganrog and who later, on Chekhov's recommendation, got a job at Gavrilov's warehouse. Alexey played the violin and the zither and took part in the musical parties at Chekhov's house.

look embarrassed, too. His eyes fixed stolidly on the wall, he told him in a bass voice what his homework was, then gave him a push with his elbow and said, "Goodbye, Kisselev." And without shaking hands left the room. Quite obviously, a socialist.'

Among Chekhov's friends were two musicians—Alexander Ivanenko, a contributor to *The Alarm-Clock*, who played the violin (Chekhov characterised him as a born failure and, according to Michael, used him as his model for Yepikhodov in *The Cherry Orchard*), and Marian Semashko, a cellist of the Moscow Opera House Orchestra, both of whom took part in the weekly 'musical parties' at Chekhov's house. Mary, who was teaching at a girls' private school and taking art lessons, was responsible for introducing Chekhov to Lydia Mizinov, a beautiful eighteen-year-old girl, who became an intimate friend of Chekhov's family, and Sophia Kuvshinnikov, a woman of forty who was married to a police surgeon and who was taking painting lessons from Levitan, with whom she was having an affair.

Chekhov was often present at Sophia Kuvshinnikov's weekly parties at her flat under the watch-tower of a fire station. Sophia had converted her flat into a very arty place. Instead of sofas she had soap-boxes covered with cushions and instead of curtains—fishing nets. Her parties were attended by doctors, musicians, artists and writers. Dr. Kuvshinnikov himself was never seen at them. Only about midnight would he suddenly appear at the dining-room door with a fork in one hand and a knife in the other and announce solemnly: 'Ladies and gentlemen, won't you come into the dining-room and have something to eat?' Mrs. Kuvshinnikov treated her husband with the becoming artless comradeship of an 'advanced' woman.

'Dmitry Kuvshinnikov,' she would cry ecstatically, rushing up to her husband; and, turning to her intellectual friends, she would go on: 'Ladies and gentlemen, look at the wonderful expression on his face!' And after returning from a long summer painting trip with Levitan, she would fling her arms round her deceived husband's neck and cry: 'Dmitry Kuvshinnikov, let me shake your honest hand! Ladies and gentlemen, look what an honest face he has!'

Kuvshinnikov certainly did his best to live up to his wife's opinion of him, though the fact that all her friends knew of her affair with Levitan put rather a heavy strain on his forbearance. It was a situation that Chekhov watched with the detached eye of the creative artist and which he rather unwisely used four years later (in 1892) in his story *The Grasshopper*, which brought about the only serious quarrel between him and Levitan.

At the beginning of 1888, however, Chekhov was still very far from thinking that any story of his might be taken seriously by his friends. He finished *The Steppe* at the end of January, leaving the story purposely unfinished in case he wished to go on with it and turn it into a novel. Grigorovich had urged him to write a novel about a seventeen-year-old boy who shoots himself in the attic of his house. 'The whole environment', he wrote to Chekhov on December 30th, 1887, from Nice, where he was recovering from his attack of angina pectoris, 'and all the motives that led up to his suicide seem to me to be infinitely more important than the reasons which forced Werther to take his life. Such a subject deals with one of the most important problems of our time, and I am sure your book will be an instantaneous success as soon as it is published.' Chekhov felt that Grigorovich's subject was a very tempting one, but also a very difficult one. 'You judge for yourself,' he wrote to Grigorovich on January 12th, 'but you forget that the writers of your generations possessed not only talent but also erudition, schooling, phosphorus and iron, while our contemporary writers have nothing of the sort and, to be quite frank, we should be glad that they do not deal with serious problems. Offer them your boy and I am sure that X, without realising it himself, will perpetrate a libel, a blasphemy and a lie, Y will make him the hero of a cheap and tendentious story, and Z will explain his suicide as being a result of some psychosis. To be able to deal adequately with such a subject one must be able to endure suffering [a remarkable anticipation of one of the main themes of *The Seagull*], but our modern writers only know how to whine and slobber.' He returned to this subject again in his next letter to Grigorovich of February 5th. 'The suicide of your Russian boy', he wrote, 'is a specific phenomenon unknown in Western Europe. The artist's entire energy must be concentrated on two things: man and nature. On the one hand, physical weakness, nervousness, early sexual maturity, a passionate desire for life and truth, dreams of future activities which should be as wide as the steppe itself, restless analysis, poor knowledge side by side with a rich imagination and, on the other, an endless plain, a harsh climate, an ignorant, stern people with its distressingly bleak history, Tartar domination, bureaucracy, poverty, ignorance, etc. Russian life weighs heavily upon the Russian; it is just as if he had to carry a rock weighing a ton on his shoulders. In Western Europe people perish because they find life cramped and stifling, in Russia because they find life too spacious. There is so much space that a little man has not got the strength to find his way about. That's what I think of Russian suicides.' But in the same letter Chekhov indicated that he was considering Grigorovich's subject as a possible line of development in the life of Yegorushka, the main character in *The Steppe*. 'Eventually', he wrote, 'my nine-year-old boy will get to Petersburg and Moscow and will most certainly come to a sticky end.' And in his letter to Pleshcheyev of February 9th he again spoke of his intention to carry on with *The Steppe*. 'The stupid Father Christopher dies,' he wrote. 'Countess Branitskaya goes from bad to worse. Varlamov [the millionaire wool merchant] continues to live a senseless sort of life.' As for Dymov, who, Pleshcheyev thought, might well be made into a tragic figure, Chekhov considered that such characters were created to become revolutionaries, but, he added (and this shows how little he was at the time aware of the strength of the revolutionary forces in the country), 'there will never be a revolution in Russia, and Dymov will end up either as a drunkard or in prison'.

Chekhov never wrote a continuation of *The Steppe*. Having failed in his attempt to write a novel, he could scarcely have been expected to undertake so difficult a task as carrying on with the life story of Yegorushka. Besides, the whole structure of *The Steppe* is such that it could not be fitted into a novel without making it lopsided: the whole story only occupies a few weeks in the life of Yegorushka, and its real hero is not Yegorushka at all but the steppe itself, and it would have been impossible to shift the interest from the steppe to the little boy.

9

Quite early in 1888 Chekhov began to make preparations for his summer holidays. He had at first intended going on a trip down the Volga with Pleshcheyev and Korolenko, but nothing came of it. He then decided to take his family to the Ukraine, as by that time he had had enough of Babkino. To Maria Kisselev he wrote: 'Father has grown lyrical of late and declares categorically that in view of his advanced years he would like to say goodbye to his native country.'

In March he was already beginning to feel the call of spring, though it was still very cold in Moscow. 'We have still 15–20 degrees of frost,' he wrote to Pleshcheyev, 'and the poor birds are already on their way to Russia. They are driven by their longing for their native land and their love of it. If the poets had known how many millions of birds fall victims to their love for the places of their birth, how many of them freeze to death on their way there, how much they suffer in March and April after their arrival in Russia, they would long ago have written poems about it. Put yourself in the place of a corncrake which does not fly but walks all the way, or a wild goose which gives itself up alive so as not to freeze to death. Life is certainly not easy in this world!'

He spent most of his time at home, but on February 19th he went to the première of his one-act comedy *Swan Song* at Korsh's theatre, and on February 21st he went to see Lensky[1] playing Othello at the Maly Theatre. He had paid six roubles twenty copecks for his ticket, he wrote to Pleshcheyev, but the acting was not worth one rouble. 'The production was good, the acting conscientious, but the chief thing— jealousy—was missing.' His work on *The Steppe* had left him so exhausted that he could not do anything except—write his famous one-act comedy *The Bear*. 'If the people on *The Northern Herald* knew that I was writing light comedies', he wrote to the poet Polonsky, 'they would anathematise me! But what am I to do if my fingers are itching and simply force me to commit some tra-la-la? However much I try to be serious, nothing comes of it, and always the serious alternates with the vulgar with me. I suppose that's fate. But, seriously, it is quite possible that that "fate" is merely a symptom showing that I shall never become a serious creative artist.'

Leykin visited Moscow at the beginning of March and he and Chekhov left for Petersburg on March 11th. At that time he had already stopped writing for *Fragments* (his last contribution to Leykin's weekly appeared on December 5th, 1887), though he still corresponded with its editor occasionally. All the way in the train Leykin got on his nerves with his incessant bragging. The moment Chekhov fell asleep Leykin would wake him with some stupid question or some boastful story. 'Do you know', he would ask Chekhov, whose works had so far not been translated into any foreign language, 'that my *Christ's Bride* has been translated into Italian?' Fortunately, there was Suvorin in Petersburg and this time Chekhov stayed at his place, enjoying all the amenities of a millionaire's home, driving about in a fine carriage and drinking champagne, but, as he wrote to Maria Kisselev after his return to Moscow, that only made him feel a bounder.

At Suvorin's house he was given a large room of his own, with an open fireplace, a lovely writing desk, and a servant to look after him. His servant wore better clothes than he and had most imposing manners. 'I felt queer,' he wrote to Michael, 'seeing this man tiptoeing round me reverentially and trying to anticipate my slightest wish.' He found that the life of a famous author had its serious drawbacks. For one thing, living with Suvorin he could not come home drunk

---

[1] Alexander Lensky, the famous producer and actor of the Moscow Maly Theatre.

(he usually did a lot of drinking during his Petersburg visits) or bring his friends with him. Then Suvorin kept talking literature to him till three o'clock in the morning. All day long, indeed, they went on talking literature, and Chekhov found Mrs. Suvorin, who preferred to talk about her migraine and about her clothes, a great relief. Chekhov would walk about Suvorin's study, while Suvorin would discuss Herzen's famous revolutionary periodical *The Bell*, published in London between 1857 and 1865. Again Mrs. Suvorin would come to Chekhov's rescue by talking in a bass voice or beginning to bark. Suvorin's little children followed Chekhov about, staring at him all the time and expecting him to say something unusual. 'In their opinion', Chekhov wrote to Michael, 'I am a genius, for didn't I write a story about Kashtanka?' It was during this visit to Petersburg that Suvorin quite seriously proposed that Chekhov should marry his little daughter, who was still in her early teens.

'Wait five or six years, my dear fellow', Suvorin said, 'and marry her. What better wife do you want? For my part I don't want a better son-in-law.'

And to show Chekhov that he was quite serious he promised to let him have half the profits from *New Times* as a dowry.

This proposal, however fantastic, caused Chekhov a great deal of unpleasantness. Rumours were spread that he had made up his mind to marry a millionairess and he began to receive abusive letters from all over Russia.

He spent eight days in Petersburg and returned convinced that Suvorin was 'the most remarkable man of our time'. In Moscow he resumed his writing and his medical practice. 'I have just returned from a visit to a patient,' he wrote to Alexander on March 24th, 'at the house of Countess Keller. My patient was the children's nurse and I received three roubles, but I had the great good fortune of talking to her ladyship.' Suvorin was issuing another volume of his stories, including *Happiness*, *The Rolling Stone*, *The Steppe*, and *The Kiss*, under the general title of *Stories*. His volume *In the Twilight* was selling well and together with the money he received from *The Northern Herald* for *The Steppe* he had about one thousand five hundred roubles, though by April most of it had already been spent. Still, he had three hundred roubles saved (put away by Mary) and with that money he hoped to be able to leave for his summer holidays with his family.

This time he rented a cottage in the grounds of a country house near the Ukrainian town of Sumy, belonging to a Ukrainian landed family whom Ivanenko, himself a native of Sumy, recommended to him.

Michael, who had earned about eighty roubles by copying out lectures and writing stories for children's magazines, had decided to pay a visit to Taganrog, and Chekhov persuaded him to make a detour and inspect the summer cottage he had rented. Michael's report, when it arrived, was far from satisfactory. He found the estate neglected; there was a huge puddle in the yard in which enormous pigs were wallowing and ducks swimming about. The garden was more like an overgrown wood, and the Lintaryovs, the owners of the estate, whose ancestors were buried in the garden, were rabid liberals who treated him as a conservative because he was wearing his student's uniform. Chekhov, however, had already made all his arrangements to leave for the Lintaryov estate at the beginning of May and he decided to take a chance. He was in one of his black moods: it was raining, he was worried about money (he had only seventy-five roubles left of the three hundred), and he was dissatisfied with the progress of the story (*Lights*) he was just then writing for *The Northern Herald.* 'I am a coward and quite morbidly sensitive,' he wrote to Pleshcheyev on April 9th. 'I am afraid to rush things and to appear in print. I can't help feeling that my readers will soon get tired of me and that I shall become a mere purveyor of fiction. This fear of mine is well founded, for I have been publishing stories for a very long time and I still don't know where my strength and weakness lie.' And a few days later he wrote to Alexander: 'I haven't any money again and I seem to have forgotten how to write. I am thinking of applying for a job at a chemist's.' About a week later he again wrote to Alexander: 'I have just enough money for the journey, but what we shall eat in Sumy I don't know. I shall have to catch fish and feed our ancient parents on it.'

There was another reason that most likely contributed to Chekhov's depression before he left for his summer holidays on May 5th, 1888. On March 24th the writer Vsevolod Garshin, who was only thirty-three at the time, committed suicide by throwing himself down the well of the stairs at his home. Chekhov had a very high opinion of Garshin. 'Such people as the late Garshin', he wrote to Pleshcheyev, 'I love with all my heart.' He did not know Garshin personally, having only exchanged a few words with him once. Shortly before his death he had been to see him twice, but both times he did not find him at home (Garshin was on a short visit to Petersburg at the time). He only saw the well of the staircase. Garshin was one of those highly sensitive writers whose pessimism expressed the prevailing mood of the Russian intellectuals of his day. Apart from being grateful to Garshin for his enthusiastic appreciation of *The Steppe*,[1] Chekhov could not but sympathise with the feeling of hopeless despair of a writer of such sterling honesty as Garshin, though he certainly did not share Garshin's views about the utter hopelessness of combating evil as expressed in his famous short story *The Red Flower*. The Russian educated classes of the last two decades of the nineteenth century, however, were so steeped in the defeatist kind of pessimism that was characteristic of Garshin's writings that they even read it into Chekhov's works, and this view, against which Chekhov repeatedly protested in vain, has attached itself particularly to Chekhov's great plays so that even today it is generally accepted as true. Garshin's short stories, whose main feature is a simple plot with a small number of characters, undoubtedly served Chekhov as a model for his own early short stories.

Chekhov's melancholy mood soon passed away. These quick changes of mood—a short period of black depression followed by a period of heightened enjoyment of life—were typical of Chekhov at that period when his natural high spirits could still cope satisfactorily with the inroads his illness was steadily making on his health. He invited Pleshcheyev and Suvorin as well as many others of his friends to visit him in the Ukraine, and in addition he planned to visit Suvorin at his summer residence in the Crimea and to go to Samarkand across the Caucasus with Suvorin's eldest son Alexey. He was always advising his friends to travel to some far-away country, like India or Japan, and his proposed journey to Samarkand was his own first attempt to undertake such a trip. All these plans helped him to recover from his fit of depression, and at Easter we find him indulging in his usual pastime of listening to the ringing of the Moscow churchbells and attending the services in the Moscow churches. There was, besides, a welcome change in the weather: the sun shone and the trees were green again. He even found time to write a story for Suvorin's paper and so get the money he badly needed.

On his arrival with his mother and sister at the Lintaryov estate Chekhov was pleasantly surprised to find that Michael had completely misled him. The place was lovely, their cottage clean, the furniture comfortable, the rooms large and bright, and there was no trace of the big puddle with the pigs and ducks. Babkino, Chekhov felt, was not a patch on it. 'The noises of the night alone', he wrote to his brother

[1] Pleshcheyev wrote to Chekhov on March 10th: 'Garshin is simply in raptures over your *Steppe*. He read it through twice. I met him at the house of some friends and he made me read aloud the passage where the peasant who is in love with his wife tells the story of his wedding. There are, however, people who do not approve of it. Garshin told me of one of these and was highly indignant . . . because it was obviously a case of professional jealousy. It was one of our young writers—a wretched little fool.'

Ivan, 'could make one go off one's head with delight.' But what appealed to Chekhov most of all was the big river Psyol with its islands on which fishermen as rabid as he were fishing all day. There was also a huge pond which was separated from the river by a dam and an old-world water-mill. It was very hot, the tulips and the lilac were in bloom, the nightingales, hoopoes and cuckoos were singing, and at nightfall 'a mysterious bird', which could hardly ever be seen in the rushes where it was hiding, cried 'like a cow locked up in a barn, or the last trump awakening the dead'. The bird, whose cry Chekhov had never heard before, was a bittern. Chekhov soon made friends with the local fishermen and gave himself up to the delights of his favourite sport. He also discovered that rowing was quite a wonderful exercise. He rowed daily, 'and every time', he wrote to Leykin, 'I come more and more to the conclusion that it exercises the muscles of your arms and trunk, and partly those of your legs and neck, and that it is therefore as good as any other athletic exercise'. And he let Kisselev into another secret: the miller's daughter was such a beauty 'that one simply has to cry for help from sheer desire'. She was, he added the information, 'plump and just like a rich raisin cake', and she seemed to spend all her time at the window, waiting for something.

But it was the Lintaryov family that made the greatest impression on Chekhov. 'The family', he wrote to Suvorin, 'is worthy of a special study. The mother is a very kind old woman who has been through a great deal in her life; she reads every number of *The European Herald* and *The Northern Herald* from cover to cover and has read novelists I have never heard of; she attaches particular importance to the fact that at one time the artist Makovsky lived in her cottage and that now a young writer is living there; she reads Schopenhauer and drives to church to listen to the singing of the choir; and when she talks to Pleshcheyev she feels a holy tremor running through her whole body and she rejoices every minute that she has been deemed worthy of seeing a great poet.

'Her eldest daughter [Zinaida], a woman doctor, is the pride of the family and the peasants look upon her as a saint,' Chekhov went on. 'She is indeed quite an extraordinary woman. She has a tumour on the brain and because of it is totally blind, suffers from epileptic fits and chronic headaches. Though she knows what awaits her, she talks stoically and with amazing coolness of her death which is near. As a doctor, I am used to seeing patients who are going to die soon and I always have an uncomfortable feeling when they talk, smile or cry in my presence; but here when I see the blind woman on the terrace laughing, joking or listening to the reading of my *In the Twilight*, it is not so much the fact that she will die that strikes me as strange as that we ourselves should be so little troubled about our own deaths to write *In the Twilight* as though we are never going to die.

'The second daughter [Helen] is also a doctor. She is an old maid, plain, quiet, shy, and infinitely kind. She loves everybody, and her patients are a real torture to her, and with them she is quite neurotically conscientious. We never agree at a consultation: where she sees death I play the part of a bringer of good tidings, and I double the doses she gives. But where death is self-evident and inevitable, my colleague does not react as a doctor should. One day I received patients with her at a village surgery; one of our patients was a young peasant girl with a malignant tumour of the glands of the neck. The affection was so widespread that there could be no question of any cure. And because the girl was not feeling any pain but would in six months die in excruciating agony, the woman doctor looked at her with such a guilty expression as if she were apologising for her own good health and was ashamed that medicine should be so helpless. She practically runs the estate and knows all the details of farming. She even knows how to handle horses. When, for instance, the side-horses are getting restive, she knows what to do and instructs the driver. She is very fond of home life, which fate has denied her, and she seems to be constantly dreaming of it; when in the evening there is music and singing in the house, she walks up and down a dark avenue like an animal that has been locked up. I don't think she has ever done any harm to a living creature and I can't help feeling that she has never been and never will be happy even for one minute.

'The third daughter [Natasha], a young woman of masculine build, is strong, bony, muscular, sunburnt and vociferous. Her laugh can be heard a mile off. She is a passionate Ukrainian patriot. She has built a school at her own expense on her estate, and is teaching the peasant children Krylov's fables in a Ukrainian translation. She goes to visit the poet Shevchenko's grave as a Turk goes on a pilgrimage to Mecca. She does not cut her hair, wears a corset and a bustle, looks after her farm and the house, loves to sing and to laugh, and will not deny herself the most conventional kind of love, though she has read Marx's *Das Kapital*, but I doubt if she will ever marry, for she is a very plain girl.

'The eldest son [Paul] is a quiet, modest, intelligent, mediocre and hardworking young man, unpretentious and apparently completely satisfied with life. He was sent down from the university during his fourth term (for political reasons), but does not boast about it. He doesn't talk a lot. Likes farming and the country and lives in peace with the peasants.

'The second son [George] is a young man who has gone mad on the idea that Chaykovsky is a genius. He is a pianist. Dreams of living according to Tolstoyan precepts.'

The Lintaryov family appealed to Chekhov also because of its traditionally liberal politics (the second daughter, Helen, went so far as to warn him against Suvorin's influence). Chekhov had, therefore, every reason to enjoy his stay on the Lintaryov estate. 'I don't want to conceal from you', he wrote to Alexander, 'that we are all having a lovely time here. At least, we are all well and not getting ready to die soon. The country is glorious, better than anything you ever saw. The people are new and original, the food is cheap and plentiful, and the weather is very warm. I have plenty of leisure time. And the fish and crawfish!'

The first people to visit Chekhov were Ivanenko and Pleshcheyev. The old poet was having the time of his life. 'Everybody here',. Chekhov wrote to Suvorin, 'looks on Pleshcheyev as on a demi-god. They think themselves happy if only he vouchsafes to taste their sour milk, they present him with bouquets, he is invited everywhere, etc. . . . And he', Chekhov went on, quoting a line from a fable by Krylov, ' "just listens and eats", and smokes his cigars which give his lady admirers a headache. He is lazy and too old to move about freely, but that does not prevent the fair sex from taking him for a sail on the river, driving him to the country houses in the neighbourhood, and serenading him. Here, and in Petersburg, he represents the same thing, that is, an icon to which people offer up prayers because in the old days it used to hang among the miracle-working icons. I personally, however, besides seeing in him a good, warmhearted and sincere man, look on him only as a vessel which is filled with traditions, interesting reminiscences and good platitudes.'

Pleshcheyev was very fond of the rich food prepared by Chekhov's mother, which often disagreed with him, and he would lie on his back and moan while Chekhov did his best to alleviate his pain, not forgetting to implore him not to over-indulge himself again. He spent over a week on the Lintaryov estate and wrote a special poem to commemorate his stay with Chekhov.

Chekhov's next visitor was Suvorin. The two of them would go by canoe to the water-mill, which was surrounded by oak woods, and spend hours there, Chekhov fishing and Suvorin talking interminably.

The Lintaryovs treated Suvorin with icy politeness, which made him rather shy of visiting Chekhov again in the following summer.

At the beginning of June Alexander, now a widower, arrived with his children, but he stayed only one week, having disgraced himself at an open air performance by a conjurer and hypnotist in the public park at Sumy. He volunteered to assist the hypnotist and, being drunk as usual, had used language which made the ladies run off and drag Chekhov away with them. That, at least, was what Chekhov had told Alexander. More likely, Chekhov, knowing very well the inexcusable things Alexander was liable to say when drunk and seeing how distressed his sister Mary was, quickly ushered his friends out of the park. Alexander, who conceived the plan to marry Helen Lintaryov, whom he had only known a few days but whose desperate yearning for a home of her own did not escape him, was so furious with his family that he left the same night with his children for Petersburg. Chekhov did his best to soothe his brother's hurt feelings. 'Unreal Chekhov,' he addressed him in a letter on June 10th, which he signed 'The real Chekhov', 'how do you feel? Do you still reek of vodka? So far as we are concerned, we are very sorry we did not stay in the park to see your performance with the conjurer. I am told your intervention had quite astonishing results: the audience was completely fooled and the conjurer was very pleased. The whole estate is still roaring with laughter as they recall how you talked to the conjurer. If you had not overdone it at the very beginning everything would have been all right and the ladies would not have dragged me away from the park. I can't understand what made you so angry that you left for the station at two o'clock in the morning. I remember you were angry with me and Nicholas. You were angry with me chiefly because I had torn off the corner of the envelope of your letter to Helen Lintaryov. I did it because it never occurred to me that you might want to write something important to her. As the letter was written by you while you were drunk, I did not pass it on to her, but tore it up. If you don't like it, write her another letter, though I don't think you have anything to write her about.' And as if afraid that he had revealed his knowledge of Alexander's intentions, Chekhov went on to assure him that the impression he had made on everyone was an excellent one and that Helen Lintaryov, in particular, thought him quite an extraordinary man, 'in which belief', he added significantly, 'I am not undeceiving her. . . . You will be acting stupidly if you don't pay us another visit in August or September,' he went on. 'If you decide to come, I shall pay half your fares, only please don't be angry for nothing and don't scold Nicholas, who looked very miserable that night. I can't help feeling that with your departure his hope of leaving the Sumy district in the near future has gone, too. . . . Mary cannot forgive herself for not having remained to see the magnetic séance.'

Alexander did not give up his idea of marrying Helen Lintaryov. He first wrote to his sister Mary about it, asking her to find out what Chekhov's attitude would be to his proposed marriage. Her reply must not have been too promising, for on August 18th he decided to approach Chekhov himself. 'I want to have a family of my own,' he wrote, 'music, endearments, and a kind word when I feel tired after a hard day's work. . . . You know Helen Lintaryov better than I. Tell me whether I shall be making a fool of myself if I ask her to be my wife. I have been thinking of writing to her without any intermediaries, but every time I hesitate for fear that her refusal might offend what is still left of the best in me. And her refusal would be justified because she has only known me for such a short time.'

Chekhov dismissed Alexander's reasons for wanting to marry as pure hypocrisy. He pointed out that a family, music, endearments and a kind word could not be had by marrying the first woman one met, however decent a person she might be. All those things, he wrote on August 28th, could be obtained only by love, and if there was no love it was useless to talk of endearments. 'And', he went on, 'there cannot be any question of love, because you know Helen Lintaryov less than the inhabitants of the moon.' If, however, all Alexander wanted was a nurse for his children, then he would like him to remember that he was not a Chokhov (a transparent hint at the financial aspect of the proposed match) and that he ought to think not only of himself but also of the woman he wanted to marry. As for Helen Lintaryov, Chekhov was quite willing to admit that, being a woman, she must be very anxious to marry, but he reminded Alexander that she was a professional woman of independent means who had views of her own and that if she decided to marry it would be only for love. 'Why should she leave a comfortable home and go and live with a man she doesn't know,' he went on, 'if the natural impulse that might have made her do so, i.e. love, isn't there? She is not a seeker after sensations and adventures, but, I repeat, a free and independent woman who is absolutely honest and knows her own worth. She could only marry for love, for her own sake and for the sake of her future children, but not out of principle or philanthropy. You won't move her by the story of your life, or by your tears, or your babies, for she is one thing and your babies quite another. The position of both of you can be summed up in a few words: you are not in love with her, you just want to be married at all costs and get her to be your children's nurse; and she is not in love with you, either. Therefore you, who are proposing to ask her to marry you by letter and who are ready to pretend that you are in love with her, are as absurd as Grigory Chokhov, who sends a matchmaker to a girl he has never seen but about whom he has heard people say nice things. Imagine Helen Lintaryov's face when she reads your letter! Have you imagined it?'

Chekhov knew very well how unhappy Alexander would make Helen Lintaryov, but he did not feel himself justified in interfering in the private affairs of either of them. He therefore invited Alexander to come to visit him again in the country and stay on the Lintaryov estate for one or two months, during which time both of them would get to know each other better. 'Helen Lintaryov', he wrote, 'certainly likes you. She thinks you are an extraordinary man, so that it is quite possible that you may learn to love her (she is a very good woman) and arouse love in her. You will employ civilised methods and get married in a civilised way, like everybody else, but if you prefer the system used by the Chokhovs or Nicholas, you are not a decent man and the woman who marries you is a fool. If you decide to spend some time at the Lintaryov estate during this winter or next summer, I shall do my best to help you and even give you a dowry (twenty copecks), but for the time being I shall keep my mouth shut and I shall do my best not to place two such excellent people as Helen Lintaryov and yourself in an awkward position. I shall not say another word about it, and I have asked our sister not to say anything about it, either, and I hope to goodness mother does not put her foot in it. Keep this letter so that if one day you should really marry Helen Lintaryov (which I wish with all my heart), you may read it to your wife and ask yourselves whether I was right or not. If you don't think so, then neither of you is worth worrying about and both of you will deserve what you get, and all I shall have to say about the two of you will be that you are not decent people, but a couple of Zulus who profane marriage and decent human relationships. I shall tell the Lintaryovs that you may possibly stay with them during the winter. I am sure they will be glad. I shall procure leave of absence from Suvorin for you.' (Chekhov had obtained a job for Alexander on Suvorin's paper.)

Alexander knew very well that Helen Lintaryov would never marry him if she got to know him better (he was already an incurable dipsomaniac at the time and the Lintaryovs were teetotallers on principle). He therefore decided to drop the whole matter. 'As for my proposed marriage,' he wrote to Chekhov on September 10th, 'I am no longer thinking of it. I must confess that I was stupid to think of marrying Helen Lintaryov. Now I have become used to the idea of living alone [actually, he got married soon afterwards] . . . You were absolutely right in your letter,' he concluded, 'except for your reproach about my hypocrisy.'

Chekhov must have felt greatly relieved at such a satisfactory conclusion of the affair. Alexander was the most troublesome member of his family and Chekhov did his best to go to his assistance every time he got himself into trouble. This was the only time when he thought it necessary to intervene personally to save a woman he respected from ruining her life by marrying his brother.

10

In June Chekhov went for a trip to the province of Poltava, where he visited the estate of Alexander Smagin, a great friend of the Lintaryovs, who was also to become a close friend of his (he had nicknamed him the Shah of Persia). It was during that visit that Chekhov conceived his highly idealistic and impractical plan of founding what he called 'a climatic station' for writers, which occupied him for the next two years.

Chekhov was appalled by the bitter strife, especially in Petersburg, between the various groups of writers, who formed small coteries and did not seem to wish to make any allowance for any writer holding different views from their own. When, therefore, the novelist Kasimir Barantsevich, whom he first met in Petersburg in 1887 and whom he thought of highly, wrote to ask him to contribute a story to a volume to be dedicated to the memory of Garshin, Chekhov expressed his approval of the publication of such a volume which he thought might also form 'a connecting link between the small but scattered number of people who live by writing. The more we stick together,' he wrote to Barantsevich on April 30th, 'and the more we support each other, the more shall we learn to respect and value each other and the more will our mutual relations be based on truth. Not all of us', Chekhov went on, 'are likely to achieve happiness in the future. One need not be a prophet to be able to say that there will be more sorrow and pain in our lives than contentment and money. That is why', he concluded, 'we must all try to stick together.'

But while wishing to keep the writers in constant touch with one another, Chekhov was against the formation of groups of writers who, because they shared the same views, wished to ostracise anybody with whose views they did not sympathise. 'We cannot all feel and think alike,' he wrote to Leontyev on May 3rd, 'for our aims are different or else we have no aims, we know each other very little or not at all, and there is therefore nothing that could unite us in one single group. But do we want such a group? I don't think so. To be of assistance to a fellow writer, to respect his personality and his work, not to spread all sorts of tales about him or envy him his success, to lie to him and play the hypocrite, it is necessary . . . to be merely a human being. Let us be ordinary men, let us cultivate the same attitude to *everybody*, and then we shall not want any artificially contrived solidarity. As for the desire to establish professional solidarity among a small circle of writers, it would only result in unintentional spying, suspiciousness and control, so that, without wishing it ourselves, we should have founded something that resembled the Society of Jesuits.'

It was his desire to create this new relationship between writers, a relationship founded on mutual trust and respect for each other's views, that gave Chekhov the idea of founding his 'climatic station' by buying a cottage with a few acres of land in the Ukraine. The idea itself first occurred to him while he journeyed with the Lintaryovs for over three hundred miles across the picturesque Ukrainian country-side to Smagin's estate. It was a most successful trip. 'Laughter, adventures, mishaps, stops and meetings we had in plenty,' he described his journey to Pleshcheyev on June 28th. 'All the time we came across views which were so wonderful that it is only possible to describe them in a novel or a long story but not in a letter,' he went on. 'Oh, if only you had been with us and seen our cross-grained coachman Roman at whom one could not look without laughing, if you had seen the places where we stopped for the night, the villages we passed through, if you had drunk the horrible vodka which makes you belch as if it were soda water! What fine weddings we saw on our way, what glorious music we heard in the still evenings, and how overpowering the smell of the hay was! I could have sold my soul to the devil for the pleasure of looking at the warm evening sky, at the little streams and puddles, in which the sad, languorous sunset was reflected! What a pity you were not with us! In the carriage you would have been as comfortable as in a bed. We ate and drank every half-hour, did not deny ourselves anything, and laughed till our sides split. . . .

'We arrived at the Smagin estate at night. Our arrival led to some accidents. Recognising our voices, Alexander Smagin's brother Sergey rushed out of the house, ran towards the gates and, stumbling over a bench in the darkness, fell flat on the ground. Alexander, too, rushed out of the house and in the darkness knocked his head against an old chestnut tree. After a most cordial and joyful meeting, there was a lot of loud, aimless laughter, and this laughter repeated itself regularly every evening.

'The Smagins' estate is huge and plenteous, but old and neglected and dead like last year's cobwebs. The house has subsided, the doors do not open, the tiles on the stove are falling on top of each other and form all sorts of angles, young shoots of plum and cherry trees peep out from the holes in the floors. In the room where I slept a nightingale built its nest between the window and the shutter, and while I was there little naked nightingales hatched out from their eggs. On the threshing floor a pair of solid-looking storks have built their nest. In the apiary lives an ancient grandad who can still remember Cleopatra of Egypt. Everything is old and rotting away, but poetic, sad, and beautiful to the highest degree.

'Smagin's sister', Chekhov continued his exciting story, 'is a wonderful, once beautiful, and very kind and gentle creature, with a gorgeous black plait and with an expression which six or eight years ago was probably ravishing, but now brings sad thoughts to one's mind. ...'

Chekhov spent five days on Smagin's estate and returned to Sumy through the Gogol country, so that his trip was in a way a literary pilgrimage as well. It was the beautiful Ukrainian countryside that gave Chekhov the idea of founding his 'climatic station' there. 'When for whole weeks you see nothing but trees and streams, when you have to take shelter from a storm and defend yourself against vicious dogs,' he wrote to Suvorin on his return to Sumy on June 28th, 'you can't help acquiring new habits, however clever you may be, and everything new produces a reaction in your organism which is much more violent than that produced by any of Dr. Bertenson's prescriptions. Under the influence of the countryside and through meeting people who in the majority of cases are excellent people, all the Petersburg tendencies fade into insignificance. Any writer, far from his native heath, will only remember Petersburg when, having made his acquaintance with the wide open spaces and having met all sorts of different people, he exclaims, "No, we don't write what is wanted!" And all that, taken together, is sure to have quite a miraculous effect on the nerves.'

On August 14th he told Leontyev that he had definitely made up his mind to found his 'climatic station' for the writing fraternity. 'I shall drag you there', he wrote, 'by a lasso, if need be.' Suvorin, he added, liked his idea and had decided to found such a 'station' at his house in Theodosia. A week later, after returning from another trip to the Poltava province in search of a cottage, Chekhov wrote to Pleshcheyev that he wanted his friends to look on his little plot of land as their own where they could retire for a rest. 'If I succeed in buying it,' he declared, 'I shall build small cottages on the bank of the river and lay the foundations of a literary colony.'

At the end of August he was already negotiating for the purchase of a cottage and accepted Suvorin's offer to advance him one thousand five hundred roubles, provided, Chekhov insisted, he did not interfere with his repayments of the loan or allow him any rebates or concessions, 'for otherwise', he wrote, 'you will put me in a very difficult position. Hitherto, whenever I owed someone money, I could not help becoming hypocritical about it, a very nasty psychopathic state. Generally speaking', he explained characteristically, 'I am very fastidious about money matters, and when I tell lies, it is against my will. When you became a close friend of mine, my fastidiousness became morbidly acute and my work for your paper for the sake of money lost its real value for me, and I fell into the habit of promising more than I actually intended to carry out; I began to be afraid that our relationship might be spoilt by the thought that I needed you as a newspaper owner and not as a man, etc. etc. All this is silly and offensive and merely goes to show that I attach great importance to money, but I am afraid I can't help it'.

In April 1889 he was still dreaming of founding his 'climatic station' for writers, but the death of his brother Nicholas later in the year and his hurried departure for Sakhalin the year after put an end to his 'great plan', which he would, anyway, have found it impossible to realise. His preoccupation with it for two years seems to have been mainly due to two causes: first, his own desire for congenial company during the summer months in the country; and, secondly, his friendship with Suvorin, which for a time cut him off from the more progressive forces in Russia. His failure to realise at a time when he was still greatly influenced by Tolstoy's teachings that the fierce divisions among the writers of his day were caused by the ruthless suppression of every opinion that was inimical to the reactionary régime which was supported by his friend Suvorin, was merely a passing phase in his development as a writer. When he finally broke with Suvorin and attached himself to the *Russian Thought* camp, his idea of a 'climatic station' lost its point, for by that time he realised that evil could never be defeated by non-resistance which always implied a tacit compromise with it, even if it assumed the innocuous form of a 'climatic station'.

II

Before leaving for the Crimea, Chekhov entertained Barantsevich at his country cottage. Barantsevich, who specialised in novels of lower-middle-class life, was a shy, baldheaded man; in spite of his mild manners, however, he was a most pitiless extirpator of crawfish, in which passion Chekhov indulged him to the full. Two other acquaintances Chekhov made in the early summer of 1888 were university professors. The first was Vassily Vorontsov, a doctor by training and an economist by choice, who, like Pleshcheyev, was looked upon as a 'demi-god' by the Lintaryovs. Chekhov described him as 'a very clever, political-economic figure with a Hippocratic expression, who, immersed in thoughts of the future of Russia, keeps eternally silent'. Chekhov was at the time working on the plot and the characters of *The Wood Demon* (he hoped to write the play during his stay with Suvorin at Theodosia), and Vorontsov, as would appear from the following description of him in a letter to Pleshcheyev, must have supplied him with certain aspects of Professor Serebraykov's character. 'The man', Chekhov wrote, 'is weighed down by his dry intellectual work and is saturated with other people's thoughts and opinions.' To his great surprise, however, Vorontsov one evening joined in the dances at Lintaryov's house, which made Chekhov decide that he was really a nice, though unhappy, man whose intentions were 'pure'. The other acquaintance was Vladimir Timofeyev, a young chemistry professor of Kharkov University, a gay and cheerful young man, with whom Chekhov liked to have a drink on the quiet.

It was with Timofeyev that Chekhov tried out his unsuccessful experiment of getting drunk, which he described in his letter to Suvorin of October 18th, where he also discussed his own and Alexander's drinking habits. Suvorin had written to him complaining of Alexander's drunken bouts. Chekhov had regretfully to admit that his eldest brother was an incurable drunkard, but he excused him on the ground that his drunkenness was a psychosis like 'morphinism, onanism, nymphomania, etc.' He professed to be puzzled about the causes that drove Alexander to become a dipsomaniac. 'There are no drunkards in our family,' he wrote. 'My father and grandfather sometimes got very drunk when they had visitors, but that never interfered with their work or prevented them from going to morning mass. Drink made them good-humoured and witty. My brother, the schoolmaster, and I never drink *solo*, we are not experts on drinks, and we can drink as much as we like without ever waking up with a headache. This summer a Kharkov professor and I decided to get drunk. We drank and drank and in the end gave it up as a bad job. Next morning we woke up as if nothing had happened.'

Chekhov left for his visit to Suvorin in the Crimea on July 10th. He took with him all his notes on *The Wood Demon*, which he decided was going to be a 'literary' play, since he was absolutely convinced that the stage could only be saved by 'literary' plays. 'We must try as hard as we can', he wrote to Suvorin later in that year, 'to take the stage out of the hands of businessmen and put it into the hands of literary people, otherwise the theatre is doomed.' He deplored the lack of literary education among the contemporary writers. Pleshcheyev had written to tell him that a story by one of his oldest and closest friends, Vladimir Gilyarovsky, was to be published in *The Northern Herald*. 'I am glad for Gilyarovsky,' Chekhov wrote in his reply on July 6th. 'He is a fine fellow and not without talent, but he lacks a literary education. He has a terrible weakness for generalities, pathetic words, and high-flown descriptions, convinced that without those ornamentations it is impossible to write. He feels the presence of beauty in other people's works and he knows that the chief charm of a story lies in its simplicity and sincerity, but he just cannot be simple and sincere in his own stories: he lacks courage. He is like those believers who do not care to say their prayers in Russian but always say them in Slavonic, though they realise that Russian is nearer to the truth and the heart.'

Chekhov found the journey across the Crimea very disappointing, but he changed his opinion when he reached the mountains with the vineyards growing on their slopes and the tall poplars in the valleys below. In the moonlight everything appeared so strange and fantastic to him that it reminded him of Gogol's story *The Terrible Vengeance*. He arrived in Sebastopol at night. Next morning he was struck by the colour of the Black Sea, which he thought defied all description and reminded him of blue vitriol. He travelled to Yalta by sea, and the town where he was to spend the last years of his life struck him as a cross between a European seaside resort (it reminded him of the views of Nice he had seen on photographs) and a Russian market town. 'Cow-

like hotels in which unhappy consumptives are pining away; impudent
Tartar faces; bustles with a very frank hint at something very nasty;
idle rich in search of some cheap adventure; the reek of cheap scent
instead of the smell of cedars and the sea; a miserable, filthy harbour;
melancholy lights of ships on the horizon; the empty chatter of young
ladies and their male escorts who came here to enjoy the beauties of
nature they don't know anything about—all that', he wrote to Mary,
'produces such an over-poweringly cheerless impression that you
start accusing yourself of being prejudiced and unfair.' He arrived in
Theodosia on July 18th at five o'clock in the morning and was again
disappointed to find that it was a little, dreary, 'greyish-brown' town
with a few wretched trees and not a trace of grass: everything was
burnt up by the hot sun. But there was the sea, and he felt so happy
when he plunged into it that he 'burst out laughing with delight'. The
Suvorins had been expecting him for some time and he found his room
prepared for him. Within an hour of his arrival they dragged him off
to lunch at the house of a Tartar dignitary, where he met all the local
notabilities, including the famous marine painter, Ivan Ayvazovsky.

Chekhov soon gave up the idea of writing his play during his stay
with the Suvorins, for it was impossible to do anything while Suvorin
was talking. And Suvorin went on talking all the time. Indeed,
Chekhov felt that it was as impossible to be silent in Suvorin's house
as it was impossible to be abstemious in a fashionable restaurant in
Petersburg. 'We talk and talk and talk,' he wrote to Leontyev from
Theodosia on July 18th, 'and we shall probably finish up by dying of
inflammation of the tongue and the vocal chords. . . . Little by little
I am being transformed into a talking machine. We have already
solved all the problems and marked out a vast number of new problems
no one has ever thought of.' Mrs. Suvorin, too, possessed the gift of
the gab and, though she talked a lot of nonsense, she could also be
intelligent and interesting when she wished, which was particularly
tantalising since one never knew what she was going to say next. At
night she sat on the seashore and wept, and in the morning she laughed
and sang gipsy songs.

Life at the house of a millionaire newspaper proprietor was certainly
very pleasant. Chekhov got up at eleven a.m. and went to bed at three
a.m. 'Siestas on the beach, Chartreuse, *cruchons* [a mixed drink made
of white wine and brandy or rum and fresh fruit], fireworks,
bathing, gay suppers, trips in the country, songs—all that', Chekhov
wrote to Mary on July 22nd, 'makes the days so short that you hardly
notice them; time flies and my head dozes off to the murmur of the

waves and refuses to work. The days are hot, stifling, Asiatic.' After a little while of this sort of life, however, Chekhov began to feel that if he did not want to be totally submerged by it he would have to leave at once.

During one of his trips Chekhov visited the 'fairy-tale' estate of the painter Ayvazovsky, who was an old man of seventy-five at the time, and, Chekhov discovered, a curious amalgam of a general, a bishop, an artist, an Armenian, a dear old grandfather and an Othello. He had a young and beautiful wife whom he kept under strict supervision. He was a friend of sultans, shahs and emirs. He had also been a friend of Pushkin, though he had never read his poetry, and had given Glinka several themes for his opera *Ruslan and Lyudmila*, though he could not read a note of music. When Chekhov asked him what books he liked best, he replied very ingenuously: 'What do I want to read books for, if I have my own opinions?'

On July 23rd, Chekhov left on his journey to Samarkand with Suvorin's eldest son Alexey. They went by sea first to Kerch and then to Sukhum. At Sukhum he paid a visit to the New Athos monastery where he met the bishop of Abkhasia, who travelled through his diocese on horseback, and bought two little icons for his mother and aunt. Abkhasia struck him as an earthly paradise. 'Nature is so marvellous here', he wrote from Sukhum to Suvorin, 'that it nearly drives me mad with ecstasy and despair. Everything is new, fairy-like, silly and poetic. Eucalyptuses, tea bushes, cypresses, cedars, palm trees, donkeys, swans, buffaloes, dove-coloured cranes, and, above all, mountains, mountains, mountains. I am sitting on a balcony watching the Abkhasians walking past dressed in costumes of masquerade capuchins; across the road is a boulevard with olive trees, cedars and cypresses, and behind it is the blue sea. It's frightfully hot. I am stewing in my own sweat. The red cord of my vest is wet with perspiration and the red dye is trickling down my chest; my shirt, forehead and armpits are wringing wet. I save myself from the heat by a dip in the sea. . . . If I spent a month in Abkhasia, I'd write about fifty fascinating stories. Thousands of subjects for stories peep out of every bush, the shadows and half-shadows on the mountains, the sea and the sky. I can't forgive myself for not being able to paint.'

Chekhov spent only three days in Sukhum. On July 28th he left for Poti on board the cargo boat *Dir*, which nearly collided with the English steamer *Tweedy* (the *Dir* captain's seamanship was not particularly brilliant, for the December after she got wrecked on the rocks near Alupka on the Crimean coast). Chekhov could not sleep and had gone on the bridge where, he wrote to Michael, 'a warm but unpleasant gust of wind nearly blew my cap off. The boat was lurching and rolling. The mast in front of the captain's cabin on the bridge was swaying slowly and regularly like a metronome; I did my best not to look at it, but my eyes refused to obey me and together with my stomach insisted on following everything that moved. The sea and the sky were dark, no land was to be seen, not a light anywhere.

'Behind me was a window,' Chekhov continued; 'I looked through it and saw a man with the face of Paul Lintaryov. His eyes appeared to be fixed on some invisible point and he kept turning the wheel just as if he were performing the Ninth Symphony. Beside him stood the fat little captain in brown shoes, whose figure and face reminded me of Cornelius Pushkaryov. He talked to me about the Caucasian settlers, the stifling heat, the winter storms, and at the same time gave quick glances at the dark horizon that separated us from the land.

' "You're keeping her to port again," he said in passing to someone, or "We ought to be able to see the lights here. Do you see them?"

' "No, sir," someone replied out of darkness.

' "Go on deck and have a look."

' "Aye, aye, sir."

'A dark figure loomed out on the bridge and without hurrying climbed somewhere aloft. In another moment a voice shouted:

' "I can see them, sir!"

'I looked to the left where there ought to have been the light of the lighthouse, but I couldn't see anything. I took the glasses from the captain, but again I could see nothing. Half an hour, an hour passed. The mast was still swaying slowly and regularly, the boat creaked, the wind tried again to blow my cap off. I was not seasick, but a feeling of vague apprehension took hold of me.

'Suddenly the captain gave a start and with the words, "Blast her!" ran off to the back of the bridge. "To port!" he roared. "To starboard! Ahoy, there! Ahoy-y-y!"

'I heard some incomprehensible words of command; the boat shuddered and creaked. "Ahoy-y-y!" roared the captain. A bell began ringing on the bow, people were running on the deck, cries of alarm. The *Dir* shuddered again, puffed and was apparently trying to reverse her engines.

' "What's the matter?" I asked, feeling a sickly sensation of terror. There was no reply.

' "Wants to collide with us, blast her!" I heard the loud shout of the captain. "To po-o-ort!"

'Red lights appeared at the bow of the boat, and suddenly, amid the uproar, I heard the siren of another boat. Now I understood: we were going to collide! The *Dir* puffed, shuddered and did not seem to move, waiting to be sunk. Here a small mishap happened to me, which lasted for no longer than half a minute, but which worried me terribly. For half a minute I was convinced that I had been instrumental in sending the ship to the bottom. [What happened was that during a sudden roll of the boat, Chekhov lost his balance and caught hold of the handle of the engine-telegraph, which gave. He tried to put it back to its original position, but did not know how to do it.] When I thought that everything was lost, red lights appeared to starboard and the silhouette of a steamer began to loom out of the darkness. A long black shape sailed past, guiltily blinking her red eyes and guiltily blowing her siren.

' "Good Lord, what boat is that?" I asked the captain.

' "The *Tweedy*," he replied.'

Chekhov went back to his cabin, and when he woke up the *Dir* was entering the bay of Poti.

His trip came to a sudden end when he and Alexey Suvorin reached Baku. Suvorin's son had received a telegram from his father about the sudden illness of his brother, who died a few days later from diphtheria, and he hurried back to the Crimea, Chekhov returning to Sumy on August 7th. He had travelled from Poti to Batum, and from there to Tiflis and Baku. From Batum to Tiflis the road was, Chekhov thought, 'original and poetic',—mountains, tunnels, rivers, rocks and waterfalls; but from Tiflis to Baku it was, in Chekhov's words, 'a bald patch covered with sand and created for Persians, tarantulas and weasel-spiders; not a single tree, not a blade of grass, everything horribly dreary'. As for Baku and the Caspian Sea, Chekhov felt that he would not live there for anything in the world. But on his return journey he was rewarded by the picturesque Georgian military road, which, he decided, was not a road but 'pure poetry, a wonderful, fantastic fairy-story written by Lermontov's Demon and dedicated to Tamara'. The description seems to have appealed to him, for he repeated it in his letters to Leykin and Barantsevich. 'Imagine', he wrote to the latter, 'that you are at a height of eight thousand feet. Now, try to imagine that you walk up to the edge of an abyss and look down; far, far below, you see its narrow bottom with a meandering white ribbon—that's the grey, growling Aragva; on the way to it your eyes meet little clouds, woods ravines, and cliffs. Now raise your eyes a little and look straight ahead: mountains, mountains, mountains with insects crawling on them—

those are cows and people. Look upwards and you will see a terribly deep sky. A fresh mountain breeze is blowing. Now imagine two high walls and between them a long, long corridor; the ceiling is the sky, the floor—the bottom of Terek; along the bottom a snake of ashen-grey colour is moving sinuously. On one of the walls is a ledge along which your carriage is being driven at a terrific speed. The snake is angry, it growls and bristles. The horses are tearing along like devils. The walls are high, the sky is still higher. From the top of the walls leafy trees look down on you curiously. Your head swims. That is the Daryal gorge.'

12

On his return to Sumy Chekhov found a gloomy letter from Barantsevich, full of doubts and dark forebodings about the future of Russian literature. Chekhov refused to share Barantsevich's pessimism. He felt that it was the duty of a writer to write and not to worry about what was going to happen. So far as he was concerned, all he wanted was to keep his independence. But to be independent a writer had to possess courage. He severely criticised his friend Lazarev-Gruzinsky for being afraid to give his temperament free play, for a writer's true talent, he maintained, could be recognised only by his passion and by the mistakes he made. 'Women, in particular,' he wrote to Lazarev-Gruzinsky, 'ought to be described in such a way as to make the reader feel that your waistcoat is unbuttoned and that you are wearing no tie.'

Chekhov returned to Moscow on September 5th and sat down to write. He owed Suvorin four hundred roubles, which he wanted to repay as soon as possible. Before the end of the year he finished two long stories, *Name-Day* and *A Nervous Breakdown*. In both his medical knowledge came in useful. He was proud of the fact that his women friends were struck by the truthfulness of his description of childbirth in the first story. He was no less pleased with his correct description of mental disorder in his second story. It was Pleshcheyev who had asked him to contribute a story to the Garshin volume *The Northern Herald* was planning to publish. The request put him in a quandary, since he had already promised to supply a story to a similar volume planned by Barantsevich. But in the end the matter was settled amicably and Chekhov wrote his story—*A Nervous Breakdown*—for Pleshcheyev. 'Today', he wrote to Suvorin on November 11th, 'I have finished my story for the Garshin volume. . . . In it I gave my opinion about such rare people as the late Garshin. . . . I talk a lot about prostitution, but do not solve anything. Why does your paper ignore the problem of prostitution? It is such a dreadful evil. Our Sobolev Lane is a veritable slave market.' Two days later he wrote to Pleshcheyev: 'I think that as a medical man I have described the mental disorder correctly in accordance with all the rules of psychiatry.'

He had, in addition, outlined the first draft of the plot and characters of *The Wood Demon*, thoroughly revised *Ivanov* for its Petersburg production at the Alexandrinsky Theatre and, as a relaxation from his usual work, contributed several editorial articles to *New Times*, including his defence of the Moscow shop-assistants against their employers who had succeeded in annulling the Sunday-closing by-law of the Moscow Town Council (*Moscow Hypocrites*), an obituary notice on the Russian Central Asia traveller N. M. Przhevalsky, and an article on the Moscow beggars. In this article on Przhevalsky ('such a man as Przhevalsky', he wrote to Helen Lintaryov on October 28th, 'I love with all my heart') Chekhov touched on a subject which preoccupied him greatly at the time, namely the absence of a serious purpose in Russian contemporary literature. It was not without reason, he pointed out in his article, that men like Przhevalsky, Stanley and Livingstone became legendary figures. 'In our sick time,' he wrote, 'when . . . even our best men sit about without doing anything and justify their idleness and debaucheries by the absence of a definite purpose in life, such pioneers are as necessary to us as the sun itself. . . Their personalities are living documents which show our society that besides the people who go on arguing about pessimism and optimism, who write mediocre novels, cheap dissertations and unwanted projects, who lead an immoral life because they deny the existence of any serious purpose in life and tell lies for the sake of making a living, that besides our sceptics, mystics, neurotics, Jesuits, philosophers, liberals and conservatives, there are people of a different order, people who have a clearly defined purpose in life for which they are ready to sacrifice themselves. If the positive characters created by literature are valuable educational material, then the characters created by life itself are quite priceless. Such men as Przhevalsky are particularly valuable because the meaning of their lives and achievements and their moral worth are accessible even to the intelligence of a child. It has always been so, for the nearer a man is to truth the more intelligent and simple he is.'

This theme—the theme that every work of art must have a serious purpose—was soon to become one of Chekhov's most strongly held beliefs, and his most abiding works, especially his great plays, become meaningless if that is overlooked.

There were no great changes in Chekhov's life during the autumn and winter of 1888. Nicholas was as difficult a problem as ever with his periodic drinking sprees, his inability to settle down to work and his disappearances from home. At that particular time he also got himself into trouble with the police for failing to do his military service and all the worries about it devolved on Chekhov. 'What a nuisance it is', he exclaimed in a letter to Suvorin, 'to be the head of a family!' Money was as scarce as ever, though the Pushkin Prize of five hundred roubles, which the Academy of Science awarded him in October, did help a little. The Pushkin Prize made him walk about 'like a man in love', he wrote to Suvorin. His family and friends overwhelmed him with congratulations. 'Mother and father', he told Suvorin in the same letter, 'talk awful rot and are indescribably happy. My sister, who watches over my reputation with the singleminded sternness of a lady-in-waiting, nervous and ambitious. goes about spreading the glad tidings among her girl friends. Leontyev talks of literary Iagos and countless enemies my five hundred roubles will bring me. Lensky and his wife have invited me to dinner; I met a lady, another admirer of the arts, who also invited me to dinner; the headmaster of our Artisan's School came to congratulate me and offered to buy a copy of *Kashtanka* as "an investment". . . . And the X's, Y's and Z's who work for *The Alarm-Clock* and the popular press are terribly excited and look with hope upon their future. I repeat again: the newspaper story writers, second-raters and third-raters, ought to erect a monument to me and at least present me with a silver cigarette-case, for it was I who paved the way for them to the serious periodicals and to laurels and the hearts of decent folk. So far that is the only thing I have done, and everything I have written and for which I have been awarded the Pushkin Prize will not live in the memory of men for ten years.'

This curious under-estimation of his achievements in literature was not just modesty on Chekhov's part. On the contrary, he was absolutely convinced that the short stories he had written were worthless. 'Everything I have written', he repeated in a letter to Lazarev-Gruzinsky on October 20th, 'will be forgotten in five or ten years; but the road I have laid down will endure—therein lies my only achievement as a writer.'

The explanation of Chekhov's inability to appreciate the stories which had made him famous is not as difficult as it might appear. Like every creative writer, Chekhov was not so much concerned with what he had written as with what he still had in mind to write. 'Everything I have written till now', he wrote to Suvorin on October 27th, 'is just rubbish in comparison with what I should like to have written and should have written with enthusiasm. . . . I have a whole army of people in my head who are imploring me to be released and are only waiting for a word of command. The subjects I have in my mind are jealous of those I have already used, and I can't help feeling vexed at having made use of the rubbish, while what I consider to be good should be lying about in the storehouse of my mind like so much junk.'

On November 3rd Chekhov went to the opening of the Society of Art and Literature founded by Stanislavsky. It is characteristic of Chekhov's attitude to the future founder of the Moscow Art Theatre and the man who was to make him famous as a playwright that, in referring to the Society of Art and Literature in his letters, he never mentions Stanislavsky by name, although by that time Stanislavsky was already well known as one of the most brilliant amateur actors and producers in Moscow. To be sure, the very title of the Society of Art and Literature sounded pretentious to Chekhov, a view in which he was confirmed at the opening ceremony of the Society.

'I am putting on my evening suit', he wrote to Suvorin, 'to go to the opening of our Society of Art and Literature to which I am invited as a guest. What the aims and resources of the Society are I don't know. All I know is that at the head of the Society is Fedotov, the author of many plays. They did not elect me as a member, and I am very glad they didn't, for I certainly do not want to have to pay twenty-five roubles membership fee for the right to be bored. Lensky will be read-ing my stories.' And on his return from the opening, he added this characteristic note: 'I have just come back from the ball. The aim of the Society is "unity".[1] One German scientist trained a cat, a mouse, a sparrow-hawk and a sparrow to eat off the same plate. That German had a system, but the Society has none. The whole thing was a frightful bore. A young lady sang, Lensky read one of my stories (incidentally, after the reading a man said aloud, "A very weak story!" and the editor of *The Alarm-Clock* was stupid and cruel enough to address him with the words, "And here is the author himself. Let me introduce him to you!" which made the poor fellow sink through the floor with confusion), we danced, were entertained to an execrable dinner and were cheated by the waiters. If actors, artists and writers really compose the best part of our society, then it is a great pity.

[1] The official aim of the Society was 'to aid in the promotion of knowledge of art and literature among its members, help in the development of good taste, and foster the growth of theatrical, musical, literary and artistic talents'.

What sort of Society of Art and Literature can it be, if it is so poor in colour, desires and intentions, so poor in taste, beautiful women and initiative. They put a Japanese effigy in the entrance hall, hang a carpet over the banisters, and they think that that is artistic. If the artistic decorations of their premises go no further than a museum effigy with a halberd and shields and fans on the walls,[1] if all that is not just an accident but part and parcel of the artistic feelings of the founder of the Society, then he is not an artist but a pompous ape.'

The last remark was certainly aimed at Stanislavsky himself. Chekhov detested what he called the 'Gavrilov' background of Stanislavsky; he could not but have the utmost contempt for Stanislavsky's literary background; and he never had anything good to say for the Moscow amateur actor which Stanislavsky was at the time. Nor was Chekhov far wrong about the Society of Art and Literature. Within one year Fedotov, the artist Sollogub, and the opera singer Kommissarzhevsky left the Society, and Stanislavsky had to carry on as best he could. What Chekhov failed to realise was Stanislavsky's selfless devotion to the art of the stage and his ability to transform the 'pompous ape' in him into a great artist. But it is impossible to blame Chekhov for being unable to detect greatness in a man who, like himself, achieved it only after a long and gruelling struggle with his own not inconsiderable imperfections of character.

Chekhov, besides, had no particular affection for the stage as it then was. 'I like putting on a play', he wrote to Suvorin on November 18th, 'as I like catching fish or crawfish. You cast your line and wait to see what will come of it. And you go for your royalties to the Society of Playwrights as you go to have a look at your creel: how many perch and crawfish have been caught during the night? It is quite a pleasant pastime.' Chekhov always assumed a pose of indifference when something he wanted badly was not within his reach, and it is certainly one of the greatest ironies of the theatre that the man whom he had misjudged so badly should have been the very man who brought about a complete reorganisation of the theatre in Russia and who made his own plays accessible to the theatregoer.

13

The time of the performance of *Ivanov* at the Alexandrinsky Theatre was now drawing near and Chekhov managed to get off to

---

[1] Those were all the props from Stanislavsky's production of *The Mikado*.

ANTON CHEKHOV AND MAXIM GORKY AMONG THE MEMBERS OF THE
MOSCOW ART THEATRE IN YALTA (1900)

Petersburg for a fortnight at the beginning of December. He stayed with Suvorin again, and, as usual, had a very hectic time. 'In Petersburg', he wrote to Leontyev shortly after his return to Moscow, 'I was torn to pieces and driven like a post-horse. I drove about the town, walked, ate and drank without stopping. Suvorin', he added, 'is an extraordinarily sociable and sincere man.'

It was during this visit that Chekhov met Chaykovsky for the first time. He found the composer to be an extremely nice man and, he afterwards wrote slyly to Helen Lintaryov, 'not at all a demi-god'; he tried to interest him in George Lintaryov, who was at the time studying at the Petersburg Conservatoire. Two things, however, spoilt Chekhov's visit to Petersburg. The first was his meeting with Grigorovich, who had completely recovered from his serious illness. There was always something false and insincere in Chekhov's relations with Grigorovich. His first almost hysterical letter to the old man, while understandable in the circumstances, put their relations on a footing of disciple and master that was completely unrealistic and that Chekhov found difficult to keep up. Not wishing to offend Grigorovich, he committed himself to statements which he must have known were not true. Thus in his letter of January 12th, 1888, he went so far as to bracket Grigorovich with Gogol, Tolstoy and Turgenev as one of those writers who would not be forgotten 'so long as there are woods and summer nights in Russia and plover and snipe utter their cries'.

It is not surprising that Grigorovich should have been deceived by these extravagant terms of speech and assumed that he had a right to play the mentor to a young writer of genius he had 'discovered', but who did not seem to be sure of himself and who did not heed his warning to stop writing short stories, especially for newspapers. Chekhov, always quick to resent any encroachment on his freedom, was getting tired of the old man's constant admonitions, and although he met Grigorovich, he did not this time go to see him at his house. That seemed quite an undeserved slight to Grigorovich who complained to Suvorin that Chekhov had become proud and conceited. When Suvorin wrote to Chekhov about it, Chekhov replied that he did not think it necessary to pay visits to 'the great ones of this world' and that, anyway, it was not conceit but laziness that had prevented him from paying the visit to Grigorovich.

It was a poor excuse (on December 24th he did write a letter of apology to Grigorovich, the last letter he ever wrote to him), and on January 6th, 1889, Chekhov put an end to the tiresome business of fawning upon a person he never really respected either as a man or as a writer by telling Suvorin quite frankly that he thought Grigorovich a fraud. 'I am very fond of Grigorovich,' he wrote, 'but I do not believe that he really is anxious about me. He is a tendentious writer himself and only pretends to be an enemy of tendentiousness. I can't help thinking that he is terrified of losing the respect of people he likes, hence his quite amazing insincerity.' The final break came eight months later with the rejection of *The Wood Demon* by the Literary and Dramatic Committee, which had to pass a play before it could be performed on the Imperial stage and of which Grigorovich was chairman. In his letter to Suvorin of October 17th after the final rejection of his play on the ground that it was merely a story written in dialogue, Chekhov denied that he had used Suvorin as a model for Professor Serebryakov and hinted that Grigorovich had invented it all. 'Oh, how glad that Grigorovich is!' he wrote. 'And how glad all those gentlemen would be if I had put arsenic in your tea or been exposed as a spy of the Third [political] Department.'

Chekhov found the exorcising of such a literary ghost as Grigorovich a somewhat unpleasant but not very difficult operation. But exorcising the Taganrog past from Alexander's life proved a much harder and, indeed, quite an impossible task. Already on November 8th Alexander had written to tell him the news that he had found a woman who agreed to share his turbulent life, a mutual friend of theirs, Natalie Golden, a sister-in-law of the poet Pushkaryov, who had left Moscow for Petersburg four years earlier in search of a job and whom Chekhov had at the time described to Leykin as 'an intelligent woman, honest and decent in every sense'. In acknowledging the news of his brother's second 'illicit marriage' (Alexander married Natalie a year later), Chekhov wrote that he was expecting 'an interesting epic with children, changes of residence, calomel, etc.'

How interesting an 'epic' Alexander's second extra-marital venture proved to be Chekhov found out only on his arrival in Petersburg. He was so angered and disgusted by what he saw that he left Petersburg without saying goodbye to his brother. 'What made me so indignant the very first time I came to see you', he wrote to Alexander on January 2nd, 1889, 'was your *horrible* and absolutely inexcusable treatment of Natalie and the cook. I hope you will forgive my saying so, but to treat women, whoever they may be, like that is unworthy of a decent man. What heavenly or earthly power gave you the right to make them your slaves? Language of the foulest kind, shouts, reproaches, rows at breakfast and dinner, constant complaints about your hard life and your damnable work—are these not expressions of the coarsest despotism? However worthless or culpable a woman might be, however intimate your relations with her might be, you have no right to sit in her presence without trousers, or be drunk in her presence, or utter words which even factory workers would not use in the presence of women. . . . Nor will a man who respects a woman allow himself to be seen by his parlour-maid without trousers, and shout at the top of his voice, "Katya, fetch the chamber-pot!" . . . There is the same difference between a woman who sleeps on a clean sheet and one who sleeps on a filthy one and roars with laughter when her lover ——, as between a drawing-room and a low pub. . . . You claim that decency and good manners are prejudices, but one must have some regard at least for something, a woman's weakness or one's own children. . . . You can sink as low as you please, but you must take care that your children do not get hurt. You can't use foul language in their presence with impunity, or insult your servants, or shout viciously to Natalie, "Go to hell out of here! I'm not keeping you!" '

This sort of thing, as Chekhov was not slow to point out to Alexander, was all too reminiscent of the way their own father treated their mother. To be reminded of it at the moment when he was contemplating settling in Petersburg with his mother and sister was particularly distasteful to him. Suvorin had offered him a salary of six thousand roubles a year if he agreed to accept a job on his paper. Chekhov did not take the offer seriously since he had already made it clear to Suvorin that he would never accept it. But the rumour of the offer had spread (Chekhov himself was incautious enough to tell some of his friends about it) and his intention to settle in Petersburg permanently revived a previous rumour that he intended to marry Suvorin's daughter. 'My partiality for Petersburg and my journeys there,' he wrote to Suvorin on December 26th (at the time he was supervising the production of Suvorin's play *Tatyana Repina* at the Maly Theatre), 'the actors and their wives explain by the fact that you have a grown-up daughter whom I want to marry.' His friends in the liberal camp got worried, and on December 31st Pleshcheyev wrote to warn him that those who sympathised with him did not approve of his intention to join 'the *New Times* army of impudent scoundrels and mercenary trash'. Pleshcheyev also hinted that Chekhov's articles in *New Times* might lead people to believe that he approved everything published in that paper. Chekhov's reply was very cautious. He did not deny that he might join the staff of *New Times*, but he argued that his previous association with journalists, far from having a detrimental effect on him, had certainly been useful. He might agree to work for

Suvorin's paper, he added, if Suvorin offered him one thousand roubles a month, in which case he intended to fight hard for his independence and for his views on how a paper should be run; he might even accept one thousand a year, but in that case he would merely agree to read manuscripts. He would devote himself heart and soul to those for whom and with whom he would have to work and he did not think that that would have any evil effects so far as he was concerned.

Chekhov could dismiss Pleshcheyev's worries about the influence of Suvorin's politics on him with a clear conscience. There never was any danger of his playing the double game Suvorin played by pretending to Chekhov that he remained faithful to his old liberal ideas while supporting the most reactionary policies of the Russian Government in his paper. Chekhov certainly showed a curious ignorance of practical affairs at this period of his life, due partly to his personal liking for Suvorin and partly to his dissatisfaction with Moscow. What worried him most was the problem of his medical practice, for he had realised that the time had come for him to give it up, at least as a regular occupation. His Moscow practice was chiefly among his impecunious friends who could not afford to pay him anything even if they had thought of doing so. Chekhov was very touched when Palmin, who was badly hurt by a fall during one of his drunken bouts and whose miserliness was notorious, sent him a bottle of perfume costing three and a half roubles (Chekhov liked to sprinkle himself with scent), although that did not pay for the money he had to spend on cabs to take him to the other end of the town where the poet lived. As for the patients who did pay him, their small fees made little difference to his income. And when, at the end of 1888, Chekhov's literary work demanded much painful concentration from him, his medical practice became a real nuisance.

In 1888 the weather at Christmas was particularly fine. 'It is a pity', Chekhov wrote in his last letter to Grigorovich on December 24th, 'that the Russian people are so poor and hungry, for otherwise Christmas with its snow, white trees and frost would have been the most beautiful season of the year in Russia. It is a season when God himself, it seems, would go for a drive in a sleigh.' And yet he had to spend Christmas day with a patient who died while he was with him. No wonder he wrote to Suvorin in December: 'Generally speaking, I am sick of my life here, and at times I am beginning to *hate*, which has never happened to me before. Long stupid talks, visitors, people coming to me with all sorts of requests, the two- or three-rouble tips from my patients which do not pay for my cab fares—in short, such an unholy mess that it is surprising I don't run away from home. People borrow money from me and forget to pay it back; they waste my time. . . . All I need now is an unhappy love affair.'

A month later he got that, too.

14

Suvorin came to Moscow for the première of his play in the middle of December, and on January 18th, 1889, he and Chekhov left for Petersburg, where Chekhov wanted to be present at the rehearsals of his new version of *Ivanov*. On January 24th, that is to say, a week before the first performance of his play at the Alexandrinsky Theatre, he paid a visit to Khudekov, who had been to see him in Moscow to ask for a story for the *Petersburg Gazette*. (Chekhov wrote for him *The Shoemaker and the Devil*, which was published on December 25th.) It was his first visit to Khudekov's, and, as was his habit, he was pacing the newspaper owner's study and discussing something, when the door opened and a young girl came in. It was Lydia Avilov, Khudekov's sister-in-law, who had been married to a civil servant a short time before and who was already the mother of a little boy. Chekhov knew nothing about it and, when introduced, walked up eagerly to her, retaining her hand in his and, according to Lydia, looking at her with surprise. Later, when Lydia had told him that she was married and had a son, Chekhov bent over her and looked into her eyes.

'How difficult it is sometimes to explain or even to perceive the true meaning of some happening,' Lydia writes in her reminiscences of Chekhov, *Chekhov in My Life*. 'And as a matter of fact nothing did actually happen. We simply looked closely into each other's eyes. But how much there was in the look we had exchanged! I felt as if something had burst in my soul, as if some rocket had exploded there— brightly, joyfully, triumphantly, rapturously. I had no doubt that Chekhov felt the same, and we looked at each other surprised and happy.'

An interesting sidelight on the authenticity of Lydia's story is thrown by her recorded remark of Chekhov's about what he considered to be at the time the aim of a writer. 'A writer', she records Chekhov as saying, 'is not a little twittering bird. . . . If I live, think, fight and suffer, then all this is reflected in whatever I happen to write. I will describe life to you truthfully, that is, artistically, and you will see in it what you have not seen before: its divergence from the norm, its contradictions.' Now, the divergence from the norm, as already remarked, was what Chekhov just then regarded as the distinguishing characteristic of a creative writer, a fact Lydia could not possibly have known at her first meeting with him.

But quite apart from Lydia's evidence, the inexplicable change in Chekhov's plans brought about by that unexpected meeting with a young woman of whose existence before his visit to Khudekov's he had no idea, is sufficient proof of the truth of her story. He had planned to settle in Petersburg and was even ready to accept some sort of a job on Suvorin's paper. All those plans he now gave up. Not only that, but he never visited Petersburg again during the whole of the next year in spite of the fact that his regular visits to Petersburg had by that time become a necessity to him. When he did visit it at the beginning of 1890, it was only to make his final arrangements for his journey to Sakhalin. The journey itself, which has puzzled his biographers as it had puzzled his family and friends, remains a complete mystery unless, as a modern Russian biographer remarks, there was 'a deep personal reason to account for it'. This reason could only have been his love for a young married woman which he concealed from everybody as he concealed all his intimate feelings from the world; for during that Tolstoyan period of his life Chekhov could not but regard a situation of that kind with dismay and abhorrence, and since his love for Lydia was too strong to be controlled, he undertook a long and arduous journey as the only cure for it. But the real paradox of the situation was that his journey to Sakhalin produced the opposite effect: it did not cure him of his love—it cured him of his Tolstoyan obsessions.

There were, no doubt, other reasons why Chekhov should have regarded the situation in which he found himself after his meeting with Lydia Avilov with dismay. There was, to begin with, Alexander's experiment in an extra-marital union, which raised a storm in Chekhov's family that by itself would have been quite enough to prevent him from following in his brother's footsteps; there were the almost insuperable difficulties of obtaining a divorce from the ecclesiastical courts, which refused to grant a divorce to Alexander's first 'civil' wife, who, like Lydia, had a son by her first husband; and even if that could have been settled satisfactorily, could he undertake any further obligations at a time when he found it so hard to provide for his own family? Besides, there was his illness, the grave nature of which he knew, though he concealed it from his family and friends. Still, at the time, that is, in January 1889, it was undoubtedly his

Tolstoyan faith that was the decisive factor in his decision 'to tear this love out of his heart', to use Masha's phrase in *The Seagull*. In *The Wood Demon*, which he wrote in 1889, he actually dealt with a similar situation, and he left no doubt as to what he considered Helen's duty to her aged husband to be.

Tolstoy's rigidly inhuman attitude to a peccant wife was certainly shared by Chekhov in the years preceding his journey to Sakhalin. When at the beginning of 1890 Tolstoy's *Kreutzer Sonata* was published Chekhov hailed it almost as a revelation. 'Didn't you really like *The Kreutzer Sonata?*' he asked Pleshcheyev in his letter of February 15th, 1890. 'I won't go so far as to claim that it is a work of genius, for I am no judge of that, but in my opinion you won't find anything among the things that are being written in Russia and abroad today to equal it in the importance of its main idea or the beauty of execution. Even disregarding its artistic merits, which are quite striking in places, we must be thankful to it for stimulating thought to the highest degree. When reading it, you can scarcely restrain yourself from exclaiming, "That's true!" or "That is absurd!" No doubt, the novel has regrettable faults. In addition to those you have enumerated, it has a fault for which I cannot forgive its author, namely, the daring with which Tolstoy treats of things he does not know anything about or does not want to know anything about out of sheer obstinacy. His pronouncements about syphilis, reform schools, women's feeling of disgust for sexual intercourse, etc., can not only be disputed, but simply show him to be an ignorant man who during his long life has not bothered to read one or two books written by specialists. But these faults are of no account whatever, for you don't notice them at all because of the great merit of the novel as a whole, and even if you do notice them you are merely sorry it has not escaped the fate of all human efforts, none of which is completely perfect or free from blemishes.'

Chekhov could not swallow those of Tolstoy's statements which his own training and experience as a doctor had proved to be false; but there was no doubt at all that he agreed with the whole underlying moral trend of the novel, that is to say, with Tolstoy's dogma of chastity. It was only his Sakhalin experiences, bringing him face to face with the stark facts of human suffering, that convinced him of the total inadequacy of Tolstoy's philosophy to deal with those facts. 'Before my journey to Sakhalin', he wrote to Suvorin on December 18th, 1890, '*The Kreutzer Sonata* was an event in my life, but now it just seems silly and ridiculous to me. Goodness only knows whether as a result of my journey I have grown up or gone off my head.'

Chekhov returned a different man from Sakhalin, and his journey to that Island of Lost Souls was in reality a pilgrimage in search of his own soul, though he may not have realised it at the time. And the visible sign of his intellectual maturity was his complete renunciation of Tolstoy's philosophy of life made evident in his own renunciation of *The Wood Demon* which he refused to allow to be published or performed. But at the beginning of 1889 he was entirely under the influence of Tolstoy's moral teachings and the only sensible thing he could do after his meeting with Lydia Avilov was to run away. As usual, however, he gave quite a different explanation of his hurried exit from Petersburg after the great success of *Ivanov*, the first night of which at the Alexandrinsky Theatre on January 31st turned out to be one of the greatest personal triumphs of Chekhov's life.

'I ran away from Petersburg', he wrote to Barantsevich on February 3rd, 'because I was utterly exhausted. Besides, I felt ashamed all the time. When I am not successful I am much braver than when I am successful. Success turns me into a coward and I feel a strong desire to hide myself under a table.' What he implied was that the great success of *Ivanov* at the Alexandrinsky Theatre had driven him out of Petersburg. In his letter to Helen Lintaryov, written on February 11th, he went much further in revealing the real reason for his flight from Petersburg, though he still pretended that the success of *Ivanov* was the cause of it. 'I could not wait for George to leave Petersburg with me,' he wrote, 'because I simply had to leave at all costs. I ran away from strong sensations as a coward runs away from a battlefield.' But that the 'strong sensations' he had run away from had nothing to do with the success of *Ivanov* is proved by the fact that a few days before the first night of *Ivanov*, when he was not at all sure whether his play would be successful or not, he had written to Mary that he would leave Petersburg on February 1st, that is, immediately after the first performance of the play on January 31st.

Chekhov often resorted to a 'white' lie in order to conceal something he would not divulge to anyone for anything in the world. He did it with his illness and he did it on many other occasions when to tell the blunt truth would have involved him in all sorts of unnecessary and difficult explanations. On January 20th, for instance, he failed to keep an appointment with the poet Polonsky, he and Leontyev having stayed the whole evening with Pleshcheyev. Ignorant of Chekhov's previous engagement, Pleshcheyev told Polonsky about it. When told that Polonsky was very much hurt by what he took to be a personal slight, Chekhov sent off the following note to Pleshcheyev: 'Even according to holy writ a lie is sometimes a way to salvation—I shall therefore tell a lie and put the whole blame on Leontyev.'

15

The year of 1889 was a year of personal tragedy and literary disaster for Chekhov. His brother Nicholas died, his work on his novel was wasted and his play *The Wood Demon* failed—nothing seemed to go right. In his literary work he seemed to have reached a parting of the ways. 'Korolenko', he wrote on September 14th to Pleshcheyev, who expressed the view that Korolenko, whom Chekhov admired so much, was shilly-shallying and would not progress any further, 'and I have reached the stage when fate will have to decide whether we are to go up or down. Shilly-shallying is quite natural in such a situation. Even a temporary standstill would be in the order of things.' He hoped that Korolenko would overcome his difficulties; and as for himself, he was quite sure that he would never give in without a fight to the death. 'I may not have what Korolenko has', he wrote, 'but I have something else. I have made many mistakes in the past, and where there are mistakes there is also experience. Besides, my field of battle is much bigger and richer than his; except for a novel, poems and political denunciations, I have tried everything. I have written long and short stories, one-act comedies, leading articles and humorous stories. If I can no longer go on writing long stories, I can try writing short ones; if my short stories are bad, I can dash off a one-act comedy, and so ad infinitum, till the day of my death. So that however much I may feel inclined to look upon Korolenko and myself with the eye of a pessimist, I refuse to give up hope for a moment, for so far I can see no sign either for or against. Let us wait for another five years. I expect the situation will become much clearer then.'

What he needed was time. 'I'm sure', he wrote earlier to Suvorin, 'that if I were to live another forty years and all that time read, read and read, and learn to write with talent, that is, briefly, then I'd fire off such a big gun at all of you that it would make the heavens shake. Now I am just the same lilliputian as the rest.' He read a lot, as usual, including Marcus Aurelius's *Meditations* in a Russian translation, which he sent on to Alexander Lensky with the request not to pay any attention to his copious marginal notes, but read everything without skipping, 'for everything', he wrote, 'is equally good'. His *Ivanov* seemed to have raised a veritable storm in Russia, and he was receiving a great number of anonymous and signed letters about his play. He had even been told by one indignant correspondent that a young student had shot himself after seeing a performance of it.

Pleshcheyev had paid him another visit in Moscow and, as usual, gorged himself on his mother's rich pasties and been sick. At Shrovetide he gave a special dinner: sour cabbage, radishes, olives, mixed salad, kidney beans and pancakes. He went to another ball given by the Society of Art and Literature. He was drinking rather heavily at the time (he seems to have taken to drink in a big way in Petersburg after his meeting with Lydia Avilov) and that was followed by a violent attack of haemorrhoids accompanied by profuse bleeding. He 'celebrated' the arrival of Lent by going to a party, where he drank all night, returning home at half-past ten in the morning and sleeping till five o'clock in the afternoon. On February 16th he attended a farewell dinner at Korsh's theatre, which, like every other theatre in Russia, was closed during Lent. 'Actresses are delightful people,' he wrote to Suvorin on February 20th. 'I was so much in love with them last night that I felt deeply moved and even exchanged farewell kisses with some of them. They have a certain nobility of character which actors seem to lack. The men who dedicate themselves to the sacred art have not got their purity of spirit. There is a great deal of the flunkey in their words, glances and actions. Still, that is not true of all of them. I did not drink a lot,' he added, evidently in explanation of the morning-after character of his letter, 'but I drank rather unwisely, mixing my liqueurs with brandy, so that now I feel an empty void in my stomach; it is as if there were an abyss with cold walls inside me. I feel like putting a lot of needles in a glass of cold water, then shaking it up vigorously and drinking it all down, but the needles would have to be sour.' A fortnight later he went to one of the big restaurants on the outskirts of Moscow to listen to the songs of gipsy women. 'These savage jades can certainly sing beautifully,' he wrote to Suvorin on March 5th. 'Their singing resembles a train hurtling over a high embankment in a raging blizzard: a lot of howling, screaming and thumping.' He was doing his best in a rather conventional, homœopathic, way to rid himself of the 'strong sensations' he had brought back from Petersburg, though the rumours of his intended marriage to Suvorin's daughter, illogically enough, worried him. 'Why are they spreading these slanderous stories about me in Petersburg?' he wrote indignantly to Leontyev on March 11th. 'What good can it do to anyone? That a slanderer will lose my respect may not seem to be particularly important; that I despise slanders and the "idealists" who spread them, may not be important, either; but, after all, I could get really angry and something rather unpleasant might happen. I am so angry about these slanders,' he went on, 'not because you write to me about them, but because everybody writes to me about them, and the students repeat them. All the students are talking about my impending marriage to a millionairess. Disgusting!'

At the beginning of March he went to Kharkov to inspect an estate Suvorin thought of buying. He was glad to find that his books were selling very well there and that his plays, too, were popular. On his return to Moscow he was elected a member of the committee of the Society of Playwrights, whose meetings he attended conscientiously. On March 15th Nicholas, who had been living apart from his family, fell ill, and it soon became clear that he had contracted an acute form of consumption and that his days were numbered. Chekhov dreamt that he had been awarded the order of Stanislaus third class, and his mother told him that it meant that he would have to bear the cross. He felt that for once his mother's rather crude predictions would come true, for the painter was undoubtedly in a very bad way.

Chekhov decided to take his brother to Sumy as soon as possible (he could not afford to take him to the Crimea). They left on April 24th. On the previous evening Chekhov attended a committee meeting of the Society of Playwrights, which went on till one o'clock in the morning. He then walked home with one of the committee members discussing 'plays and distilleries'. He did not go into the house, however, but stood for a long time by the gate watching the sunrise. He then went for another walk, wandered into a low-class pub, where he watched a game of billiards between two experts, after which he went off to an even less respectable place where he talked to a student of mathematics and the band, and then he went back home again, had a glass of vodka and something to eat and at six o'clock in the morning went to bed.

In Sumy Nicholas's illness progressed steadily to its inevitable conclusion. Chekhov knew very well that he could do nothing to save him, and at times he was sorry he was a doctor and not an ignorant layman. It was a particularly fine spring. He got up early, went to bed early, ate a lot, wrote and read, and indulged in his favourite pastime of fishing and catching crawfish. 'The weather is beautiful,' he wrote to Suvorin on May 4th. 'Everything is singing, blossoming and sparkling with beauty. The garden is almost entirely green, even the oak-trees are in leaf. The trunks of the apple trees, pear trees, cherry trees and plum trees have been painted white against the worms and they are smothered in white blossom which makes them look astonishingly like brides at a wedding: white dresses, white flowers, and such a sweet look of innocence as though they were ashamed of people admiring them. Every day sees the birth of myriads of new creatures. Nightingales, bitterns, cuckoos and other birds fill the air with their cries at all hours of the day and the night, and they are accompanied by the frogs. Every hour of the day and the night has its own peculiar charm. Thus, at nine o'clock in the evening the garden is filled with, quite literally, the roar of cockchafers. The nights are full of moonlight, and the days of sunshine. I am for that reason in a most excellent mood, and but for the coughing artist and the mosquitoes, I should have felt a real Potyomkin [Leontyev had nicknamed him a Potyomkin of literature]. Nature is a very good sedative. It puts you at peace with the world, that is, it makes you indifferent. And in this world', he added significantly, 'it is necessary to be indifferent. Only indifferent people can see things clearly, be fair, and work—that, of course, applies only to people who are honourable and intelligent; egoists and brainless people are indifferent as it is.'

So far Chekhov had not written a single story. He had begun writing his short story about 'an infamous woman', *The Princess* (a religious woman of high rank who visits a monastery regularly and makes a nuisance of herself, but is under the impression that she is conferring a great favour upon the monks), in November 1888, but only finished it in March 1889, when it was published in *New Times*. Suvorin accused him of having grown lazy, but Chekhov quite rightly claimed that he was not working less than he had done three or five years before. 'To work and have the appearance of working between nine o'clock in the morning and lunch and from tea till bedtime has become my routine,' he wrote to Suvorin, 'and in this respect I am a regular civil servant. But if my work does not result in two long stories a month or in an annual income of ten thousand roubles, it is not the fault of my laziness but of my psychic and organic constitution: I don't love money sufficiently for medicine and I have not enough passion, that is, talent, for literature. The fire burns feebly and steadily in me, without flashes or crackling, and that is why I never write four or five printed sheets in one night, or, carried away by my work, do not go to bed when I feel sleepy; I do not therefore commit any extraordinary stupidities nor any strikingly brilliant things. In this respect, I am afraid, I am very like Goncharov, whom I do not like and who is ten times more talented than I. There is not enough passion in me, and to this you must add the following crazy obsession that has come over me: for the last two years

Fame

I have grown tired of seeing my things in print, I have grown indifferent to reviews, talks about literature, slanders, failures, large fees—in short, I have become a damn fool. I am suffering from a sort of stagnation of the spirit, and I cannot help feeling that it is due to my personal life. I am not disappointed, tired or depressed, but somehow everything has suddenly lost its interest for me. I'll have to pull my socks up,' he repeated Suvorin's first admonition to him.

Except that Chekhov grossly exaggerated the period during which he had felt a 'stagnation of the spirit', which seemed to have only come to a head after his last visit to Petersburg, his phrase that 'somehow everything has suddenly lost its interest for me' seems to be an admirable description of his state of mind and is, surely, not unconnected with his meeting with Lydia Avilov. He was certainly hard at work on his ill-starred novel. In addition, he was studying French and German, his ignorance of foreign languages worrying him no less than his inability to write a novel. It was a very hot summer, and Suvorin spent six days at Chekhov's cottage at the end of May. Shortly after Suvorin's departure for the Tyrol, where it was arranged that Chekhov was to join him, Paul Svobodin, an actor of the Alexandrinsky Theatre who played Count Shabelsky in the Petersburg production of *Ivanov* and with whom Chekhov became great friends, arrived with his nine-year-old son. Svobodin, who seems to have been an even greater practical joker than Levitan, helped to raise Chekhov's drooping spirits. He would dress up in a frock-coat, boiled shirt and top hat and stand fishing solemnly for hours on the bank of the river. He and Chekhov would also go off to the neighbouring town of Akhtyrka and take a room at the hotel, Svobodin pretending to be a count and Chekhov his valet. It was the sort of mild fun that reminded Chekhov of his old mystification tricks and still amused him.

In June Alexander and his family arrived, and during his stay in the country with Chekhov he got married to Natalie. Leaving Alexander to look after Nicholas, Chekhov went off with Svobodin and the Lintaryovs to pay a visit to Smagin, but this time their journey was not as pleasant as the year before. It was a cold day, and half-way to Smagin's estate it began to rain. They arrived late at night soaked to the skin and went straight to bed. 'I shall never forget the muddy roads, the grey sky and the tears on the trees,' Chekhov wrote to Pleshcheyev on June 26th. 'I say I shall never forget, for next morning a peasant arrived from Mirgorod with a wet telegram: 'Kolya has died.' You can imagine what I felt. I had to rush to the station, change trains and wait for eight hours for my connexion and then wait again at Romny from

7 p.m. till 2 a.m. I went for a walk in the town. I remember sitting in the park. It was dark, terribly cold, and excruciatingly boring, and behind the brown wall where I was sitting actors were rehearsing some melodrama.'

He was back on the 17th and found Nicholas lying in his coffin 'with a beautiful expression on his face'. At first Nicholas had been very irritable and lost his temper with everybody, but a month before his death a strange change came over him: he became very gentle and affectionate and talked all the time about how he would start painting again when he recovered from his illness. Although he received the last sacrament a week before he died, he firmly believed that he would recover. According to the local custom, he was carried by Chekhov and his brothers to church, and from the church to the cemetery, in an open coffin, the women in the funeral procession carrying the lid of the coffin. He was buried in the village cemetery, 'a very quiet and cosy place', Chekhov wrote to a friend, 'where birds are always singing and the air is full of the fragrance of sweet-smelling grass'. They put a cross on his grave immediately after the burial, 'a cross', Chekhov wrote, 'that can be seen for miles'.

16

The death of Nicholas left Chekhov at a loose end. While his brother was alive there was at least something that kept him tied to one place, but after Nicholas's funeral the restlessness he felt after his last Petersburg visit got the better of him and he could no longer stay in one place for more than a few weeks. He should have gone to join Suvorin in the Tyrol, but that would have meant being constantly in the company of the one man who could easily have guessed his state of mind and the reason for it. As usual, he found other reasons for not wanting to go abroad. 'I want a rest,' he wrote to Pleshcheyev on June 26th from Sumy, 'and the running to museums and Eiffel towers, jumping from one train to another, daily meetings with the garrulous Grigorovich, hasty dinners, drinking, and chasing after excitement—all that is hard physical labour. I'd much rather live for some time in the Crimea, where I might be able to do some work.' On July 2nd, however, he wrote to Suvorin that he would join him in the Tyrol after spending a few days in Odessa, 'whither I am drawn by an unknown power'. He had just then heard from Peter Sergeyenso, his old schoolmate and former fellow contributor to *The Alarm-Clock*, that the Moscow Maly Theatre was on tour there, and he decided that he might as well try to find distraction with one or another of the actresses. He was a fortnight in Odessa, spending most of his time with the young and pretty actress, Glafira Panova.

'Thanks to certain circumstances,' he wrote to Leykin after his return to Sumy, 'I spent a great deal of money in Odessa and I had to abandon my plans for going abroad and go to Yalta instead.' But it is much more likely that he had gone to Yalta because the 'cure' he sought had failed. For he had intended to leave Odessa for Yalta long before he had run out of money. 'I had already packed my things,' he wrote to his brother Ivan on July 16th on board the ship that was taking him to Yalta, 'and went to the theatre to say goodbye, but they kept me there. One took my hat, another my walking-stick, and all of them began begging me to stay so warmly and earnestly that a stone would not have been able to resist. I had to stay.' And he went on to give the following circumstantial account of the way he spent his time in Odessa (the names he mentions are all of actors and actresses of the Maly Theatre): 'I got up at eight or nine o'clock and went for a bathe with Pravdin. In the bathing pavilion I had my shoes cleaned (I have a new pair of shoes, by the way). Then I had coffee in the restaurant on the beach near the stone steps. At twelve o'clock I went for Panova and took her to Zambrini's to eat ice-cream (sixty copecks), then I accompanied her to her milliner's and to other shops, where she bought lace, etc. The heat, of course, was quite unbearable. At two I saw Sergeyenko and then I went on board the *Olga Ivanovna* for lunch, chiefly for the sake of the borshch and sauce. At five I had tea with Cleopatra Karatygina, which was always a very merry and gay affair; after tea, at eight, we all went to the theatre. Behind the scenes, I looked after the coughs of the actresses and made my plans for the following day. Lensky's wife, always worried about expenses; Panova, searching with her black eyes for those she wanted; the fat Grekov, always asleep and always complaining of being tired; his wife, a sickly-looking lady, imploring me not to leave Odessa; the pretty maid Anyuta, in her red blouse, who opened the door to us, etc. etc. After the performance a glass of vodka in the downstairs bar, then wine in the cellar, while waiting for the actresses to go to Karatygina's for tea. Again we drank tea and went on drinking it a long time, till 2 a.m., talking all sorts of nonsense. At two I saw Panova off to her room and then went back to mine, where Grekov was waiting for me. I drank more wine with him and talked about the Don district (he is a Cossack) and the stage. And so till daybreak. Then the barrel-organ was started up again and the music of the day before repeated. All the time I did not seem able to do without female company, and I became completely effeminate, practically wore skirts myself, and not a day passed without the virtuous Lydia Lensky telling me with a meaningful look how Medvedeva had been afraid to let Panova go on tour and how Pravdina (also a very virtuous but rather nasty-minded woman) was spreading all sorts of tales about her (Lydia), who was apparently accused of conniving at wrong-doing. Last night's parting was a very touching affair. I got away with difficulty. They made me a present of two ties and saw me off to the boat. I had got used to them, and they had got used to me, and, as a matter of fact, we were sorry to part.' He did not really know what he was going to Yalta for, he told Ivan. 'I am feeling bankrupt and indifferent,' he wrote. 'I go on living mechanically and without thinking.'

From Sebastopol to Yalta the sea was choppy and many passengers were seasick. But Chekhov was a good sailor and he even had dinner on board, though, he told Mary, he did fear that he would be sick at the table on the plate of his neighbour, the daughter of the Governor of Odessa. In Yalta he stayed at a very nice villa within a few yards of the sea. He did not like the town better on his second visit than on his first. This time, in fact, he found things much worse, for he had many acquaintances and had to listen to all sorts of 'clever nonsense' to which he had to reply at length. Many students came to see him, bringing their heavy manuscripts for him to read. Most of them were in verse: pretentious, clever, noble and third-rate. He enjoyed his bathing in the morning, but in the afternoon he suffered from the great heat. Every day he made up his mind to leave, but somehow could not. There were lots of 'young ladies' in Yalta, but none of them was pretty. There were lots of writers, but none of them had any talent. The only things that made his life bearable were the sea and the ambling horses on which he liked to go riding. He had a narrow escape from death or serious injury while bathing when a peasant nearly hit him over the head with a long, heavy pole, used as an aid to swimming. During the three weeks of his stay in Yalta he spent most of his money, returning to Sumy with only forty roubles in his pocket.

It was in Yalta that he made the acquaintance of Helen Shavrov, a writer in whose literary career he was to take a great interest. She was only a girl of fifteen at the time. Chekhov was walking along a street in the residential part of the town when three young girls came out of the gate of a house and one of them approached him with the question, 'Are you Chekhov?' and introduced herself and her two sisters.

Chekhov accepted their invitation to a picnic on the beach, during which Helen Shavrov gave him one of her stories to read. Chekhov liked her story and, after correcting it, sent it on to Suvorin, who published it in *New Times*. That was the beginning of her literary tutelage by Chekhov, which went on for many years.

Chekhov did not altogether waste his time in Yalta. He finished his *Boring Story* which he had begun already in March. 'The story', he wrote to Pleshcheyev from Yalta, 'is a little boring because of the heat and my rotten, melancholic mood. But the theme is new and it will probably be read with interest.' He was back in Sumy on August 12th and left with his family for Moscow on September 3rd. They travelled in the same compartment as Professor Nicolai Storozhenko, a well-known 'liberal' and a friend of Goltsev's who was to be responsible for the rejection of *Uncle Vanya* by the Dramatic and Literary Committee of the Maly Theatre ten years later. Storozhenko had been one of Mary's lecturers and examiners, and all the way, Chekhov wrote to Helen Lintaryov, she was pretending not to know her brother and Semashko, who was travelling with them. 'To punish such pettiness of mind,' Chekhov wrote, 'I began telling them in a loud voice how I had served as a cook in the house of Countess Keller and how good my employers had been to me; every time I had a drink I bowed to my mother and wished her to find a good place in Moscow. Semashko pretended to be a valet.'

Back in Moscow, Chekhov took another three weeks in revising *A Boring Story* before he sent it off to 'the clinic for women's diseases', i.e. *The Northern Herald*, where, he told Suvorin, he was 'consultant physician-in-chief'. He hoped his story would produce some violent abuse 'from the enemy camp', he wrote to Pleshcheyev, 'for in our age of telegraph and telephones abuse is the sister of advertisement'. The story did arouse great discussion in the literary journals, but little real abuse. It was rightly considered to be the most important work Chekhov had so far produced.

17

The main work Chekhov wrote after his return to Moscow was his play *The Wood Demon*. Since it was to be written in quite a new way as a 'lyrical comedy' or 'comedy-novel' (the vagueness of these terms which Chekhov only used in connexion with *The Wood Demon* clearly shows that he was still very much at sea about what he called the 'architecture' of such a play), he took to visiting the theatre regularly to study afresh those laws of dramatic art which seemed to conflict with the sort of play he wanted to write. On September 26th he also went to the Bolshoy Theatre to see a performance of Glinka's *Ruslan and Lyudmila*.

On October 14th the composer Chaykovsky paid Chekhov a visit. A day earlier, taking advantage of Chaykovsky's presence in Moscow, Chekhov had written to ask his permission to dedicate *Gloomy People*, the new volume of short stories Suvorin was publishing, to him. 'This month', he wrote, 'I am about to publish a new volume of my stories, which are as boring and dreary as autumn, the artistic elements in them being thickly interwoven with medical ones. But that does not discourage me from asking your permission to dedicate it to you. I hope you will not refuse, because this dedication will, first, give me great pleasure and, secondly, will to a certain extent satisfy the deep feeling of respect for you which makes me think of you daily.' He also asked Chaykovsky for his autographed photograph.

Chaykovsky brought him his photograph on the following day himself. He inscribed it: 'To A. P. Chekhov from his ardent admirer P. Chaykovsky. Oct. 14th 89'. Chekhov returned the compliment by giving Chaykovsky his own photograph, inscribed: 'To Peter Ilyich Chaykovsky, a souvenir from his devoted and grateful admirer Chekhov'. But Chaykovsky had another and more important reason for visiting Chekhov. He was planning to write an opera based on an incident in Lermontov's novel *A Hero of Our Time*, to be known by the name of the heroine of that incident, Bella, and he wanted Chekhov to write the libretto for it. 'But please', Chaykovsky said in discussing the libretto with Chekhov, 'don't let us have any processions with marches. To tell you the truth, I don't like marches.'

Chekhov accepted Chaykovsky's proposal. He even inscribed the volume of stories he gave the composer, published in the same year by Suvorin under the title of *Stories*, 'To Peter Ilyich Chaykovsky from his future librettist 14/x 89 A. Chekhov'. But, naturally enough, nothing came of Chaykovsky's proposal; for, to begin with, Chekhov was hardly the man to write a romantic libretto for a romantic composer, and, besides, such a libretto would have to be written in verse, and with the exception of two or three doggerel poems of a satiric kind Chekhov had never written any verse, and, in fact, was quite incapable of writing verse.

In spite of the failure of *The Wood Demon*, performed on December 27th in Moscow at Abramova's Theatre, on which Chekhov had counted so much to help him out with his ever-dwindling funds, his financial position during the last months of 1889 was not bad. His books as well as *Ivanov*, just then revived in its revised version at Korsh's Theatre, and *The Bear* were bringing him in a steady income and he was beginning to feel like a *rentier*. 'I live tolerably well,' he wrote to Pleshcheyev on October 21st, 'and occasionally there are even a few good moments, but, on the whole, to use the language of the stock exchange, my mood is sluggish'. In Moscow, too, he was besieged by budding authors, especially playwrights, who brought him their manuscripts. He could not bring himself to refuse anyone (the memory of his own struggles for recognition was always fresh in his mind), though sometimes, as he said himself, he felt like shooting the lot. The constant stream of visitors was another nuisance and he often felt like running away to the North Pole, where he understood there were no visitors. His family, too, seemed to be disintegrating. Nicholas was dead, Ivan lived at his school, and now Michael had finished his law course at the university and was looking for a job. 'I don't like it,' Chekhov wrote to Suvorin, and indeed what he wanted most was a sense of security which his family alone was able to give him, especially during his illness, which in December recurred with particular intensity. His whole family fell ill with influenza, and he, too, caught a chill, accompanied by a hacking cough and a discharge of blood from the lung. Again he became obsessed by his fear of loneliness, aggravated by sleeplessness and persistent fits of coughing, which used to wake Michael in the next room. He would not hear of calling in a doctor, though in a letter to Lensky he went so far as to admit that he was beginning to suspect that his illness was not influenza 'but some other abomination'. It was during those sleepless nights that he was tortured by the thought of the futility of his literary work. 'There is not a single line', he wrote to Suvorin at the end of December, 'that has a serious literary significance in my eyes. There has been a great deal of hard work in my past, but not a single minute of serious work. I long passionately to hide myself away somewhere for five years and devote myself to serious spade work. I have to learn my job, learn it from the very beginning, for as a literary man I am an absolute ignoramus; I have to write conscientiously, competently and with feeling, write not five sheets in one month but one sheet in five months. I must leave my home, I must live on seven or eight hundred roubles a year and not on three or four thousand as I am doing now, I must get rid of lots of things, but I am afraid there is more Ukrainian laziness in me than courage.'

It was during those awful nights of illness and terror that he also fought in vain against a feeling he could not overcome, a feeling for a woman which he considered morally reprehensible, but which he was unable to suppress either in Odessa or in Yalta. He had to run away from it to the other end of the world, where he might also achieve that complete break with his past which he considered necessary before he could become the sort of writer he wanted to be. A complete withdrawal from the world of men held more terrors for him than his present life. What he wanted was a withdrawal that would not entail any separation from mankind. He wanted to go to a place where he could study mankind in its most degraded and pitiful form, and by such a study learn to bear his own suffering with fortitude and equanimity. He decided to go to Sakhalin.

Part Four

SAKHALIN

I

The last three months before his departure for Sakhalin Chekhov devoted to an intensive study of all the available material which had a direct or indirect bearing on his proposed journey. He consulted over a hundred different authorities on criminal law, the history of Russian prisons and Siberian convict settlements, the history of the colonisation of Siberia, the geological, zoological and other scientific data on Sakhalin and the Russian Far East, the official documents on the administration of Sakhalin, the accounts of Russian and foreign travellers about their discoveries on the island, etc. Among the English and American works he consulted were translations of William Broughton's *Voyage of Discovery to the North Pacific Ocean performed by H.M.S. Providence and her tender*, published in London in 1804, and the articles, published in *The Century Illustrated Magazine*, and books on the Siberian prisons by the American traveller George Kennan, who had visited Tolstoy after his Siberian journey in 1871 and whose works, though forbidden in Russia, were translated into Russian abroad and reached Chekhov in all sorts of 'illegal' ways. Chekhov was also interested in the question of prison reform, and among the books he read on this particular subject were Elizabeth Fry's memoirs.

He began collecting the materials for his journey in Petersburg, where he spent a whole month from January 7th to February 7th, keeping away from most of his friends and acquaintances and making copious extracts from books and documents. On January 20th he paid a visit to the head of the Prison Department, Mikhail Galkin-Vrasky, hoping to obtain from him official assistance for his visit to Sakhalin. In the letter which he handed to Galkin-Vrasky he stated that he wanted to visit Eastern Siberia and the island of Sakhalin for 'literary and scientific reasons'. The interview was extremely friendly, but the official 'assistance' he asked for he never received. What Galkin-Vrasky did, however, was characteristic of the policy of the Russian Government: he sent a secret order to the Governor of Sakhalin to prevent Chekhov from meeting certain categories of political prisoners.

Chekhov never discussed his reasons for going to Sakhalin with his friends, though here and there in his letters of that time one does catch a glimpse of the true reason for his journey. Thus, writing to Maria Kisselev, who was in Petersburg at the time, he asked jokingly: 'Was my future wife from whom I am running away to Sakhalin satisfied with the Indian present I gave her?' The reference is to Maria Kisselev's little daughter, but why should Chekhov have used just that particular phrase if he were not running away to Sakhalin from anyone? Again, in reply to a letter from a Moscow acquaintance who wrote that he had heard a rumour that Chekhov was going to Sakhalin to study the conditions of life among the convicts, Chekhov wrote: 'It is quite true that I am going to Sakhalin, but not because of the convicts. I want to erase a year or a year and a half from my life.' Again, on March 22nd he wrote to Leontyev: 'Don't put any literary hopes on my Sakhalin journey. I am going there not for the sake of observations or impressions, but simply for the sake of living for six months differently from the way I have lived till now.' And only a week before starting on his journey he wrote to Suvorin that he had dreamt he was running away from a wolf. The point is not the particular dream he had (though that, too, is not without some significance), but that it should have impressed him sufficiently for him to write about it to Suvorin. Even Chekhov, it seems, could not keep the great secret of his journey to himself without now and then throwing out obscure hints about it. When Suvorin told him bluntly at the beginning of March that his journey was just a silly whim in which he persisted out of sheer obstinacy, he replied that he, too, was quite convinced that his journey would not be of any value either to literature or to science. 'I have neither Humboldt[1] nor even Kennan plans. All I want is to write one or two hundred pages and in that way repay however little a part of the debt I owe to medicine which, as you know, I have treated most shamelessly. Perhaps I shan't be able to write anything, but nevertheless the journey does not lose its aroma for me: while reading, looking around me and listening, I shall learn and get to know a lot. I have never gone on a long journey before, and thanks to the books I have had of necessity to read now, I have already learnt a great deal of what every man ought to know on pain of forty strokes of the birch and which I was too ignorant to know before.' Even if his journey were nothing but a whim, he would not lose anything by it. If it did not give him anything at all, it would give him two or three days at least which he would remember all his life with pleasure or bitterness. All that, he admitted, was very unconvincing, but it was no more

---

[1] The German scientist and explorer Friedrich von Humboldt was invited by the Russian Government in 1829 to study the geological and geophysical data of Asiatic Russia.

unconvincing than what Suvorin wrote. 'For instance,' he went on, 'you write that no one really wants Sakhalin and that it cannot be of interest to anyone. Is that really so? Sakhalin may be uninteresting and unwanted only to a society which does not send thousands of people there and does not spend millions on it. After Australia in the past and Devil's Island today, Sakhalin is the only place where colonisation by convicts can be studied; the whole of Europe is interested in it, and you say we do not want it? . . . From the books I have read and am reading it is evident that we have let millions of men rot in prisons, let them rot there barbarously, without reason; we have driven men in manacles for tens of thousands of miles, we have infected them with syphilis, we have corrupted them morally, we have multiplied the numbers of criminals, and put the blame for it all on the red-nosed prison officials. Now the whole of educated Europe knows that it was not the fault of the prison officials but of all of us, but we don't seem to care, the whole thing is not of the slightest interest to us. . . . We are doing a great deal for our sick, but we do nothing for our prisoners. No, I assure you, Sakhalin *is* interesting and it is our duty to know all about it, and the pity of it is that I am going there and not someone who knows more about these things and who is more capable of arousing the interest of our society in it. I personally am going there for a trivial reason.'

Chekhov was merely stating the bare truth; for the personal problem that made him undertake his journey *was* trivial when compared with the great human problem of the convict settlements and prisons on Sakhalin.

The preparations for his journey did not, however, prevent him from taking part in a number of social distractions. On the contrary, it seems that once he had taken the decision 'to run away' he felt much easier in his mind and was more ready to counter the anxious enquiries of his friends and family with a lighthearted joke. Even in Petersburg, where he was for obvious reasons very careful to pay as few visits as possible (he even pretended to have left town a fortnight earlier than he actually had done), he went to the theatre three times and to a dog show. 'I went to a dog show today,' he wrote to Mary on January 14th. 'I went there together with Suvorin, who is standing at my desk now and is saying: "Tell them that you went to a dog show together with the notorious cur Suvorin."' Suvorin certainly had his moments of cynical frankness, though he kept them mostly for his diary. The plays Chekhov saw in Petersburg were Tolstoy's *The Power of Darkness*, produced by Davydov for an amateur company,

Ostrovsky's *The Poor Bride* and Turgenev's *The Bachelor*, the last two plays performed at the Alexandrinsky Theatre. He found the playing of the professional actors at the Imperial Theatre 'wooden and soulless'. He also paid a visit to the studio of the famous painter Repin. On his return to Moscow he dined with the famous actress Yermolova, who nine years before had rejected his play *Platonov*. 'A wild flower,' he wrote to Pleshcheyev, 'having found itself by chance in a bunch of carnations, becomes more fragrant by its association with its aristocratic neighbours. So, having dined with a star, I felt a halo round my head for two days afterwards.'

The necessity of earning some money on which his family (which was to spend the summer on the Lintaryov estate) was to live while he was away made Chekhov write a story for *New Times*, published on April 1st under the title *Devils* and republished later under the title *Horse Thieves*. Suvorin criticised this story for its 'objectivity' and 'indifference to good and evil', but Chekhov pleaded that he was mainly interested in 'theft as a passion' and that he counted on his readers to supply 'the subjective elements'. He was, that is to say, interested in the problem of theft as he would be interested in the problem of cancer. As a doctor, it would never have occurred to him to waste words on the undesirability of cancer and he did not see why he should do so about the undesirability of stealing horses. Here his doctor's training had certainly misled him, for it is impossible to dissociate human conduct from its purely moral consequences. To present it as dispassionately as he did in this and in some of his other stories, made him an easy target for the less well-disposed of his critics, especially those who belonged to the 'liberal' camp whom he never hesitated to abuse himself. It is not surprising, therefore, that *Russian Thought* should have dismissed Chekhov in its March number as 'a high priest of unprincipled writing'; nor is it surprising that Chekhov, whose Tolstoyan principles had led him to undertake what at times seemed even to him quite an absurd journey of about ten thousand miles under the most primitive conditions, should feel outraged by such a cavalier way of dismissing him in one short sentence. He dashed off a furious letter to Vukol Lavrov, the owner and editor-in-chief of *Russian Thought*, in which he indignantly repudiated the accusation of being an unprincipled writer as a libel. 'I have never blackmailed anyone,' he wrote to Lavrov on April 11th, 'nor libelled anyone, nor informed on anyone, nor lied to anyone, nor flattered nor insulted anyone; in short, I may have written many stories and articles I'd be glad to throw into the waste-paper basket because I don't consider them good enough, but I have never written a single line of which I need be ashamed.' He admitted that his entire literary activity consisted of a succession of mistakes, sometimes gross mistakes, but that was because he was not a good writer and not because he was a good or bad man, for to him an unprincipled writer was equivalent to a scoundrel. If, however, Lavrov considered him to be unprincipled because of the 'lamentable fact' that, as an educated man who had so often appeared in print, he had done nothing that had been of any use to the agricultural boards, the new law courts, the freedom of the press and freedom in general, then *Russian Thought* was as much to blame as he, for it did not accomplish anything more in that direction—and that was neither their fault nor his. Chekhov went on quite inconsequentially to cite his excellent personal relations with his friends, and even brought forward the strange excuse that he was a doctor and not a writer. The truth is that at heart Chekhov felt that the accusation of lack of principle was largely justified, which indeed explains why he was so furious and why he would have nothing to do with *Russian Thought* for the next two years. It also explains the plaintive reason he gave for writing his letter. 'One does not usually reply to criticisms,' he declared, 'but in this particular instance it is not criticism but a libel. I should not have replied even to a libel, were it not that I shall be shortly leaving Russia on a journey from which I may never return, and I have not the strength to refrain from a reply.'

There is no trace of anger in his letter to his friend Leontyev, who a little earlier had also accused him of lack of moral principles. 'Do I really differ so much in my conception of morality from people like you', he wrote, 'that I deserve to be reproached for it? You can't possibly have in mind some abstruse higher morality, for there is no higher or lower morality but only one, namely the one given us at the time of Jesus Christ, which prevents people like you or me or Barantsevich from stealing, lying, etc. Now, if I am to trust my conscience, I have during the whole of my life, neither by word nor by deed, neither in my stories nor in my one-act comedies, ever coveted my neighbour's wife, nor his manservant, nor his maidservant, nor his ox nor any other animal; I never stole, nor played the hypocrite, nor flattered the powerful and curried favour with them, nor blackmailed anyone, nor lied to anyone. It is true I was lazy, I loved to laugh, eat and drink a lot, I fornicated—but that is my own affair and it does not deprive me of the right to think that, so far as moral principles are concerned, I am no whit different from any other ordinary man. I am neither a hero nor a scoundrel, I am just like most people; I have sinned a lot, but I have paid for my sins by those inconveniences which they bring. If, however, you want to scold me for not being a hero, then for goodness' sake don't let us hear any more about it, and instead of your abuse let me hear your charming tragic laughter [Leontyev had a high-pitched laugh which Chekhov called tragic and which in time got on his nerves]—that will be much better.'

Leontyev's objection to his conception of 'artistic values' Chekhov dismissed by saying that he was tired of hearing people talk about them, since it seemed to him to be merely a continuation of the scholastic disputes of the Middle Ages. 'When people talk to me about artistic and inartistic values, or about what is scenic or not scenic, or about tendencies, realism and so on, I am at a loss what to say, I nod half-heartedly and reply with banal half-truths which are not worth a farthing.'

Shortly before he was due to leave Moscow for the Far East, Chekhov received the news that *The Northern Herald* had stopped publication for lack of funds. That was a serious blow to him, as he had counted on getting about three hundred roubles from it to cover some of his travelling expenses and another fifty roubles a month for his family. But Suvorin once again came to his help by giving him an advance of one thousand five hundred roubles.

2

No man setting out on so hazardous a journey felt less thrilled at the unknown adventures and dangers awaiting him than Chekhov did when he left Moscow for Sakhalin on April 19th, 1890. He had another discharge of blood from his diseased lung, which he ascribed to the strain of the preparations for his journey, the packing and, perhaps, also to the farewell parties at which he had drunk rather immoderately. He had bought himself a sheepskin, an army officer's waterproof leather coat, a pair of topboots, a penknife 'for cutting sausages and killing tigers', as he told Suvorin, and a revolver. Thus 'armed from head to foot', he took the train for Yaroslavl at eight o'clock in the evening. His itinerary was as follows: from Moscow to Yaroslavl by railway; from Yaroslavl to Perm by boat, first on the Volga and then on the Kama; from Perm to Tyumen by railway; from Tyumen to Lake Baykal by coach; across the lake by boat and then again by coach to Sretensk; from Sretensk by boat down the Amur to the Pacific port of Nikolayevsk, and from there across the Gulf of Tartary to Sakhalin.

ANTON CHEKHOV IN 1894

On his return journey he hoped to pay a visit to Japan and from there return home either via America or the Suez Canal.

It was characteristic of Chekhov that even in the midst of the preparations for his journey he found time to carry out a request he had received through his uncle Mitrofan from the mayor of Taganrog to send his books to the public library of his native town, thus inaugurating a special branch of the library bearing his name, which he kept supplying with books during the next fourteen years of his life. He was seen off at the station by Levitan, Dr. Kuvshinnikov and his wife Sophia, Dr. Kuvshinnikov giving him a bottle of cognac which Chekhov was to open only when he reached the shores of the Pacific. His mother and sister accompanied him part of the way to Yaroslavl. It was pouring with rain when he arrived in Yaroslavl and the first thing he did on the boat was to go to bed. When he woke up next morning the sun was shining and the Volga no longer looked so dismal. He liked the great expanse of the river, the water meadows, the monasteries basking in the sun, and the white churches. White gulls were skimming the surface of the water, cows were grazing on the banks, and from time to time he caught the sound of the cowherd's horn. He sailed past Pless where Levitan and Sophia Kuvshinnikov had spent the previous summer together, and he saw the house with the red roof in which they had lived, and the churchyard with the church rising above the trees which Levitan had immortalised in his famous painting 'A Haven of Rest'.

The Kama did not impress him as much as the Volga, and, besides, the further East he travelled, the colder it got. There were strips of snow on the banks and iceflows on the river. The change in the weather had an immediate effect on his mood: the sounds of the accordions which floated across the muddy water from the bare banks with their bare trees seemed dismal to him, and the men in torn sheep-skins, standing motionless on the barges, looked as though they were frozen with grief. He did not feel like talking to the passengers, though he did observe them closely, his interest being particularly aroused by a group of peasants who were emigrating to Siberia.

'It can't be any worse,' one of them said, smiling with his upper lip only.

The remark seemed to have been addressed to Chekhov, who did not know what to say in reply.

'It can't be any worse!' the peasant repeated.

'It will be worse!' another peasant, not a Siberian settler, replied from a nearby seat. 'It will be worse!'

The only thing Chekhov enjoyed on the boat was the caviare which he consumed in huge quantities. The cities on the Kama looked dull to him and their inhabitants, he thought, must all be occupied in manufacturing clouds, boredom, wet fences and mud. He arrived in Perm at two o'clock in the morning. It was cold and raining. He was still coughing and spitting blood. He took the train to Tyumen, on the other side of the Ural mountain chain, stopping in Yekaterinburg for three days. It was snowing. The local inhabitants terrified him: they were all so big, with prominent cheek-bones, broad shoulders, tiny eyes and huge fists. They seemed to him to be a cross between Ural cast-iron and the great sturgeon, to have been born in the local foundries and delivered not by midwives but by mechanics. All night long watchmen raised an awful din by banging their iron plates. There were some cousins of his mother's living in the town, but as they belonged to the well-to-do branch of the family, they were not very keen on a closer acquaintance with their poor relation.

In Tyumen, where he hoped to catch a boat for Tomsk, he found that the first boat left only on May 18th, which meant waiting over a fortnight, so he decided to hire a coach and go by road. This was the beginning of his nightmare journey of several thousand miles over the worst roads in the world. The strain of the first days of that horrible drive caused another discharge of blood from his lung which made him feel dreadfully depressed. The monotonous Siberian plain merely deepened his depression. It was cold, the woods were bare, and the snow still lay on the ground; the lakes were ice-bound. He left Tyumen on May 3rd, and on May 9th it was snowing heavily. The only sign of spring he could see was the presence of enormous numbers of wild ducks, geese, cranes and swans. The woods seemed to be teeming with black-game and hazel-grouse. There were also great numbers of hares which did not scuttle away at the approach of the carriage, but watched it roll past with curious eyes, standing on their hind legs with their ears pricked. Chekhov liked the Siberian peasants, whose houses were spotlessly clean and who seemed to be well off, as well as the fare he got at the farmhouses where he stopped for the night, especially the very tasty bread the peasants baked. What he did object to was the ducksoup which was one of the staple dishes of the countryside. He was forced to fall back on milk and eggs for his meals, but after a few days he got tired of it. He could not drink any vodka, for he found the Siberian brand distasteful, and that worried him a little as he had a theory that vodka was absolutely necessary on the road because it stimulated the brain which grew dull and inert from constant travelling.

Sakhalin

He found the tales of the dangers of the Siberian roads exaggerated and his revolver an unnecessary luxury. He was involved in one adventure, though, which might have ended tragically for him. This is his own account of it in one of his letters home:

'They drive very fast here, but that seems to be their regular practice, and indeed in winter they drive even faster. Once we nearly ran over an old woman, and another time we nearly drove into a gang of convicts. Now let me tell you of an adventure which befell me because of the Siberian fast driving. Only I must ask Mother not to wail or moan, for everything ended happily. On the night of May 6th, at dawn, I was being driven by a very nice old man in a small, open carriage and pair. I was dozing and watching the gleaming, snake-like flames in the fields and the birchwoods. The dead grass, which is usually set alight here, is damp and burns very slowly, and that is why the snake-like flames creep along leisurely, dying down and blazing up again. Every time a flame flares up, a cloud of white smoke rises over it. It is a beautiful sight to see the flames suddenly setting a tall clump of grass on fire: a fiery column seven feet high rises above the ground, a huge cloud of smoke goes up and suddenly disappears as though swallowed up by the ground. It is more beautiful still to watch the flames creeping through a birch wood; the whole wood is lit up and the white trunks stand out clearly and the shadows cast by the trees spring to life and move along with the moving flames. Suddenly I heard the quick rattle of wheels. A mail-cart, drawn by a team of three horses, was coming straight at us at a terrific pace. My driver made haste to turn right and, as the mail-cart drove past us, I could just make out the huge, heavy cart with its coachman returning home after delivering the mail. It was followed by another mail-cart, also careering along at a terrific speed. Again we hastened to turn right, but to my horror the mail-cart did not turn right but left. I had scarcely time to say to myself, "Goodness, we're going to run slap into each other", when I heard a crash, the horses became entangled in one huge, heaving black mass, my carriage rose up into the air, and I was flung out of it in the middle of the road with my trunks falling on top of me. But that was not all. A third mail-cart came flying on top of us. That ought really to have reduced me and my trunks to pulp, but, fortunately, I was not asleep and had not broken any bones in my fall, so I was able to jump up rapidly and had just enough time to rush aside. "Stop!" I yelled to the third mail-cart. "Stop!" The third cart ran into the second and stopped. Then a fourth cart appeared, but that one was stopped in time. If I had been asleep or if the third mail-cart had been a little closer to the second, I should have returned home an invalid or as the headless rider. What happened was that the first driver, anxious to get home, was driving as fast as he could, while the drivers of the other two carts had fallen asleep, leaving their horses to follow the first cart blindly as there was no one to keep them in check. The moment they had recovered from the shock of the collision, my old driver and the drivers of the mail-carts began swearing at each other furiously. You can't imagine how lonely I felt among that wild, blaspheming horde, beside the near and distant flames which were consuming the grass without making the cold night air one whit warmer. As I listened to the shouts and looked at the broken shafts and my poor trunks scattered in the road, I could not help feeling that I was in a different world and that I might at any moment be trampled to death. . . . At last my old driver began tying the broken shafts and the torn harness together with bits of string and the leather belts from my trunks. Somehow or other, after many stops to repair the broken carriage, we reached a village. . . .'

Five or six days later it started to rain and it rained day and night. The roads turned into muddy swamps, and the coachmen refused to drive by night. Chekhov's most hair-raising experience was the crossing of the flooded Siberian rivers. On reaching a river in the evening, he and his driver would start shouting for the ferry. The wind howled, the rain came down in torrents, icefloes moved slowly down the stream. Fortunately, there were bitterns in the rushes along the banks and the now familiar booming of that mysterious bird brought back memories of the Lintaryov estate and made him feel less lonely. In about an hour the huge shape of the ferry would loom out of the gathering dusk, its huge oars reminding him of the claws of a craw-fish. The crossing was a very slow business, and every time Chekhov would be overcome by a terrible feeling of loneliness, and it seemed to him that the bitterns were booming on purpose, as if to say: 'Don't be afraid. We are here. The Lintaryovs have sent us here from the Psyol.'

On May 7th his driver told him that the Irtysh had flooded the water meadows and that they would have to wait till the floods had subsided. Thinking that his driver had said it because he did not want to travel by night over muddy roads, Chekhov refused to wait. But soon they drove up to what looked like an enormous lake with here and there a few bushes sticking out of the water. In the distance strips of snow could be faintly discerned: that was the bank of the Irtysh. Chekhov realised that it would be wiser to return, but his stubbornness asserted itself and, besides, he was overcome by an even stronger feeling: an irresistible urge to take his chance come what may. It was something he had already experienced when he had plunged off a yacht into the Black Sea during his stay with Suvorin at Theodosia and which he was to experience again on his return from Sakhalin when he used to jump off the bow of the boat into the Indian Ocean and swim to the stern where a rope was lowered for him. A sort of psychosis, he thought it was. But, perhaps, it was more like a wager with fate: if he survived, his illness would not kill him too soon; if not, it was just as well.

The drive across the flooded countryside was a real nightmare: all the bridges had been carried away by the floods and on reaching them Chekhov had to alight and help his driver to replace the missing planks. It was pouring with rain all the time, and it took them hours to reach the Irtysh. The bank of the river was low, bare and slippery, and the white-flecked waves dashed against it furiously and at once rebounded, as though, Chekhov thought, they hated to touch a place so loathsome that only toads and the souls of murderers could live there. The river, too, did not roar like any other river in full spate, but made strange hollow sounds as though knocking on coffins on its bed. It was a curious and incongruously romantic image that occurred to Chekhov again and again in the ferryman's cottage where he spent the night. Next morning he crossed the Irtysh by boat as it was too windy to use the ferry. It was again pouring with rain, but he had to wait for an hour till a carriage arrived and took him to the nearest village where he dried himself and had tea. On May 12th he reached the river Ob which had also overflowed its banks and flooded the countryside. The wind had abated and for the first time he enjoyed the ten miles in the boat. Fifty miles from Tomsk he had again to take a boat across the Tom river. There was still snow on the ground, and to Chekhov's astonishment a thunderstorm broke during the crossing and a strong wind whipped up huge waves. The boatmen, caught by the storm in the middle of the river, wanted to row to some willow bushes and wait there till the storm had passed over. But one of the men in the boat remarked that if the weather did not improve they might have to wait a whole night in the boat. They decided to take a vote, and the majority being in favour of sailing on, the boatmen accepted the decision. It was getting dark, the wind was rising, the bank was still far off and the willow bushes, too, were by that time left far behind. Chekhov thought that if the boat capsized, he would first throw off his sheepskin, then his leather coat, then—but the bank was getting nearer and nearer, the boatmen plied their oars more cheerfully, and within seven yards of the bank Chekhov, too, cheered up. 'How nice it is to be a coward,' he reflected. 'He needs so little to cheer him up!'

He reached Tomsk on the evening of May 15th and stopped there for a whole week. He found half of the town under water and the other half buried in mud. He could see no sign of the poplars about which he had been told in Moscow; nor were there any nightingales: only magpies and cuckoos. He was rather pleased to see his one-act comedy *The Proposal* advertised on the hoardings, but found life in the town very dull. 'To judge by the drunkards with whom I've got acquainted here,' he wrote home, 'and the clever people who come to pay me their respects, the inhabitants of Tomsk are a very dull lot. At any rate, they make me feel so depressed that I have given orders not to admit anyone to my room.' He went to the steam-bath, sent his linen to the laundry, bought some chocolate, and sat down to write his impressions of the journey for *New Times*. He bought himself a carriage with a retractable top which he hoped to sell on reaching the Amur (he did sell it at a considerable loss), but it was not sprung and it had to be repaired twice on the way. In Tomsk he had an unexpected visitor in the person of the assistant commissioner of police. For a moment he wondered whether the authorities were going to send him back, but the visit was a purely literary one. The police officer had written a play and he wanted Chekhov to read it. He also showed Chekhov a gold nugget and asked him for vodka. Every educated person Chekhov met during his journey across Siberia always asked him for vodka. After a few glasses the assistant police commissioner got very talkative and told Chekhov that he was having an affair with a married woman whom he hoped to marry after his application for divorce, which he produced, had been approved by the Czar. He ended up by offering to take Chekhov on a tour of the Tomsk brothels. Chekhov went. He returned at two o'clock in the morning, feeling thoroughly disgusted with himself.

3

Chekhov had now travelled across the whole of the immense Siberian plain, and the problem that occupied him most was the fate of the people who for their political or criminal offences had to spend the rest of their lives in exile in Siberia. 'I don't like it', he wrote in one of his articles, 'when an exile, a man of education, stands at a window and gazes silently at the roof of the opposite house. What is he thinking about all the time? I don't like it when I hear him talking to me about all sorts of trifles while all the time he is saying to himself, "You'll be going back home, but I won't." I don't like it because I feel infinitely sorry for him just then.

'I am convinced,' Chekhov went on, 'that in fifty or a hundred years life sentences will be regarded with the same feeling of abhorrence and bewilderment as we regard the tearing of nostrils or the cutting off of a finger of the left hand. . . . For the last twenty or thirty years educated and thinking people in our country have been repeating the phrase that every criminal is the product of the society in which he lives, but how indifferent we are to this product! The reason for this indifference to prisoners and to the people who languish in exile, which is quite inconceivable in a Christian country and in a Christian literature, must be sought in the lack of education among our jurists. They graduate from a university only to be able to try a man and sentence him to imprisonment or exile; having entered the Civil Service, they receive their salaries and merely try people and pass sentences on them, but it is not part of their duties to know what happens to the criminal after his trial or what imprisonment and Siberia mean to him. That's the job of the red-nosed jailers!'

After spending a great deal of time in finding out the opinion of the local inhabitants about the exiles who lived among them, Chekhov came to the conclusion that the great majority of the more or less educated exiles lived a modest and retiring life. When they arrived at their places of exile they looked bewildered and lost. They usually began by selling their belongings, and after two or three years most of them were destitute and a great number of them were dead. Those who did adapt themselves to the conditions of their new life got jobs of one kind or another, but never earned more than thirty or thirty-five roubles a month. Gradually, they followed the example of the local intelligentsia and took to drink. With the exception of the bad public-houses, the family baths, and the large number of brothels, there were no places of entertainment of any kind. The exile, therefore, either spent the long autumn and winter evenings at home or went to visit one of the local inhabitants to drink vodka, and after consuming two bottles of vodka and half a dozen bottles of beer, one of them would ask the usual question: 'Shall we go *there*?' that is, to a brothel. What could the exile do to distract himself? He could either read some useless book like Ribot's *Diseases of the Will* or put on a light pair of trousers on a sunny spring day—that was all. Ribot was not particularly exciting, and, besides, Chekhov asked, was it really worth while reading about the diseases of the will if he himself had no will of his own? Light trousers were cold, but, still, it made a change!

From Tomsk Chekhov travelled in the company of two army officers and an army doctor, who were also bound for the Amur district. He had now reached the *taiga*, the belt of forest land which stretches for thousands of miles across Siberia, and as the country was hilly as well as thickly wooded, the roads did not dry as quickly as on the Siberian plains, with the result that his carriage sank axle-deep in mud and often overturned as it fell into a big hole in the road. But at long last he could see signs of spring: the fields were green and the buds on the trees were opening up. The nightingales were singing. When he approached Krasnoyarsk he seemed to be entering a new world. The mountains surrounding the town reminded him of the Caucasus, and the town itself surprised him by its fine, clean streets, its stone houses and its large, elegant churches. The mountains and the Yenissey river, which he found much more beautiful and impressive than the Volga, had compensated him a hundredfold for the inconveniences he had suffered on the road. He thought Levitan a fool not to have come with him.

It was getting very hot, and travelling from Krasnoyarsk to Irkutsk he was plagued by the heat and the dust, but at least he could now sleep in his carriage at night. Till then he had not been sleeping for a whole day and a whole night, and by lunchtime on the second day he would feel very tired and in the evening what he called his 'inquisition' would begin. After five cups of tea, his face would start burning and his whole body seemed to droop with fatigue; his eyes would be sticky with sleep; his feet in the heavy topboots would begin to itch, his brain would refuse to work. . . . If he spent a night at an inn, he would immediately sink into a heavy sleep; if he travelled, he would doze off in his carriage in spite of the bumps and the jolts only to be wakened by his driver on reaching the next post stage. His drivers would not even have to pull him by the sleeve, the heavy smell of garlic that issued from their mouths being quite sufficient to waken him. It was only after Krasnoyarsk that he really enjoyed his sleep in the carriage, though such a sleep never really refreshed him.

He spent a week in Irkutsk, which he thought was quite a European city. It had a theatre, a museum, a park in which a band played, and good hotels. He left it on June 11th, travelling along the banks of the Angara and admiring the picturesque views. It was warm and sunny. The mountains, covered with woods, were magnificent and reminded

him of the views of Switzerland he had seen. He was no longer coughing, and felt unusually well. He was charmed by the beauty of Lake
Baykal, which was turquoise blue and more transparent than the
Black Sea, and its wooded, mountainous shores, with tall cliffs jutting
out into the water. He spent two days on the shores of the lake before
crossing it in a steamer (it is about eighty miles across). He then
travelled again by carriage to Sretensk through the most beautiful
countryside he had ever seen: a mixture of Switzerland, the Don
country and Finland.

He arrived in Sretensk on June 20th and went on board a steamer
for a journey of over a thousand miles on the Amur to the Pacific
coast. At last he could take off his heavy boots and shiny blue shirt and
dress decently. He travelled in a first-class cabin, and the journey to the
Pacific coast took him ten days. Life in the Amur region reminded him
of the stories he had read about America. The banks of the river were so
wild, so 'original' and picturesque that he felt a strong desire to stay
there for good. It was very hot, and the nights, too, were warm.
Through his binoculars he could see countless numbers of wild duck,
geese, loon, heron and all sorts of wild fowl with long beaks. There
was a gold rush in the district and everybody talked of nothing but
gold. He met many gold prospectors (one of them even insisted
on his seeing his sick wife and forced him to take some money for his
visit). But what really amazed him was the freedom with which people
expressed their opinions. No one seemed to be afraid to talk, for there
was nowhere he could be exiled to. He had also been meeting many
Chinese (China was just across the river) and found them to be a
most good-natured and courteous people. A Chinese merchant with
whom he shared his cabin on the last stage of his journey told him that
in his country they had their heads chopped off on the slightest
provocation. He thought it a big joke. Unfortunately, he took opium
and raved all night so that Chekhov could hardly sleep.

4

On his arrival in Nikolayevsk on July 3rd Chekhov was beginning
to wonder whether he would after all be admitted to Sakhalin. The
thought worried him and the stories he heard on board ship of the
fierce winter in that part of the world and the no less fierce customs
spoilt his enjoyment of the broad river and the magnificent scenery.
Nikolayevsk presented a picture of desolation. Half of the houses in

the town were uninhabited and crumbling away. There were no hotels and he had to stay on board his boat for two days. When she returned to Khabarovsk, he decided to go on board the s.s. *Baykal*, which was to take him to Sakhalin, though she was not due to sail for another four days. But first he went to the local club, where he had dinner and listened to conversations about gold, the antlers of the spotted deer (a very valuable commodity used as an aphrodisiac in China), a juggler who had recently visited Nikolayevsk, and a Japanese dentist who pulled out teeth with his bare hands. While he sailed down the Amur he had a curious feeling that he was not in Russia at all but in Texas or Patagonia. It seemed to him that not only nature but the whole way of life was quite different from what he was used to, and that the people who came from Russia were foreigners. Even the priests he came across were either gold prospectors themselves or dealers in gold and they were no more honest in their transactions than the members of their flocks. And what really amazed him was the local moral code. It seemed that gallantry to women was raised almost to a cult, and yet from what he could gather people did not think it wrong for a man to sell his wife to a friend. Neither were there any social prejudices of any kind, and exiles or ex-convicts were treated like equals, but that did not prevent people from openly boasting of having shot a Chinese tramp in a forest or from organising a lynching party to hunt down a runaway convict.

He left the club and was rowed across to the s.s. *Baykal*, a medium-sized liner which sailed between Nikolayevsk, Vladivostock, Sakhalin and the Japanese ports. He was glad to find a comfortable and clean cabin on board. There was even a piano in the saloon. The attendants were all Chinese, who were called 'boys' in the English fashion. Having read of the storms and icebergs in the Gulf of Tartary, which separated the mainland from Sakhalin, he expected to meet whale-hunters on board, speaking in hoarse voices and chewing tobacco, and he was pleasantly surprised to find that his fellow passengers were educated people, and that the captain, too, was an educated man who had been sailing the northern Pacific for thirty years and who was able to supply him with a great deal of interesting information for his proposed book on Sakhalin. The Captain, he thought, had a greater right than Othello to speak of 'antres vast, and deserts idle, rocks and hills whose heads touch heaven'.

The *Baykal* weighed anchor on July 8th. She had three hundred soldiers under the command of an officer and a party of convicts on board. One convict, Chekhov noticed, had with him his five-year-old daughter, who held on to his chains when he walked up the gangway. There was also a woman convict in the party, who attracted general attention because she was accompanied to Sakhalin by her husband. One morning Chekhov went out for a walk on the forecastle and he saw soldiers, women and children, two Chinese and convicts in chains all asleep, huddled up together for warmth and their clothes covered with heavy dew. A soldier stood in the middle of that heap of human bodies, leaning with both hands on his rifle and also fast asleep.

It was a calm, sunny day. In the cabin it was very close and on deck it was hot. On the right bank of the river a forest was on fire, and Chekhov watched the huge red flames shooting out of what looked to be an impenetrable wall of green foliage. A cloud of black smoke hung motionless over the forest. Everything around was dead still, no attempt being made to deal with the fire, as though, he thought like the hero of *The Wood Demon,* no one cared whether the trees perished or not. At six o'clock in the afternoon they were already in the Gulf of Tartary, and Chekhov caught his first glimpse of the convict island which looked like a long, misty strip on the horizon. He felt as though he had reached the end of the world. As the Gulf of Tartary was very shallow and no reliable charts existed, the captain decided to anchor in the Amur estuary.

Early next morning they resumed their journey along the coast of the mainland, studded with mountain peaks covered with a blue haze from the forest fires. The smoke from those fires, Chekhov was told, was sometimes so thick that it was even more dangerous than fog. It was again a hot sunny day, and as they passed through the narrowest part of the Gulf of Tartary both the mainland and the coast of Sakhalin could be clearly seen. At two o'clock they entered the large bay of Castri, where they stayed till the following day. The moment the boat had anchored, a sudden thunderstorm broke, and Chekhov was surprised to see the waters of the bay turn a bright green colour. The rest of the day he and the chief engineer spent fishing from the deck.

At midday on July 10th they left for Sakhalin. The day was again quite unusually bright and sunny. A school of whales was calmly sailing up the gulf in a long line, and as he watched the fountains of water rising over their heads Chekhov thought it an extraordinarily 'original' sight, but he could not really enjoy it, as he was now beginning to be worried about his reception in Sakhalin, particularly as the officer who was in command of the soldiers on board the *Baykal* had told him that, as he was not on an official mission, he had no right to go near the prisons or the convict settlements. When at nine o'clock in the evening the *Baykal* cast anchor off Alexandrovsk, the administrative centre of Sakhalin, Chekhov could not see the landing stage because of the dense smoke of five large forest fires on the island. He could only make out the lights of the harbour, two of which were red. It was a fantastic sight. To the left he saw the monstrous beacons of the forest fires belching flames and sparks, with ranges of mountains rising above them, and behind the mountains—the red glow of more fires. It looked to him as if the whole of Sakhalin was on fire. To the right the black contours of a big promontory blotted out the sea. On its top a lighthouse threw a strong beam of light into the darkness, and beneath it three sharp-pointed reefs—the Three Brothers—rose ominously from the spray of the white breakers. And everything was covered in a pall of black smoke. Just like hell, Chekhov thought.

A cutter with a large barge in tow bringing a gang of convicts to unload the cargo came alongside.

'Don't let them on board,' Chekhov heard a voice shouting from the bridge. 'They'll clean us all out at night!'

'That's nothing,' the chief engineer said to Chekhov, noticing the depressing effect the coast of Sakhalin had made on him. 'You wait till you see Dui. There the cliffs rise sheer from the sea, with black gorges and layers of coal. A dismal coastline. We used to bring parties of two or three hundred convicts to Dui and I saw many of them burst into tears at the sight of that coast.'

Chekhov spent the night in his cabin. At five o'clock in the morning he was awakened by the cry, 'Get up, sir! The cutter is leaving for the last time. We're sailing in a few minutes!'

He dressed hurriedly and went down into the cutter. Beside him sat a young official with a sullen, sleepy face. The cutter sounded her siren and they sailed towards the landing stage, a wooden pier in the shape of the letter T. The cutter was towing two barges with convicts who looked sullen and tired. Their faces were wet with dew. There were a few Caucasian mountaineers among them, their tall fur hats pulled over their eyebrows.

The young official introduced himself. He was, it seemed, a poet who spent the long winter nights writing 'liberal' verse. Otherwise, however, he was no different from any other Sakhalin official. Chekhov heard a woman one day address him as Mr. D. 'Don't you dare call me Mr. D.,' he shouted at her. 'I'm "sir" to you!' Chekhov tried to find out from him what life on Sakhalin was like, but he just sighed and said darkly: 'You'll find out for yourself soon enough.'

In the bright morning sun the coast did not look as forbidding as the night before. The huge unsightly promontory with the lighthouse on top, the Three Brothers, the tall, sheer cliffs, the transparent mist on the mountains and the smoke from the forest fires had a strange fascination of their own. On the pier about fifty convicts, some of them wearing long coats and others grey tunics, were standing about without apparently having anything to do. As Chekhov alighted from the cutter, all of them took off their hats, an honour, he reflected, which had never been bestowed on any writer before. The convicts put his luggage on a cart, a man with a black beard mounted the box, and Chekhov drove off.

'Where shall I drive you to, sir?' the convict with the black beard asked, taking off his hat.

Chekhov asked him if he knew of any rooms to let in town.

'Yes, sir,' the man replied.

The road from the pier to Alexandrovsk was excellent by Siberian standards, but everything else looked bleak and dismal. The mountains and hills which surrounded the valley were covered with burnt stumps or dead trunks of larches, and except for weeds and grasses the valley itself was bare of vegetation; there was not a single fir or maple or oak to be seen—only a few spindly larches, the unmistakable sign of a marshy ground and a fierce climate.

Alexandrovsk was a town of three thousand inhabitants. Its churches, houses and pavements were all built of wood. The prison near the main street looked, to Chekhov's surprise, just like an ordinary army barracks. His driver brought him to a little house in the only Alexandrovsk suburb and he was shown round five big, clean rooms and a kitchen—all empty. The landlady, a young peasant woman, brought in a table and a stool and that was all the furniture she could give him. An hour later she brought in the *samovar*.

'What a place to come to,' she said with a sigh.

She herself had come to Sakhalin as a little girl with her mother and father, a convict who was still serving his prison sentence, and married an ex-convict who owned two houses, several horses and cows and employed many labourers. Chekhov had tea and then went for a walk round the suburb. At the end of it he came across a small house with a front garden and a brass plate on the door. Next to the house was a little shop. He went in to buy some food. The shop belonged to a former officer of the guards who had been found guilty of murder by a Petersburg court twelve years before. He had served his sentence and was now keeping a shop and carrying out all sorts of official duties for which he was paid a regular salary. His wife, a 'free' woman of a good family, was working as a nurse at the prison hospital. One could buy everything in his shop, including sickles and saws and women's hats of 'the latest fashion' from four and a half to twelve roubles apiece. While Chekhov was talking to the shop assistant, the former guards officer came in wearing a silk jacket and a coloured cravat. He introduced himself and invited Chekhov to lunch. At the ex-guardsman's house he met four Sakhalin officials, one of whom, an old man with white side-whiskers, reminded Chekhov of Henrik Ibsen. He had been a doctor at the hospital, and a short time before he had been involved in an unpleasant scene with General Konotovich, the governor of the island, during an inspection of cattle in the harbour. Next day he sent in his resignation. During lunch, which consisted of soup, roast chicken and ice-cream (there was also wine), the doctor kept abusing the administration of the island and contradicting everybody who had a good word to say for Sakhalin in general.

'Don't believe a word they tell you,' he warned Chekhov, and, as subsequently appeared, with good reason. 'They're merely throwing dust in your eyes.'

Chekhov accepted the doctor's offer to stay at his house, and as soon as he moved in the doctor showed him a big bundle of various petitions against local officials which he had sent to the authorities on the mainland 'in defence of truth'.

'The General won't like your staying with me,' he warned Chekhov.

But when Chekhov paid him an official visit on the following day, General Konotovich was not at all dismayed by his choice of lodgings. 'I'm glad', he said, 'you're staying at the house of our enemy. You'll be able to find out all about our shortcomings.' He gave Chekhov full permission to go anywhere he liked, but he asked him to wait for the arrival of the Governor-General, Baron von Korf, before starting on his investigation.

5

Chekhov found it difficult to adjust himself to life in Sakhalin. Before he got up in the morning all sorts of unusual sounds reminded him where he was. Convicts marched past the open windows of his room clanking their chains; the local military band began practising the marches they were going to play on the arrival of the Governor-General, the flautist playing a tune from one military march, the

Sakhalin

trombonist from another and the bassoonist from a third; the doctor paced his room in great agitation as he composed the petition he intended to hand to the Governor-General, which, he hoped, would result in the impeachment of the entire administration of the island. When he went out into the street after breakfast the scene that met his eyes was certainly 'original': a party of native Gilyaks walking to the police station, with every mongrel in town running after them in full cry (the dogs seemed to bark only at the natives, because, as Chekhov found out later, they wore dogskin boots); a group of convicts, clanking their chains and escorted by soldiers with perspiring faces and rifles slung over their shoulders, dragging a heavy barrowload of sand with little boys hanging on behind; a convict in a long grey prison coat going from house to house selling bilberries. There were convicts everywhere, mostly without chains or escort, walking in groups or singly. At first he could not help feeling a little apprehensive, but he soon got used to these outcasts of humanity.

The Governor-General arrived on July 19th on board a man-of-war. He was met by a guard of honour and a big crowd of officials, including the doctor in a black frock-coat and petition in hand, settlers and convicts. The band struck up its cacophonous march, and an ex-convict, a venerable-looking old man and one of the most prosperous settlers on the island, offered the Governor-General the traditional bread and salt on a silver dish of local manufacture.[1] As he watched the festive crowd Chekhov was surprised to see no young men among it, which meant that as soon as the children grew up they left the island.

On July 22nd the Governor-General sent for Chekhov and asked him what his business on the island was. Chekhov explained that he had no official authorisation to visit the island, but that he intended to study the life of the prisoners and the settlers for literary and scientific reasons.

'Haven't you been sent by some scientific society or some paper?' Baron von Korf asked.

Chekhov had the correspondent's card Suvorin had given him in his pocket, but as he did not intend to publish any articles on Sakhalin in *New Times* nor deceive the people who had shown full confidence in him, he did not produce it.

[1] The name of this local celebrity, who was always held up as an example of the success of the administration's colonisation policy, was Potyomkin. He owned two shops, forty horses and nine head of cattle. Chekhov had tea with him one day and was shown round his house: the rooms were clean and there was even a picture cut out of an illustrated magazine on the wall, which reminded him of similar pictures in his father's house in Taganrog, 'Marienbad, sea bathing near Libau'.

'I give you permission to go anywhere you like and to speak to any-one you like,' Baron von Korf said. 'We have nothing to hide. You are at liberty to inspect anything here. One thing only I cannot permit you,' he added, as instructed by Galkin-Vrasky, 'and that is to have any communication with political prisoners.'

Next day Chekhov was present at the dinner given in honour of the Governor-General by General Konotovich. In reply to the toast to his health, Baron von Korf went so far as to claim that the convicts on Sakhalin were treated better than anywhere else in Russia or in Europe, a statement which Chekhov thought was irreconcilable with such well-known facts as starvation, widespread prostitution among the women convicts (most of whom were never imprisoned), and the particularly brutal kind of corporal punishment inflicted on the convicts (male and female) often without the knowledge, and even contrary to the direct orders, of the governor of the island.

In the evening the little town was illuminated. Soldiers, settlers and convicts thronged the streets, in the garden of the governor's residence a band was playing, and a salute was fired from a gun, which blew up. In spite of these festivities, Chekhov did not notice any real signs of merriment. The people wandered about like shadows and were as silent as shadows. A prison, Chekhov reflected, remained a prison even in the light of fireworks, and music heard by a man who would never return home merely increased his unhappiness.

Chekhov paid another visit to the Governor-General before the latter left the island, and took down at his dictation a highly optimistic and quite astonishingly unrealistic account of the treat-ment of the prisoners, according to which 'no prisoner was ever put in chains, or had his head shaved, or was escorted under armed guard'. He then began his own investigation. The weather was certainly ideal for his work. The days were mostly bright and sunny and the evenings warm, with a glowing sunset, a dark-blue sea, and a white moon peeping out from behind the mountains. On such an evening he liked to go for a drive in the valley on the smooth road alongside of which ran a narrow-gauge rail track for trolleys. The further from Alexandrovsk he drove, the narrower did the valley become, and, as it grew darker, the burdocks, which grew to a gigantic size on the island, began to look like tropical plants and the mountains seemed to move closer and closer on all sides. In the distance he could see the glow of the forest fires. The moon rose. Suddenly a spectral figure appeared in the distance and seemed to be floating rapidly towards him. For a moment he was panic-stricken: the terror, which often overwhelmed him at night, seized him with even greater force. Then he discovered that it was only a convict in a white coat speeding along on a trolley which he pushed from behind with a large pole.

'Isn't it time we went back?' Chekhov asked his driver, still unable to shake off his feeling of terror.

The driver turned back towards the town, then he looked up at the mountains and the forest fires.

'It's an awful place to live in, sir,' he said. 'It's much better at home in Russia.'

6

Chekhov spent two months in the central part and one month in the southern part of the island (the northern part is uninhabitable because the ground there is permanently frozen). He got up at five o'clock in the morning and went to bed late at night. He took a census of the whole population, visited every settlement, went into every cottage, and spoke to everybody. For the census he used his own card-index system (he had the cards for it specially printed at the police headquarters). Each card had thirteen entries: the name of the settlement, the number of the house, the official status of the settler, his name, surname, etc., his age, religion, place of birth, the year of his arrival on the island, his main occupation, whether he was illiterate or not, whether he was married or single, whether he was in receipt of a government grant, and, finally, whether he suffered from any illness. In registering the children, Chekhov was interested to find out whether they were illegitimate or not and how many of them were adopted. The children knew everything about the sordid side of the life on the island, the hunting down and sometimes shooting of the runaway convicts, the hangman, the chains, the cat, and the 'cohabitants' (the official name given to the ex-convict who was permitted to choose one of the women convicts to live with him). In one settlement Chekhov came across a ten-year-old boy with a pale freckled face.

'What's your father's name?' he asked.

'Don't know,' the boy replied.

'What do you mean? You live with your father and you don't know his name? You ought to be ashamed of yourself.'

'He isn't my real father.'

'Oh? Why not?'

'He's my mother's cohabitant.'

'Is your mother a married woman or a widow?'

'She's a widow. She came here for her husband.'

'How do you mean—for her husband?'

'She killed him.'

'Do you remember your father?'

'No, I'm illegitimate. I was born in prison.'

All Sakhalin children were thin, pale and listless. They went about in rags and were always hungry. The women, who composed 11.5 per cent of the convict population, were considered important from the point of view of the colonisation of the island, for they were all of the child-bearing age. They were mostly sentenced to transportation for crimes of passion. 'I'm here for my husband', or 'I'm here for my mother-in-law', were the usual replies Chekhov received. Most of them were murderesses, the victims of love and family despotism. Even those of them who had been found guilty of arson or counterfeiting were victims of love, for it was their lovers who had induced them to commit their crimes. The pick of the women convicts usually went to Alexandrovsk where they first arrived. Some of them became servants of local officials, others were placed in what Chekhov called 'the harems' of the prison warders and clerks, but most were distributed among the wealthier ex-convict settlers. Few of them ever got married because either they or the settlers were already married. A woman convict, Chekhov discovered, was regarded by the authorities in quite a special way: she was both a human being and a creature whose position was even lower than that of a domestic animal. The governor of the island, addressing a group of settlers in Chekhov's presence, said: 'I shall see that you get your fair share of women.' And an official once said to Chekhov: 'It is a pity they send us the women in the autumn and not in the spring. In winter a woman has nothing to do and she is only a burden to the peasant. That is why some farmers are so unwilling to take a woman in the autumn.' So, Chekhov reflected, people talked of horses when fodder happened to be expensive in winter. 'Human dignity', he wrote in his book *Sakhalin*, 'and a woman's natural feelings of modesty and shame are not taken into consideration at all; it is taken for granted that all that has been destroyed in a woman convict by her disgrace or, at any rate, during the time she spent in the different prisons on her way to Sakhalin.' On the other hand, many a woman convict told Chekhov that her life with one of the settlers was much happier than her life with her husband, because, being free to leave her 'cohabitant', she was treated with more respect and consideration by him. But her 'freedom' to leave a settler, Chekhov found, was more often than not earned only after several doses of the birch, since the authorities frowned on such 'loose behaviour' because it was likely to interfere with their 'colonisation programme'.

'Because of the scarcity of women on the island', the Governor-General told Chekhov, 'the peasant has to plough, cook, milk his cow and mend his clothes himself, so that if he gets a woman he does his best not to lose her. Look how he dresses her up. The ex-convicts think a lot of their women.'

'Which does not prevent them from walking about with black eyes,' the governor of the island, who was present at the interview, remarked dryly.

The position of the 'free' women who accompanied their husbands to Sakhalin was, Chekhov discovered not without surprise, much worse than that of the women convicts, mainly because they did not receive any government grants. 'From constant starvation,' Chekhov wrote in *Sakhalin*, 'mutual recriminations over every morsel of bread and the certainty that things would not improve in the future, the free woman makes up her mind that delicate feelings are out of place in Sakhalin and goes to earn five or twenty copecks, as one of them told me, "by my body". Her husband, too, gets hardened and all that does not seem to be of any importance to him. As soon as one of his daughters reaches the age of fourteen or fifteen she, too, is put into circulation; their mothers trade with them at home or give them to rich settlers or prison warders as mistresses. And that happens the more easily since the free woman has nothing to do all day.' Chekhov was shown a path leading from a settlement to one of the Sakhalin prisons which was made by the hundreds of free and convict women who many years previously had gone regularly to sell themselves to the convicts for a few coppers. That path, he noticed, was still in perfect condition.

Chekhov was as thorough and conscientious in his investigation of the Sakhalin prisons as in his inspection of the settlements. He was present at the punishment of a prisoner with ninety strokes of the cat, for, though he knew that such a scene would haunt him for days (for three nights, in fact, he dreamt of the hangman and the block), he overcame his own feelings of horror and disgust in order to be able to study the effect of such a punishment on those who inflicted it even more than on the prisoner himself.

'Corporal punishment', Chekhov summed up his impression ot tne flogging in *Sakhalin*, 'has a coarsening and brutalising effect not only on the prisoner but also on those who are present at its administration. Even educated people are not immune. At least I did not notice that

the attitude to flogging of officials with university education was any
different from that of army orderlies or those who graduated from
military or theological colleges. Some of them get so used to the cat·
and the birch and become so coarsened that in the end they even
derive enjoyment from a flogging.'

The remarkable fact Chekhov established after a thorough investigation of the way in which corporal punishment was administered in
the Sakhalin prisons was that the governor of the island himself knew
very little about it. General Konotovich was a humane but ineffectual
man who refused to confirm any punishment by the birch or the cat.
His subordinates, however, paid little attention to his orders and the
prison governors accepted birching as a regular practice, while the
warders made money by blackmailing the richer convicts, who were
birched every time they refused to pay up.

Chekhov was not deceived by the fine sentiments of the Governor-
General—he never took anything for granted—and during the two
months he spent in Central Sakhalin he saw, as he wrote to Suvorin on
September 11th, *everything*. 'The question is,' he wrote, 'not *what* I
saw, but *how* I saw.' His visit to Dui prison, where he saw the convicts
who were chained to iron wheel-barrows, had convinced him that not
only the convicts, but also the Russian Government, were shamelessly
cheated by the owners of the coal mines, who got all the benefits of
forced labour without carrying out their contractual obligations. He
realised the futility of the administration's efforts to colonise the island
in the same way as Australia had been colonised, for it completely dis-
regarded the natural resources of the island, such as its deposits of cual
or its fishing industry, and concentrated on turning it into an agricultural colony for which its soil was not suited. But what interested him
above all was the human problem. How, for instance, did Tolstoy's
theory of non-resistance to evil stand up to the realities of Sakhalin?
Did the convicts' non-resistance to the evil of flogging or forced
labour or blackmail or prostitution transform them or those who were
responsible for those things into better men? It did nothing of the sort.
On the contrary, it turned them into bigger brutes than they had been
before. And yet if there was anything in the doctrine of non-resistance
to evil, Sakhalin was the place where its beneficent results ought to
have been apparent to everybody.

One result of his visit to Sakhalin was, therefore, his complete
renunciation of Tolstoy's teachings as false to life and human experience. But there was another even more important result. The
question that presented itself to him was not only what was to be done

to prevent human beings from being turned into beasts, but the much more personal one of what was he as a writer to do to achieve the 'serious' purpose of art of bringing about a change of heart in man. He had known long before he set foot on Sakhalin of the atrocities committed there in the name of justice, but the three months he spent on the island showed him that there was all the difference in the world between knowing a thing objectively and feeling it subjectively. Sakhalin had taught him the difference between an emotional experience and an intellectual attitude. It was only the former that was liable so to affect a man's views as to change his whole outlook on life. The serious purpose of a work of art was not to preach higher moral standards but to awaken in the reader or spectator a realisation of the cruelties and injustices of his own life by evoking in him the same feelings, both good and bad, that animated the characters in a story or a play. It was therefore the art of evocation, the art of bringing about a catharsis through a powerful emotional experience, that from now on became one of the great aims of Chekhov as a writer. And in the final achievement of that aim his visit to Sakhalin had played a vital part.

7

Chekhov left Central Sakhalin on September 10th, but his work was already done and he spent a great deal of his time in the southern part of the island (which was only ceded to Japan after the Russo-Japanese war) on walks and picnics. He left on board the *Baykal*, which sailed from Alexandrovsk at nine o'clock in the evening. Standing in the stern of the boat, he bade a last farewell to the sombre little world guarded by the Three Brothers, which in the darkness reminded him of three black monks, listening to the roar of the breakers which drowned the noise of the boat's engines. A little later he saw the lights of the dreaded Voyevod prison, and then the lights of Dui. Soon Central Sakhalin had vanished from sight, and he had a curious feeling as though all he had seen was a bad dream.

He went down to the saloon feeling ill at ease, but, as had happened to him often before, a chance meeting soon dispelled his gloom. For among the passengers on the boat was the wife of a naval officer who was returning to Vladivostok, which she had left because of a cholera scare. The lady possessed a most enviable disposition: she would burst into peals of gay laughter on the slightest provocation. It was just what Chekhov needed so badly. Soon he as well as a Japanese businessman and a Russian priest, whom he also found in the saloon, were convulsed with laughter. 'Never at any other time', Chekhov wrote in describing that scene, 'had there been so much laughter in the Gulf of Tartary. Next morning the priest, the Japanese businessman, the naval officer's wife and I met on the deck for a talk. Again there was laughter, and all that was needed was that the whales should thrust their snouts out of the water and, looking at us, start laughing, too.'

The weather was sunny and warm. Through his binoculars Chekhov could clearly see the woods and the grass on top of the cliffs of the still unexplored and uninhabited part of Sakhalin. On September 12th the *Baykal* entered the bay of Aniva, formed by the two projecting tongues of land at the southern extremity of the island, and cast anchor off Korsakov Post, the administrative centre of southern Sakhalin. Chekhov spent only a month there, during which he visited most of the settlements and inspected the prisons.

On the whole, he found that, in spite of their gravity, the crimes committed by the convicts were rather ordinary and uninteresting. He had only met two murderers who seemed 'original'. In central Sakhalin there was a convict named Kislyakov, who had helped him with the census, a regimental clerk, who had murdered his wife with a hammer and then given himself up to the police. Kislyakov told Chekhov that his wife had been a very beautiful woman and that he was very much in love with her. But one day they quarrelled and he vowed before an icon to kill her. Since that day, and to the very day of the murder, an unseen power kept whispering in his ear, 'Kill her! Kill her!' His work in prison consisted of making little wooden sticks, but he found even that too hard an occupation and hired another convict to do it for him, while he himself 'gave lessons', that is, did nothing at all. He was very fond of talking and philosophising. 'Where there are fleas, there are also children,' he used to repeat in a sugary baritone voice every time he saw children. When Chekhov was asked in his presence why he was taking a census, Kislyakov replied, 'To send you all to the moon. Do you know where the moon is?' And when one evening he and Chekhov were returning to Alexandrovsk, he suddenly blurted out, 'Revenge is a most honourable thing.'

In southern Sakhalin Chekhov met a tall, spare, venerable-looking man with a long beard, who was employed as a clerk at the police headquarters. His name was Pishchikov. He, too, was serving a life sentence for the murder of his wife. The motive of the murder was jealousy. Pishchikov's wife, a young, educated woman, had been friendly with a Turkish prisoner of war before her marriage. Pishchikov had known all about it. Indeed, it was he who had carried the girl's letters to the Turk and helped to arrange their meetings. After the Turk had gone home, the girl became attached to Pishchikov because he had been so kind to her and eventually married him. And it was only when she was about to give birth to their fifth child that he was overcome by a sudden murderous fit of jealousy and flogged her to death.

Pishchikov was an extremely obliging and courteous man. He was very conscientious about his work, but very reserved and self-centred. Chekhov paid a call on him, but he was out at the time. He lived in a small room, which he kept very tidy. His bed was meticulously clean and covered with a red woollen blanket. Over the bed hung a framed portrait of a woman, probably of his wife.

Sakhalin certainly provided Chekhov with a unique opportunity of studying human nature in its worst as well as in its best manifestations. Most of the officials on the island he found both callous and unscrupulous. In their treatment of subordinates they did not seem to recognise anything except blows, the birch and foul language, while in the presence of their superiors they were eager to show how well educated and even 'liberal' they were. One day Chekhov was having lunch with an official, a university man, in a particularly picturesque part of southern Sakhalin. An old convict, the caretaker and gardener of the place, was waiting on them at the table, and when he made some trifling blunder the official called him a fool. Chekhov glanced at the inoffensive old man and reflected bitterly that all the educated Russian had so far succeeded in doing about prison reform was to reduce the prisoners to the condition of serfs.

At the same time, Chekhov found not a few intelligent and humane people among the officials, which he thought to be a sufficient guarantee that there could be no question of a return to the conditions described by Dostoevsky in *The House of the Dead*. During his stay on the island, for instance, a prison governor risked his life to save a convict who had been carried out to sea in a storm. Generally speaking, any act of crying injustice and inhumanity was sooner or later exposed. Among the convicts Chekhov observed the prevalence of the vices and perversions that were usually found among people who were deprived of their freedom and forced to live in crowded and unhealthy surroundings. A particularly obnoxious practice was the scribbling or scratching of obscene words on walls, fences and benches. What amazed Chekhov was that even old men with one foot in the grave, as they told him, found a curious kind of release from their hopeless existence in uttering a string of obscenities. On Sakhalin even the love-letters, Chekhov discovered, were disgusting.

He introduced, as one of the Sakhalin officials afterwards expressed it, 'something new, something that was not at all like what we were used to', into the brutish life of the convict island. His sympathy and loving-kindness had an instantaneous effect on those he met, whether at a dinner, or in a settlement, or in a prison, as many letters he received from Sakhalin on his return to Moscow testify. For some of the settlers he even provided material help, little as he could afford it. He bought a calf for one of the ex-convicts, who wrote to him a year later: 'Looking at the heifer which is still growing and which is worth forty roubles today, I thank you daily from the bottom of my heart and I shall always offer up prayers to God for you.'

In Korsakov Chekhov paid a visit to the Japanese consul, whom he found to be an extremely urbane and well-read man. He went three times from Korsakov to Nai-Buchi, a settlement on the shores of the Pacific. While he was there a boat with six American whalemen, whose ship had been wrecked in a storm, was washed ashore. The Americans returned with Chekhov, where they embarked with him on board the Russian boat *Petersburg* for Vladivostok.

In his last letter home from Korsakov, Chekhov wrote: 'I am tired of Sakhalin. I have spent three months there and I saw no one except convicts or people who only talked of convicts, prisons and the cat. It is a dreary life. I hope to leave for Japan soon and from there for India. . . . On Sakhalin, from the very day of my arrival the weather has been sunny and warm; at present light cold and hoar frost occur in the mornings, there is snow on one of the mountains, but the earth is still green, the leaves have not fallen from the trees, and everything is perfect just as in the country in May. So you see, Sakhalin isn't such a bad place after all! . . . I am well except for attacks of dizziness accompanied by dimness of sight and after each attack I have a splitting headache. I had such an attack yesterday and today my head aches and I feel a heaviness in my whole body. I have also been suffering from haemorrhoids.'

Chekhov did not go to Japan after all, because of a cholera epidemic there, but went straight to Vladivostok. This is his own description of his journey home in a letter to Suvorin: 'I stopped at Vladivostok. About the Maritime Province and generally about our Far East coast with its fleets, problems and Pacific Ocean dreams I can only say one thing: terrible poverty! Poverty, ignorance and utter ineptitude which would make anyone yield to despair. Out of every hundred men

ninety-nine are thieves who are a disgrace to the Russian name. The
first foreign port we stopped at was Hong Kong. A beautiful bay and
such sea traffic as I never saw even on pictures. After leaving Hong
Kong, our boat began to roll. She was sailing without ballast and sometimes she had a list of 38 degrees, so that we were afraid that she might
capsize. I was not sea-sick, and this discovery gave me a pleasant
surprise. On the way to Singapore we buried two men at sea.[1] When
you watch a dead man, wrapped in sail cloth, turn a somersault before
hitting the water, and when you remember that the sea is over a mile
deep, you become frightened and for some obscure reason you begin
to think that you, too, will die and be thrown into the sea. . . . I remember very little of Singapore, for when we passed it I was in a very
melancholy mood and felt like crying. Then we arrived in Ceylon. In
that paradise I travelled more than a hundred miles by rail and had my
fill of palm groves and bronze women.'

It was in Ceylon, Michael records, that Chekhov 'received a de-
claration of love from a beautiful Indian woman in a palm grove'. This
statement is characteristic of the naïve, almost adolescent level of most
of Michael's reminiscences of his famous brother. In his letter to
Suvorin Chekhov described his affair with the Indian girl in quite
different terms. 'When I have children', he wrote, 'I shall say to them
not without pride: "Once in my life I made love to a black-eyed Indian
girl—and where? In a coconut grove on a moonlit night!" '

Chekhov summed up the impression of his journey in these words:
'The Lord's earth is beautiful. There is one thing, however, that is not
so beautiful, and that's us. How little justice there is in us, and how
little humility! How badly we understand the meaning of the word
patriotism! We, the papers tell us, love our country, but how do we
show this love of ours? Instead of knowledge—arrogance and im-
measurable conceit, instead of honest work—laziness and filth. We
have no sense of justice and our conception of honour goes no further
than "the honour of the uniform", a uniform which is too often to be
seen in the docks of our courtrooms. We must work, and the rest can
go to the devil. And the main thing is—we must be just, for if we are
just the rest will come of itself.'

[1] The incident is described by Chekhov in his story *Gusev*, published in *New Times* on
December 25th.

Part Five

YEARS OF MATURITY

Chekhov returned to Moscow on December 8th, 1890. He had travelled from Vladivostok by way of Odessa in the company of a young midshipman, the son of an acquaintance of his, Baroness Ixul von Hildebang, a publisher of cheap 'people's editions' of the Russian classics, and a Siberian bishop who stayed with him for a time in his new flat in a 'good' residential quarter of Moscow into which his family had moved during his absence. The first thing he did on his return was to organise a collection of books for the Sakhalin schools which, as he wrote to a correspondent, existed 'only on paper', the children receiving all their education from their prison environment. He wanted to leave for Petersburg immediately, for he hoped to meet a number of influential people there who might help him in his educational work; but the now inevitable recurrence of his illness in an acute form kept him in Moscow for a month. He was running a high temperature, coughing, and, what really worried him, suffering from heart attacks. 'Ever since I returned home', he wrote to Leykin, 'I have been suffering from the so-called intermittent activity of the heart: every minute my heart stops beating for a few seconds and I feel as though there were a rubber ball in my chest. This happens every evening; in the mornings it is not so bad.' His heart attacks were accompanied by a general feeling of exhaustion and indifference. He decided to take a short rest in the country, and his stay with the Kisselevs in Babkino for about a week brought about the expected relief.

From Sakhalin Chekhov brought a large number of documents, which he intended to use for his book on the convict island as well as several presents from convicts, including plaster of Paris figures and a little copper handbell. In Ceylon he bought two mongooses, which were a great success in his household at first, though later on their inquisitiveness and fondness for breaking crockery proved too much even for so great an animal lover as Chekhov, who was forced to dispose of them to the Moscow Zoo.

'The Christmas holidays', Chekhov wrote to Suvorin, 'I couldn't have spent worse. First of all, there were my heart attacks; secondly, my brother Ivan arrived on a visit and fell ill with typhoid fever;

thirdly, life in Moscow after my Sakhalin labours and the tropics appears so boring and commonplace to me that I feel like screaming; fourthly, the need of earning money interferes with my book on Sakhalin; fifthly, I am getting thoroughly tired of my Moscow friends and acquaintances, and so on.' He left for Petersburg on January 7th, but during his short stay in Moscow he did manage to finish his story *Gusev*, 'conceived', as he wrote to Suvorin, 'on Ceylon' (he had dated it: Colombo, November 12th).

Before he left for Petersburg, Chekhov learnt that Pleshcheyev had inherited a fortune of two million. 'Pleshcheyev's figure with his two million inheritance appears comic to me,' he wrote to Suvorin. 'What the hell does he want them for? To smoke cigars, eat fifty pastries a day and drink soda water three roubles a day should be sufficient.' But Pleshcheyev's inheritance had a curious sequel. Alexander wrote to Chekhov on December 30th that the story that went the rounds in Petersburg literary circles was that he was thinking of marrying Pleshcheyev's daughter. The literary fraternity in Petersburg certainly did not miss a single chance of discrediting Chekhov, whose rise to fame his fellow-writers could never forgive him. 'I am surrounded by an atmosphere of ill-will, very indefinite and utterly incomprehensible to me,' he wrote to Mary on January 14th from Petersburg. 'They invite me to dinners and pour vulgar dithyrambs into my ears and at the same time they are ready to devour me. Why? Goodness knows. If I had shot myself, I should have given great pleasure to nine-tenths of my friends and admirers. And what a petty way they have of expressing their petty feelings! Burenin abuses me in an article,[1] though it is against all the rules for a paper to abuse its own contributors; Maslov (Bezhetsky) refuses to come to Suvorin to dinner; Leontyev spreads all the slanderous stories that are invented about me, and so on. All this is terribly stupid and boring. They are not people, but a kind of fungoid growth.'

But his reputation was so firmly established that they all fawned on him. Even Grigorovich hastened to pay him a visit to save something from the wreck of their old friendship. 'Grigorovich came to see me yesterday,' Chekhov wrote to Mary in the same letter. 'He kissed me, told lies and kept asking me about Japanese women.'

He spent three weeks in Petersburg, paying calls on all sorts of influential people whom he tried to interest in his scheme to help the Sakhalin children. 'I am terribly tired,' he wrote to his brother Ivan

---

[1] Burenin, the chief columnist of *New Times*, published an article on January 11th in which he referred to Chekhov as 'a mediocre writer', adding that 'such mediocrities, losing the ability to look straight at life, run off to Siberia and from Siberia to Sakhalin'.

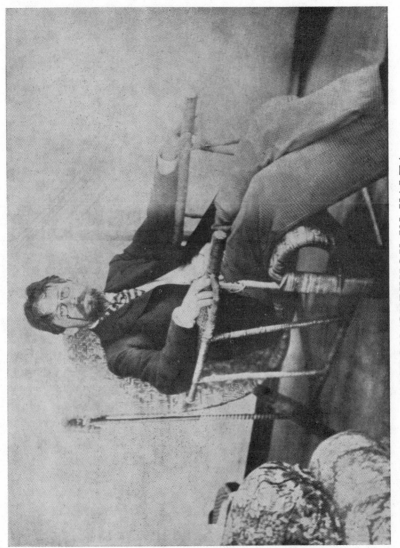

ANTON CHEKHOV IN YALTA

on January 27th. 'All day long from 11 a.m. to 4 a.m. I am on my feet; my room is crowded with friends and acquaintances. My journey to Sakhalin has assumed an importance which I never expected: State Councillors and Regular State Councillors come to see me. They are all waiting for my book and prophesying its success, but I have no time to write!' And to his sister he wrote earlier: 'I am as tired as a ballerina after five acts and eight scenes. Dinners, letters I am too lazy to answer, conversations and all sorts of nonsense.' Still, he found time to go to the theatre, have a talk to Chaykovsky; go to Svobodin's birthday party, where he drank more than he should, buy birthday presents for Alexander's boy Anton, and listen to Suvorin's interminable talk. He bought many books for the Sakhalin schools and collected many more from the Petersburg publishers and writers. His own books were selling well. He got four hundred roubles from Suvorin, who promised to give him more in May when the fifth editions of *In the Twilight* and *Stories* were to be published. He also arranged with Leykin for the publication of a revised second edition of *Motley Stories*.

On his return to Moscow on January 30th he got ready the second edition of *Motley Stories*, 'throwing overboard', as he wrote to Suvorin, more than twenty stories and including six stories from *Innocent Speeches* and one story, *The First Class Passenger*, published four years earlier in *New Times*. He then sat down to write his first challenge to Tolstoyan philosophy and, more specifically, to *The Kreutzer Sonata*, his long story *The Duel*. But the approach of spring made him feel restless. He went off for a few days to Babkino (soon after the first performance of his one-act comedy *The Proposal*, written in November 1888, on the stage of the Maly Theatre on February 20th). But when he returned to Moscow he found that he could not get on with *The Duel*. His restlessness increased and there was a strange touch of sadness about it: he felt an irresistible urge to go back to Petersburg, as though there was someone he had forgotten to see, or perhaps deliberately avoided seeing, when he was there a short while ago. On March 5th he received an invitation from Suvorin to go abroad with him, and he made up his mind at once to accept it. He was running away again, and in the very excitement with which he accepted Suvorin's invitation one can sense the tension under which he had been labouring all the time. 'My heart leaps for joy,' he wrote. 'Not to go now would be an act of folly on my part, for when shall I get such a chance again?' And to the utter astonishment and consternation of his family he went off on his first trip to Europe, though only a few days earlier he had been planning to visit Ivan at his new school in the country. On March 13th he was in Petersburg again, and five days later he was already in the train with Suvorin and his eldest son Alexey, bound for Vienna.

In Petersburg he paid a visit to an exhibition of Levitan's paintings. 'Levitan', he wrote to Mary, 'is celebrating the birthday of his magnificent Muse. His painting, "A Haven of Rest", has created a sensation.' He had also been to see Eleonora Duse as Cleopatra in Shakespeare's *Antony and Cleopatra*. 'I have just been to see the Italian actress Duse in Shakespeare's *Antony and Cleopatra*,' he wrote to Mary on March 17th. 'I don't understand Italian, but she played so well that it seemed to me that I understood every word. A remarkable actress. I have never seen any actress like her before.'

2

Chekhov left Petersburg on March 18th and arrived in Vienna at four o'clock in the afternoon on the following day. His first impression of a western European country is summed up in the following significant phrase in his letter home from Vienna on March 20th: 'It seems strange that here you can read everything and talk about anything you like.' He thought the Vienna of the last decade of the nineteenth century one of the most beautiful cities he had ever seen. 'The streets here', he wrote in the same letter, 'are wide and elegantly paved, there are lots of boulevards and squares, the houses are all of six or seven stories and the shops are not shops but a dream! There are milliards of cravats alone. And what amazing things in bronze, porcelain and leather! The churches are enormous, but they do not oppress you by their heaviness; they caress your eyes because they look as if they had been woven in lace. The cathedral of St. Stephen and the Votiv-Kirche are especially lovely. They are not buildings but wedding-cakes. The Parliament, the Town Hall and the University are magnificent. Everything is splendid, and it was only yesterday that I realised that architecture is an art. In Vienna this art is not found here and there as with us, but stretches for miles and miles.' Even the Vienna cabs were not cabs but sumptuous carriages, and as for the cabbies, they were 'well-dressed dandies in top-hats who read newspapers on their boxes'. The only criticism Chekhov had to make was that they charged him for his rolls at the restaurants. The Vienna women were all 'beautiful and elegant'. Everything, in fact, was 'devilishly elegant'.

This curiously uncritical attitude, which was so unlike Chekhov, shows in what a state of high nervous tension he was and how guilty he felt to have left his family with practically no money. 'I am ashamed', he wrote home, 'to have abandoned you again. But never mind! I shall soon be back and I shan't leave you again for a whole year.' And in one of his letters from Venice he even went so far as to ask his father to forgive him for not having said goodbye to him before he left for his trip abroad.

It was Venice that made the greatest impression on Chekhov. It was there that he felt himself in a world of true romance.

'One thing I will say,' he wrote to his brother Ivan on March 24th, 'never in my life have I seen a city more remarkable than Venice. It is full of enchantment, radiance and the joy of life. Instead of streets and lanes there are canals, instead of cabs—gondolas; the architecture is amazing, and there isn't a place which is not of historic or artistic interest. You sail in a gondola and see the Palace of the Doges, the little house where Desdemona lived, the houses of famous artists. . . . And the churches are full of the most wonderful paintings and sculptures. In short, pure enchantment. . . .

'All day long', Chekhov continued, 'I sit in a gondola and sail along the streets or wander about in the square of St. Mark's. The square is as clean and smooth as a parquet floor, and the church itself defies all description. I feel the amazing beauty of it all and revel in it. . . .

'Merezhkovsky, whom I met here, is beside himself with enthusiasm. It is not difficult for a poor and humble Russian to go off his head in this world of beauty, riches and freedom. One would like to stay here for ever; and when you stand in a church and listen to the organ you want to become a Catholic. . . . The tombs of Canova and Titian are magnificent. Here great artists are buried like kings in churches; here art is not held in contempt as it is in Russia.'

Chekhov also paid a visit to the famous Venice glass-works. 'Your bottles', he wrote to Ivan, whose school was attached to a glass factory, 'are such monstrosities compared with the bottles they make here that it makes me sick to think of them.'

His excitement is perhaps best conveyed in the following short letter he wrote to Maria Kisselev on March 25th: 'I am in Venice. Put me in a lunatic asylum. Gondolas, the square of St. Mark's, water, stars, pretty Italian women, evening serenades, mandolines, Falernian wine—in short, it's all over with me! The ghost of beautiful Desdemona sends its smile to the chairman of the agricultural board [Maria Kisselev's husband]. Antonio.'

His letters home are written in the same vein of childish ecstasy: the stars, the canals, the gondolas and the music ravished his soul so that he almost felt like crying. As a postscript he added that the picturesque road from Vienna to Venice did not impress him. 'The mountains, chasms, snow-capped peaks I saw in the Caucasus and Ceylon are much more impressive than they are here,' he wrote.

Fortunately, it started pouring with rain on March 26th and Chekhov's enthusiasm for *Venezia la bella* somewhat abated. A saner outlook asserted itself. He went to see Titian's *Madonna*, and the first note of criticism crept in: he thought it a pity that the Italians showed so little discrimination and hung fine pictures like that alongside of others of less lasting value. He next visited Bologna, where he saw Raphael's *Cecilia*, and Florence, where the *Venus of Medici's* ample waist made him think how ugly she would have looked in a modern dress. In Rome the weather was still bad. He visited the Vatican and St. Peter's and returned to his hotel so tired that his feet felt as if they were stuffed with cottonwool. 'At dinner at my hotel', he wrote to Maria Kisselev on April 1st, 'two Dutch girls sat opposite me: one looked like Pushkin's Tatyana and the other like her sister Olga. I kept looking at them all through dinner and imagined a little white house with a tower, excellent butter, wonderful Dutch cheese, Dutch herrings, a venerable old pastor, a sedate teacher—and I felt like marrying a Dutch girl and being painted with her outside our clean little house.

'I saw everything,' he went on. 'But', he added, his excitement entirely worn off, 'just now I feel tired and I wish I could have some cabbage soup with buckwheat porridge. Venice fascinated me and I nearly went off my head there, but when I left bad weather and Baedeker took her place.' The thing that astonished him in Rome was the cheapness of ties. 'Ties', he wrote to Maria Kisselev, 'are remarkably cheap here. So frightfully cheap that I may even start eating them. One franc a pair.'

In Naples, where he arrived on April 4th, Chekhov and his two companions stayed at a harbour hotel, from where they had an excellent view of the sea, Vesuvius, Capri and Sorrento. In the morning they rode up a mountain to the monastery of St. Martini, and the magnificent view reminded him of the view he saw from a railway carriage in Hong Kong. He liked the Naples shops almost as well as the shops in Vienna. On the morning of April 6th he visited Pompeii and was surprised at the ability of the ancient Romans to combine simplicity with comfort and beauty. Then he climbed Vesuvius. 'It was the excellent red wine I had at lunch that made me decide to go up Vesuvius,' he wrote home on April 7th. 'We reached the foot of the mountain on horseback. As a consequence certain parts of my body feel as though I had been in the Third Department and been given the cat there. What a torture it is to climb Vesuvius! Ashes, mountains of lava, congealed waves of molten minerals, and every kind of filthiness. You go forward one step and back half a step. Your heels ache, your chest is heavy. You walk, walk and walk, but it is still far from the top. . . . The climb began at half past two and ended at six. I stood at the edge of the crater. The ground all round me was covered with a layer of brimstone that never stopped smoking. From the crater came a white, stinking smoke, sparks and red-hot stones were flying about, and beneath the smoke Satan lay and snored. There was a strange jumble of sounds: you could hear the waves breaking against a rocky shore, peals of thunder, the rumble of a train, and the clatter of wooden planks. It was very terrifying and at the same time I was overcome by a desire to jump down the crater. Now I believe in hell. . . . The descent was as difficult as the ascent. I sank up to my knees in ashes and got terribly tired. I rode back to our hotel through little villages and holiday resorts; there was a delicious fragrance in the air and the moon was shining.'

He was now beginning to be worried by the expense of his journey, for the Suvorins stopped at the most expensive hotels and dined at the most expensive restaurants. If he had travelled alone, he reflected ruefully, the trip would have cost him three hundred roubles, whereas now he already owed Suvorin over a thousand. He decided to give up the idea of buying a cottage in the Ukraine for his 'climatic station'. 'I have postponed the purchase of the cottage till 1895,' he wrote to Natasha Lintaryov on April 11th. 'I have been spending so much money that I shall soon ask you to lend me twenty copecks.'

From Naples Chekhov and his companions went to Nice, where his first experience of the roulette table cost him eight francs. He also went to the theatre to see a French operetta. 'The baritone', he wrote home, 'made his bed and put a chamberpot under it; the audience roared with laughter.' He next paid a visit to Monte Carlo, which, he thought, was very like 'a very beautiful thieves' kitchen'. He lost forty francs at the roulette table and decided to go a second time to try his luck. 'The game is terribly exciting,' he wrote home on April 15th. 'After my first visit Suvorin junior and I started thinking and thinking and in the end we invented a system which we were sure could not possibly fail. We went to Monte Carlo yesterday, taking five hundred francs each. The very first time I won two gold pieces, then more and more, till my waistcoat pockets were bulging with gold. Never before did I see so much gold and silver. We started playing at five o'clock and by ten o'clock I did not have one franc left in my pocket. The only thing I still had left was the pleasant thought of my return-ticket to Nice. That's how it is, ladies and gentlemen. I expect you will say, "What a disgusting way to behave! We're so hard up and he's gambling away all his money there!" You're absolutely right, and I give you permission to cut my throat when I return home. Personally, however, I'm completely satisfied with myself. At least I shall now be able to tell my grandchildren that I've played at roulette and am familiar with the feelings aroused by that game.

'Near the casino with the roulette tables', he went on, 'there is another roulette—the restaurants. They fleece you there terribly, but the food is excellent. Every portion is a marvellous composition before which one must kneel reverently, but which one must never attempt to eat. Each little bit is richly garnished with artichokes, truffles and all sorts of nightingales' tongues. . . . And, dear Lord, how contemptible and horrible this life with its artichokes, palms and the scent of orange blossoms is! I love luxury and riches, but the roulette luxury here creates the impression of a water-closet luxury. There is something in the air which is an affront to your feeling of decency and which makes everything so cheap—nature, the murmur of the waves, the moon.'

It was only Venice that he remembered with pleasure. He was, in fact, tired of his whole trip. He was tired of his luncheons and dinners. He was tired of sleeping in hotels. 'Siberia,' he wrote home from Nice on April 17th, 'where travellers do not lunch, dine or sleep, is much better in this respect. There you don't eat, but you feel as if you had a pair of wings.'

Chekhov spent Easter in Paris. He arrived there at twelve o'clock on Friday, April 19th (May 1st, according to the new style), and went immediately to the World Exhibition. But he only saw the Eiffel Tower, as all the exhibition buildings were occupied by the military in expectation of disturbances in connexion with the May Day demonstrations. The police were dispersing the large crowds in the streets. Chekhov stood watching a crowd running away when he felt himself grabbed from behind by a policeman and pushed roughly on to the pavement. Five days later he went to the Chamber of Deputies to hear a statement by the Minister of the Interior on the serious labour disturbances in Fourmies, where many workers were killed and injured.

By that time he was getting thoroughly tired of his tour. Before he left Moscow his pince-nez had got broken and he was beginning to find his short-sightedness a real hindrance to his enjoyment of Paris. He went to the Salon exhibition and could not see half of the pictures. He found, however, that, compared to the French landscape painters, Levitan was a king. He left Paris, where he met Pleshcheyev, whose offer of a loan he declined, on April 28th (May 11th), having seen all there was to see, even, he wrote to a correspondent, 'naked women'. In his absence his family had taken a summer cottage near Alexin in the Kaluga province, where Michael had a job as a tax assessor. On May 3rd he joined them there.

3

In the small four-roomed cottage Michael had rented at the edge of a birchwood near the little town of Alexin, Chekhov felt as if he were confined in a fortress. 'My family is large,' he wrote to Suvorin, 'and I, who live by my pen, am like a crawfish who has been put in a basket with other crawfish: I feel cramped for space. But for that I should have felt well contented.' His family, in fact, was larger than ever, for now he had his father with him, too. Pavel, who was sixty-seven at the time, had left his job at Gavrilov's warehouse at last and became a regular member of Chekhov's family. Occasionally, more from habit than anything else, he would squabble with his wife, or, what was worse, would express so outrageous an opinion that Chekhov, whose illness had made him very irritable, would lose patience with him. It was not surprising, therefore, that Chekhov should have felt unhappy in the cottage, especially as the cold weather forced him to stay indoors, where there was hardly room to move. In spite of all these inconveniences, he did his best to concentrate on his work, devoting three days a week to his book on Sakhalin, two days to writing a novel (the novel is only mentioned once in his correspondence so that he must have given it up very soon), and one day to what he called 'smaller things'. He had evidently decided to put off his work on *The Duel* for the time being. But there was something wrong with him. He lost all zest in life. 'I'm sick of life,' he wrote to Suvorin. At first he accepted Suvorin's explanation that all he wanted was something to engage his interest, something that would bring 'balm' to his soul, though he gave it, not unintentionally perhaps, a literary twist. 'Yes,' he wrote to Suvorin on May 10th, 'you are right, my soul does want balm. I feel

like reading something serious, and all the recent Russian criticism
does not satisfy me. I wish I could read something new about Pushkin
or Tolstoy—that would have been real balm for my idle mind.' He was
envious of Michael, who had just published a translation of a story by
Ouida. 'Why don't I know foreign languages?' he wrote to Suvorin.
'It seems to me that I'd have made an excellent translator; when I read
translations, I keep transposing and changing the words in my mind
and I get something light and ethereal like lace.'

He had also his usual money worries. He owed Suvorin eight
hundred roubles for his trip abroad and two hundred roubles for his
Moscow flat. The summer cottage cost him another 90 roubles, and all
he got on his return to Moscow was three hundred roubles from the
Society of Playwrights, a blessed though quite inadequate windfall,
most of which were royalties from his *Bear*.

But Chekhov had always been lucky with his summer holidays, and
this time, too, his luck held. He invited Levitan and Lydia Mizinov
to visit him at the cottage. They travelled by boat and struck up an
acquaintance with a passenger, a young landowner, whose estate was
only a few miles from Chekhov's cottage. Learning from them that
Chekhov lived so near, Kolossovsky (that was the name of the landowner) sent two carriages to the cottage with an invitation to Chekhov
and his family to visit his estate at Bogimovo. His invitation was
gratefully accepted, and Chekhov was pleased to find that Bogimovo
was a most charming old country house with a magnificent park, long
lime-tree avenues, ponds, a small river, and a tumbledown water-mill.
The rooms in the house were enormous. There was a drawing-room
with columns and a ballroom with a music gallery. And what was most
surprising of all, the top floor was to let for one hundred and sixty
roubles. Chekhov made up his mind at once to take it. He himself
occupied the large drawing-room with the columns. The sofa on which
he slept was of such vast dimensions that it could easily accommodate
twelve persons. He got up at five o'clock. ('When I am old', he wrote
to Suvorin, 'I shall get up at four o'clock. All my ancestors rose before
cockcrow. And I have noticed that people who get up early are usually
very fussy, so I expect that I, too, will be a very fussy and fidgety old
man'). After a cup of coffee, which Michael prepared for him, he would
sit down to write at the window-sill and not at the table, for he liked
to look out into the garden every now and then. He worked till
eleven o'clock and then went out for a walk into the woods to gather
mushrooms or to the ponds or the stream to fish or put in his creels.
At one o'clock he had lunch, Michael being called upon to show his

culinary talents by devising some specially appetising dish. After lunch he would usually have a nap, and then sit down to work till the evening. He had also many patients, who, as in Babkino, came to consult him from all over the countryside. 'Oh, how sick I am of my patients!' he wrote to Suvorin at the end of his stay at Bogimovo. 'A land-owner in the neighbourhood has a nervous breakdown and I am dragged down there in an old boneshaker. But most of all I am tired of the country women with their babies and the powders I have to weigh out for them.'

Before he had moved to Bogimovo, his mongoose ran off into the woods. 'My mongoose', he wrote to Suvorin on May 18th, 'has bolted into the woods and hasn't come back; I expect he must be dead by now.' But on June 3rd the mongoose was found, which gave Chekhov an opportunity to read Suvorin a lecture on the benefits of freedom: 'My mongoose has been found,' he wrote to Suvorin. 'A hunter with hounds found it in a stone quarry; but for a fissure in the quarry, the hounds would have torn it to pieces. It wandered about the woods for eighteen days. In spite of the climatic conditions which must have been terrible for him, he grew fat—such is the effect of freedom. Yes, sir, freedom is a great thing!' The mongoose, incidentally, showed its prowess one day in a fight with an adder, which Chekhov obligingly umpired.

Part of the Bogimovo mansion was occupied by other holiday-makers, with whom Chekhov got very friendly; one of them was Vladimir Wagner, a future professor of zoology, who was just then writing his doctorate thesis on spiders and whom Chekhov nicknamed 'the little spider'. They spent whole evenings together discussing questions like the survival of the fittest, natural selection, degeneration, and so on. It was Wagner's views that Chekhov put into the mouth of the naturalist von Koren in *The Duel*. Wagner lived in Bogimovo with his young wife and aunt. The other guests in the house were the landscape painter A.A. Kisselev and his family. Chekhov was, therefore, again in the familiar surroundings of decaying landed gentry forced to let part of their ancestral mansion to members of the professional classes.

It was a very hot summer and every day he went for a swim in the river. He also organised picnics in the woods. After one of these picnics, at three o'clock in the morning, he and Kolossovsky went for a drive. The horses bolted and overturned the landau, which was smashed to bits. Chekhov was thrown out, but fortunately got off with only a few scratches.

The symptoms of his illness appeared much earlier that year. Already in June he began coughing and suffering from fits of giddiness. 'In spite of the fact that my inside is full of dry and wet murmurs,' he wrote to Lydia Mizinov on June 12th, 'I bathe and go for walks, but I am still alive.' And a week later: 'I am coughing and seeing spots before my eyes, but I am all right for all that.' On his return to Moscow in September he went so far as to admit to Suvorin that he was sorry he had not gone to Theodosia, as he was losing weight. But even in summer his family, and especially his mother, must have realised that he had T.B. Chekhov was quick to detect the reason for his mother's uneasiness. His illness had made him very irritable, and his mother's hidden fears increased his irritation. Almost daily there were angry scenes at table. His father's obtuseness and sanctimonious self-righteousness added fuel to the flames. 'Quarrels at table', he wrote on July 5th to Mary, who was visiting the Lintaryovs at the time, 'occur seldom as before: only at lunch and dinner.' It may well have been during one of these quarrels that a fortnight later Pavel had a slight apoplectic stroke.

Most of the day, however, Chekhov was shut up in his room, writing. He had to raise enough money to pay back his debt to Suvorin and have something over to pay his rent in town and the country and provide for the upkeep of his family. 'To improve my circumstances,' he wrote to Suvorin on August 6th, 'that is to say, to make them different or better, is quite impossible. There are sick people who are cured by a simple and drastic method, namely, "Arise and take up thy bed and walk." But I haven't the strength to take up my bed and go away, and therefore it's no use talking about it.'

In June he sent Suvorin his short story *Peasant Wives*, one of his most ruthless studies of a type of a sanctimonious bully and hypocrite. His insight into human nature had by then so deepened that he could dispense with the need of pointing a moral or using objectivity merely as an excuse for providing a photographic copy of reality. But he was not as successful in this integration of message and character in *The Duel*, his major work of 1891, serialised in *New Times* from October 22nd to November 27th. His main object in writing *The Duel* was to shatter Tolstoy's argument in *The Kreutzer Sonata* that the ideal of Christian love was incompatible with sexual love. Having completely shaken off Tolstoy's influence, he was now ready to challenge the main tenets of his teachings, beginning with his ideas of the relations between the sexes and (in the following year) his dogma of non-resistance to evil. 'Alas,' he wrote to Suvorin on August 30th, 'I shall never be a follower of Tolstoy! In women I first of all admire their beauty; and in human history—culture which finds expression in carpets, sprung carriages, and refinement of thought.' And more directly and incisively, commenting on Tolstoy's *Afterword* to *The Kreutzer Sonata* in his letter to Suvorin on September 8th: 'Tolstoy denies immortality to mankind, but, dear me, how much personal there is in all that! I read his *Afterword* the day before yesterday, and, say what you like, it is more stupid and more stifling than [Gogol's] *Letters to a Governor's Wife*, which I despise. The devil take the philosophy of the great men of this world! All great and wise men are despotic like generals, and discourteous and indelicate like generals, because they are quite sure that they won't be punished. Diogenes spat in men's beards, knowing very well that nothing would happen to him because of it; Tolstoy calls doctors blackguards and shows his utter ignorance when he discusses great problems, because he is the same Diogenes who will not be hauled off to a police station and whom the papers will not dare to abuse.[1] So to hell with the philosophy of the great men of this world! All of it, with its afterwords and letters to a governor's wife, is not worth one mare from *Kholstomer*.'

Chekhov's final break with Tolstoy's teachings could hardly have been more aptly expressed than in this preference for Tolstoy the artist who wrote the story of the horse Kholstomer to Tolstoy the moralist who wrote *The Kreutzer Sonata*. *The Duel*, though it is a much greater as well as a much more profound work than *The Kreutzer Sonata*, suffers from the same fault as Tolstoy's story that it is artistically unconvincing. The sudden reconciliation of its hero and heroine indeed bears a striking resemblance to the same *deus ex machina* device Chekhov had used in his Tolstoyan stories and particularly in the first version of *The Wood Demon*. That was, however, the last time the preacher in Chekhov got the better of the artist.

4

On his return from Bogimovo to Moscow in September 1891 Chekhov went through one of the worst mental and physical crises of his life. The atmosphere at home was getting more and more strained. He had moved to another flat in the same house, but it was not much

---

[1] Chekhov was wrong: in November 1891 the reactionary daily *Moscow Gazette* used the article on the famine, *A Fearful Problem*, which Tolstoy wrote for the London *Daily Telegraph*, to launch a vicious attack on Tolstoy accusing him of being a revolutionary, which might have had very serious consequences even for a man in his unassailable position.

larger than the old one and he still had his family on top of him. He had paid off his debts, but he still had not enough money to carry on. And now he had to cope not only with his mother but also with his father, both of whom were anxious that he should marry a rich girl and set up in practice and not waste his time in writing stories. They had always insisted that he should not sacrifice his profession to his scribbling, and the events had proved them right, for there he was again without a penny in his pocket worrying himself to death because he could not pay the rent. That sort of thing was getting on his nerves so much that he could stand it no longer. 'I must run away from home for at least a fortnight,' he wrote to Suvorin in October. 'From morning till night I am in a state of unendurable irritation. I feel as though someone were scraping my soul with a blunt knife, and outwardly this expresses itself in my going to bed as early as possible and my avoidance of conversations. Whatever I do seems to lead to nothing; everything seems to drop out of my hands.' Alexander, in one of his rare moments of insight, wrote to Chekhov at this time: 'What you miss is the tender care which only a woman can give to the man she loves.' And it was no doubt the great store of tenderness and affection in him that was turning sour for lack of an outlet. He had not yet trained himself to put up with his loneliness or to reconcile himself to a life with people who, though they were as much attached to him as he was to them, had not the slightest understanding of his thoughts and feelings and who even pitied him in their hearts for refusing to accept their own primitive ideas of right and wrong. And it was characteristic of him that he did not blame anyone but himself for everything. 'If I am a doctor,' he wrote to Suvorin a week after he had expressed his wish to run away from home, 'then I must have patients and a hospital; if I am a writer, I must live among the people and not on Little Dmitrovka Street with my mongoose. I must at least have some social and political life, however little, for this life within four walls without nature, people or a motherland, without health or appetite, is not a life but a kind of —— and nothing more.' He pegged away steadily at his Sakhalin book, but though he wrote and wrote, he did not seem to be getting any nearer to the end. 'The completion of this work', he wrote to a correspondent, 'seems as remote to me as the time when all men will become chaste in accordance with the prescription of Pozdnyshev [the hero of *The Kreutzer Sonata*].'

It was in this mood of black despair and desolation of spirit that he threw himself into the work of providing relief for the famine-stricken provinces of Russia. The famine of 1891 became sensational news all

over the world because of Tolstoy's challenge to the Russian Government, which, for reasons of external and internal policy, tried to hush
up the desperate condition in which millions of peasants found themselves after a disastrous drought and the consequent failure of their
crops. High officials, like the governor of the Nizhny-Novgorod
province, went so far as to blame the peasants for the famine, which,
he asserted in a widely circulated press interview, they had brought
upon themselves by their laziness and habitual drunkenness. 'To talk
of laziness and drunkenness now is as strange and tactless as to try to
teach a man to behave reasonably when he is gravely ill,' Chekhov
wrote to Suvorin. 'People who are well fed', he went on, 'invariably
display a certain amount of arrogance, which chiefly expresses itself
in lecturing the hungry. If a man resents consolation at a time of great
misfortune, how much more will he resent being lectured at and how
insulting such a lecture must seem to him. According to them, a peasant
who owes fifteen roubles in taxes is a worthless fellow who has no
right even to have a drink. Why don't they count up the debts owed
by cabinet ministers, leaders of the nobility and bishops? Think of the
money owed by the officers of the Life Guards alone! Only the tailors
know that.' Long before Tolstoy decided to organise his soup kitchens
for the starving peasants, Chekhov had begun agitating among his
Moscow acquaintances to raise a fund for the famine sufferers. But
from the very outset he found his task beset with difficulties. On the
one hand, the Government would only allow the Red Cross and the
local church authorities to organise relief work among the peasants,
and, on the other, the people he approached refused point blank to
contribute anything to his famine-relief fund because most of it would
find its way into the pockets of the officials handling it. Chekhov,
however, argued that with a little goodwill on both sides relief measures
could be organised without the interference of officials. He remembered
that a certain Lieutenant Yegorov he used to know in the early 'eighties
in Voskresensk was the chairman of an agricultural board in one of the
famine-stricken districts of the Nizhny-Novgorod province and he
decided to get in touch with him. He wrote him a letter at the beginning
of October proposing to go down to see him in order to discuss on the
spot what was best to be done to help the peasants. As he did not know
Yegorov's address, his letter miscarried and he had to wait till Suvorin
arrived in Moscow and cabled to the Nizhny-Novgorod governor for
Yegorov's whereabouts. In Moscow Suvorin fell ill with influenza and
Chekhov caught the infection. 'I am coughing, my head aches and I
have a pain in my back,' he wrote on November 7th to Smagin, who

was still trying to get a cottage for him in the Ukraine. 'I took castor oil and am now sitting in the Slav Bazaar with Suvorin, who has also got the flu. He gave it to me.' But a few days later it became evident to him that his illness was much more serious than influenza. On November 18th he wrote to Suvorin, who was back in Petersburg: 'I am beginning to think that I shall never be as well again as I was. Medical treatment and worries about my physical condition fill me with something like disgust. I shall not call in a doctor. I shall continue to take quinine, but I shall not allow myself to be medically examined.' His coughing interfered with his sleep and he spent most of his nights reading. 'Every night', he wrote to Suvorin, 'I wake up and read *War and Peace*. I read it with avidity and naïve surprise as though I had never read it before. It is remarkably good. The only parts I don't like are those which deal with Napoleon. The moment Napoleon comes on the scene the narrative becomes strained and you feel that Tolstoy had to resort to all sorts of tricks to prove that Napoleon was more stupid than he really was. Everything Pierre, Prince Andrey or the totally worthless Nicolai Rostov does or says is good, intelligent, natural and moving; but everything Napoleon thinks or does is unnatural, unintelligent, inflated and insignificant. When I settle in the provinces (which I dream of doing day and night), I shall spend all my time practising medicine and reading novels.' And, characteristically enough, he added this note on the state of medicine at the time of the Napoleonic wars: 'If I had been with Prince Andrey I should have cured him. It is strange to read that the wound of a prince, a rich man, who had a doctor at his bedside day and night and who was nursed by Natasha and Sonia, should have exuded a corpse-like smell. How awful the state of medicine was in those days! While writing his great novel Tolstoy could not help being filled with hatred of medicine.' By the middle of December he was getting better, but by that time he realised that he could no longer neglect his illness and that he would have to leave Moscow and settle in the country. 'I suffered from a vicious attack of influenza for a whole month,' he wrote to Natasha Lintaryov on December 14th. 'At first it affected my head and legs and I had to take to my bed, and then it went to my lungs. I coughed frantically and got as thin as a smoked herring. It was terrible! A whole month I sat at home, or rather lay in bed or walked about, and there was so much work to do. I have now made up my mind to get out of Moscow.' He sent Mary off to the Ukraine to buy the cottage Smagin had already inspected for him. 'If', he wrote to Smagin, 'I don't settle permanently in the country this year, or if the purchase of the cottage should for some reason fall through, I shall have myself to blame should my health suffer. I feel as though I had become warped like an old cupboard, and that if I spend another season in Moscow and keep indulging too much in my scribbling exercises, Gilyarovlsky will write a beautiful poem, celebrating my entry into the kind of cottage where you can neither sit down, nor get up, nor sneeze, but just lie down and do nothing in. I simply *must* leave Moscow.' And to his old friend, the architect Franz Schechtel, he wrote: 'I live just as I used to live before. I am not married. I am still not rich. The influenza has all but shattered me. I cough, I have grown thin and I look, I am told, like a drowned man. I have decided to submit to necessity: to buy a cottage in Poltava province and settle there for good. Away from Moscow! I shall spend nine months in the cottage or abroad and the other three months in hotels in Moscow or Petersburg.'

That winter Zinaida Lintaryov, the blind lady doctor who had a tumour on the brain, died, and Chekhov wrote an obituary notice of her in *New Times*. His aunt Feodossia had died earlier of consumption, and on October 26th Palmin, the close associate of his *Fragments* days, also died. 'This autumn', he wrote to Natasha Lintaryov, 'I had to bury quite a few people and I somehow grew indifferent to the deaths of my friends, but your family sorrow has made a very painful impression on me. Zinaida did well to die, that is true enough, but I am sorry for her all the same. Still,' he added, 'it's no use brooding on it, for we shall all die one day.'

In spite of his serious illness, Chekhov went on with his plans for helping the starving peasants. Together with Yegorov he decided to buy up the horses the peasants were selling for food in order to give them back to them in spring, for otherwise, unable to till the ground, they would be faced with another famine the following year. He collected money from all his friends and acquaintances and sent it to Yegorov, who bought the horses. The whole transaction was conducted in dead secret for fear that the authorities might stop it. He also asked Yegorov to organise free dinners for school children and promised to raise the necessary money. Tolstoy's courageous action in organising soup kitchens aroused his unfeigned admiration. 'What a marvellous man Tolstoy is!' he wrote to Suvorin on December 11th. 'Among the men of our time he is a giant, a Jupiter. His article on the soup kitchens in the volume published by the *Russian Gazette* in aid of the famine sufferers is full of such practical advice that, according to Sobolevsky [the editor of the *Russian Gazette*], it should really have been published in the *Government Gazette*.' Chekhov took an active part in the publication by the *Russian Gazette* of a volume of stories, poems and articles in aid of the famine-stricken districts, but his illness prevented him from contributing anything of his own.

In addition to his two stories, *Peasant Wives* and *The Duel*, Chekhov published in 1891 two long articles in *New Times*: *The Conjurers* and *In Moscow*. The first, which he wrote together with Vladimir Wagner in Bogimovo, is an attack on the director of the Moscow Zoo, the mismanagement of which Chekhov had occasion to expose many years before in several of the notices he wrote for *Fragments*. It was written in defence of a pamphlet by the well-known Russian scientist, Professor Timiryazev ('a man', Chekhov wrote in 1902, 'whom I greatly honour and respect'), criticising the recently established botanical station at the Moscow Zoo. Chekhov, however, enlarged the scope of his article by attacking the zoo itself, to which he referred as 'the graveyard of animals'. His other article, published in *New Times* on December 7th, was a brilliant and merciless exposure of a Moscow highbrow.

Before the end of 1891 Chekhov wrote two more stories, both of which were published in January of the following year and both of which bear unmistakable marks of having been written at a time of great mental and physical stress. The first story, *The Wife*, published in the January number of *The Northern Herald*, which had passed to new proprietors, dealt with the topical subject of the famine, and is a study of one of those highly placed people who seemed to be determined to do their utmost to undermine any private effort to help the starving peasants. The second story, *The Grasshopper*, published in the first number of the new monthly *North* in January 1892, was a blunder from beginning to end and brought about his quarrel with Levitan and Mrs. Kuvshinnikov. The story was a blunder because it violated one of Chekhov's own rules never to put his own friends into any of his stories or plays. He had criticised Markevich, the author of the play *The Whirl of Life*, for doing just that, because, he maintained, an author who put his friends into a novel or a play could not see further than his nose. If he put Levitan and Mrs. Kuvshinnikov in his story it was because he wrote it at a time when, as he wrote to M. Albov, the new editor of *The Northern Herald*, his head refused to work. It is true that a number of Chekhov's biographers seem to find Levitan and his mistress a little too squeamish and too apt to discover likenesses where there were none. Chekhov himself, when the storm broke over his head, is reported by Michael to have said: 'My grasshopper is a pretty young girl, while Sophia Kuvshinnikov is neither so pretty nor so young.' But that is beside the point. The trouble was that Chekhov not only took his triangle from life, but endowed his characters with the same mannerisms of speech, so that none of his friends could possibly have mistaken the source of his story. Michael himself thought that the situation in the Kuvshinnikov household was too much for Chekhov and, as he put it, 'Anton secretly condemned the behaviour of Sophia Kuvshinnikov and, unable to restrain himself, wrote *The Grasshopper*'. It was certainly a bad blunder on Chekhov's part, but of a kind that loses its importance with the passage of time. The story itself is a brilliant study of the artistic milieu of Moscow (or any other big city, for that matter) and its main theme—the facility with which people overlook real greatness and fool themselves into mistaking tinsel for gold—is admirably developed. Chekhov never suspected the trouble he was letting himself in for with his story. He was innocent of malice or spite, and it was its theme that attracted him. 'I am sending you', he wrote to Vladimir Tikhonov, the editor of *North*, on November 30th, 'a little sentimental love story for family reading.' The statement was made with his tongue in his cheek: he liked to have his joke with his editors. He first entitled the story *Philistines*, then he altered the title to *A Great Man*, but even that title did not satisfy him. 'I really don't know what to do with the title of my story,' he wrote to Tikhonov on December 14th. 'I don't like *The Great Man*. We must find another title for it. Call it——' and he took the first word of Krylov's fable *The Grasshopper and the Ant*: *Poprygunya*—jumpety-jump, that is, the onomatopoeic adjectival noun describing the grasshopper. The English translation of the title of the story is therefore incorrect. It would be more appropriate to translate it as *The Butterfly*, that being a much apter description of the character of its heroine.

Before the end of 1891 Chekhov wrote his last one-act comedy *The Anniversary*, based on a short story (*A Helpless Creature*) he had written four years earlier.

5

Since his meeting with Lydia Avilov in January 1889, Chekhov had been only three times to Petersburg: once in 1890 before his journey to Sakhalin and twice in 1891 after his return from Sakhalin and before his first journey abroad. He had apparently made up his mind to go there in October, but, significantly, he asked Suvorin not to tell anyone of his visit as he wished to live there 'incognito'. A week later he changed his mind and wrote to Suvorin that he would not come to Petersburg after all. In December his health improved and, as his royalties were beginning to come in, he recovered from his depression and decided to go to Petersburg at once. He arrived there on December 27th and stayed for about a fortnight.

He met Lydia Avilov again on January 1st. All during the three years he had not communicated with her. Lydia had written to him shortly after their first meeting, but as he did not remember her married name (at least that was the excuse he gave her), he did not reply to her letter. 'There is one thing I feel guilty about,' he wrote to her on March 19th, 1892. 'It is this. One day I received a letter from you in which you asked me something about the idea behind an unimportant story of mine. Being only little acquainted with you at the time and having forgotten that your married name was Avilov, I tore up your letter and appropriated the enclosed stamp—that is how I generally deal with inquiries, especially those from women. But afterwards when you reminded me of your letter, I recalled your signature and felt guilty.' They met at the house of Lydia's brother-in-law, Sergey Khudekov, on the occasion of the celebration of the 25th anniversary of the foundation of his paper, the *Petersburg Gazette*. 'Yesterday', Chekhov wrote to a friend on January 2nd, 'I made merry at the anniversary of the *Petersburg Gazette*. . . . Khudekov offered me forty copecks a line and gave me an advance of two hundred roubles, though I did not ask him for it.' That is the only reference to the anniversary dinner to be found in Chekhov's letters, but it is quite evident that in accepting the invitation to it Chekhov must have expected to meet Lydia there.

'I recalled my first meeting with Chekhov', Lydia writes in *Chekhov in my Life*, 'and that inexplicable and strangely unreal feeling which suddenly made us so close to one another, and I was wondering whether he would recognise me now. Would he remember? Would that intimate feeling of closeness be reborn in us again, the feeling which three years ago blazed up so brightly in my soul?' Chekhov did remember, and as they ran into each other accidentally in the crowd of guests, they at once 'stretched out their hands to one another happily'.

There is no reason to doubt Lydia's account of that meeting. Chekhov who had felt so constrained at home that he found it difficult to talk to anyone, suddenly felt free and happy again. His excitement is well conveyed in Lydia's description of the dinner, and that is something that she could not possibly have invented. But one incident connected with their second meeting she left rather obscure, and one cannot help feeling that she did so designedly. 'An obliging friend', she writes, 'told Michael [that is, her husband] that after the anniversary dinner Chekhov went to a restaurant with friends where he got drunk and boasted that he would take me away from my husband, make me get a divorce and marry me. His friends were said to have encouraged him, and almost carried him on their shoulders in their enthusiasm. Michael was furious.'

Now, it is undoubtedly true that Chekhov had a gay time in Petersburg. One of the symptoms of his last attack of illness, aggravated by influenza, that really worried him was that he had completely lost his taste for vodka and could not even have the two glasses he usually drank before going to bed. But his health had so improved in Petersburg that he regained his taste for wines and hard drinks. 'Yesterday', he wrote to Smagin on January 4th, 'I visited all sorts of Arcadias and filled myself with champagne.' He was also at a gay birthday party given by Leontyev at which everybody including Chekhov seemed to have got drunk. In a letter to Vladimir Tikhonov on January 24th Chekhov wrote: 'I can vaguely remember your silhouette on the box of the cab. The finale of Leontyev's birthday was brilliant.' And in another letter to the same correspondent on February 22nd he added the following details: 'You needn't worry about having gone too far at Leontyev's birthday party. You were drunk and that was all. You danced when everybody else danced, and your imitation of Caucasian trick-riding on the box of the cab aroused nothing but general satisfaction. As for your criticism, it must have been very severe because I can't remember a word of it. The only thing I do remember is that Vvedensky [a literary critic] and I roared with laughter at something you said.' It was certainly a very gay party with a strong literary flavour at which the novelist who had spread the slanderous story that had made Lydia's husband so angry might well have been present. Chekhov did not go to any restaurant after the dinner. He and Hieronimus Yassinsky, a Petersburg journalist and novelist, went to Leykin's.

Chekhov's attitude towards Leykin had not changed, but there was never any question of a final break between them. Leykin still hoped to get some stories out of Chekhov, and Chekhov kept up a desultory correspondence with Leykin in which he refrained from discussing literature. 'Leykin', he told a friend, 'has his faults like all of us, but . . . he is not a snob. To him a writer always comes first.' It was during this visit that Leykin made Chekhov a present of two dachshund puppies which, christened Quinine and Bromide, replaced the mongooses that had to be given away to the Moscow Zoo. Chekhov was so grateful for the dogs that he wrote four stories for *Fragments*, which was perhaps what Leykin had in mind when making his present.

There is, therefore, a serious discrepancy in the story Lydia had been told, as Chekhov was not slow to point out. '*Your letter*', he wrote to Lydia, '*both distressed and perplexed me.* You write about some sort of "strange things" which I am supposed to have said at Leykin's, and then you beg me not to talk of you "in that way" out of respect for a woman, and, finally, you even go on to say that "for such a confidence alone it is easy to be covered with dirt". *What does it all mean?* Me and dirt? . . . *My dignity does not permit me to justify myself; besides, your accusations are so vague that I don't know what exactly I have to apologise for. But from what I gather it has something to do with a story someone has spread about me. Am I right? I ask you earnestly (if you trust me as much as the people who spread those stories about me) not to believe anything people in your Petersburg tell you. Or, if you can't help believing them, believe everything they say about me: that I am married to a woman with five millions, that I have affairs with the wives of my best friends, etc. For goodness sake, calm yourself.* If I am not sufficiently convincing, have a talk to Yassinsky who went to Leykin's with me after the anniversary dinner. Both of us, I remember, talked a lot about what nice people you and your sister were. We were both a little tipsy after the dinner, but even if I had been as drunk as a cobbler or had gone mad, I should never have lowered myself to "that way" and "dirt" (how could you have brought yourself to use that horrible word?), being restrained by my ordinary sense of decency and by my respect for my mother, my sister and women in general. To speak badly of you and in the presence of Leykin, too! *However, what does it matter? To defend myself against gossip is . . . useless. Think what you like of me.*'

The italicised passages in the above letter is all that Lydia quotes of it in *Chekhov in my Life*. As can be seen, Lydia had suppressed everything in the letter (including the already quoted passage about her first unanswered communication to Chekhov) that might suggest any more intimate relationship at that particular period of their friendship. It is, however, obvious that she must have discussed her unhappy private life with him. She had promised to send him her stories for his criticism, but, as appears from the first letter he wrote to her from Moscow on February 21st, she refused to see him again. 'As a matter of fact', Chekhov wrote, 'I ought to criticise your story very severely because you did not want to come to see me, but—may Allah forgive you!' And he added after criticising her story: 'However, I see that

I have not restrained myself and have revenged myself on you for treating me like a lady-in-waiting of the time of Catherine the Great, that is, for refusing to discuss your story with me and insisting that I should write to you about it.' And in reply to Lydia's protest against his rather drastic suggestions for improving her story, he wrote to her on March 3rd: 'Why are you angry with me? It worries me.' It was only a fortnight later that Lydia told him about the scandalous story that was being spread about him and her. What were Chekhov's feelings towards Lydia when he met her for the second time? He told her several years later.

'Remember our first meetings? And, do you know—do you know that I was deeply in love with you? Seriously in love with you? Yes, I loved you. It seemed to me there was not another woman in the world I could love like that. You were beautiful and sweet and there was such freshness and dazzling charm in your youth. I loved you. I thought only of you. And when I met you again after our long separation it seemed to me that you were more beautiful than ever, that you were quite a different person, quite a new person, and that I must get to know you again and love you even more—in a new way. And that it would be even harder to leave you. . . .'

But leave her he had to. There was his relief work for the famine sufferers he had still to complete; there was the question of the country cottage he simply had to buy, for he knew that his state of health would no longer permit him to live in Moscow; and there was, besides, his family, the 'benignant tumour' he always carried about with him and which of late was showing signs of turning malignant. Could he, even if Lydia had shown any sign of reciprocating his feelings (and so far she had refused even to meet him), undertake the added responsibility of keeping a wife and three children, a 'civil' wife, as the polite phrase had it, too, with all the scandal *that* would have created? The whole thing was impossible. 'I knew that you were not like other women,' he was to tell Lydia a long time afterwards, 'and that the love one feels for you must be pure and sacred and must last all one's life. I was afraid to touch you so as not to offend. Did you know that?' Chekhov would never have made such a statement if he had not been convinced from the very start that his love for Lydia was doomed. He could do nothing about it. It was hopeless.

Chekhov left for Yegorov's district in Nizhny-Novgorod province on January 14th. While he was there about twenty hundredweights of rusks arrived from Petersburg for distribution among twenty thousand people. 'Our philanthropists', he wrote to Suvorin, 'want to feed five thousand people on five loaves of bread—according to the gospels.' His plan to buy up the horses from the peasants was not progressing very satisfactorily, either. The starving peasants had killed and eaten most of their horses in the autumn, with the result that the prices of horses had risen steeply. 'It seems', he wrote to Suvorin, 'that the peasants will be left without horses after all—on which let me congratulate the public.' He visited every famine-stricken village, and on the night of January 17th he and his driver were overtaken by a blizzard, lost their way and were nearly frozen to death. He returned to Moscow on January 22nd unable to bend down or write; he had caught a cold while sleeping under a ventilator in Nizhny-Novgorod and for a few days he could not leave his house. But on February 2nd he recovered sufficiently to accompany Suvorin to his native village in the Voronezh province, where he found the famine relief organised on much better lines than in Nizhny-Novgorod. Suvorin did his best to organise soup kitchens for the peasants, but it seems he was not as good a hand at that kind of work as Tolstoy. 'So far as soup kitchens, etc., are concerned,' Chekhov wrote to Mary, 'we talk a lot of nonsense and we are as naïve as babes; this observation does not refer to myself but to that bronze bust which stands on the desk in my study. We talk frightful rot and get into a temper when it is pointed out to us that we talk rot and don't understand anything. In the morning we are in an excellent mood, but in the evening we say, "What the hell did we come here for? I shall never be able to do anything here," etc.' This is the first time Chekhov had spoken with such contempt of Suvorin, whose bronze bust adorned his writing desk.

Except for the little money he had collected, Chekhov's efforts for the relief of the famine did not amount to much. He could not even bring himself to write the article he had promised Yegorov to publish.

'I have begun writing this article dozens of times,' he declared in a letter to Yegorov on March 29th, 'but every time it has turned out so false that I could not carry on with it. I don't mean that I was telling lies in my article, but there was a kind of forced and false tone such as I cannot bear either in my own or in other people's articles. So it seems that my journey to you has been wasted. Yes, my journey was useless so far as you are concerned, but I cannot help recalling it with pleasure. It will be useful to me, for it has left me with not a few interesting impressions.'

Disappointed with Mary's failure to buy a cottage with a small plot of land in the Ukraine, Chekhov gave a deposit of two hundred roubles to the owner of a small estate near the village of Melikhovo in the Serpukhov district of the Moscow province before he left for Voronezh and completed his purchase on his return to Moscow. The haste with which he bought the estate (he had not even bothered to inspect it) shows how terrified he was of a recurrence of his illness if he stayed in Moscow another winter. The estate was within two and a half hours' journey by rail from Moscow and six miles from the railway station of Lopasnya. It cost him fourteen thousand roubles, of which he paid down four thousand roubles he borrowed from Suvorin, promised to pay, in the spring, another four thousand, which he hoped to raise on a mortgage, and undertook to pay the rest within ten years at 5 per cent interest. At the beginning of March he moved into his country house, a ten-roomed bungalow with a veranda, where he was to spend the next six years of his life.

'I have bought a large and unwieldy estate,' he wrote to Alexey Kisselev on March 7th, 'which in Germany would have earned its owner the title of a duke. Two hundred and thirteen acres divided into two plots of land. Over one hundred acres are woodland which in twenty years' time will look like a real wood. At present it is just covered with shrub. . . . An orchard. A park. Large trees. A long lime-tree avenue. Newly built sheds and barns which look all right. The hen-run is made according to all the latest scientific rules. A well with an iron pump. The whole estate is shut off from the world by a wooden fence. The yard, the orchard and the threshing-floor are also separated from each other by wooden fences. The house has both good and bad points. It is larger than our Moscow flat, it is light and warm, it has an iron roof, is built on a good site, with a veranda leading into the garden, large Italian windows, etc. Its bad points are that it is not sufficiently lofty or new, that it has a rather stupid and naïve appearance, and abounds in bedbugs and black-beetles which can only be got rid of in one way— a fire; nothing else seems to have the slightest effect on them.

'We have hotbeds. In the orchard, about fifteen feet from the house, is a pond over a hundred feet long and thirty-five feet wide, with crucian and tench, so that I shall be able to fish from the window of my study. There is another pond behind the yard, but I haven't seen it yet. The other plot of land has a stream, but I suspect it must be a wretched one. About two and a half miles from the estate is a broad river with fish. Fourteen acres have been sown with rye. We shall sow oats and clover. The clover seeds we have already bought, but I have still to find the money for the oats.'

The livestock on the estate included three horses, one cow and two dogs. There were also ten 'sickly' hens.

The first thing Chekhov did was to put his newly acquired property in order. Every member of his household was mobilised and given his allotted task. (The purchase of the estate, Chekhov told Alexander, had brought about 'a family reconciliation'.) Michael came down from Alexin and was appointed 'manager in chief'. Workers were hired to repair the chimneys and the floors. 'I am beginning to appreciate the fine points of capitalism,' Chekhov wrote to Suvorin. 'To remove the oven in the servants' quarters and install a kitchen stove in its place, then remove the stove in the kitchen and replace it by a Dutch stove costs only twenty roubles. The price of two shovels is only twenty-five copecks. To refill the ice-cellar you have to pay only thirty copecks a day to a labourer. A young workman, literate, sober and a non-smoker, whose duties include ploughing, cleaning boots and looking after the hotbeds, is paid five roubles a month. The repair of the floors, the putting up of wooden partitions, the papering of the walls—all that is cheaper than mushrooms. And I am free to do as I like. But if I had paid for this work even one quarter of what my leisure is worth to me, I should have been financially ruined, for the number of stove-men, joiners, carpenters, etc., never seems to come to an end. . . . I am promised a good harvest and riches, but what do I want it for? I'd rather have five copecks now than a rouble later on. I have to sit down and work. I shall have to earn at least five hundred roubles to pay for all this. Half of it I have already earned.' In spite of his financial worries, Chekhov liked his life in the country. 'To live in the country', he wrote to Suvorin five days later, 'may be uncomfortable, especially now that the roads have become impassable, but what is taking place in nature just now is so marvellous and moving that it repays all the discomforts by its novelty and poetry. Every day all sorts of surprising things seem to happen. The starlings have arrived, everywhere I can hear the ripple of water, and on the thawed patches green grass has already appeared. The day seems to go on for ever. You might be in Australia, for you seem to live on the very edge of the world. You feel calm, contemplative and animal-like in the sense that you do not regret yesterday and are not eager for tomorrow. . . . Watching the spring, I am overcome by a desire that there should be a paradise in the next world. In short, there are moments when I feel so well that I check myself superstitiously and think of my creditors who will evict me from my newly acquired Australia one day. And serve me right!'

Chekhov was not by any means a mere idle spectator of the feverish work that was going on on his estate. He shovelled snow into the pond in anticipation of the happy moment when the fish would be jumping out of it; he dug ditches; he planted trees and busied himself in the house, supervised the putting up of bookshelves in his room, and so on. 'At first', he wrote to Suvorin, 'my bones ached from physical work, but now I have got used to it. I am afraid that as a worker and a landowner I am worse than useless. All I am good for is to shovel snow into the pond and dig ditches. When I knock in a nail, it is always crooked.'

'We get up at 7 a.m. and go to bed at 8 p.m.,' he wrote to Lydia Mizinov on March 29th. 'We also eat a lot. On the whole, I can promise you that in about a year we shall be proper pigs. I do a lot of physical work. My muscles are getting stronger and I'm gaining in strength every hour, so that when my estate is sold at a public auction I shall get myself a job at Solomonsky Circus as an athlete.'

He also found time to read a lot. It is very rarely that Chekhov gives any particulars about his reading, or indeed about the immense amount of thought he put in as a preliminary to his writing at this and at subsequent periods of his life. But on March 11th, a week or so after he had moved into his little country house, he wrote to Suvorin: 'I have just read Leskov's *Legendary Characters*. Heavenly and piquant. A combination of virtue, piety and obscenity. But very interesting. Read it, if you haven't read it already.' He had also been reading Pisarev's criticisms of Pushkin again. 'How awfully naïve,' he wrote in the same letter. 'The man debunks Onegin and Tatyana, but Pushkin remains intact. Pisarev is the grandfather and the father of all our modern critics, including Burenin. The same pettiness in debunking, the same cold selfish wit and the same coarseness and indelicacy in his attitude to people. It is not Pisarev's ideas, which do not exist, but his coarse tone that is liable to make his readers coarse and beastly. His attitude to Tatyana, in particular, and her charming letter, which I love so much, appears to me simply abominable. He reminds me of a tiresome, captious public prosecutor. However, to hell with him!'

It is interesting that Chekhov's attitude to an 'aesthetic' critic like Merezhkovsky was no less contemptuous. 'The enthusiastic and pure-minded Merezhkovsky', he wrote to Suvorin on another occasion, 'would do well to exchange his quasi-Goethe-like régime, his wife and his "eternal verities" for a bottle of good wine, a sportsman's gun and a pretty girl. His heart would beat better.'

He also read Alphonse Daudet's latest novel *Rose et Ninette* and was amused by Daudet's role as a moralist who demanded that a married couple who hated each other should not be given a divorce. 'Frenchmen', he wrote to Suvorin, 'had got tired of naked girls. So they want a little moral amusement for gastronomic reasons.'

Chekhov did not forget his intention to devote himself to medicine in the country. He had brought a whole cartload of medicines with him and his medical practice began almost as soon as he had installed himself in his country house. 'From the very first days of our settling down in Melikhovo', Michael records, 'everyone in the neighbourhood got to know that Anton was a doctor. Patients began to flock to our house or were brought in carts, and he himself had often to travel for miles to see a patient. From early morning women and children waited outside the house. He would come out to them, examine each patient and never send anyone away without his medicine. Our sister Mary acted as his "assistant". He spent a great deal of money on medicines and had a regular chemist's shop at home. He would often be awakened at night to attend to a patient. I remember one occasion when late at night some people brought in a peasant they had picked up in the road whose stomach had been pierced with a pitchfork. The peasant was taken into Anton's study, where I happened to be sleeping, and laid on the carpet in the middle of the floor. Anton busied himself a long time with him, examining his wounds and putting on bandages.'

Shchepkina-Kupernik tells this characteristic story of Chekhov's medical practice at that time:

'Approximately a year before I made Chekhov's acquaintance, I went to see my former nurse, who lived in a village not far from Chekhov's Melikhovo estate. She had consumption, and I became very worried and began asking her whether there was a doctor in the village and whether he had any medicines.

'"Don't worry, my dear," she replied. "We have a doctor here who is much better than any of your Moscow doctors. He lives about four miles from here, Anton Pavlovich does. He's such a nice man, such a nice man! He gives me my medicine and he doesn't charge me anything for it." '

Chekhov himself claimed that his good relations with the peasants were due entirely to his medical practice. 'The peasants and the shopkeepers', he wrote to Suvorin in May, 'are already eating out of my hands. One had a discharge of blood from the throat, another had his arm injured by the fall of a tree, a third had a little daughter who was ill. Without me they would be lost. Now they bow to me respectfully, just as Germans do to their pastor, and I am very nice to them, so that everything is perfect.' And another time Chekhov wrote to Suvorin that when he walked through the village the women treated him with great kindness and consideration 'as if I were a saintly half-wit'. Many years later he wrote to Lydia Avilov: 'I live in peace with the peasants. They never steal anything from me, and when I pass through the village the old women smile and cross themselves. I always talk to all of them, except to the children, as I would to my friends and acquaintances. I never raise my voice. But the chief cause of our good relations is medicine.'

7

It was only a few months after his arrival in Melikhovo that Chekhov was called upon to deal with a threatened cholera epidemic. He immediately offered his free services to the agricultural board of the Serpukhov district and was given a medical sector comprising twenty-five villages, four factories and one monastery. In his white coat of military cut and peaked cap he drove daily round his sector on a tour of inspection, explaining to the peasants how to deal with the epidemic, attending the regular meetings of the district medical council, keeping a careful case-book of his patients, and organising special barracks for cholera patients. 'I have declined the offer of a salary,' he wrote to Suvorin, 'as I was anxious to preserve even a little freedom of action for myself, and because of that I haven't a penny. I am waiting for our rye to be threshed, and till then I shall subsist on my *Bear* and mushrooms.' Chekhov's begging from the rich involved him in all sorts of humiliating situations. The Countess Orlov-Davydov, who lived in his sector, received him, when he came to discuss the building of cholera barracks for her workers, as though he had come to ask her for a job. He felt hurt and told her that he was a rich man. He told the same lie to a bishop, who refused to let him have a room for any patient who might contract cholera in his monastery.

Luckily for Chekhov, the cholera epidemic never reached his sector, though in the sector next to his there were seven cholera cases.

But in spite of the cholera epidemic, Chekhov's first summer at Melikhovo was a happy one. To the son of a former serf it must have been a very exciting experience to own an estate. The feeling of property, he told Suvorin, was certainly a great thing, and so was the power of habit. Pavel, with the typical mentality of a slave, reacted to the fact of being the father of a landowner in his own slavish fashion: he began, to Chekhov's annoyance, talking of being the 'master' and treating the servants as his former owner had treated him and his father when they were still serfs. He even expected, on the strength of his father's job as the manager of Count Platov's estate, to be made manager of his son's estate. But the conflict with his father did not come to a head till the following year. For the time being they were all too busy settling down in their new surroundings for any serious quarrel to arise. 'It is wonderful', Chekhov wrote to Suvorin, 'how pleasant it is not to have to pay rent for a flat. . . . Everybody here already considers me as one of them, and when people pass through Melikhovo they stop at my place for the night. Add to this that we have bought a new comfortable carriage with a hood, helped to build a new road so that we have no longer to travel through the village, dug a new pond. . . what else do you want? In short, till now everything has been new and interesting, but what is going to happen in future I don't know. It's already cold and snowing, but I don't feel like going to Moscow. So far I have not felt bored. The intelligentsia here is very charming and interesting. Above all—honest. The police alone are unsympathetic.' Even the various misadventures on the farm had their amusing side. 'Our gander', Chekhov wrote to Natasha Lintaryov in June, 'jumped on the back of one of our farm women and hung on to her kerchief. Our cook Darya, drunk as usual, dropped the eggs from under our geese so that only three hatched out. Our pig has a nasty habit of biting people and eating our Indian corn. Our horses have eaten up our red cabbage during the night. We bought a calf for six roubles and she keeps on serenading us in a low bass voice. Our pious parents are fasting and continue to shine sanctimoniously at lunch and dinner. In the pond all sorts of salamanders and green devils have made their appearance. In short, all that is left for your Midian King to do is to utter a wild war-cry and run off to a desert.' The most amazing occurrence on the farm was the transformation overnight of a recently bought young mare, 'mated', as Chekhov explained to a correspondent, 'in the presence of reliable witnesses', into an ancient gelding. The mystery, however, was not so difficult to explain: the young mare was stolen and replaced by a gelding of exactly the same colour.

Chekhov, who was too good a fisherman to be satisfied with a pond, missed a good river badly. 'But what is there to be done about it?' he

wrote to Alexey Kisselev. 'I must console myself with the words of
Voltaire, who said that in Russia there are nine months of winter and
three months of foul weather. In winter the river cannot be seen under
the snow and in foul weather its absence is a great convenience.'

What did annoy him was the thought that he had to go on writing
for money. 'My soul yearns to soar,' he wrote to Suvorin in June
'but I am forced to lead a life that is centred round the rouble and the
copeck. . . . That makes me look on my writing as a contemptible
occupation, and I do not respect what I write; I feel apathetic and I am
bored with myself, and I am glad I can fall back on medicine, which at
any rate I do not practise for the sake of money. I ought really to take
a sulphuric-acid bath so as to take my skin off and then grow a new
one.'

There were his regular visitors, without whom he could not live.
Levitan spent a few days with him, and he accompanied the painter on
a shoot. It was during that visit that the often-quoted incident with the
woodcock occurred. Levitan fired at a woodcock and winged it. The
bird fell into a puddle. Chekhov picked it up and examined it: a long
beak, large black eyes and beautiful plumage. The woodcock looked
at him with surprise and he did not know what to do with the poor
bird. Levitan had a pained look on his face. He closed his eyes and said
with a tremor in his voice: 'Knock its head on the butt of the gun,
there's a good fellow!' Chekhov replied that he could not bring himself to do so. Levitan twitched his shoulders nervously, winced and
implored Chekhov to kill the bird. In the end Chekhov complied.
'There was one beautiful creature less in the world,' Chekhov concluded his description of the incident in a letter to Suvorin, 'and two
fools returned home and sat down to supper.'

Chekhov was not sentimental in his love of animals. He would
catch mice in a special trap and take them to the woods, where he would
release them. (He did the same thing many years later in his house in
Yalta.) But that did not prevent him from taking drastic measures when
necessary. 'Find out in a shop a good remedy for mice,' he wrote to
Mary in October 1894. 'The little beasts have devoured the wallpaper in
the drawing-room four feet from the floor.' He had a strong fellow-
feeling for all animals, and, as his stories show, he was able to project
himself into their minds almost as well as Tolstoy. Needless to say, he
felt no such attachment to fish, though one of the last stories he wrote
for *Fragments* is of a crucian which fell in love with a beautiful girl who
had bathed in its pond and, unable to commit suicide (there were no
pike in the pond), turned pessimist and took his revenge on humanity

by biting a poet. The unsuspecting poet went to Petersburg, where he infected all the other poets with pessimism, since when, Chekhov ended his story, 'all our poets have begun writing gloomy and despondent verse'. This is an interesting comment on those critics who accuse Chekhov himself of being a pessimist.

Chekhov condemned blood sports and quoted Shakespeare with approval on the subject. 'If you see Leskov,' he wrote to Suvorin in December 1892, 'tell him that in Shakespeare's *As You Like It*, Act II, Sc. i, there are a few excellent lines about hunting and, generally, killing animals.' And a year later he quoted the passage in full in a letter to Gorbunov-Posadov, editor of Chertkov's *Intermediary Press* and a staunch follower of Tolstoy.

The remarkable thing about Levitan's visit to Melikhovo at the beginning of April 1892 was that it happened three months after the publication of *The Grasshopper*. At the time, then, Levitan, who must have read the story, did not take the transparent hint at his relations with Sophia Kuvshinnikov seriously. It was only after he had gone back to Moscow that, incited by Sophia, he quarrelled with Chekhov. 'Yesterday I was in Moscow', Chekhov wrote to Lydia Avilov on April 18th, 'and was nearly stifled there with boredom and all sorts of abominations. Can you imagine it? An acquaintance of mine, a woman of forty-two, recognised herself in the twenty-two-year-old heroine of my *Grasshopper*, and the whole of Moscow is accusing me of libel. Their evidence seems to be mainly based on a number of external similarities: the lady paints, her husband is a doctor and she lives with an artist.' Chekhov's resentment of the scandalous imputation on his integrity as a writer was all the stronger because he realised that there was some substance in it.

In his letters to Lydia Mizinov, Chekhov used to tease her about Levitan's pretended passion for her. That was one of the standing jokes of the Chekhov family, but in June 1892 he had another reason for keeping up this pretence of an affair between her and Levitan, for she had fallen in love with Chekhov, and one evening in June she must have misunderstood a jocular remark he had made (he always used extravagant expressions of love to her) and given herself away. Next day, on her return to Moscow, where she had a job on the town council and took lessons in acting from Fedotov, she wrote a letter in which she apologised for her stupid behaviour. 'Putting aside all false vanity,' she wrote, 'I should like to tell you that I feel very sad and that I want to see you very much. I am sad, Anton Pavlovich, because you must have been unpleasantly surprised by my behaviour shortly

ANTON CHEKHOV IN MELIKHOVO 1897
(On his return from the Moscow Clinic)

before I left for Moscow. I admit that I behaved like a silly girl. Isn't it really absurd to have forgotten myself so much as to take a joke seriously. Anyway, I don't suppose you will blame me for it very much since you must have discovered long ago what my feelings for you are.' And in another letter she wrote: 'You know perfectly well what my feelings towards you are and that is why I am not at all ashamed to write to you about it. I know, too, that you are either completely indifferent or just sorry for me. My dearest wish is to cure myself of the awful state in which I find myself, but I can't do it alone. Please help me. Don't ask me to come to Melikhovo and don't try to see me. This may not be important to you, but it may help me to forget you.' Chekhov did his best to help her. His letters to her were a mixture of extravagant protestations of love ('You have turned my head so much that I am quite ready to believe that twice two makes five') and expressions that bordered on the unprintable, and one cannot help feeling that his freedom of language was 'put on' to make it quite clear to her that, while he valued her friendship, there could be no question of any love between them. The point is of some importance in view of the stories that were spread after the publication of *The Seagull* that the unhappy love affair between Nina and Trigorin was autobiographical and that his friendship for Lydia Mizinov was in danger, as one modern Russian biographer of Chekhov has put it, of developing into 'something more serious', but that, mindful of his obligations to literature, he decided 'to sacrifice his personal happiness'.

Apart from Lydia Mizinov and Levitan, Chekhov had all his usual visitors at Melikhovo, including Alexander and his wife and children, Semashko and Ivanenko, Natasha Lintaryov, Smagin, Suvorin, Gilyarovsky and the actor Svobodin, who died suddenly during a performance later in the year and in whom Chekhov lost one of the very few people whom he could call a real friend.

8

With *Ward No. 6*, the only major work he wrote in 1892 (it was begun in March and finished about two months later), Chekhov entered upon his last period as a creative writer. Unlike *The Duel*, with which he started his polemic against Tolstoy's philosophy of life, *Ward No. 6* is a fully integrated work of art, the serious purpose of which is not arbitrarily imposed upon its characters but flows easily and imperceptibly out of them. That Chekhov did not achieve this full integration of idea and character without careful thought becomes clear from his letter to Suvorin of October 25th in which he first formulated the aim a writer ought to strive to achieve. All writers who were generally recognised as 'eternal' or simply 'good' and not just as 'charming and talented' (a phrase he used in *The Seagull* to describe the type of writer Trigorin was), possessed, he maintained, one important characteristic in common: they all knew where they were going and they invited their readers to follow them, and their readers, too, felt 'not with their mind but with every fibre of their being' that they had some definite aim. The best of them were realists and painted 'life as it is', but because each word they wrote was permeated with the consciousness of a higher aim, the impression their readers obtained from their works was not only of 'life as it is' but also of 'life as it should be'. 'He who wants nothing, fears nothing and hopes for nothing,' Chekhov declared, 'cannot be an artist.' The great feature of the works Chekhov wrote during the last eleven years of his life, and particularly of his last four plays, is the remarkable way in which he fused these two principles of a work of art. To his contemporaries, however, the 'definitive aim' of his work tended to become obscured by the artistry with which he painted the life they knew. The deeper his perception of life and the greater the sensibility with which he described the agony of the human heart, the more instantaneous was the impact of his story and play on his readers and spectators, who were so absorbed in the fate of his characters that they completely overlooked the purpose for which he had created them. The best illustration of this is provided by *Ward No. 6*. Chekhov wrote the story as a condemnation of the main tenet of Tolstoy's faith—non-resistance to evil. Its hero, Dr. Andrey Ragin, a non-resister to evil by nature as well as conviction, is shown by Chekhov to be himself a perpetuator of evil and, finally, its victim. But Chekhov was not going to be involved in a polemic with the followers of Tolstoy. On July 8th, that is, while he was still engaged on writing the story, he advised Suvorin to cut the 'tirade' about Tolstoy out of a story of his. 'Today', Chekhov wrote, 'a reader cannot help wincing at the mention of a woman wearing a crinoline or a bustle, and I daresay that in ten or fifteen years' time a reader will consider in exactly the same way any discussion of Tolstoy's philosophy. . . . Tolstoy may be a great man, but he is not worth wasting your time on, particularly when you are writing a story, that is, when you are most free and objective.' Chekhov was therefore determined to disguise the chief aim of his story, namely his attack on Tolstoy's dogma of non-resistance to evil, so as to ensure that *Ward*

No. 6 should not lose its interest or its importance as a work of art, when, as he rightly anticipated, Tolstoy's philosophy within a comparatively short time lost its hold over people. And so successful was he in disguising it that Vladimir Chertkov, Tolstoy's main propagandist, asked his permission to reprint the story in one of his *Intermediary* booklets of popular fiction. He was anxious to publish it, Chertkov wrote to Chekhov on January 15th, 1893, because of 'the humanity, importance and topicality of its ideas', and it never apparently occurred to him that by publishing the story he would be undermining people's belief in his master's teaching. Chekhov saw the irony of it; and being, above all, a fair-minded person, he at first refused Chertkov's request on the ground that the story would be included in a new volume of his stories. It was only when the request was repeated that Chekhov gave his consent for his story to be published by the *Intermediary Press*.

Ward No. 6 indirectly played an important part in Chekhov's life by facilitating his return to the liberal camp. He was becoming more and more disgusted with Suvorin's reactionary politics and he was anxious to attach himself to a periodical of liberal views. Unfortunately, the only periodical of that nature was *Russian Thought*, which Chekhov had gone out of his way to abuse for its supposed narrow-mindedness and dishonesty at a time when his friendship with Suvorin was closest. His quarrel with Vukol Lavrov before his departure for Sakhalin in 1890, however, seemed to preclude any approach to him in 1892. Still, Chekhov decided to take the first step towards burying the hatchet and he asked Svobodin to tell Lavrov, who was a close friend of his, that he would be glad to contribute a story to *Russian Thought*. To Chekhov's surprise, Lavrov sent him a most friendly letter assuring him that any work of his would always find a cordial welcome in the pages of *Russian Thought*, regretting the 'unhappy misunderstanding' that had arisen between them and declaring himself to be one of his 'most fervent admirers'. Chekhov had already offered *Ward No.* 6 to another Moscow journal and received an advance of five hundred roubles for it, but he took his manuscript back on the specious plea that he had never received the proofs, returned his advance and sent it to *Russian Thought*. How pleased he was with his return to the liberal fold can be seen from the following passage in his letter to Lydia Mizinov on June 28th: 'I have a sensational piece of news: *Russian Thought* in the person of Lavrov sent me a letter full of delicate feelings and assurances. I am touched, and but for my horrible habit of not replying to letters, I should have replied that I considered the misunderstanding that occurred between us at an end. At any rate, I am sending the liberal story I began while you were here, my child, to *Russian Thought*. Well, well!' *Ward No. 6*, published in the November number of *Russian Thought*, thus inaugurated a close partnership and friendship with Lavrov and Goltsev which was to last till Chekhov's death.

One of his stories, *In Exile*, published in May 1892 in *World Illustration*, provoked a characteristic protest from Chekhov. 'Will you be so kind as to point out to the people in your office', he wrote to the editor of the magazine, 'that the advertisement in which I am described as "highly talented" and in which the title of my story is printed in letters of poster size, has made a most unpleasant impression on me. It looks like an advertisement of a dentist or a masseuse and is, besides, in bad taste. I know the value of advertisements and I am not against them, but I consider modesty and literary standards in his relationship to his readers and fellow-writers to be the best and most effective advertisement for a literary person.'

Three short stories which Chekhov wrote for Leykin, in acknowledgment of the promise to send him two dachshund puppies, were published in *Fragments* in May and June under his old pseudonym of 'A Man Without a Spleen', and the fourth, *A Fish in Love*, under the pseudonym of 'Starling' he only used on that occasion. Chekhov repaid the advance he received from Khudekov by his brilliant study of an adolescent girl *After the Theatre*, published in the *Petersburg Gazette* under the title of *Joy* on April 7th. His contributions to *New Times* included the short story *Terror*, published on December 25th, and the article *From What Illness Did Herod Die?*, a most curious medical dissertation based on some apocryphal references in the Russian *Lives of the Saints*. Finally, Chekhov published his story *Neighbours* in the July supplement of *The Week*, a liberal journal edited by Mikhail Menshikov, who, like Suvorin, was to end up as a rabid reactionary. The story has the line: 'If you ever want my life, come and take it', which Lydia Avilov sent as her message to Chekhov and which he later made Nina send as her message to Trigorin in *The Seagull*. Chekhov did not like this story, because, as he explained to Suvorin, it had neither a beginning nor an ending. 'It should never have been published,' he wrote.

This short list does not exhaust Chekhov's literary work in 1892. During that year he also wrote his long story with a political slant, *An Anonymous Story*, published in the following year in the February and March numbers of *Russian Thought* (he had begun it as far back as 1887, but did not finish it because he feared that the censorship would never pass it), and he began writing his long story *Three*

Years (his last attempt to write a novel), which he only finished three years later.

'I have to write and write, post haste,' he wrote to Suvorin on December 8th, 'for not writing means living on credit and feeling depressed. I am writing something in which there are a hundred characters, summer, autumn, and I get mixed up, lose the hang of it, forget. . . . The devil take it!'

The most curious work Chekhov did in 1892 was the production of an abbreviated version of Dumas's *Monte Cristo*, which Suvorin intended to publish but did not. He also wanted to adapt a Sudermann play, but whether he did so or not and what play he had in mind it is impossible to say. He had, besides, an 'interesting subject' for a comedy under the unusual title of *Cigarette-Case*, which he never wrote.

On October 30th Chekhov left hurriedly for Petersburg. Suvorin was suffering from attacks of giddiness and getting very worried about it. Chekhov did not think there was anything seriously the matter with him, but (he wrote to Leontyev) 'if things are really as bad as Suvorin thinks, it would be such a loss to me that it would make me older by ten years'. As it turned out, Chekhov was right. There was nothing wrong with Suvorin. His attacks of giddiness, Chekhov thought, were 'almost normal' for a city dweller of his advanced age. Chekhov spent only a short time in Petersburg, 'eating and drinking and devouring vast numbers of oysters', he wrote to a friend, 'and I am very sorry there is not an oyster big enough to eat me for my sins'. It was during this visit that he saw Leskov and gave him a thorough medical examination. He found that Leskov was suffering from fatty degeneration of the heart and that his condition was extremely precarious. He left Petersburg by the middle of November, promising to be back within a month for a longer stay, and this time he kept his promise, returning on December 19th.

It was during his second visit that Chekhov inaugurated the so-called 'literary dinners' which were a direct result of his unsuccessful attempt to found his 'climatic station' and which took place at irregular intervals till 1901. It was one of his fondest illusions that by getting writers of different political and ideological views together he would succeed in eliminating their misunderstandings and personal enmities. The first 'literary dinner' took place in a Petersburg restaurant at six o'clock on January 12th, 1893. 'The dinner', Chekhov wrote to Michael next day, 'was a great success. In addition to the younger writers, there were present Grigorovich and Suvorin. The dinner was

my idea, and now the writers will meet and dine every month.'
Chekhov even wrote a highly optimistic report of the dinner for *New
Times*.

On the whole, he enjoyed his stay in Petersburg, although he was
ill part of the time. He dined with several of his literary friends, including Leykin and Bibilin, arranged with Tolstoy's son Leo to go
to the Chicago Exposition, and tried to raise some badly needed
money. He paid a visit to Repin's studio, and found the famous painter
engaged on a large picture of Christ in the garden of Gethsemane.
Repin was worried by the question whether there was a moon in
Gethsemane that night, and Chekhov volunteered to make inquiries
about it. On January 23rd he wrote to Repin: 'I have discussed the
question of whether there was a moon in the garden of Gethsemane
with a young theologian who is a student of ancient Jewish literature,
etc. Today I received a letter from him which I am enclosing. It has
two or three references which you may find useful. The writer of the
letter is a sensible man and a good scholar. If he cannot answer this
question, then it can only mean that other students of theology cannot
answer it, either. As for astronomers, I doubt whether they could tell
you anything definite about it. At any rate, I think it is safe to assume
that there was a moon. I can see your picture very clearly,' Chekhov
concluded, 'which means that it has made an impression on me. And
you said it was a boring subject.'

Chekhov's interest in such obscure theological problems as of what
illness Herod died of and whether there was a moon in the garden of
Gethsemane seems to indicate a much stronger link with his family
background than he would have cared to admit himself. It was the
sort of problem that would appeal very strongly to an obscurantist
like his father.

9

Did Chekhov meet Lydia Avilov during his visit to Petersburg in
December 1892 and January 1893? From a letter Chekhov wrote to
Lydia on March 1st, 1893, it is quite clear that he did not. And yet
Lydia herself describes a meeting with him after the 25th anniversary
dinner of the *Petersburg Gazette* in January 1892, and before their next
meeting in February 1895. As Chekhov did not visit Petersburg
between January 1893 and February 1895, his meeting with Lydia
must have taken place during his brief visit in October 1892. He had
already been corresponding with her 'in secret', as Lydia put it,

addressing his letters to her *poste restante*, in itself an acknowledgment on his part of a relationship that had to be concealed from her husband. The meeting took place at her sister's house, and from her account of it Chekhov could no longer have been in doubt that she was in love with him. It ended abruptly, a message having been brought that Lydia's little son was taken ill. Chekhov promised to call at her sister's next day to find out how the child was. Did he call? It is impossible to say, but from the letter he wrote to Lydia in March it seems certain that they must have met much more often than Lydia cares to admit in *Chekhov in my Life*. Chekhov's letter was in reply to an angry letter from Lydia accusing him of being 'spiteful', of not visiting her sister because he was angry with her, of forgetting her name and mistaking her for someone else and of not keeping his promise of writing to her in the country. All these accusations certainly suggest a relationship that had gone much further than one would suspect from Lydia's own account of her first three meetings with Chekhov. In his reply he wrote: 'I am not going to justify myself, because I am afraid I couldn't. All the same, I'd like to say that if I did not go to your sister's, it was not because I was afraid to meet my worst enemy there, but because—I confess it to my shame—I am a very dissolute and undisciplined fellow. I made up my mind dozens of times to call on her in the evening, but every time I was prevented by dinners, suppers, visitors and all sorts of unforeseen events. To tell you the truth, I wanted very much to call on your sister if only because I like to visit her. And I wanted to meet you there, too. However improbable that may sound to you, it is true. I wanted to say something nice to you about your stories and . . . to tell you that at a party at Baroness Ixul's someone proposed to read one of your stories, but that I strongly objected to it. Here is something else you can blame me for.

'I live in the country. I've grown old and uncouth. In the drawing-room next to my study people are playing music and singing love-songs and that is why I am at present in so elegiac a mood, which explains the peaceful and quiet tone of this letter. . . . You're wrong in describing your letters as neurotic. It isn't time yet for you to write such letters. Wait till you have become a great writer and begin publishing long novels in *European Herald*. It will be your turn then; you will succumb to the mania of grandeur and will look upon fellows like me from above and write this sort of sentence in your letters: "Only one idea, the idea that I am serving sacred, eternal and imperishable art has stopped me from committing suicide!" However, I think I'm writing nonsense. Sorry. And so', Chekhov concluded his letter, 'I am no longer angry with you and I shall be glad if you will write something to me.'

The mention of the mania of grandeur was not accidental, for in the spring of 1892 he was working on *The Black Monk*, published in January 1894 in *The Artist*, a monthly edited by Fyodor Kumanin, an old friend of his. The story, he explained to a correspondent, was 'a medical one, *historia morbis*. I deal with the mania of grandeur in it'.

Chekhov returned to Melikhovo from Petersburg towards the end of January, summoned by a message that his father was gravely ill. Pavel was suffering from arterio-sclerosis. He had attacks of giddiness, convulsive spasms in the legs and paralysis of the hands. Mary, too, was ill, and Chekhov, who had brought her home from Moscow, spent two sleepless nights at her bedside. In Petersburg he had taken to smoking cigars and he liked them so much that he indulged in three cigars a day in spite of his hacking cough, which was particularly bad in the mornings. He had, besides, a recurrence of the violent convulsions from which he had suffered as a young student and which occurred every time he went to bed after a hard spell of work. One day he went to his room for his usual afternoon nap and shortly afterwards rushed out of the house into the garden and began walking about excitedly and rubbing his forehead.

'Have you had one of your attacks again?' Michael asked.

'No,' Chekhov replied. 'I've had an awful dream. I dreamt of a black monk.'

At the time he was working on the last chapters of his book *Sakhalin*, and the Three Brothers, the ominous-looking reefs at the entrance to Korsakov which reminded him of three black monks, might well have been the cause of his dream, a kind of subconscious flashback to his state of mind at the time of his arrival in Sakhalin, which became concentrated and intensified into that frightening phantom of a black monk rushing at him out of a whirlwind. (The description of the monk in the story is amazingly vivid.) In reply to Suvorin, who wondered whether the story expressed his state of mind at the time, Chekhov wrote on January 25th, 1894: "I don't think there is anything wrong with my mental health. It is true I have no particular desire to live, but that is not an illness in the strict meaning of the word, but most probably something transitory and natural in the present circumstances of my life. In any case, if a writer depicts a mentally deranged person, it does not follow that he is sick himself. I wrote *The Black Monk* not under the influence of any gloomy thoughts but with cool deliberation.

I simply wanted to depict the mania of grandeur. The monk who comes rushing along across the field appeared to me in a dream and, on awakening, I told Michael about it.'

He had just sent in the report of his medical practice to the local medical council, from which it appears that he had 578 patients between July 21st and December 18th, 1892, an average of 4.9 patients a day. His surgery hours were rather unusual: from five to nine o'clock in the morning, but, in addition, he paid visits to patients at every hour of the day and night. And he did it all without payment. He had, besides, inspected several factories during the same period, and in his report he emphasised the need of making such inspections as frequently as possible in spite of the reluctance and occasionally open hostility of the factory owners to any supervision of their sanitary arrangements. (His story *A Woman's Kingdom*, published in January 1893 in *Russian Thought*, is based on his first-hand experience of factory life.) Having sent off his report, he sat down to write *The Black Monk*. He had been rereading the works of Turgenev, and it is interesting that Turgenev's supernatural story *The Dog* should have appealed to him particularly.

'Dear me,' he wrote to Suvorin in appraisal of Turgenev's works, 'what a magnificent novel *Fathers and Sons* is. Bazarov's illness is so powerfully done that I felt weak when I read it and I had a feeling as though I had caught the infection from him. And Bazarov's end? And his old parents? And Kukshina? It's all devilishly well done. A work of genius. I don't like anything in *On the Eve* except Helen's father and the finale. The finale is full of a feeling of tragedy. *The Dog* is very good. *Assya* is nice. *A Backwater* is rather botched and unsatisfactory. *Smoke* I don't like at all. *A Nobleman's Nest* is weaker than *Fathers and Sons*, but its ending is simply a miracle. Except for the old woman in *Fathers and Sons*, i.e. Eugene's mother, and mothers in general, especially society women, who are all, however, similar to one another (Lisa's mother, Helen's mother), and Lavretsky's mother, a former serf girl, and the peasant women as well, all Turgenev's women and girls are intolerable because of their artificiality and, forgive me, their falsity. Lisa and Helen are not Russian girls, but sc of pythians (Delphian oracles), delivering themselves of prophecies and full of pretensions which do not suit them. Irene in *Smoke*, Odintsova in *Fathers and Sons*, all of them lionesses, burning, avid, insatiable, searching for something—they are all just nonsense. When you remember Tolstoy's Anna Karenina, all these Turgenev ladies with their alluring shoulders vanish into thin air. The negative female characters, where Turgenev caricatures a little (Kukshina) or where he jokes (the description of the balls), are wonderfully delineated. . . . His descriptions of nature', Chekhov concluded, 'are good, but', he added not surprisingly, 'I can't help feeling that we are already getting tired of such descriptions and that we want something different.'

But although Chekhov liked Turgenev's story *The Dog*, his own *Black Monk* provides the reader with a much greater thrill just because it is based on a careful scientific study of mental disorder. Gorky reports Tolstoy as saying about Chekhov: 'His medicine is a hindrance to him. If he had not been a doctor, he would have written much better.' *The Black Monk* shows how wrong Tolstoy's judgment was about Chekhov's debt to medicine, though, oddly enough, in *Sakhalin* his medical training was a disadvantage to him inasmuch as it prevented him from applying his creative genius to what he considered to be only a 'scientific' work.

Chekhov interrupted his work on *The Black Monk* in April, as he had to go to Moscow to raise some money from *Russian Thought*, which owed him five hundred roubles for the second instalment of his *An Anonymous Story*, published in the March issue of that periodical. He had dinner at Lavrov's. 'Alas,' he wrote to Suvorin on the following day, 'some time ago I wrote abusive letters to Lavrov and now I am a renegade! It is pleasant to dine at Lavrov's. A typical Moscow mixture of the patriarchal spirit and modern culture. We drank five glasses of vodka, and Goltsev proposed a toast to the union of literature and scholarship. We drank Madeira, champagne and liqueurs, and Lavrov proposed a toast to his dear friend A. P. Chekhov and exchanged kisses with me. We smoked fat cigars.'

Chekhov did not suspect how very soon his new friendship with Lavrov would bring about a rift in his old friendship with Suvorin. Shortly after his return to Melikhovo he was shocked to learn that, following the publication of an attack on *New Times* by *Russian Thought*, Suvorin's son Alexey, the companion of his travels in the Caucasus, slapped Lavrov's face. 'Alexey Suvorin', he wrote to Mary, 'has slapped Lavrov's face. He came specially to Moscow to do it. This means that everything is now at an end between me and Suvorin, although he goes on writing whining letters to me.' And three weeks later he wrote to Alexander in a reference to his relations with Suvorin: 'The old building is beginning to crack and is bound to collapse. I am sorry for the old man, who wrote a repentant letter to me, and I shall probably not have to break with him finally.'

It was at this time that the situation at home was becoming so strained that Chekhov was no longer able to cope with it and even contemplated running away to Petersburg. 'My nerves are in a terrible state,' he wrote to Alexander in the same letter. 'I haven't any money and I shall never have any, neither have I the courage nor the ability to live, my health is bad, and I don't think I shall ever enjoy high spirits again.' And a fortnight later, in a letter to Suvorin, after complaining of his attack of haemorrhoids which made it impossible for him either to sit down or to walk about and which increased his feeling of irritation to such an extent that he felt like putting a noose round his neck, he added: 'It seems to me that no one wants to understand me, that they are all stupid and unfair, and I fly into a rage and say all sorts of silly things.' He had now made up his mind to give up his projected visit to the Chicago Exposition with Tolstoy's son, as he could not afford it. There were moments, however, when he would suddenly recover from his depression. 'Today,' he wrote to Schechtel on April 19th, 'as the weather was warm, I walked to the village to see a woman patient; I walked through a wood, the sun was hot, and I felt myself a king for two whole hours.' The arrival of the two promised dachshunds from Leykin on April 15th also helped to cheer him up. 'The dachshunds', he wrote to Leykin, 'have created a sensation here and everybody is talking about them. Many thanks.'

Chekhov was again in Moscow by the middle of May, but he fell ill there and had to return home hastily. 'I have dozens of different illnesses, with haemorrhoids at the head of the list,' he wrote to Schechtel on May 20th. 'I'm trying to cure myself by abstinence and solitude, i.e., I'm doing my best to listen as little as possible to what people are saying to me and to speak even less. I'm sick and tired of talk and I'm sick and tired of my patients, especially the women, who seem to be particularly stubborn and stupid.' Among his patients were many consumptives, one of whom—a woman—died, and that must have intensified his feeling of depression. By the middle of June the rows with his family became so violent and so unpleasant that Alexander, who had come down from Petersburg on a short visit, could not bear it and went back without even saying goodbye to his brother. On the station, however, he scribbled a letter to Chekhov, which to a certain extent lifts the veil on that particular period of Chekhov's domestic life. 'Looking at you and that rotten life of yours,' he wrote, 'I suffered all the time. Mother said that I offended her by going away, as she hoped that I would "talk you round". She told me that you were a very sick man. After you had driven off to see a patient before dinner, sister cried because of the scene you had during the harnessing of the horse. Mother does not understand you. She will never understand you. She is greatly worried because she is convinced that you are physically ill and therefore irritable. Father was complaining to me in the wood yesterday that no one obeyed his orders. He is a clever fellow: grandfather was the manager of an estate, ergo. . . .' To make sure Chekhov kept 'his soul alive' Alexander advised him to leave Melikhovo at once, since if he stayed their father would be sure 'to devour your soul as rats devour tallow candles. And', he added, 'it won't take him long to devour it, either'. Chekhov himself, it seems, had been thinking of taking a furnished flat in Petersburg, and Alexander offered his services to get the flat for him. 'If mother, with her loving heart,' he wrote, 'thought that you were so angry yesterday because you objected to her feeding the dogs, then it means that you can do nothing about it. As for father, nothing will change him. Of that I am certain. Your relations with sister Mary are false. One kind word from you, and she will be all yours. She is afraid of you. . . .'

A month later Alexander inquired whether Chekhov still wanted to settle in Petersburg, but by that time the worst was over. 'I went through a terrible time in spring,' Chekhov wrote to Suvorin on July 28th. 'Haemorrhoids and a most disgustingly neurotic state of mind. I lost my temper and felt bored, and my family would not forgive me my moods, and hence daily squabbles and a longing for solitude. And the spring was vile and cold. And I had no money. But summer came and everything vanished as if by magic. We're having a wonderful summer. Lots of warm, sunny days and plenty of water—such a happy combination probably happens only once in a hundred years. The harvest is marvellous. Millet, which rarely ripens in the Moscow province, is now as high as my waist. . . . Last autumn I dug a pond and planted trees round it. Now thousands of small crucians are already swimming about in it. And we have quite good bathing, too. Last spring I gave up smoking and drinking, but now I smoke one or two cigars a day, and find that it is much healthier not to smoke at all.'

He had completed his book on Sakhalin by then. 'I had been writing it a long time,' he told Suvorin, 'but all the time I felt that I was not following the right road. At last I discovered where I was wrong. I wished to convert people by my *Sakhalin*, but at the same time I was hiding something and restraining myself. The moment I began to describe what a strange fellow I felt myself to be on Sakhalin and what awful swine some of the officials were, I felt at ease and my work progressed rapidly. . . . The first chapters will be published in the October issue of *Russian Thought*.'

When at the beginning of January 1894 Suvorin referred in a jocular vein to the 'solidity, dullness and erudition' of the first chapters of *Sakhalin*, Chekhov replied that his book was an academic work. 'Medicine', he wrote, 'cannot reproach me now with unfaithfulness: I have paid my debt to learning and to what the old writers used to call pedantry. And I am glad that this coarse convict's coat, too, will hang in my literary wardrobe. Let it hang there!'

There is certainly a discernible touch of priggishness in Chekhov's attitude to what he regarded as his scientific work. According to Rossolimo, Chekhov even entertained the idea of a lectureship at Moscow University on the strength of his book. 'During my talks with Chekhov', Rossolimo writes, 'we discussed the question whether in his lectures to his students a professor ought to describe not only the different symptoms of a disease but also the patient's personal experience of it. "For instance," Chekhov said, "I suffer from gastric catarrh and I know perfectly well what it feels like. If I were a lecturer, I should have tried to make my students understand the subjective feelings of a patient, and I'm sure it would be very useful to them." I liked the idea,' Professor Rossolimo continues, 'and I proposed that he should take the necessary steps to obtain the post of a lecturer, which entailed the getting of a doctorate degree. "But", Chekhov said, "I have written no medical thesis. Shall I offer them my *Sakhalin* instead?" "Why not?" I replied. "That's simple enough." He agreed that I should talk the matter over with the Dean of the Medical Faculty, Professor I. F. Klein, which I did. However, I was completely unsuccessful, because, when I put my proposal to him, the Dean glared at me over his glasses and, without saying a word, turned his back on me and walked away. I told Chekhov about my failure and instead of an answer he burst out laughing. After that he gave up the idea of an academic career.'

The whole idea, in fact, was preposterous, and it can only be explained by Chekhov's genuine respect for medicine and his curious underestimation of the importance of his own literary work.

10

In the winter of 1893 Chekhov's health rapidly deteriorated. He coughed incessantly and complained of headaches and sleepless nights accompanied by palpitations. Again he stopped smoking and drinking for a time, and again he was beginning to wonder whether he would not after all have to live in the Crimea. At any rate, it was becoming abundantly clear to him that his hopes of an improvement of his health in the country had not been realised. The news of his illness had spread to Petersburg, and Leykin was going about telling everybody that Chekhov was dying of consumption. The story, when it reached him in Melikhovo, infuriated him and he denied it vehemently. 'My cough has grown worse,' he wrote to Suvorin in November, 'but it is still a long way from consumption.' And a little later: 'I have no consumption and I haven't had a discharge of blood from my throat for a long time. Why Leykin is spreading all these strange and unnecessary rumours in Petersburg only God who created fools and gossips knows.' He kept up the pretence for two more years, and even then he merely hinted cautiously to a close friend like Schechtel that the reason why he could not think of marriage was because 'there are germs inside me, rather insidious kind of lodgers'. In the meantime he was trying to get as much out of life as he could. While the weather was mild he was out in the open as much as possible, planting trees and bulbs, and trying to make good the depredations in his newly planted apple orchard wrought in the previous winter by the hares; and when the cold weather set in, he took frequent trips to Moscow, where a small circle of friends celebrated his arrival with so much enthusiasm that he nicknamed himself Avelan (after the Russian admiral who commanded the naval squadron which visited Toulon in 1893 in connexion with the conclusion of the Franco-Russian alliance and who was dined and wined both in France and Russia for that reason). His friends included the two editors of *Russian Thought*, Lavrov and Goltsev; the elderly managing director of Moscow's liberal daily *Russian Gazette*, M. Sablin, known as 'grandpa', who was greatly attached to Chekhov; the novelist and playwright Ignatius Potapenko, with whom Chekhov was on very friendly terms at the time; and three young girls—Lydia Mizinov, who was twenty-three just then, Tatyana Shchepkina-Kupernik, who was twenty, and her great friend Lydia Yavorskaya, an actress at Korsh's theatre, who was twenty-one. When 'Avelan' arrived, the so-called 'general naval manœuvres' began: theatre and concert parties, dinners at restaurants, and so on. 'The other day', Chekhov wrote to Suvorin in November, 'I returned from Moscow, where I spent a fortnight in a sort of a daze. I was nicknamed Avelan because my life in Moscow was a succession of feasts and new acquaintanceships. Never before did I feel so free. To begin with, I have no flat and I can live where I like; secondly, I have still no passport;[1] and, thirdly, girls, girls, girls. . . . All the summer I was worried about money, but now that my expenses have grown less, I am no longer worried and I have a feeling of freedom from money, i.e. I am beginning to think that I can manage on two thousand a year and that I can write or not as I please.'

Chekhov first met Potapenko, who was four years older than he and who had already been twice divorced, during his visit to Odessa in 1889 and found him so dull and uncongenial a companion that he dreaded his visit to Melikhovo at the end of July 1893. But when Potapenko arrived in the company of Sergeyenko, Chekhov changed his opinion of him. 'The expression "the god of boredom" I applied to Potapenko', he wrote to Suvorin, 'I now take back. Apart from everything else, Potapenko sings very charmingly and plays the violin. I was not at all bored with him even when he did not sing or play.' Potapenko was a frequent visitor to Melikhovo, bringing champagne and port with him, and in his company Chekhov, who was beginning to complain of feeling old, regained some of his youthful high spirits. He appreciated Chekhov's love of a joke and was as eager as Chekhov to play the fool. (Chekhov abominated 'serious' conversations and the look of self-importance people who engaged in such conversations assumed when solving 'eternal' problems.) Curiously enough, what Chekhov so admired in Potapenko, who at his best was only a third-rate writer, was the facility with which he wrote. 'Potapenko', he wrote to Suvorin, 'is an extraordinary man. He can write sixteen pages a day without a single correction. Once he earned one thousand one hundred roubles in five days. In my opinion, writing at a terrific speed is not, as Grigorovich thinks, a blemish but a special gift.' In his diary Suvorin described Potapenko as 'a third-rate talent, but very productive', and he might have added that with Potapenko it was his third-rateness that was the direct cause of his great productivity. It was through Chekhov that Potapenko met Lydia Mizinov, with whom he had a love affair which bears a close resemblance to Trigorin's love affair with Nina in *The Seagull*. At the time, however, Chekhov knew nothing about it, although already in October Leeka, as Lydia Mizinov was affectionately known among her friends, gave Chekhov a hint of her pregnancy. 'I have', she wrote to him, 'only three or four months more in which to see you, and afterwards I will most probably never see you again.'

It was Yavorskaya who caught Chekhov's fancy in a mild way

---

[1] Chekhov shortly obtained a permanent passport instead of the temporary one issued on the strength of his medical diploma by accepting a nominal post at the Ministry of Health for a month, thus securing for himself the recognised position of a retired civil servant.

during his frequent visits to Moscow in the winter of 1893 and 1894. He visited her so often in her dressing-room that all sorts of rumours about his 'latest love affair' were soon spread in Moscow. Even Shchepkina-Kupernik thought Chekhov's attitude to the young actress was different from his attitude to any other young woman of their acquaintance. 'There was a sort of flirtation going on between them,' Shchepkina-Kupernik writes in her reminiscences of Chekhov. 'I remember she was at the time acting in an Indian drama, in which she knelt before her chosen one, saying, "My only one, my inscrutable one, my wonderful one. . . ." And every time Chekhov came to see her and entered her blue drawing-room, she knelt on the carpet and, holding out her arms to him, exclaimed, "My only one, my great one, my wonderful one!" Echoes of this I later found in *The Seagull*,' Shchepkina-Kupernik concludes, 'when Arkadina kneels before Trigorin and calls him her only one, her great one, etc. Yavorskaya's parts in *La dame aux camélias* and in *The Whirl of Life* also found a reflection in *The Seagull*. But the similarities are only superficial ones.'

The fact, however, remains that Chekhov was 'interested in Yavorskaya as a woman' and that, while he found her company congenial, he was entirely blind to her many serious blemishes of character. He recommended her to Suvorin as a fine actress and 'extremely nice woman', and for some years she acted the leads at Suvorin's theatre in Petersburg. Suvorin left this unflattering opinion of her in his diary: 'Yavorskaya is entirely compounded of affectation, envy, vice and lies.' It was Yavorskaya who had spread the story that Chekhov had used her as the prototype for Ariadne in the story of that name, published in 1895 in the December issue of *Russian Thought*. Whether true or not, it certainly shows that in the end she realised that Chekhov had seen through her.

At the beginning of March 1894 Chekhov left for the Crimea. However much he tried to conceal the real nature of his illness from his friends, he made up his mind to do something about it, and the Crimea was the only place where he could hope to obtain some alleviation from it. Potapenko and Leeka had left earlier for Italy and France. In Yalta it was already spring, and the fine weather brought about an improvement in his health. 'In general', he wrote to Suvorin, 'I am all right, though I still cough and suffer from occasional heart attacks and haemorrhoids.' He received a letter from Leeka, who was in Germany, in which she again hinted darkly at her condition. 'I should like to get to my destination as soon as possible,' she wrote, 'and have a good look at Berlin, too, for I shall soon be dead and not be able to see anything again.' Chekhov tried to comfort her as best he could (he did not seem to have guessed even then what was the matter with her). In his reply he also gave her some particulars about his life in Yalta. 'The local aristocracy', he wrote, 'is putting on a performance of *Faust,* and I go to the rehearsals and enjoy the sight of a whole flower-bed of black, red, flaxen and chestnut heads, listen to the singing and have dinner at the house of the headmistress of the local girls' school. I go to bed at ten, get up at ten, and after lunch I have a rest— it's a boring life; in the north spring is much better than here, and not for a single moment can I forget that I simply have to sit down and write. I have worried myself so much by constantly thinking of the work I ought to be doing that for the last week I have been suffering from an intermittent pulse. A horrible sensation. It is warm, sunny, the trees are opening up, the young ladies are yearning for love, but still the north is much better than the Russian south, in spring at any rate. Nature in the north is sadder, more lyrical, more Levitan-like, while here it is neither the one nor the other, like good and sonorous but cold verses. Owing to my heart attacks, I have not drunk wine for a whole week and that makes me take an even poorer view of everything here.' He had been to a concert and regretted that he had never studied singing (Leeka had ostensibly gone to Italy and France to study singing). 'I, too, could have roared,' he wrote to her, 'for my throat abounds in rattling noises and I'm told I have a true octave. I should have had a regular income and success with the ladies.'

Instead of writing a play in the Crimea, he wrote one of his shortest stories of that period—*The Student*—which he afterwards claimed to be one of his favourite stories and one of the most perfect from the point of view of technique. He made that claim in order to rebut the accusations of pessimism which were being brought against him more and more frequently, for the story ends on a highly optimistic note. As he was just then also evolving his new dramatic technique, he spent a great deal of his time discussing the stage with Nadezhda Medvedeva, one of the leading actresses of the Maly Theatre and, as Stanislavsky testifies, one of the shrewdest and most intelligent judges of the actor's craft.

He left Yalta on April 3rd and was back in Melikhovo on the 6th. Although the weather was excellent, he was already thinking of going away somewhere and making plans with Suvorin for a trip on the Volga. His cough was not so bad as it had been when he had left for the Crimea and he had also put on weight. He had a curious experience, though. While walking with his neighbour, Prince Shakhovskoy, he nearly fainted. 'I felt as if something in my chest had got loose,' he wrote to Suvorin; 'there was a sudden sensation of warmth and tightness, a ringing in the ears, and, remembering my heart attacks which went on for a long time, I said to myself: there is a good reason for it. I walked quickly to the verandah, where some visitors were waiting for me, thinking all the time what a nuisance it would be if I were to collapse and die in front of strangers. But the moment I had taken a sip of water in my study, I felt better. So, you see, you're not the only one to suffer from fits of giddiness.' That happened at the end of April. In May he had completely recovered. He attended a conference of country doctors of the Moscow province, and on his return to Melikhovo, while driving through the woods in the moonlight, he felt as though he were coming back from a love assignation. 'I can't help thinking', he wrote to Suvorin, 'that proximity to nature and idleness are the indispensable elements of happiness; without them no happiness is possible.'

He was busy on his estate, laying down new paths, planting flowers, cutting down dead trees, keeping the dogs and chickens out of the garden, and supervising the building of a little cottage in his orchard. On June 12th he went to Moscow, where he spent a few days with Suvorin and arranged to go abroad with him. He was thinking of going to Spain and even to Africa. He wanted to live, he told Suvorin, and he felt drawn somewhere by some unknown force. By the end of June his little cottage was finished, and though it was very small, he was pleased to have at last a place to which he could retire from his family and visitors. It was in June, too, that he was elected a member of the council of the local agricultural board. At the end of July Potapenko returned from abroad. By that time Leeka had had her baby (which later died) and Potapenko had finally broken with her. But he never said a word about it to Chekhov. On August 2nd he and Chekhov went on a trip on the Volga, their ultimate destination being Taganrog. But their plans underwent a sudden change as a result of an unexpected meeting in Nizhny-Novgorod. 'Our journey on the Volga', Chekhov wrote to Suvorin on August 15th, 'ended rather strangely. Potapenko and I went to Yaroslavl, intending to go by train to Tsarytsin [Stalingrad], then to Kalach and from there down the Don to Taganrog. . . . But in Nizhny we met Sergeyenko, the friend of Leo Tolstoy. The heat, the dry wind, the noise of the Fair and Sergeyenko's conversations made me feel so stifled and bored and sick that I grabbed my trunk and fled ignominiously to—the station. Potapenko after me. We went back to Moscow, but we were ashamed to go back home without having been anywhere. We decided to go somewhere—even to Lapland. But for Potapenko's divorced wife we should have gone to Theodosia, but, alas, "our wife" was there. So after talking the matter over, we counted up our money and went to Sumy.'

They spent a week on the Lintaryov estate, and by the middle of August Chekhov was back in Melikhovo. 'The Psyol was lovely,' he wrote to Suvorin. 'Warm, spacious, lots of water and greenery, and excellent people. We spent six days there, eating, drinking, going for walks and doing no work. My ideal of happiness, as you know, is idleness. Now I am back in Melikhovo. A cold rain, leaden skies, mud. . . . I have received bad news from Taganrog. My uncle is very ill and there seems to be no hope of recovery. I shall have to go to Taganrog to see what can be done for him and to console his family.'

II

Chekhov left for Taganrog on August 24th. He found his favourite uncle Mitrofan dying, and after spending six days at his bedside, left for Theodosia, where he found Suvorin ill, the sea stormy, and a cold north-easterly wind blowing through the magnificent, but unheated, mansion. 'I sleep under three blankets,' he wrote to Natasha Lintaryov, 'and am having bad dreams. It's frightfully cold. I envy the lucky people who buy an estate in the north and live there. I cough and am beginning to take snuff from sheer boredom.' (Leeka had been taking snuff before she left Moscow, and Chekhov makes Masha in *The Seagull* take snuff, too.)

In Theodosia Chekhov received some good news from Petersburg which made him decide to go to France with Suvorin. He had been getting very contradictory reports about the state of his accounts from Suvorin's publishing house. He himself had been under the impression that he had paid off his debt to Suvorin long ago and he was surprised to learn that he still owed him seven thousand roubles. He asked Potapenko, who had gone to Petersburg, to look into the matter, and in Theodosia he received a new account according to which he owed Suvorin not seven thousand but less than a thousand roubles, and, in addition, there were still the royalties on six thousand copies of his books due to him. He was rich! 'My new account', he wrote to Natasha Lintaryov, 'has bewildered me—ought I not to go abroad and have a good time there?' And abroad he went for the second time. He stopped in Lvov, where he bought two volumes of

Shevchenko's poetry and went to an exhibition of Ukrainian paintings, which he found dull, though undoubtedly patriotic. His next stop was Vienna, where he arrived on September 18th. All he had to say about the Austrian capital this time was that the bread there was delicious. He bought himself an ink-well and a deerstalker. From Vienna he wrote to Leeka. He got her reply in Abbazia. She gave him her address in Montreux, told him that she would be glad to see him, but warned him not to be surprised at anything. It was raining in Abbazia, and, as can be gathered from his story *Ariadne*, he was not particularly impressed with that 'paradise on earth', as he had been led to believe it was. 'The sea here is worse than at Yalta,' he wrote to Schechtel, whom, incidentally, he thanked for his present of a fireplace (he had it transferred to his Yalta house afterwards), 'and the whole of Abbazia, which has only recently come into existence [as a holiday resort], reminds me of Maupassant's novel *Mont Auriol* (an excellent novel). There are lots of Russians here, but I have only made one Russian acquaintance, and she, too, is only a wet-nurse.' On September 22nd he left for Trieste, where it was also raining at first, but later it cleared up and he went for a sail round the harbour to inspect the ocean-going liners. His next stop was Venice, but 'the Queen of the Adriatic' had lost her glamour for him. All he had to record of his visit was that he got nettle-rash and bought himself a glass painted in the colours of the rainbow, three silk ties and a tie-pin. In Milan, where he spent a few days, he inspected the cathedral, which he found so beautiful that it made him frightened, the Victor Emmanuel gallery, and the crematorium ('a pity', he wrote to Mary, 'they don't burn heretics there, that is, people who eat meat on Wednesdays'). Two things he did like in Italy, though. The beer, he thought, was wonderful. 'If we had such beer in Russia', he wrote to Mary, 'I would have become a drunkard.' The other thing he admired greatly was the Italian actors. 'We in Russia', he wrote in the same letter from Milan, 'have never seen such fine acting. I went to an operetta and an Italian stage adaptation of Dostoevsky's *Crime and Punishment*, and remembering our actors, our great, cultured actors, I came to the conclusion that there was not even lemonade in their acting.' He had also paid a visit to the circus (of which he was very fond) and listened to the singing of budding opera stars. 'There are many foreign girls à la Leeka here,' he wrote, 'who come to learn singing in the hope of fame and riches. The poor things scream at the top of their voices from morning till night.' What he did find really enchanting was the magnificent Lombardy landscapes with which, he thought, nothing in the whole world could compare. He next spent a day in Genoa, where he was impressed by the great number of ships in the harbour. He also visited the famous cemetery (he had a morbid attachment to cemeteries) with its hundreds of monuments. 'Not only the deceased', he wrote to Natasha Lintaryov, 'but even their inconsolable widows, mothers-in-law and children are represented there life-size.' He was impressed by the large crowds in the streets of Genoa at night, and it is indeed very probable that, as he mingled with the crowds, the idea of the world-soul in Konstantin Treplyov's play in *Th. Seagull* first occurred to him. There is certainly more than a hint at that in Dorn's speech in the fourth act of the play.

It was in Nice that he got Leeka's letters and learnt of the unhappy issue of her affair with Potapenko. 'I feel very, very miserable,' Leeka wrote to him. 'Don't laugh. There is not a trace left of the Leeka you knew, and I cannot really say that you are to blame for it. . . . If you are not afraid to be disappointed, you may come. There is nothing left of the former Leeka. In less than six months my whole life was completely changed. . . . Still, I don't think you will cast a stone at me. It seems to me that you were always indifferent to people and their weaknesses and shortcomings'. In his reply, written on October 2nd, Chekhov protested that he was not indifferent to people and asked her to cheer up and take care of her health. But he did not go to see her in Switzerland, giving as his excuse that he was with Suvorin, who had to go to Paris. On the same day, in a letter to Mary, he expressed his opinion of Potapenko's treatment of Leeka in four words: 'Potapenko is a swine.'

Chekhov spent about a week in Nice. It was sunny and warm, but the fine weather did not seem to have any effect on his cough, which continued to plague him. 'I am coughing and coughing and coughing,' he wrote from Nice to Goltsev on October 6th. 'But I feel well enough. I find travelling abroad very bracing.' He was busy writing *Three Years*, 'a story of Moscow life', on which he had been working intermittently for the past three years (the first random notes relating to the story were jotted down by Chekhov during his first journey abroad in 1891). After a few days in Paris, he was back in Moscow on October 15th and immediately sent off the following characteristic note to Shchepkina-Kupernik: 'At last the waves have thrown the madman on the shore . . . and he holds out his arms to the two white seagulls . . .', that is, to her and Yavorskaya. He spent four days in Moscow, going through the proofs of *Sakhalin*, lunching and dining with his friends and having his photograph taken at a fashionable Moscow photographer's. It was Fyodor Kumanin who took him, Shchepkina-Kupernik and Yavorskaya to be photographed. To commemorate the occasion they decided to be photographed together. There was a great deal of laughter while the photographer was arranging the group, and at the crucial moment Chekhov turned away and pulled a long face. The resulting picture he christened 'The Temptation of St. Anthony'.

The second journey abroad did not improve Chekhov's health. He looked haggard and he had got very thin. His cough never left him, and, as he put it in a letter to a friend, he had got so used to it that he did not notice it any longer. 'It was clear', Michael records, 'that he now realised himself the seriousness of his illness, but, as before, he never complained to anyone about it and tried to hide it even from his fellow-doctors and, perhaps, deceive even himself.' To his protégée Shavrova he wrote from Melikhovo on December 2nd: 'I am perfectly all right. My story *Three Years* will be published in the January number of *Russian Thought*. I thought of writing one thing and got something quite different, not silken as I wished but satiny. You are an expression-ist. You won't like it. Oh, I'm sick of writing one and the same thing! I want to write about devils, terrible, volcanic women, sorcerers, but, alas, all they want is stories about Ivan Gaviloviches and their wives.'

The death of Alexander III and the accession to the throne of Nicholas II had revived hopes of a more liberal régime, but Chekhov did not share those hopes because he had no faith in the Russian educated classes. Five years earlier he had stigmatised the Russian intelligentsia in a letter to Suvorin as 'snails and woodlice' who were 'flabby, apathetic, dejected and colourless' because life had lost its meaning for them. And in December 1894 he wrote to Suvorin: 'As I listen to the conversations of our educated people I realise to what an extraordinary extent they are naïve, superstitious and ignorant. They seem to have been intimidated at school and they are afraid to have an opinion of their own. They have so little faith in themselves that if they give Yermolova an ovation one day they are ashamed of it the next. However,' he concluded, 'they are expecting something and hoping for something, and when they meet each other they smile.' When Suvorin asked him what he thought a Russian ought to want, his reply was that he ought to want something, anything. 'What he should first of all have', he wrote, 'is some sort of desire, some sort of temperament. One gets sick to death of these spineless do-nothings.'

In Melikhovo Chekhov resumed his medical practice. He was also summoned to serve on the jury in the Serpukhov court and was very favourably impressed with the way the jury system worked in Russia. He was further appointed inspector of the school in the neighbouring village of Talezh whose teacher he used as his model for Medvedenko in *The Seagull*. Alexander came down to Melikhovo for a short visit. 'He is a sick, suffering man,' Chekhov wrote to Suvorin on November 27th about his eldest brother. 'When he is drunk, it is distressing to be with him, and when he is sober it is also distressing, for he is ashamed of what he has been saying and doing while he was drunk.'

It was in November 1894 that Chekhov sent a letter to Goltsev that is as tantalising as it is mysterious. The letter, headed 'highly confidential', reads:

'I cannot come to Moscow, for the roads are bad and, besides, I have just returned from Serpukhov where I was serving on a jury and I am snowed under with work. Do me a favour as a friend and see that everything that is necessary is done. Raise two hundred roubles from someone and send it to the prodigal son. Keep this letter a secret and don't show it to anyone. I shall return the two hundred roubles at the beginning of December.

'If you cannot get the money from anyone, then send the following telegram to Suvorin at once: "Petersburg, Suvorin, telegraph two hundred roubles *Russian Thought* for transference to me. Chekhov." Suvorin will send you the money, for I am at present negotiating a business deal with him. Get it for me at the office and send it to the aforementioned son. Of course, when you meet him—not a sound.

'Forgive me, dear friend, for troubling you. Perhaps I shall not remain in your debt and do you a favour, too, one day.

'Give my regards to Vukol.

'Chekhov.

'I am ashamed to trouble you, but I really do not know what else I can do.'

Who was the 'prodigal son'? And what was his relationship to Chekhov? Goltsev's reply contains no clue to the mystery. 'The money has been sent *for you*,' Goltsev wrote on November 28th. 'Lavrov asked me to tell you this. He thinks (I'm afraid it is only too true!) that you won't see the end of it.'

Chekhov's extreme secretiveness was always a puzzle to his family and friends. Was there another and more over-riding reason for it than his illness? It is impossible to say except that there were secrets in his life which he felt he had to keep at all costs. His relationship with Lydia Avilov was another such secret. On December 30th he wrote to Alexander: 'If you happen to be at the office of the *Petersburg Gazette*, try and find out the address of Lydia Avilov, the sister of Mrs. Khudekov. And, please, find out quietly, without any talk.' Alexander sent Lydia's address to him, but the reason why he wanted it remains obscure. He knew how reluctant Lydia was to receive any letters from him at her home. He had been addressing his letters to her *poste restante.* The last time he wrote to her was on March 1st, and his letter seemed to have remained unanswered. Was he becoming uneasy about it? Was he afraid that Lydia was so angry with him that she did not want to write to him again? It is impossible to say for certain what his motives were, but there can be no doubt that Lydia occupied quite a special place in his thoughts.

In the same letter to Alexander there is this revealing reference about Pavel: 'Father moaned all through the night. Asked why he was moaning, he replied: "I saw Beelzebub." '

12

In 1895 Chekhov returned to the stage with the completion of *The Seagull.* It was in the previous year that a number of disconnected incidents occurred which were to be fused by the alchemy of his genius in his great stage masterpiece. There was the affair between Leeka and Potapenko, his visit to Genoa, his appointment as inspector of the Talezh village school and his meeting with its teacher. But so far none of these incidents seemed to be of the slightest literary interest to Chekhov, who was thinking of writing his comedy, *The Cigarette Case,* which certainly had nothing to do with any of them. Then in 1895 two incidents occurred which together with the others combined to provide the bare bones, the 'skeleton', as he called it, of the great play whose central idea (and it is well to emphasise that point) has nothing whatever to do with any of them. The two last incidents were connected with Levitan and Lydia Avilov.

Chekhov's quarrel with Levitan went on for over two years, and their final reconciliation was brought about by Shchepkina-Kupernik, who persuaded Levitan to accompany her to Melikhovo. All the way Levitan was terribly agitated, Shchepkina-Kupernik recalls in her reminiscences of Chekhov, sighing and infecting her, too, with his fear that they might be doing 'something silly'. At last they drove up to the house, the dogs began to bark, Mary ran out on the verandah, followed by Chekhov, well wrapped up and peering to find out who his late visitors might be. 'A small pause,' Shchepkina-Kupernik describes the meeting between the two old friends, 'then a firm handshake and—they began talking of the most ordinary things—the state of the roads, the weather—just as if nothing had happened.'

The actual date of the reconciliation can be determined with the utmost exactitude. Pavel noted down Levitan's arrival in his diary as his first entry for 1895. 'January 2. Anton drove to dine with our priest. Tatyana Shchepkina-Kupernik and I. I. Levitan arrived when we were already in bed.'

The year 1895 began dismally for Chekhov. 'I am coughing,' he wrote to his cousin in Taganrog at the beginning of January. 'If I get seriously ill, I shall have to spend six months or a whole year in Taganrog, for the air of my native city is the most healthy air.' He also told his cousin that he intended to celebrate the anniversary of Moscow University on January 12th in Moscow, but that it would most probably be a very modest celebration, as he was no longer keen on 'drunken solemnities', preferring sleep to drink. 'I slept as soundly at midnight on New Year's Eve', he wrote, 'as on any ordinary day.' On January 4th Chekhov went off to Moscow and on January 10th he wrote to Suvorin: 'I am feeling out of sorts and I expect I must have caught a cold. My devilish cough has given me the reputation of a sick man and everyone who meets me thinks it his duty to ask, "Haven't you been losing weight recently?" But as a matter of fact I am quite well and I only cough because I have got used to coughing.' He went to see Levitan at his studio. 'Levitan', he wrote to Suvorin on January 19th, 'is one of the best Russian landscape painters, but there is no longer the feeling of youth in his work. He is no longer painting like a young man but like a brilliant technician. I can't help thinking that it is women who have worn him out. These dear creatures give their love to men, but take just a little thing in return: their youth. It is impossible to paint a landscape without pathos, without enthusiasm, and enthusiasm is impossible if a man has over-eaten himself. If I had been a landscape painter, I should have led an almost ascetic life: I should have had a woman once a year and eaten once a day.' And in reply to Suvorin's bantering remark that he was hardly the man to preach continence, Chekhov wrote: 'Good heavens, women may rob a man of his youth, but they never did it to me. In my life I have always been a shop-assistant rather than a shopkeeper, and fate has not favoured me very much. I had few love affairs and I am as much like Catherine II as a walnut is like a battleship.'

It was in the same letter that Chekhov at last confessed that for reasons of health he would have to go away somewhere for eight or ten months, as otherwise he was sure to die. 'My whole chest rattles,' he wrote, 'and my haemorrhoids are so bad that it would make even the devil sick. I simply must have an operation. To hell with literature.

I ought to have devoted myself to medicine. Still, I really ought not to say that, for I owe the happiest days of my life and my best friends to literature.'

Chekhov met Lydia at a shrove-tide literary party at Leykin's. He arrived in Petersburg at the beginning of February. In *Chekhov in my Life* Lydia Avilov tells how when they drove home in a sledge after the party Chekhov kept teasing her. She asked him how long he would stay in Petersburg and he thought that he might stay another week, and he added that he would like to see her every day.

'Come and see me tomorrow evening,' Lydia suddenly proposed.

Chekhov looked surprised.

'At your place?'

And for some time (according to Lydia) they remained silent.

'Do you expect many visitors?' Chekhov asked.

'On the contrary, none at all. My husband has gone to the Caucasus. My sister never comes to see me in the evenings. We shall be all alone and we shall be able to talk and talk.'

Chekhov went, but the unexpected arrival of two friends, so brilliantly described by Lydia in her reminiscences of Chekhov, spoilt any hope either of them might have had of coming to an understanding. When at last they were left alone, they were both worn out, and Lydia listened listlessly to his sudden avowal of love for her. He took her hand and almost immediately relinquished it with, what looked to her, a feeling of disgust.

'Oh, what a cold hand!'

He then suddenly changed his mind and told her that he would not see her the next day as he had promised. 'I shall be leaving for Moscow tomorrow,' he said. 'That means that we shan't see each other again.' And as she dragged herself out of the chair and went to the door to see him off, he repeated: 'So we shan't see each other again.' Lydia said nothing, but just shook his hand listlessly. It was only as she watched him run downstairs that she summoned enough strength to call to him: 'Anton Pavlovich!' He stopped, raised his head, waited a minute, and then started running down the stairs again. She said nothing.

But Lydia's account of their two meetings in Petersburg seems to be incomplete. From the letter Chekhov wrote to her on the following day it would appear that she had invited him to have dinner with her, but as she did not repeat the invitation, he concluded that she did not want to see him. 'You were wrong to say that I was awfully bored at your place,' Chekhov wrote on February 14th. 'I was not bored but a little depressed because I could see from your face that you were tired of your visitors. I wanted to have dinner with you, but you did not repeat your invitation, and again I could not help concluding that you were tired of visitors. I am sending you my book and thousands of cordial wishes and blessings. Write a novel. Devotedly yours, Chekhov.' And on the following day, he returned the manuscripts of her stories he had taken with him from her flat with the letter of criticism she quotes in her reminiscences.

Till then it had been Lydia who had held back because she was overcome by misgivings of the dreadful consequences to her and her three children of an open break with her husband. But after Chekhov's departure from Petersburg, 'a sudden gale', as she expressed it in *Chekhov in my Life*, had swept away all her hesitations. What she did was to order a pendant for a watchchain in the form of a book from a jeweller's and have it engraved on one side: 'Short Stories by Chekhov', and on the other: 'Page 267, lines 6 and 7'. The lines were from Chekhov's story *Neighbours* and read: 'If you ever want my life, come and take it.' She asked her brother in Moscow to take it to Goltsev at the office of *Russian Thought* with the request to send it on to Chekhov. There can be no doubt whatever that Chekhov got Lydia's pendant and that it was the pendant that gave him the idea of Nina's message to Trigorin in Act III of *The Seagull*. In fact, he gave the pendant to Vera Kommissarzhevskaya at one of the rehearsals of the play at the Alexandrinsky Theatre in 1896. He did not take it back, because of his flight from Petersburg after the failure of his play. In May 1897 Kommissarzhevskaya asked him what she was to do with it, and in his reply (published in 1949 for the first time) Chekhov told her that when she got tired of it she should send it back to Melikhovo.

Lydia was waiting for a reply to her message to Chekhov, but she waited in vain. It was too late. He was ill. 'I am suffering from frequent headaches,' he wrote to Suvorin in February, 'accompanied by dizziness and dimness of sight. This illness is called scotoma. And now I am either lying down or wandering about and I don't know what to do with myself. I can't afford a doctor.' And some time later to Leykin: 'My heart attacks have got me down. I cough as frequently as in winter.' As for marriage, he wrote to Suvorin at the end of March: 'If you insist, I am quite willing to get married. But these are my conditions: everything is to remain as it was before, that is, she will have to live in Moscow and I in the country, and I shall go to see her every now and then. For happiness which goes on from day to day, from one morning to another, is something I shall not be able to endure. When people tell me the same thing every day in the same tone of voice, I become furious. For instance, I become furious in the company of Sergeyenko, because he is very like a woman ("intelligent and sympathetic") and that is why I can't help feeling in his presence that my wife may be like him. I promise you to be an excellent husband, but give me a wife who, like the moon, would appear in the sky not every day: because I am married, I shall not become a better writer.'

On April 29th Levitan was again in Melikhovo, and next day Pavel noted down in his diary: 'Anton, Mary and Levitan went for a walk in the woods and returned at ten o'clock in the evening.' That summer Levitan was painting in the Novgorod lake district. He had gone there with Sophia Kuvshinnikov and Shchepkina-Kupernik, and they lived in a country house on the shore of a lake. Levitan had by then got thoroughly tired of his Sophia and had gone to live in the neighbouring country house of a rich Petersburg society woman with whom he proceeded to have an affair. It was at that country house that he attempted to commit suicide at the beginning of July. A telegram was sent to Chekhov, who was at the time tending his roses and, generally, pottering about on his estate. He immediately left to attend on his friend. According to Michael, he was met by Levitan, who was wearing a black bandage round his head, which he tore off 'during an explanation with the ladies'. Then, Michael continues without explaining who 'the ladies' were, Levitan took his gun and went off to the lake. He returned to 'his lady' with 'a seagull he had shot for no reason and threw it at her feet'. Michael adds: 'Mrs. Kuvshinnikov claimed that it happened with her, but that is not true.' The whole story, in spite of Michael's assertion that Chekhov himself had told it to him, has an apocryphal air about it. All Levitan's love affairs were the subject of the most extravagant gossip, and Michael's story certainly does not explain who 'the ladies' were with whom Levitan had had an explanation on Chekhov's arrival or how it was that on Levitan's return with the shot seagull there was only one 'lady' there. Levitan himself left a much more plausible explanation of his attempted suicide. On July 13th he wrote to his doctor: 'I can tell you as my doctor the whole truth, knowing that it will go no further. My melancholia had gone so far that I tried to shoot myself, and now a doctor has been attending me for about a month, cleaning my wound and changing my bandage.' Levitan had attempted to commit suicide before in a fit of depression, and there is no reason to doubt his statement. Be that as it may, this final incident—Chekhov's visit to Levitan who lived at a country house on the shore of a lake—provided the last link in the chain of incidents which led him to write *The Seagull*. He spent about a week with Levitan, then went off to Petersburg for a few days and was back in Melikhovo on July 14th, but did not start writing his play till October. In August his first meeting with Tolstoy took place.

13

Chekhov's reluctance to meet Tolstoy in spite of Tolstoy's frequently expressed desire to meet him was due entirely to his growing hostility to Tolstoy's teachings, and not, as an American biographer of Tolstoy naïvely expressed it, to his losing courage 'when he came in sight of the aristocratic towers of Yasnaya Polyana'.[1] He explained his attitude towards Tolstoy's philosophy of life in unmistakable terms in his letter to Suvorin of March 27th, 1894. 'Tolstoy's morality', he wrote, 'no longer moves me. In my heart I regard it with hostility, which is of course not fair. I have peasant blood in my veins and I cannot be impressed by a peasant's virtues. Since childhood I have believed in progress and I could not help believing in it, for there is a vast difference between the time when I was whipped and the time when people stopped whipping me. I liked intelligent people, courtesy, sensitiveness, wit, and I was as indifferent to the fact that people fingered their corns and that the rags round their feet exuded a suffocating odour as to the fact that young ladies went about in curling papers in the morning. Tolstoy's philosophy had exercised a strong appeal to me and held sway over me for six or seven years; it was not its general theses, which I knew before, that impressed me so much as the Tolstoyan manner of expression, the reasonableness of it and, I suppose, it exerted a sort of hypnotic influence on me. Now something in me keeps protesting; my sense of fair play tells me that there is more love of humanity in electricity and steam than in chastity and abstention from meat. War is evil and the courts of law are evil,[2] but it does not follow that because of that I must walk about in bast-shoes and sleep on a stove with a labourer and his wife, etc. etc. But that is not important. It is not a question of being "for" or "against" anything; what matters is that for one reason or another Tolstoy no longer exists for me, that he is no longer in my heart, and that he went out of it, saying, "I leave thy dwelling empty." I am now exempt from having anyone billetted upon me. I am sick of every kind of argument, and nitwits like Max Nordau I read with disgust. People who are sick of a

[1] Ernest J. Simmons, *Leo Tolstoy.*
[2] Chekhov was referring to the political trials in Russia.

fever do not want to eat, but they want something, and they express their vague desire by saying, "I'd like something nice, something sour." So I, too, want something sour. And it is not just accidental, for I notice the same sort of feeling all round me. It is as though all of us had been in love and had fallen out of love and were now looking for some new diversions. It is quite possible, and indeed it looks like it, that the Russians will again go through a phase of enthusiasm for the natural sciences and that the materialistic movement will again become fashionable. Natural sciences are performing miracles today and they may march upon the people, like some invader, and conquer it by their grandeur and overwhelming force.'

In his *House with an Attic* he summed up his case against the followers of Tolstoy in one devastating sentence. 'The people', the hero of the story says, 'have been entangled in a great chain, and you do not cut through that chain but merely add new links to it'.

Holding such views of Tolstoy's teaching, it is not surprising that, in spite of his great admiration for Tolstoy as a creative artist, Chekhov for two years resisted all attempts to persuade him to see the great man. On March 3rd, 1893, the novelist A. I. Ertel, whose novel *The Gardenins* Tolstoy had greatly admired, told him that Tolstoy would like to see him, but he replied that he was too busy. 'I am afraid', he wrote to Mary about a month later, 'that if I go to Moscow Sergeyenko will drag me off to Tolstoy, but I shall go to Tolstoy without any guides.' In August of the same year he wrote to Suvorin: 'I wanted to go to see Tolstoy and I was expected there, but Sergeyenko was lying in wait for me in order to go with me, and I do not want to be obliged to him for my acquaintance with Tolstoy.' In July 1894 he again wrote to Suvorin: 'I don't feel like going to Yasnaya Polyana. My brain refuses to work and does not want any serious impressions. I'd much rather have a bathe in the sea and talk all sorts of nonsense.' In December of the same year he was just about to pay a visit to Tolstoy when (he wrote to Gorbunov-Posadov) he was kept back at the office of *Russian Thought* and forced to write a story. He hoped, however, to call on him before January 10th. But it was not till August 8th, after Gorbunov-Posadov had paid a visit to him in Melikhovo before going to Yasnaya Polyana himself, that Chekhov at last paid his long delayed call on Tolstoy.

On the whole, Chekhov was pleased with his visit to Yasnaya Polyana. He spent a day and a half there and his impression, he wrote to Suvorin in October, was excellent. 'I felt entirely at ease, just as if I were at home, and my talks with Tolstoy were also entirely free and easy.'

It was during that visit that Chekhov heard extracts from the first draft of *Resurrection* read by Chertkov and Gorbunov-Posadov. Tolstoy discussed it with Chekhov (he gave him a copy of it to read at home), who suggested several corrections in the description of the scene in court which were incorporated in the final draft of the novel.

What struck Chekhov rather forcibly was the way Tolstoy's daughters were devoted to their father. That, at any rate, he thought, was a sign that Tolstoy did possess some great moral force, for, if he had been insincere, his daughters would have been the first to treat him sceptically. 'A man can deceive his fiancée or mistress as much as he likes,' he wrote to Suvorin, 'and even a donkey appears a philosopher in the eyes of a woman in love, but daughters are quite a different proposition.'

Tolstoy's first impression of Chekhov was curiously indeterminate. He liked him very much and he even went so far as to declare (in a letter to his son Leo) that he thought Chekhov must have a good heart, but, he added, 'so far he has given no evidence of possessing a definite point of view', a remark that would certainly have infuriated Chekhov and made him even more reluctant to keep up his association with Tolstoy than he had been to start it.

Whether it was because of the strain of his visit to Yasnaya Polyana or because, as he suspected, he had caught a cold there, Chekhov returned home with a splitting headache. 'The whole of the right side of my head aches,' he wrote to Suvorin: 'hair, skin and bones. I had some of my teeth extracted, swallowed antiprin, phenacitin, quinine, but nothing was of any avail. Never before had my head ached for so long.'

Chekhov paid his second visit to Tolstoy six months later (on February 15th, 1896) with Suvorin, with whom he had just returned from Petersburg. 'Passing through Moscow in February, I paid a call on Tolstoy,' Chekhov wrote in the diary he began keeping that year. 'He was irritable, spoke harshly of the decadents, and for half an hour argued with Chicherin [a Russian sociologist who became a member of the first Russian revolutionary government in 1917], who, it seemed to me, talked a lot of nonsense all the time. Tatyana and Maria [Tolstoy's daughters] were laying out patience; having thought of something, both asked me to take out a card and I showed each of them separately the ace of spades, which made them look unhappy; there happened to be two ace of spades in the pack of cards. Both of them are extremely nice and their attitude to their father is very touching. The countess criticised the painter Ge all the evening. She, too, was irritable.'

Suvorin supplies a few more details of Chekhov's second visit to Tolstoy. 'Yesterday', he recorded in his diary on February 16th, 'Chekhov and I paid a visit to Tolstoy. There was also Professor Chicherin there. There was an argument about Ge's picture of Christ. Tolstoy said to Chekhov: "I am sorry I gave you my *Resurrection* to read." "Why?" "Because I have changed everything in it completely. Not a stone of the original version remains." "Are you going to let me read it now?" Chekhov asked. "I shall when I have finished it." '

Chekhov enjoyed his visit to Tolstoy. 'I spent two hours with him with pleasure,' he wrote to Korolenko. But it is significant that immediately after his first and second visits he should have begun writing stories directed against Tolstoy's philosophy of life: *The House with an Attic* after his first visit, and *My Life*, in which he exposed with devastating effect the tragedy of the people who tried to put Tolstoy's teaching into practice, after his second visit.

14

Chekhov completed the first version of *The Seagull* on November 20th, 1895, having written most of it in the small cottage he had built for himself in Melikhovo. In December he read it to a large gathering of friends in Moscow. The reading took place in Yavorskaya's blue drawing-room. It was the only time Chekhov ever read a play of his in public (the well-known photograph of him reading *The Seagull* to the company of the Moscow Art Theatre was merely a posed picture), and that alone shows how eager he was to find out what impression the new type of drama he had invented would make on his friends. The result was a great blow to him. Nobody seemed to know what to make of it. Korsh, who regarded Chekhov as *his* author because he was the first to put on *Ivanov*, and Yavorskaya, who hoped to get a part in the play, were expecting the sort of play they were used to and were terribly disappointed. 'The impression the play has produced', Shchepkina-Kupernik writes, 'can be compared with Arkadina's reaction to Treplyov's play: "Something decadent. . . ." The play surprised everybody by its novelty of form and, of course, those who like Korsh and Yavorskaya recognised only the showily dramatic plays of Sardou, Dumas, etc., could not possibly have liked it. I remember the loud arguments and Yavorskaya's insincere expressions of delight and Korsh's astonishment. "My dear fellow," Korsh said, "but it isn't dramatic: you make your character shoot himself behind

CHEKHOV'S PORTRAIT BY JOSEPH BRAZ

the scenes and don't even give him a chance of making a speech before his death!" I also remember Chekhov's embarrassed and stern face....'

There can be no doubt that Chekhov was greatly disappointed with the reception of his play and, as usual, his first reaction was to blame himself. 'It seems that I am not destined to become a dramatist,' he wrote to Suvorin on December 13th. 'I'm unlucky. But I don't lose heart because I can still go on writing my stories. In that sphere I feel at home, but when I write a play I feel troubled as though someone were standing over me.'

But how unlucky he was with *The Seagull* Chekhov was only to learn a year later in Petersburg. In the meantime he sent the play to Suvorin, who was immediately struck by the similarity between the Nina-Trigorin episode in the play and the Leeka-Potapenko love affair. Chekhov decided to revise the play thoroughly, and he was busy working on it for the next three months. In spite of the criticisms of his play, however, he was determined to have it put on, and at the beginning of January 1896 he went to Petersburg to make arrangements for its production in the autumn at the Alexandrinsky Theatre.

He spent a fortnight in Petersburg, seeing Potapenko almost daily as well as many others of his literary friends, including Korolenko and Mamin-Sibiryak, whom he thought 'a very sympathetic fellow and an excellent writer'. He did not see Lydia Avilov, but he sent her a letter on his return to Melikhovo, where he was summoned on some business in connexion with the Talezh village school he was building. 'Having learnt from your sister that you have just published a book,' he wrote to her on January 17th, 'I was about to pay a call on you to receive your dear child from your own hands, but fate decided otherwise: I am back in the country again. I received your book on the day I left Petersburg. I haven't had time to read it yet, but to judge by its appearance it has been most charmingly produced and indeed looks very nice. After the 20th or the 25th January I shall be in Petersburg again and I hope to call on you then.'

Lydia had inscribed her book to Chekhov: 'To the proud master from his apprentice, L. Avilov,' and, referring to that inscription, Chekhov added: 'Why did you call me "proud master"? Only turkeys are proud. Your proud master is devilishly cold. It's twenty degrees of frost. Your Chekhov. Today is my name-day, but I am bored all the same.'

By that time Chekhov must have received the watch-chain pendant from Lydia, and quite possibly Lydia's reference to his pride was a concealed reflection on Chekhov's refusal to take her hint. He was back in Petersburg on January 24th and spent three weeks there. Did he carry out his promise to meet Lydia? According to Lydia, he did not, for she met Chekhov by chance at a Shrove-tide mask-ball, that is to say, some time in February, and she never revealed her identity to him. There is a gap of eight months between the mask-ball and the first night of *The Seagull* on October 17th, which Lydia disregards in her reminiscences of Chekhov, telescoping the two events in one chapter. At the mask-ball Chekhov had told her that he would send her a message from the stage. The message, as Lydia discovered on her return from the first night of the play, occurred in the lines which Nina asks Trigorin to look up in his book and which referred not to the actual passage in Chekhov's book but to a line in her own book, namely: 'It is not proper for young ladies to go to mask-balls.' A message like that (Chekhov must have altered the numbers of the pages while he was revising the play) is quite in character. Faced with a difficult decision, Chekhov always resorted to some roundabout way in which to indicate his own attitude. If it was improper for young ladies to go to fancy-dress balls, it was even more improper for a young married woman with three children to run away from her husband. Chekhov's reply was, besides, entirely in accordance with Lydia's conception of propriety. 'You possess an inborn moral sense,' he had said to her one day. His reply to Lydia's message was clear: there could be no question of their running away together even if he still loved her as passionately as he did three years earlier.

On his return to Melikhovo at the beginning of March, Chekhov was busy with supervising the building of the Talezh village school and working on his play and his two anti-Tolstoyan stories. At the end of March he went to Moscow for a few days to meet Suvorin. He met Suvorin again in Moscow at the end of May, when the two of them went specially to inspect the graves of the two thousand people who were crushed to death on Khodynka Common during the festivities on the occasion of the coronation of Nicholas II. It was at that time that Chekhov was beginning to be worried about his eyes. Many of his friends had noticed his curious habit of screwing up his eyes, throwing back his head and peering from under the rim of his pince-nez. Stanislavsky, who admits that he disliked Chekhov at first, thought that it indicated a supercilious attitude towards people. Actually, when Chekhov at last made up his mind to visit an oculist in June, it was discovered that he was practically blind in the right eye, following a rash on the cornea and the partial paralysis of the eye muscles. He was prescribed electric treatment, injections of arsenic and a sea cure.

Chekhov stayed in Moscow till June 20th. On his return to Melikhovo he put the finishing touches to *The Seagull* and sent it off to Suvorin. For the next six weeks he was very busy with the different social activities in the country. He built a steeple with a glass cross, which gleamed in the sun, for the Melikhovo church, and he was instrumental in opening a post office in the village, the stopping of express trains at Lopasnya station, the construction of a bridge over the river and the building of a highway. On Sunday, August 4th, the school he had built in Talezh was consecrated. The peasants from four villages welcomed Chekhov with the traditional dish of bread and salt and presented him with an icon and two silver salt-cellars. An old peasant made a moving speech (Chekhov described the scene in *My Life*) and the manager of Count Orlov's estate presented Mary with a bouquet. 'There were refreshments,' Pavel wrote in his diary, 'and a girls' choir sang songs.'

At its meeting of October 29th the Serpukhov agricultural board passed a special vote of thanks to Chekhov for building the school, and three years later the Government in the name of the Czar conferred the order of Stanislaus third class (the lowest order in the honours list of Czarist Russia) on him. This rather belated and grudging acknowledgement of Chekhov's work for education was accompanied by a rise in his social status, for in the official announcement (which came to light only recently) he was referred to as 'an hereditary nobleman', a fact which, characteristically, he never mentioned either to his friends or relations.

Before leaving for the Caucasus and the Crimea for a short holiday, Chekhov asked Potapenko to look out for a flat for him in Petersburg, as he intended to spend the winter there; he certainly never dreamt at the time that he would not wish to stay for a single day in Petersburg after the first night of *The Seagull*. Having got his play passed by the censorship after making some unimportant changes in the text (Potapenko was very helpful to him in that matter), he left for Taganrog on August 20th and, after a short stay there, took the train for the Caucasian spa of Kislovodsk, where he met many old friends as well as the Russian mystic Vladimir Solovyov, who told him that he always carried a nutgall in his pocket as the best cure for haemorrhoids. He listened to the band twice a day, ate *shashlyks*, bathed in thermal waters and joined a shooting party. On August 31st he left for Theodosia, where he stayed with Suvorin for a fortnight, 'doing nothing and bathing in an ice-cold sea', as he wrote to his cousin in Taganrog. He was back in Melikhovo on September 17th, and until his departure for Petersburg he was busy with the distribution of the parts of *The Seagull* among the cast of the Alexandrinsky Theatre. By that time it had been decided to put on the play for the benefit night of the light comedy actress Levkeyeva. It was a fatal mistake, for Levkeyeva was very popular among the sort of playgoer who would be least likely to enjoy a play like *The Seagull*. On his return from the Crimea there was a recurrence of the discharge of blood from his lungs and that always filled Chekhov with dreadful forebodings; this quite possibly prevented him from appreciating the unwisdom of putting on his play in such haste or of entrusting the production to a man like Karpov, whom he had known since 1888 and whose conventional, third-rate plays he had criticised severely in *Fragments of Moscow Life*. Karpov, indeed, was fully aware of the difficulties of producing, as he wrote to Chekhov on September 27th, 'such an unusual play, demanding exceptionally subtle acting', but in a play like *The Seagull* the producer's ability to understand the revolutionary methods of Chekhov's new dramatic technique is perhaps even more important than the acting. And, as Chekhov should have known, Karpov was the last man to understand those methods. But Chekhov was ill, and it was his tragedy as a playwright that he should have returned to the stage at a time when his illness made it impossible for him to take an active part in the production of his plays.

Chekhov arrived in Petersburg on Monday, October 7th, and spent only ten days there. The rehearsals of *The Seagull* began on the day after his arrival and at once an important change had to be made in the cast. Savina, the star of the Alexandrinsky Theatre, who was to have played Nina, backed out at the last moment and the part was given to Vera Kommissarzhevskaya. This eleventh-hour change wasted three rehearsals. Chekhov, who was present at the fourth rehearsal, realised, to his dismay, that the actors did not know their parts and, as he put it, 'acted too much'. But more ominous still was the intangible feeling of hostility of many of his literary friends who had always envied his fame and were only waiting for an opportunity to vent their spite on him. 'So far', he wrote to Mary on October 12th, 'the acting in *The Seagull* is poor. It is boring in Petersburg. Everybody is spiteful, petty, insincere. . . . I'm afraid it's not going to be a cheerful, but rather a gloomy performance. On the whole I don't feel very bright.'

On the same day Chekhov met Grigorovich, who looked very ill and, Chekhov suspected, was suffering from cancer and would soon

die. Of the three famous writers who had given him so much en-
couragement at the beginning of his literary career two were already
dead: Pleshcheyev had died two years earlier and Leskov had died on
February 21st of that year. It seemed that it was Grigorovich's turn
now, and though Chekhov might on occasions have resented Grigorovich's claim to have 'discovered' him, he could not but feel sad at the
thought that he, too, might die soon.[1]

15

The first night of *The Seagull*, on October 17th, was a complete
fiasco. The derisive laughter and booing during the first two acts drove
Chekhov out of the auditorium and he spent the last two acts of the
play in Levkeyeva's dressing-room.[2] 'During the intervals,' he wrote
in his diary, 'the theatrical officials in their uniforms came into the
dressing-room. Pogozhev with a star; a young handsome official
from the police department also came in. If a man attaches himself
to some job he knows nothing about, to art, for instance, he inevitably
becomes an official. How many people thus become parasites of
some scientific pursuit, the theatre, or painting, and wear uniforms!
The same thing happens in the case of a man who knows nothing of
life and is incapable of dealing with it. Such a man has no alternative
but to become an official. The fat actresses in the dressing-room treated
the officials with respectful good humour and did their best to flatter
them; they are like so many old, respectable housekeepers whom their
master has come to visit.' And what more damning criticism of the
actors and actresses on whom Chekhov relied for the success of his
play could be made?

Chekhov fled from the theatre after the end of his play. 'It is true',
he wrote in his diary, 'that I fled from the theatre, but that was only
after the end of the play.' Nobody knew where he was. 'At one o'clock
in the morning', Suvorin recorded in his diary on October 17th,
'Chekhov's sister arrived to find out where he was. She was very upset.
We sent messengers to the theatre, to Potapenko, to Levkeyeva
(she was giving a dinner to the actors), but he was nowhere to be
found. He arrived at two o'clock. I went to see him. "Where have you
been?" I asked. "I walked about the streets," he replied. "I couldn't
just dismiss that performance from my mind, could I? If I live for

---

[1] Grigorovich did not die till three years later, in 1899.
[2] Levkeyeva, a popular comedienne, whose benefit night it was, appeared in a light comedy
after the performance of *The Seagull*.

another hundred years, I shall not give another play to the theatre. In that sphere I am unlucky." He told me that he had decided to leave Petersburg the next day at three o'clock. "Please, don't stop me," he said. "I can't listen to all that talk." Last night after the dress rehearsal he was very upset about the play and said he wished it could be taken off. He was very dissatisfied with the acting, which, indeed, was very mediocre. Chekhov', Suvorin concluded his entry, 'is very vain, and when I explained to him my impressions of the play he listened to me impatiently.'

But Chekhov's impatience with Suvorin's criticisms was more likely caused by Suvorin's failure to grasp the meaning of the play than by his vanity. Suvorin realised that *The Seagull* was quite different from any ordinary play of direct action. 'The action of the play', he noted down in his diary, 'takes place behind the scenes rather than on the stage, as though its author was only interested in showing how the events reacted on the characters and thereby characterised them.' Having thus quite correctly analysed the main characteristic of an indirect action play like *The Seagull*, Suvorin immediately jumped to the conclusion that 'as a play, it is weak'. And it was that conviction of his that must have exasperated Chekhov.

Next morning at about ten o'clock Potapenko, who had not been at the first night of *The Seagull* either because he had anticipated its failure or because he did not want to meet Leeka Mizinov who was in the theatre with Mary, came to see Chekhov and found him writing letters.

'I'm glad you've come,' said Chekhov. 'You'll see me off to the station, won't you? I can give you that pleasure, as you were not a witness of my last night's triumph. I don't want to see any of those who were.'

'Not even your sister?' asked Potapenko.

'I shall see her in Melikhovo,' Chekhov replied. 'Let her have a good time here first. Here are the letters I've written. We shall dispose of them downstairs. I've already packed my trunks.'

'Are you going back by the express train?'

'No, I shall have to wait too long. There's a train at twelve.'

'But it's a dreadfully slow one. It takes twenty-two hours to reach Moscow.'

'So much the better. I shall sleep and dream of fame. Tomorrow I shall be in Melikhovo. Ah, there's real bliss for you. No actors, no producers, no audience, no papers. You know, you have a good nose.'

'You mean?'

'I'm referring to your instinct for self-preservation. You were not at the theatre last night. I oughtn't to have gone there, either. Oh, if you'd seen the faces of the actors! They looked at me as though I'd robbed them and gave me a wide berth. Let's go.'

They went downstairs, where Chekhov left his letters with the porter. Then they took a cab to the station. There Chekhov was already cracking his usual jokes, laughing at himself and making Potapenko laugh, too. A newsvendor on the platform offered Chekhov a paper.

'I don't read papers.' Chekhov motioned him away. 'Look,' he turned to Potapenko, 'what a good-natured face he has, and yet his hands are full of poison. Every paper has a notice of my play.'

The train was empty and Chekhov had a second-class compartment all to himself.

'Ah,' he said, 'I shall be able to have a good sleep.'

But Potapenko could see from the look in his eyes how distressed he really was.

'That's the end,' he said, as he entered the carriage. 'I shall write no more plays. As I was leaving the theatre last night, hiding my face in the turned-up collar of my overcoat, I heard one man say to another, "That's literature and not drama"; and the other added, "And bad literature at that." A third one asked, "Who's this Chekhov? Where did he spring from?" And as I was going out I overheard a shortish gentleman say indignantly, "I can't understand how the administration of the theatre allows such plays to be performed. To put on such plays is an insult!" But I just passed on, thinking, "Ah, you don't know that I wrote the play, do you?"'

'Are you sure you won't change your mind and stay after all?' Potapenko asked as the train was about to move out of the station.

'No, thanks. They'll all be coming to comfort me, looking like people who are seeing off their dear relation to a Siberian convict prison.'

The train moved off.

Potapenko was right. In spite of his laughter and jokes, Chekhov was deeply distressed. That becomes evident from the three letters he left behind for Suvorin, Mary and Michael. To Suvorin he wrote: 'Stop the printing of my plays. I shall never forget last night, but I had a good sleep and I'm leaving feeling tolerably cheerful. . . . I shall not put on my play in Moscow. *Never* will I write or produce any more plays.' To Mary he wrote: 'Last night's business neither surprised nor distressed me very much, because I had been prepared for it by the rehearsals—and I don't feel particularly bad about it.' He was more outspoken in his letter to Michael. 'My play', he wrote, 'was a terrible flop. There was a tense feeling of bewilderment and disgrace in the theatre. The actors played disgracefully. Hence the moral: don't write plays.'

In his letter to Suvorin on October 22nd Chekhov denied that he had fled from Petersburg out of cowardice. 'In your last letter [of October 18th] you call me a silly old woman three times and say that I acted like a coward,' he wrote. 'Why this defamation? After the performance I had a good dinner at Romanov's, then I went to bed and slept soundly and the next day I left for home without uttering a single moan. If I had acted the coward, I should have been running about the different newspaper offices or gone to see the actors, imploring them to treat me kindly. I should have made all sorts of useless corrections and spent another two or three weeks in Petersburg, going to each performance of my *Seagull*, trembling with excitement, covered in a cold sweat, uttering complaints. . . . When you came to see me at night after the performance, you said yourself that it would be best for me to leave Petersburg; and next morning I received a letter from you in which you said goodbye to me. Where, then, is my cowardice? I acted as reasonably and coolly as a man who makes a proposal and is rejected and has nothing else to do but leave. I admit my vanity was hurt, but the whole thing was no surprise to me, for I expected failure and was prepared for it, and I warned you about it in all sincerity.

'At home', Chekhov went on, 'I took castor oil, had a wash in cold water—and now I am ready to write a new play. I don't feel tired or irritated any longer and I have no need to fear that Davydov or Leontyev will come to discuss my play with me. I agree with your corrections and thank you for them a thousand times. Only please don't be sorry that you were not at the rehearsals. There was only one real rehearsal, and I couldn't make head or tail of anything; I couldn't see my play because of the disgustingly bad acting.'

By that time Chekhov was receiving telegrams from all sorts of people to tell him that the subsequent performances of his play were successful (the play was taken off after the fifth performance). One of these letters was from Anatoly Koni, a well-known lawyer and writer, who had seen the play at the Alexandrinsky Theatre and was deeply moved by it. 'I have known you a long time,' Chekhov wrote in reply. 'I respect you deeply and have more faith in you than in all the critics put together. I feel easy in my mind now and I no longer recall the play and its performance with a feeling of disgust.'

But a month later, having completed and sent off *Uncle Vanya* to Suvorin, he still insisted that he did not feel anything but disgust for his plays. 'You will say again', he wrote to Suvorin, 'that it is stupid, that it is my vanity, my pride, etc. etc. I know, but what can I do about it? I should be glad to get rid of my stupid feeling, but I can't do it. That is not because my play was a failure. On October 17th it was not my play but my personality that was unsuccessful. Already during the first act I was struck by one curious circumstance, namely that those with whom I had been on frank and friendly terms before October 17th, those with whom I had been dining without an evil thought in my mind, those for whom I had broken lances (as, for instance, Yassinsky) —that all of them looked very odd, damned odd. In short, what happened gave Leykin the opportunity of commiserating with me for having so few friends, made *The Week* ask, "What has Chekhov done to them?" and *The Playgoer* publish a report alleging that the writing fraternity had created a disturbance against me in the theatre. Now I have regained my habitual calm and am in as good a humour as ever, but I still can't forget what has happened as I could never forget if, for instance, someone had slapped my face.'

A little earlier he blamed Nemirovich-Danchenko[1] and Sumbatov[2] for 'suborning' him to write a play. 'The theatre', he wrote to Nemirovich-Danchenko, 'breathed malice and the air was full of hatred and I flew out of Petersburg like a bomb according to the laws of physics. . . . Lavrov and Goltsev', he added the information, 'insisted that I should let them publish *The Seagull* in *Russian Thought*, and now the literary critics will start damning me—which makes me feel as though I had to wade through a puddle in the autumn.'

It was while he was still feeling disgusted with the reception given to *The Seagull* in Petersburg that he sent Leeka 'a design for a watch-chain pendant', being a replica of the pendant Lydia had sent him, on which he asked her to look up page 73, line 1, of the catalogue of plays issued by the Society of Russian Playwrights. The reference was to a one-act play with the title of *Ignatius the Fool, or Accidental Madness*, a jocular reference to Leeka's unhappy entanglement with Ignatius Potapenko.

Summing up tne events of his life for the past two years, Chekhov wrote to Suvorin on December 2nd: 'In my personal life there has been so much unpleasantness of every kind (we even had a fire in our

---

[1] Vladimir Nemirovich-Danchenko (1858–1943), novelist, playwright, producer, and one of the founders of the Moscow Art Theatre.

[2] Prince Alexander Sumbatov-Yuzhin (1857–1927), playwright and leading actor of the Moscow Maly Theatre.

house the other day) that nothing else is left for me to do but to join the army and go to war like Vronsky[1]—only, of course, not to fight but to heal. The only bright period during that time was my visit to your place in Theodosia, as for the rest, I wish it had never happened, it was so bad.' As for the state of his health, Chekhov no longer concealed the fact that he had consumption from some of his friends, at any rate. 'I have got bacilli,' he wrote to Schechtel on December 12th, 'and I am constantly coughing, but on the whole I feel quite well and am always on the move.' Within three months the secret of his illness would no longer be a secret to anybody, but for the time being Chekhov was more worried about Levitan's health than about his own. There were rumours that Levitan was seriously ill. 'Levitan', Chekhov noted in his diary on December 21st, 'has an enlarged aorta. He wears a little sack of clay on his chest. Wonderful paintings and a passionate zest for life.' And two months later he wrote to Suvorin with that curious detachment which was characteristic of him when face to face with such an unavoidable calamity as death: 'The artist Levitan (the landscape painter) will probably die soon. He has an enlarged aorta.' During his visit to Moscow in February 1897 he examined Levitan and summed up his opinion in one sentence in a letter to their mutual friend Schechtel: 'It's hopeless: his heart does not beat, it puffs and blows.'

16

The new régime inaugurated by the reign of Nicholas II soon settled down to a ruthless suppression of all freedom of thought and expression. Chekhov found that even his letters to Suvorin were being opened by the police, and when he went to France in September 1897 he discovered that one of the results of the Franco-Russian alliance was that the French post offices refused to accept any Russian printed matter bearing a Russian address. When, on February 2nd, 1897, the police searched the house of Chertkov, confiscated the copies of the appeal he had issued with Tolstoy's approval on behalf of the persecuted sect of the Dukhobors and ordered him to leave Russia, Chekhov told Suvorin that he was sorry he could not go to Petersburg to see off Chertkov who was sailing for London. 'I have no tender feelings for Chertkov,' he wrote, 'but what they did to him makes my blood boil.'

Like Tolstoy, Chekhov was at the time preoccupied with the problem of the meaning of art, but he considered it from the point of

[1] One of the leading characters in Tolstoy's novel *Anna Karenina*.

view of the creative artist and not from that of the moralist. He found Tolstoy's ideas in *What Is Art?* neither new nor convincing. 'Old men', he wrote to Ertel, 'were always prone to see the end of the world and they always said that morality had sunk as low as it possibly could, that art had degenerated, that men had grown weak, etc. etc. In his book Tolstoy wants to persuade us that art has now entered into its final phase, that it has got itself into a rut from which it can no longer get out. All that is not new. Clever old men have been saying it in one way and another in all ages. . . .' And later in a letter to Suvorin: 'To say that art has grown feeble, that it has got itself into a rut, that it isn't what it should be, etc. etc., is like saying that the desire to eat and drink has become outmoded and is no longer what we need. Hunger, no doubt, is an old story, and in our desire to eat we have quite likely got ourselves into a rut, but we must eat all the same and we shall go on eating whatever philosophers and cross-grained old men may say.'

Far from driving the ethical principle of art to a point where it becomes indistinguishable from a denial of art, Chekhov had been concentrating on finding new and more subtle forms of dramatic expression, and Tolstoy's failure to realise that, which becomes obvious from his condemnation of Chekhov's plays and, particularly, of *The Seagull*, perhaps shows more than anything else how completely wrongheaded he was.

Chekhov's social conscience was no less developed than Tolstoy's, and that is perhaps best illustrated by the part he took in the general census of January 1897. He had just finished building one village school and was already drawing up the plans of another in the village of Novoselki when he was called on to supervise the census in his district. He had 'influenza' at the time and a bad headache, but he carried on with his allotted task, supervising the work of fifteen census officials and going round the villages himself, filling up the forms for the illiterate peasants.

An unexpected complication of the census was the threat of a bubonic plague epidemic, and in this connexion Chekhov gives a shocking picture of the state of health of the Russian working population of his time. 'It is impossible to say for certain', he wrote to Suvorin on January 17th, 'whether the plague will come to our district or not. If it comes it will hardly create a panic as both the population and the doctors have long become accustomed to the high death rate from diphtheria, typhus, etc. Even without the plague only about four hundred out of every thousand children survive to the age of five in our district, and in the villages and the factories and backstreets of our towns you will not find one healthy woman. The plague will be bad only inasmuch as it will come two or three months after the census; for the common people will interpret the census in their own way and accuse the doctors of poisoning the superfluous population so that there should be more land for their masters.'

The census was over by February 5th and Chekhov went off to Moscow for a few days. He was interested in the proposal to found a national theatre in Moscow for which Schechtel had, at his suggestion, drawn up a plan. To discuss it, he convened a meeting of Moscow writers and actors at Goltsev's office at seven o'clock in the evening on February 16th. Stanislavsky had also been invited. It was his third meeting with Chekhov. Their first meeting must have taken place at the opening of the Society of Art and Literature in November 1888, and their second more recently at a concert at Korsh's Theatre in aid of the Literary Fund where Stanislavsky had the unfortunate experience of reciting a poem and afterwards having his leg pulled by Chekhov. On that occasion Stanislavsky had parted from Chekhov in a huff, and at their meeting on February 16th their relations could hardly have improved as Stanislavsky was against the whole scheme. This is Stanislavsky's meagre description of the meeting: 'The small office of the editor of a well-known periodical. Many unknown people. The room was full of tobacco smoke. A well-known architect, a friend of Chekhov's, demonstrated a plan for building a people's home, a theatre and a refreshment-room. Rather timidly I offered my objections to the plan. Everybody listened thoughtfully, while Chekhov walked about, making everybody laugh and, to be quite frank, being rather a nuisance. That evening he looked particularly cheerful: tall, red-cheeked and smiling. At that time I did not know why he was so happy. Now I know. He was happy because something new and good was being planned for Moscow. He was glad of anything that made life more beautiful.'

Schechtel's design for a national theatre was to be exhibited at a conference of actors which was to take place in Moscow in April. In a letter to Suvorin on March 1st Chekhov wrote: 'At the conference of actors you will probably see the project for a huge national theatre which we are planning to establish. *We*, that is, the representatives of the Moscow intelligentsia (the intelligentsia has expressed its willingness to meet capital half way and capital is not averse from doing the same). Under one roof, in a neat and beautiful building, a theatre, a library, a reading room, refreshment rooms, etc., are to be housed. The plan is ready, the statutes are being drawn up, and all that is lacking is a mere trifle—half a million roubles. I have so entered into the spirit of the thing that I believe in it already.'

At the time Chekhov never dreamt that he was destined to play a prominent part in the foundation of what was eventually to become one of the most famous national theatres in Russia and that, of all people, Stanislavsky, whom he disliked and who had spoken so scornfully of Schechtel's plan, was to be closely associated with it and, through his production of *The Seagull*, ensure its existence and further development. He would have dismissed the whole thing as the ravings of a lunatic. Life has a way of playing the most fantastic tricks on those who seem to know its secrets best.

On February 19th, shortly before his return to Melikhovo, Chekhov was present at a dinner to celebrate the great anniversary of the liberation of the serfs. There could, it seems, have been no more appropriate occasion for Chekhov, whose father was born a serf, to celebrate; and yet the dinner merely deepened his feeling of bitterness for his former masters. 'The whole thing', he wrote in his diary, 'was absurd and boring. To dine, drink champagne, deliver speeches on the subject of the people's awakening, freedom and so on, while at the same time slaves in evening dress are scurrying round the table, serfs of the same sort, and outside in the street the drivers are waiting for their masters in the frost, means to sin against the Holy Ghost.'

After attending an amateur performance in Serpukhov in aid of the school he was building, Chekhov returned home where he finished his story *Peasants*, published in the April issue of *Russian Thought*. The story raised a veritable storm and got him into trouble both with the radicals and the reactionaries. The censors insisted on the removal of a page from the published story, in which Chekhov dealt with the attitude of the peasants to religion and put the blame for their illiteracy on the authorities. They threatened to put him under arrest if he refused to comply; which furnishes a striking confirmation, if one is necessary, of Chekhov's belief that a creative writer need not engage in overt propaganda to rouse the consciousness of his readers to the crying evils of his time.

A little earlier Chekhov received a letter from Schechtel, who wrote to tell him that P. Tretyakov, the founder of the National Portrait Gallery, had commissioned the painter Joseph Braz to do his portrait. On Saturday, March 22nd, he left for Moscow, intending to spend a few days there and then leave for Petersburg to sit for his portrait. He was feeling ill at the time and coughing up blood. Suvorin had arrived in Moscow, and Chekhov also arranged to have dinner with Lydia

Avilov, who was in Moscow at the time. He wrote to Lydia from Melik-hovo on March 18th, addressing her as 'Angry Lydia Alexeyevna' and telling her that he wanted to see her very much in spite of the fact that she had wished him all the best 'in any case'. At Lopasnya station he met his sister, who was coming back from Moscow for the week-end. 'He told me', Mary records, 'that he was going to Moscow and that the painter Braz was going to paint his portrait for the Tretyakov gallery. While he spoke, he was coughing. I did not like the look of his face and I thought that he ought not to pose with a face like that. At home I was met by my mother, who looked very troubled. "Antosha", she said, "has been coughing so much at night; I could hear everything through the partition. I'm so worried. I hope he won't fall ill." Father, too, looked very upset.'

On his arrival at his hotel Chekhov sent a hasty note to Lydia. 'I have arrived in Moscow earlier than I expected,' he wrote. 'When shall we meet? The weather is misty and foul, and I feel a little indisposed. I shall try to stay indoors. Won't you come and see me without waiting for me to pay you a visit?' In the evening Chekhov had dinner with Suvorin, but as soon as they sat down at the table he had a haemorrhage. Blood poured from his mouth. He asked for some ice, but as he could not stop the flow of blood, they left without dining for Suvorin's hotel, where he stayed for two days. 'Chekhov', Suvorin wrote in his diary, 'was frightened by his haemorrhage and told me that his condition was very serious. "To calm our patients", he said, "we usually tell them that their coughing is due to some upset of the stomach, and when they have a discharge of blood that it is of a haemorrhoidal origin. But no cough is ever caused by a condition of the stomach, and a discharge of blood is always from the lungs. My blood is coming from my right lung as it did with my brother and another relative of mine who also died of consumption." ' He sent for his friend, Dr. Obolonsky, who succeeded in stopping the flow of blood. On Monday morning Chekhov got up early, woke Suvorin and told him that he was going back to his hotel. He was obviously anxious about the appointment with Lydia Avilov he had failed to keep. At the hotel he had another haemorrhage and sent for Dr. Obolonsky again. The same day he wrote to Goltsev to ask him to send Schechtel's design for a national theatre, as he wanted to show it to 'a rich man'. He also wrote to Lydia, telling her what had happened. At six o'clock on the morning on Tuesday, March 25th, he had still another haemorrhage, and this time Dr. Obolonsky took him immediately to Professor Ostroumov's clinic. Suvorin went to see him twice on that day.

'Chekhov', he records in his diary, 'lies in Ward No. 16, ten numbers higher than his *Ward No.* 6, as Dr. Obolonsky observed. He laughs and cracks jokes as usual, expectorating blood into a large glass. But when I told him that I had been watching the icefloes on the river, the expression of his face changed. A few days earlier he had said to me, "When a peasant is being treated for consumption, he says, 'It's no use, sir. I shall die with the spring waters.' " '

Lydia saw Chekhov in the afternoon of the same day. She has left a record of it in *Chekhov in My Life.* Their meeting lasted only a few minutes. As he was forbidden to talk, he wrote a short note, asking her to bring him the proofs of *Peasants* from Goltsev, and after she had read the note, he took it from her and added: 'I lo . . . thank you very much.' He crossed out the 'lo . . .' and smiled. She came to see him next day, brought him the proofs and a bunch of flowers, and told him that she had received a telegram from her husband and would have to leave for Petersburg immediately. He asked her to stay another day, but she refused. On her way home, she met Tolstoy and asked him to go and see Chekhov.

Mary saw Chekhov at the clinic on March 27th. 'After spending a few days in Melikhovo', she records, 'I returned to Moscow. Usually nobody met me at the station, but this time my brother Ivan met me and told me that Anton was at the clinic and that he had a discharge of blood from the mouth. At the clinic I was taken to a special ward. Anton lay on his back. He was forbidden to talk. After exchanging greetings with him, I went up to the table to conceal my agitation. On it was a drawing of lungs. They were drawn with a blue pencil, except for the upper parts which were coloured red. I knew what it meant. . . .'

Next day (Friday, March 28th), Tolstoy paid him a visit. Chekhov was still very ill and he let Tolstoy do most of the talking. At first Tolstoy embarked on a long disquisition on his book *What is Art?* He told Chekhov that he stopped his work on *Resurrection,* as He did not like it, and that as a preliminary to writing his book on art he had read sixty books on the subject. He then switched over to the subject of immortality, which, seeing the parlous state Chekhov was in, he no doubt judged to be most appropriate to the occasion. It was here that Chekhov joined the discussion, which weakened him so much that he had another bad haemorrhage that night. 'Tolstoy', Chekhov wrote later to Menshikov, 'believes in immortality in the Kantian sense of the word. He thinks that all of us (men and animals) will continue to live in the primary cause (reason, love), the essence and purpose of which remains a mystery to us. But to me this primary cause or force presents itself in the form of a shapeless, congealed mass, my ego—my individuality, my consciousness will merge with this mass—I have no use for such immortality and I don't understand it, and Tolstoy was surprised that I did not understand it.'

Tolstoy's visit left a bitter taste in his mouth. The more he admired Tolstoy as a creative writer, the more was he beginning to detest him as a philosopher and moralist. 'For all my profound respect for Tolstoy,' he told Leontyev who visited him at the clinic a week later, 'I disagree with him about many things—many things,' he underlined emphatically, frowning and coughing with agitation.

For the next few days Chekhov's condition was critical. He, who was such a voluminous correspondent, had only enough strength to scribble short notes to Tretyakov and Braz, announcing his inability to go to Petersburg to sit for his portrait and—which is surely significant—a few lines to Lydia. 'Your flowers', he wrote, 'do not fade but are getting lovelier. My colleagues have given me permission to have them on the table. . . . You are good, very good, and I really don't know how to thank you.' By April 1st, however, his general condition had improved and he was transferred from the private Ward No. 16 to the general Ward No. 14. On that day he wrote his first long letter to Suvorin. The doctors, he reported, had definitely established that the upper part of his lungs was affected by tuberculosis and ordered him to change his mode of life. 'The first', he went on, 'I understand, but the second I don't because it is almost impossible. They will most certainly order me to live in the country, but life in the country presupposes constant trouble with peasants and animals, not to mention the weather, and to protect oneself from these worries and troubles is as difficult as to avoid getting burnt in hell. All the same, I shall do my best to change my mode of life as much as possible, and I've already made it known through Mary that I'm giving up my medical practice in the country. That will be a relief as well as a great loss to me. I shall resign from all my district jobs, buy myself a dressing-gown, bask in the sun, and eat a lot. I'm ordered to eat six times a day, and they are indignant with me at the clinic for eating so little. I'm forbidden to talk a lot, to swim, etc. etc. Till now', he added ruefully, 'I thought that I drank just enough not to be harmful, but it now appears that I haven't been drinking half as much as I might have done. What a pity!' Soon he was allowed to go out for short walks in the morning. He usually went to the ancient Devichy monastery, which had a large cemetery attached to it (seven years later he was himself buried there), either visiting Pleshcheyev's grave or going into the chapel to listen to the singing of the nuns. He left the clinic on April 10th and was back in Melikhovo on the following day.

At home he took things easy, merely carrying on with the building of the new village school. On May 1st Leontyev paid him a visit and he entered the following characteristic note in his diary: 'Leontyev paid me a visit. Thanked me for tea and dinner, kept apologising, was afraid of missing his train, talked a lot, often spoke of his wife, gave me the proofs of his new play to read, one sheet, then another, laughed, abused Menshikov whom Tolstoy had "swallowed up", assured me that he would have shot Stassyulevich [the historian and editor of the liberal monthly *The European Herald*] if the latter had taken part in a parade as president of the republic, laughed again, dipped his moustache in the cabbage soup, had very little to eat—but he is a good fellow all the same.' In a letter to Suvorin on May 2nd, Chekhov, who was occasionally driven frantic by Leontyev's high-pitched 'tragic' laugh, was much more outspoken about his friend's play. 'The play', he wrote, 'deals with the life of Russian literary people. It is full of hatred of those whose ideas Leontyev dislikes and is false from beginning to end. My impression was that it was not written by the humorist Leontyev at all, but by a cat which had had its tail trodden on by a writer.'

His life, he complained to Suvorin about the middle of May, was not particularly cheerful and the visitors who came to Melikhovo were not very interesting. He was feeling depressed. His cough had grown worse with the change in the weather, and his mother's worried looks irritated him and made him lose his temper with everybody. In the circumstances he preferred to spend most of his time at his little cottage in the orchard. 'Anton', Pavel noted in his diary in his best apocalyptic style, 'has retired to his hermitage, and is spending his time in fasting and labours, like an anchorite, shunning all worldly vanity.' To escape this sort of sanctimonious claptrap, Chekhov went off to Moscow for a few days, settled some business at the offices of *Russian Thought*, and paid a visit to Levitan, who was living at the country house of the millionaire industrialist Sergey Morozov near Moscow. 'The other day I spent some time at the country house of the millionaire Morozov,' he wrote to Suvorin on June 21st. 'The house looks like the Vatican, the footmen go about in white piqué waistcoats with golden chains on their bellies, the furniture is tasteless, and Morozov's face is expressionless—so I fled.'

On July 4th Braz arrived in Melikhovo to paint Chekhov's portrait. He brought his two nieces with him, which put even the hospitable Chekhov in a quandary as the house was full of visitors already,

Alexander having, in addition, dumped his two elder boys there. 'My house is simply crawling with visitors,' he wrote to Leykin on the day of Braz's arrival. 'There is no place for them to sleep, no linen to make up their beds, and I feel in no mood to entertain them. . . . I do nothing but wander about the orchard and eat cherries,' he added. 'I pick about twenty cherries and put them in my mouth all at once. It is tastier that way.'

Between sitting for his picture and eating cherries Chekhov read Maeterlinck. 'I have finished reading *Les Aveugles* and *L'Intruse*', he wrote to Suvorin on July 12th, 'and am now reading *Aglavaine et Selysette*. All these are strange and curious things, but the impression they produce is tremendous, and if I had a theatre I should most certainly have put on *Les Aveugles*. Its setting, incidentally, is excellent, with the sea and a lighthouse in the distance. Half of the playgoing public are fools, but one could avoid the failure of the play by printing a brief summary of its plot in the programme—just a few words about its being a play by Maeterlinck, a Belgian writer, a decadent, dealing with an old guide of blind men who dies quietly, and, not knowing that he is dead, the blind men sit waiting for his return.'

The consecration of the Novoselki school on July 13th provided a good illustration of the indifference shown by the landed gentry to one of the most important problems of the Russian peasant's life of that time. Chekhov had taken great trouble to see that all the important officials of the district were present at the consecration, but not a single person turned up at the ceremony. The only people present were Chekhov himself, his sister Mary and his brother Michael. To atone in some way for the absence of the members of the agricultural board, Chekhov did something he had never done in his life before: he made a speech, which, Michael records, 'was not very fluent'.

The painting of Chekhov's portrait was not proceeding satisfactorily. Chekhov gave Braz two sittings a day, and 'the artist', he wrote to Suvorin, 'paints and paints, but I don't think he will finish it by the 14th as he promised'. The portrait was not finished even by July 22nd, when Chekhov decided to go to Petersburg. Some time before Leykin had written that he had two husky puppies for him, and as that breed of dog was quite unknown in Central Russia, Chekhov was very anxious to get them. He had, besides, some business to transact with Suvorin, who was about to publish another volume of his stories. He arrived in Petersburg on July 23rd. 'Everybody', he wrote to Mary, 'is terribly disappointed: they expected to see a consumptive at his last gasp and suddenly they saw a man who had a moon instead of a face!' He stayed with Suvorin and went to see Leykin at his country estate on Lake Ladoga. 'I went to Leykin's to fetch the dogs,' he wrote to Suvorin, who had in the meantime left for abroad. ' "Drink some milk," he kept asking me; "it's from my own cow." He took me round his farm, telling me exactly how much he had paid for everything.'

Chekhov was back in Melikhovo on July 29th. 'There is nothing new,' he wrote to Suvorin. 'We have another drought. In Moscow I indulged in a bit of revelry and now I feel an inclination to work. After a fall from grace I always feel an access of high spirits and inspiration.' The huskies were a great success. 'They have already got used to our place,' Chekhov reported to Leykin on August 4th. 'Everybody likes them very much, especially the little bitch, which is, I think, of a purer breed than the dog. They are altogether very amusing animals.'

17

It became clear to Chekhov soon after his return to Melikhovo that there could be no question of his staying there during the winter. Already in August he was feeling the cold and coughing more than usual. As his friend Vassily Sobolevsky, the editor and owner of the liberal *Russian Gazette*, was in Biarritz at the time, he, too, decided to go there. 'Let me have a detailed itinerary,' he wrote to Sobolevsky on August 19th, 'as I have never been to Biarritz before and I feel a little diffident. You probably know that I speak all languages except foreign ones; when I talk German or French abroad, the railway guards usually laugh, and to get from one station to another in Paris is like playing at blindman's buff to me.' He intended to stay a month in Biarritz and then go to a warmer place. He arrived in Paris on September 4th. 'As far as Berlin I travelled comfortably in the company of nice people,' he wrote to Mary from Paris. 'From Berlin to Cologne the Germans nearly suffocated me with their cigars, and from Cologne to Paris I slept. All the way I drank marvellous beer. It's not beer but pure delight. I arrived in Paris yesterday and was met by Pavlovsky [the Paris correspondent of *New Times*, who was a native of Taganrog and an old acquaintance of Chekhov's]. The Suvorins are here. . . . Yesterday I walked all over Paris. I went with Suvorin's daughter to the *Magasin du Louvre* and bought myself a sweater, a walking-stick, two ties and a vest. In the evening I went to the *Moulin Rouge* and saw the famous *danse du ventre*. In a huge elephant with red eyes there is a small room which one enters by climbing a narrow spiral staircase; it is there that the *danse du ventre* is performed to the accompaniment of tambourines and a piano played by a negress.'

The weather was dull and chilly in Paris, but Chekhov enjoyed his short stay there. He arrived in Biarritz on September 8th. 'The weather is not particularly good,' he wrote to Suvorin, 'especially in the mornings, but the moment the sun appears it becomes hot and very cheerful. The *plage* is interesting; I like the crowd when it is sitting about on the sand. I go for walks and listen to the blind musicians. The town is very interesting, with its marketplace, where I saw many women cooks with Spanish faces. Life is very cheap here. I pay fourteen francs for my room on the second floor with service and everything else. The cuisine is very good, refined; but one thing is not so good—I have to eat such a lot. At lunch and dinner, all for the same price, they serve wine, *blanc et rouge*; there is good beer, good Marsala. . . . Lots of women. . . . Crowds of Russians. The Russian women are not so bad, but both the old and young men have such insipid, mole-like faces and they are all below medium height.' In his diary Chekhov noted down: 'Every Russian in Biarritz complains that there are too many Russians there.'

And here is another description of his life in Biarritz from a letter to a friend, a woman artist: 'It is very hot here after lunch. The most interesting thing is the ocean: it roars even on a very calm day. I sit on the *grande plage* from morning till evening, reading the papers, while ministers, rich Jews, society women with lorgnettes, Spaniards, poodles walk past me in a motley crowd; dresses, parasols of different colours, the bright sun, the sea, the cliffs, harps, guitars, singing—all that taken together makes me feel thousands of miles away from Melikhovo. . . . The other day I saw a bull fight at Bayonne. Spanish picadors were fighting the bulls. The angry and rather cunning animals chased the picadors round the arena like dogs. The public went mad with excitement.'

The next six and a half months Chekhov spent in Nice. He arrived there on September 25th, 1897, and left on April 12th, 1898. He stayed at the *Pension Russe* in a mean and dirty street not far from the *Avenue de la Gare*, down which he walked every day to the beach. He had a large room with an open fireplace, a large carpet, large windows facing south and a dressing-room in which he washed, all for eleven francs a day which he later got reduced to ten francs. He usually got up at seven, had his breakfast half an hour later (two eggs, two crescent-shaped rolls and a large cup of coffee), luncheon at twelve (an omelette,

beefsteak, sauce, cheese, fruits), a large cup of chocolate at half-past
two, dinner at half-past six (soup or *borshch*, fish, cutlets, chicken,
fruits), and in the evening tea with biscuits. The pension was full of
Russian ladies whom Chekhov disliked intensely. 'Life here is not
bad,' he wrote to Mary on December 14th, 'and the weather is still the
same, that is, warm and calm, but there are no roses without thorns.
The ladies who live in the *Pension Russe*, Russian ladies, are such
horrible creatures, such fools. One ugly face after another, malice and
gossip, the devil take them all.'

What he liked about Nice was the abundance of flowers. 'And the
flowers', he wrote, 'are so wonderfully hardy—they don't wilt at all.
The moment a flower begins to fade, you have only to cut off a little
bit of its stem and put it in warm water for a minute or two—and the
flower revives.' What he also admired was the courtesy and the 'culture'
of the French people. 'You have to live abroad', he wrote to his
brother Ivan, 'to appreciate the courtesy and the considerateness of the
common people. Our maid is constantly smiling at me; she smiles like
a duchess on the stage—and at the same time you can see that she is
very tired. When you enter a railway carriage, you are expected to
bow; you can't address a policeman or leave a shop without saying
bonjour. And even when you talk to beggars you have to add *monsieur*
or *madame*.' And in a letter to Mrs. Suvorin: 'Nature here does not
move me, but I am passionately in love with their culture—and culture
oozes here from every shop window and every wicker basket; every
dog smells of civilisation.' There were also the street singers he liked
to listen to and whom he found better than Russian opera singers. 'The
street singers here,' he wrote to Mary, 'who come into our yard and
give concerts under our windows for ten centimes a time, sing much
better than the singers in Mamontov's opera.'

There were certain things in France, however, that he felt bound to
criticise. 'Everything is all right here,' he wrote to Mary, 'but France
has not outstripped Russia in everything. Matches, sugar, cigarettes,
footwear and chemist's shops are all incomparably better in Russia.
The sugar here is not sweet, and, compared with ours, the French
sweets are worthless.'

He was fortunate to find a man after his own heart in Maxim
Kovalevsky, a former professor of Moscow University, who had been
dismissed for 'freethinking' and who had a villa near Nice. 'A tall, fat
lively, good-humoured man,' Chekhov described him in a letter to
Suvorin. 'He eats a lot, jokes a lot and works a lot—he's very good and
cheerful company. He bursts into peals of laughter, which is very

infectious. He lives in Beaulieu, in his own pretty villa. There is also the painter Yacoby here, who calls Grigorovich a blackguard and Ayvazovsky a son of a bitch. The other day Kovalevsky, Yacoby and I had dinner together and laughed till our sides ached—to the great astonishment of the servants.' A third friend Chekhov made in Nice was the local Russian vice-consul Yurassov, 'a decrepit old man', Chekhov described him, 'so decrepit that you ,can clearly see the joints of his skull on his bald head'. Yurassov became deeply attached to Chekhov and saw him almost every day. 'He is an excellent man,' Chekhov wrote to a correspondent, 'of exemplary goodness and inde-fatigable energy.'

While the weather in Nice was good, Chekhov was not troubled by his illness, but with the coming of the rainy season in October his health deteriorated and there was again a constant discharge of blood from his lungs. 'I feel excellent,' he wrote to Mrs. Suvorin at the beginning of November, 'and externally (as I believe) I am perfectly all right, but the trouble is that I am spitting blood. The flow of blood is small, but it lasts a long time, and my last discharge of blood, which still continues, began three weeks ago. As a consequence I have to submit myself to a strict régime: I don't leave my house after three o'clock in the afternoon, I don't drink anything at all, I don't eat hot food, I don't walk fast, I don't go out anywhere except in the street, in a word, I don't live but vegetate. And that irritates me, I am in a bad mood, and it seems to me that the Russians at dinner talk a lot of nonsense and I have to make an effort not to be rude to them. Only for goodness' sake don't tell anyone about my discharge of blood. It's between ourselves. In my letters home I tell them that I am perfectly all right, and there is no sense in writing otherwise, as I feel well, and if they get to know at home about the discharge of blood they will raise the roof.'

On December 4th he moved to a room on the ground floor on the advice of his doctors, as they found that walking upstairs was harmful to him. Before his illness had taken a turn for the worse, he had been to Monte Carlo a few times. On November 15th he noted down in his diary: 'Monte Carlo. I saw a croupier steal a gold coin.' With the improvement in the weather in the new year, his health improved, too. At the beginning of March 1898 Potapenko and Sumbatov arrived, Potapenko staying with Chekhov at the *Pension Russe*. The two arrived for the purpose of winning money at the roulette table, and Chekhov went with them to Monte Carlo almost every day. 'Sumbatov arrived to win a few hundred thousand to build a theatre,' Chekhov wrote to

Mary, 'and Potapenko arrived in order to win a million. Sumbatov
is smartly dressed, while Potapenko looks rather untidy.' As a matter
of fact, Chekhov, too, although he never mentions it in his letters, was
indulging in a little flutter at the roulette tables. He was again, as
during his first visit to Monte Carlo seven years before, trying to
invent an infallible system. 'Monte Carlo', Potapenko records, 'had a
depressing effect on Chekhov, but it would be untrue to say that he was
immune from its poison. Like every other writer, he dreamt of
being able to write without having to earn a living and he, too, could
not resist the temptation. For hours on end we pored over the paper
with pencils in our hands, trying to find a system. One day we found
it and went to Monte Carlo. Our stakes were small, but in spite of that
we lost a few hundred francs. Once again we pored over the paper,
writing down numbers. We tried another system, and one day we had
apparently found the right one. For two days we won, but on the third
we lost again. In the end Chekhov refused to listen to my theories and
sat down to work out his own system. Sometimes he refused to accompany me to Monte Carlo. I would go there alone, but an hour later,
he, too, would appear, looking a little embarrassed, stop at one of the
tables and watch the game for a long time as though checking up on
some idea of his. Then he would sit down, take out a few gold coins
and place them in a special order on the roulette table. I believe he did
win something. That is the moment when a gambler usually loses all
self-control and becomes completely obsessed with the game. Not so
Chekhov. One day he told me firmly that he was finished with the roulette and he never returned there again. His common sense reasserted
itself, and, above all, he was ashamed to waste his time on such trifles.'

That Chekhov did dream of making money by some lucky chance
and in that way ridding himself of his constant financial worries is
shown by the fact that he always bought state lottery tickets and that
even in Nice he did not fail to acquire a few Paris Exhibition lottery
tickets. But he was never lucky at that sort of thing. At the same time
he was very careful not to put himself under any financial obligation
to a rich man. It was while he was in Nice that Levitan obtained for
him a loan of two thousand roubles from Savva Morozov without his
knowledge. 'I did not want that money,' Chekhov wrote to Leeka
Mizinov in November, 'and I asked Levitan to return it in a way so as
not to offend anyone. Levitan refused to do so. But I shall send it
back, all the same. I shall wait another month or so, and send it back
with a letter of thanks. I have enough money.' Potapenko relates how
Chekhov managed to disencumber himself of the unwanted loan when

Morozov arrived in Nice in the spring. 'A few days after his arrival', Potapenko writes, 'the millionaire paid Chekhov a visit. I arrived soon after he had gone. "You would have lost your bet," Chekhov said to me. "He did say, Don't, my dear Anton Pavlovich, think that by coming to see you I want to remind you . . . and so on." He then wrote a letter in which he thanked Morozov in the most correct terms for his loan and begged him to accept the money back. And not to offend him, he added that he was anxious to repay his loan promptly so as to be able, in case of need, to take advantage of his kindness again. He put the letter and the money in an envelope, wrote the address and asked the porter of the *pension* to take it to Morozov. "He came in a carriage," Chekhov said, "and that means that he will be back at his hotel already so that it won't seem that I am returning him his money too quickly." That was the end of the story,' Potapenko concludes, 'and the millionaire must have understood, for he never came to see Chekhov again.'

It was while, as Chekhov put it, he had strayed from the path of righteousness and become a sedulous frequenter of Monte Carlo and could only think in figures, that Braz arrived in Nice to paint another portrait of him. He had finished his first portrait, but was so dissatisfied with it that he obtained Tretyakov's permission to paint another. The weather was beautiful. 'A sheer delight,' Chekhov wrote to Suvorin. 'Warm, even hot; the sky is blue and bright, the sea sparkles, the fruit trees are in blossom.' Braz hired a studio and Chekhov sat for him in the mornings. 'Braz is painting me,' Chekhov wrote to a correspondent on March 23rd. 'A studio. I sit in a chair with a green velvet back. *En face.* I'm told the portrait does justice to my tie and myself, but I find that I look as I did last year, as though I had a strong whiff of horseradish. I can't help thinking that Braz will remain dissatisfied with this portrait, though he does compliment himself on it.' And five days later to Mary: 'Braz is still painting me. He takes rather long over it, don't you think? People say it looks like me, but I don't find the portrait interesting. There is something in it which is not me and something that is me is missing.' Five years later Chekhov was much more outspoken about the Braz portrait. When it was presented to the Moscow Art Theatre in January 1903 he wrote to Olga Knipper that he was against its being hung in the theatre, as he considered it 'an awful portrait'. It was the solemn gloom exuded by Braz's picture which Chekhov detested so much and which he considered something that was not him.

18

What absorbed Chekhov's interest most during his stay in Nice, what made him, to use his own expression, 'devour' the newspapers, and what eventually brought about his final break with Suvorin, was Zola's famous open letter to the President of the French Republic, published on January 1st, 1898, in *Aurore* under the title of *J'accuse*, in which he accused the French General Staff and the War Ministry of having engineered the trial of Albert Dreyfus for treason and brought about his conviction. Captain Dreyfus, a French General Staff officer, was convicted in December 1894 of selling military secrets to the Germans on the evidence of a forged document by Major Esterhazi and sentenced to life imprisonment on Devil's Island. On December 30th, 1897, Esterhazi was tried at the instigation of Colonel Picquart, who accused him of having forged the document, the famous *borderau* that led to Dreyfus's conviction, and acquitted. It was in connexion with the acquittal of Major Esterhazi that Zola published his open letter, for which he was tried for libel and sentenced to one year's imprisonment. Zola's trial went on from January 26th to February 11th (February 7th to February 23rd, new style).

Chekhov began following the Dreyfus case during Esterhazi's trial. 'The papers are full of discussions and gossip about Dreyfus,' he wrote to his friend Dr. Korobov on November 12th. 'I am reading them very carefully, and my impression is that someone has made a bad joke.' Three weeks later he wrote to Sobolevsky: 'I read the papers all day long and in my opinion Dreyfus is innocent.' After the publication of Zola's letter and a few days before his trial, Chekhov wrote to the Russian historian Professor Batyushkov: 'Zola's letter has made every Frenchman feel that there is still justice in the world and that if an innocent man is condemned there is someone to take his part. The French papers are very interesting, but the Russian ones are no good. *New Times* is simply abominable.' Replying to a woman correspondent who asked him before the end of Zola's trial if he still thought that Zola was right, Chekhov wrote: 'And I ask you whether you can really have such a bad opinion of me as to doubt for one moment that I am on the side of Zola. All those who tried him at the assizes, all those generals and honourable witnesses, are not worth his little finger. I am reading the stenographic account of the trial,' he added, 'and I don't find that Zola was wrong and I don't know what other proof people want.'

But it was in his letters to Suvorin, the chief calumniator in Russia of Dreyfus and Zola, that Chekhov unhesitatingly declared himself to be on their side. 'The Dreyfus affair', he wrote three days after the publication of Zola's open letter, 'is boiling up again, but it has not begun to move yet. Zola is a noble soul and I,' he added ironically, but with a sharp sting in his irony against the disgraceful anti-semitic propaganda conducted by Suvorin's paper in connexion with the Dreyfus affair, 'who am a member of the syndicate [the alleged 'Jewish syndicate' which was said to have bribed Zola to write his letter], and who have already received five hundred francs from the Jews, am in raptures over his noble action. France is a wonderful country and she has wonderful writers.' And on February 6th, in a long letter in which he reviewed the whole Dreyfus affair, he declared that, even if Dreyfus were guilty, Zola would still be right, for, he wrote, 'it is not the business of writers to accuse or prosecute, but to take the part of even guilty men once they have been condemned and are undergoing their punishment. You will say: what about politics? what about the interests of the State? But great writers and artists must only engage in politics in so far as it is necessary to defend oneself against it. There are plenty of accusers, prosecutors and gendarmes without them, and, anyway, the role of Paul suits them better than that of Saul.'

As for the general reason for the anti-Dreyfus and anti-Semitic agitation in France and in the Russian reactionary press, Chekhov went to the very heart of the matter when he explained that it was merely a symptom of the troubled conscience of a people which tried to put the blame on somebody else for something of which it felt itself to be guilty. 'When something is wrong with us', he wrote in the same letter, 'we look for reasons outside us and soon find them: it's the Frenchman who is responsible for the mess in which we find ourselves, it's the Jews, it's Wilhelm. Capital, freemasons, a syndicate, Jesuits— all these are phantoms, but how they ease our troubled minds! They are, of course, a bad sign. Once the French began talking about the Jews, about some syndicate, it meant that they were feeling uneasy and that they needed those phantoms to calm their troubled conscience.... And Zola's letter and his trial spring from the same source. What do you expect? The best men of a nation must be the first to sound the alarm—and that is exactly what has happened.'

When asked by his sister-in-law what he thought of Zola after he had been found guilty, Chekhov replied: 'What counts with me first of all is the fact that the entire European intelligentsia is on the side of Zola and everything that is vile and equivocal is against him. The psychology of the French Government is clear. Just as a decent woman, having been once unfaithful to her husband, makes a number of bad mistakes, becomes the victim of a blackmailer and in the end kills herself—and all because she was anxious to conceal her first mistake—so the French Government, too, tries to break through every obstacle in its way, hits out right and left only because it does not want to admit its mistake. The whole thing', he concluded, 'will solve itself as a result of the explosion of those gases which are accumulating in the French heads. Everything will come right.'

Finally, in a letter to Iordanov he wrote from Paris on April 21st, Chekhov summed up the Dreyfus affair in the following words: 'The Dreyfus affair, it is becoming gradually clear, is a big swindle. The real traitor is Esterhazi, and the documents were fabricated in Brussels; the French Government knows all about it, including Casimir Perier [the French President, who resigned after the trial of Dreyfus], who never believed that Dreyfus was guilty and who does not believe it now—and he resigned because he did not believe it.'

Chekhov protested to Suvorin against the attitude of his paper towards the Dreyfus affair, but received no satisfactory explanation. 'I don't want to write to him,' he told Alexander, 'and I don't want to receive any letters from him in which he justifies the tactlessness of his paper by stating that he is fond of army officers; I don't want any letters from him, because I have long since found the whole thing too boring for words. I, too, am fond of army officers, but if I owned a paper I should never have permitted the printing *gratis* of a novel by Zola in the supplement and abusive attacks on Zola in the paper. Why do they do it? Because none of the people on the staff of his paper has ever known the meaning of a noble impulse and spiritual purity. Besides, whatever your opinion of Zola, to abuse him while his case is still *sub judice* is an offence against literary good manners.' He was more outspoken still in another letter to Alexander: 'Whatever you may think, *New Times* produces a hideous impression. You can't read the telegrams from Paris without a feeling of disgust; they are not telegrams but shameless forgeries. . . . It's not a paper but a zoo, a pack of hungry jackals. . . .'

Chekhov wrote four stories in Nice. The failure of *The Seagull* still rankled, and it was with real regret that he wrote to Suvorin about his estrangement from the stage: 'You have become attached to the theatre, I am apparently going further and further away from it—and I am sorry, for the theatre gave me a great deal of joy once upon a time (and I am not making so badly out of it, either; this winter my plays were performed in the provinces as never before, even *Uncle Vanya* was performed). Before,' he added significantly, 'I knew of no greater joy than sitting in a theatre, but every time I go to a theatre now I have a feeling as though someone in the gallery were going to shout "Fire!" any moment. And I don't like actors. It is my theatrical authorship that has demoralised me.'

The four stories are all to a greater or lesser extent autobiographical. When Professor Batyushkov, who had taken over the editorship of the Russian section of the international periodical *Cosmopolis*, which was published in four languages, asked Chekhov for a contribution and expressed the wish that he should write a story with an international background, Chekhov made the following revealing observation about his method of work: 'I can only write from memory and I have never written directly from nature. The subject must first seep through my memory, leaving, as in a filter, only what is important and typical.' Two of his stories—*At Home* and *Pecheneg*, published in *Russian Gazette* in November—hark back to Chekhov's childhood impressions of the Ukrainian steppe; the third—*In the Cart*, published in *Russian Gazette* in December—is based on his observations of a village school-mistress in the Melikhovo district; and the fourth—*A Visit to Friends*, published in *Cosmopolis* in February, 1898, but not included by Chekhov in the collected edition of his works—deals with one of Chekhov's favourite themes: the impoverishment of a country family, the forced sale of their estate and (the last autobiographical touch) a love affair that fails to come off.

Chekhov had planned to go to Algeria with Professor Kovalevsky, but the trip did not come off because of Kovalevsky's illness. Before leaving for Paris, Chekhov bought the works of French classical writers, three hundred and nineteen volumes in all, for the Taganrog library, which left a considerable gap in his pocket. His solicitude for the cultural life of his native city is really astonishing when one considers how unhappy he was there. In Paris he saw the Russian sculptor Antokolsky about a statue of Peter the Great which was to be erected in Taganrog during the bi-centenary celebrations of its foundation. Before he left Nice, incidentally, he saw Queen Victoria, which fact he duly reported to Mary. He spent over a fortnight in Paris (Mary had asked him not to hurry back home, as the weather was bad), and, as he noted in his diary, he had a very enjoyable time in spite of the cold, rainy weather. Indeed, he found life in Paris so 'gay and interesting' that he even decided, as he wrote to Leykin later, that the Paris climate was the healthiest climate for a man like him. He met the Khudekovs in Monte Carlo and in Paris, and he was glad to report to Mary that Mrs. Khudekov thought that he looked younger and had put on weight. He visited a big hardware shop on the Quai du Louvre with Khudekov and admired the different gardening implements which he found both 'durable and elegant'. He met many French journalists and writers and went to the theatre, where he was surprised to see a dog walking about on the stage in a drawing-room scene. He left Paris on May 2nd, and was back in Melikhovo on May 5th.

19

On his return to Melikhovo, Chekhov found a letter from Nemirovich-Danchenko, who wrote to tell him about the foundation by Stanislavsky and himself of what was first known at the People's Art Theatre, and who asked for his permission to put on *The Seagull* during its first season in the autumn. Chekhov would not hear of it. He wrote back to say that he was not going to risk another failure of his play, that there were much better playwrights to choose from, that, as a matter of fact, he was not a playwright at all, and so on. But Nemirovich-Danchenko was not put off by Chekhov's first refusal. 'If you don't give me your play', he wrote on May 12th, 'you will ruin me, for *The Seagull* is the only modern play that appeals to me strongly as a producer and you are the only modern writer who is of any interest to a theatre with a decent repertoire. . . . If you wish, I shall come down to see you before the rehearsals and discuss *The Seagull* and my plan of production with you.' Chekhov did not reply, and Nemirovich-Danchenko wrote to him again, pointing out that *The Seagull* was being put on everywhere in the provinces, that he himself knew many people who admired it and that he (Chekhov) need not come to the first night if he was worried by its reception in Moscow. Finally, he asked Chekhov point blank whether he did not think that he (Nemirovich-Danchenko) could produce his play in a satisfactory manner. But Chekhov would not commit himself. This time, however, he did answer Nemirovich-Danchenko's letter. 'I take you at your word,' he wrote on May 16th. 'You write: "before the rehearsals I'll come down and talk things over with you." All right then, come down. You can't imagine how much I want to see you and for the pleasure of seeing you and talking things over with you, I will gladly give you all my plays.'

Nemirovich-Danchenko knew Chekhov too well to risk a personal discussion of *The Seagull* with him, particularly as he had already discussed the play with him before its Petersburg production, had offered him all sorts of advice 'as an authority of the stage' and had proposed to discuss it with him again after its failure at the Alexandrinsky Theatre, a proposal of which Chekhov did not avail himself. He realised that the only way to get the play was not to wait for Chekhov's consent but to present him with an accomplished fact. He therefore put a literal interpretation on Chekhov's last sentence and wrote back on May 31st: 'So I am going to put on *The Seagull* . . . for I shall certainly come down to see you . . . expect me between the first and the tenth of July.'

Nemirovich-Danchenko never went to see Chekhov, though Chekhov wrote to him at the end of July to ask him when he might expect him. But, of course, the fact that Chekhov did not object to the interpretation Nemirovich-Danchenko put on the last sentence of his letter meant that, however reluctantly, he had consented to give *The Seagull* to the Moscow Art Theatre. It is significant, though, that not once did Chekhov mention the fact that his play was to be put on by the new theatre. His references to the Moscow Art Theatre in his letters were few and very brief. On June 12th he wrote to Suvorin: 'Nemirovich-Danchenko and Stanislavsky have opened a new theatre in Moscow; rehearsals are starting in July.' And to Sumbatov he wrote on July 6th: 'I have already exchanged letters with Nemirovich-Danchenko. In all probability he will soon be in Moscow and will come down to see me—at least he promised to.' On August 21st Nemirovich-Danchenko wrote to Chekhov that he had already discussed *The Seagull* with the actors and that he regarded the 'rehabilitation' of the play as one of his greatest services to the cause of drama. Again Chekhov did not reply. On August 24th, however, he wrote to Suvorin: 'I received a letter from Nemirovich-Danchenko. He is very busy. They have apparently had almost a hundred rehearsals, and lectures are delivered to the actors.' Brief and a little ironical, but no mention of *The Seagull*. From then on Chekhov was receiving most detailed accounts from Nemirovich-Danchenko on the progress of the production of his play, accounts that Chekhov must have read with great interest, but never once did he take the trouble to comment on them, a most unusual thing considering how eager he was to comment not only on his own but on other people's works.

Of the four stories Chekhov wrote in the spring and summer of 1898, the first—*Ionych* (it was published in the September literary supplement of the weekly magazine *Neeva*)—is perhaps one of the most perfect examples of Chekhov's genius for compressing the story of a man's life within the compass of twenty-odd pages. There are only four or five characters in the story, and yet the whole provincial town where it takes place springs to life, and the descriptive passages in it, reduced to a minimum, possess the typically Chekhovian property of evoking the inmost feelings of his characters. The other three stories—*The Man in a Case, Gooseberries* and *About Love*, all published in *Russian Thought*—were to have formed a special series of short stories, but Chekhov never wrote another story for it. The last of these—*About Love*—Lydia Avilov claims to contain many auto-biographical references to her own love affair with Chekhov. And there are indeed ample hints, if not more direct indications, in Chekhov's letters to her to justify such a claim as well as the conclusion that by giving an artistic shape and form to his secret feelings and thoughts, Chekhov had finally cured himself of his love for Lydia.

It was at the beginning of November 1897 that Chekhov wrote Lydia a letter in which he criticised her style and chided her for working too little on it. Lydia must have resented his remarks, for she did not write to him again till July 1898. Chekhov wrote back: 'I am sorry that my unnecessary severity made you feel a little sad.' Then followed the rather ominous sentence: 'You and I are old friends; at least I should like it to be so.' And after asking her not to put too exaggerated a construction on what he wrote to her, he went on: 'I ask you to be forbearing and to believe me when I tell you that the sentence with which you concluded your letter: "If you are happy, then please be more kind to me," is quite undeservedly severe.' He also told her that he could not possibly meet her, because he was busy writing and because his visitors made it impossible for him to leave Melikhovo. 'I have nothing more to write about,' he concluded, 'but as you want to see my signature with the long tail upside down, like the tail of a suspended rat, and as there is no room for the tail on the other page, I have to go over this page. Keep well. I press your hand and thank you from the bottom of my heart for your letter. Your A. Chekhov.'

A fortnight later, having in the meantime received a reply, Chekhov wrote her the letter she quotes in *Chekhov in My Life* (she does not refer to his earlier letter), in which he declared that he was tired of his writing and particularly of the literary *entourage* from which he found it impossible to escape. Then after telling her that the weather was lovely and that he felt like going away somewhere, he slipped in the remark of having written something for *Russian Thought* which he had still to revise. 'I got used to reading between the lines of Chekhov's letters,' Lydia writes in *Chekhov in My Life*, 'and now I had a feeling that he was drawing my attention to the August number of *Russian Thought* and wanted me to read it immediately.' Why did he want her to read the story? Lydia knew the answer to that question as soon as she had finished reading *About Love*. It was clear to her that Chekhov wanted to tell her that whatever had passed between them was at an end. That made her so angry that she dashed off a furious letter to him, thanking him for the honour of figuring as the heroine of one of his stories, short as it was. She then referred to a friend of his who committed all sorts of mean and despicable actions because he wanted to give a realistic description of them in his novels. 'How many themes must a writer find', she went on, 'to be able to publish hundreds of stories one after another, so that, like the bee, he must gather his honey where he may find it.' And in an obvious reference to his last letter in which he had complained of being tired of writing, she accused him of describing, coldly and dispassionately, feelings he no longer experienced: let the reader weep over them—that was what art was for!

Chekhov's reply, written on August 30th, was typical. He began by telling her that he would have to leave for the Crimea soon, that then he might go to the Caucasus and, when it got cold there, he would probably go abroad, which meant, he explained, 'that I should not be able to go to Petersburg'. Then he went on describing how he hated to go away and how he wished to have been able to spend the winter in Moscow or Petersburg, adding, as though as an afterthought: 'You are wrong about the bee. The first thing the bee sees is the bright and beautiful flowers, and it is only then that it begins gathering the honey. As for the rest—indifference, boredom, and men of talent living and loving only in the world of the imagination, all I can say is that another man's soul is a dark well.' And again the typical Chekhov touch: 'The weather is beastly. Cold. Damp. I press your hand. Keep well and happy. Your A. Chekhov.'

But, curiously enough, what Lydia seemed to resent was Chekhov's last sentence: 'Keep well and happy', although he had used it before in his letters to her. She interpreted it to mean that Chekhov was saying goodbye to her for good and that he did not want to have anything to do with her any more. Chekhov was appalled. 'I have read your letter and just don't know what to make of it,' he wrote to her on October 21st from Yalta (he had already met his future wife, Olga Knipper, at a rehearsal at the Moscow Art Theatre in September and had written to Suvorin a week before that if he had stayed in Moscow

ANTON CHEKHOV AND OLGA KNIPPER

he would have fallen in love with her). 'If I wished you happiness and good health in my last letter, it was not because I wanted to discontinue our correspondence or (which heaven forbid) because I am trying to avoid you, but simply because I always have wished you, and I still do, good health and happiness. The whole thing is really very simple. And if you read in my letters what is not there, it is probably because I can't write letters. . . . Be that as it may,' he concluded, 'don't be angry with me and do forgive me if there really was anything harsh or unpleasant in my last letter. I did not want to distress you, and if my letters are sometimes not what they should be, it is not because of any fault of mine but it just happens against my will.'

'In his reply', Lydia wrote after his earlier letter of August 30th, 'there was not one—not one—ill-tempered, spiteful line.' And that was doubly true about his letter from Yalta on October 21st. Chekhov sensed her despair and agony and, as she expressed it in her reminiscences, 'he understood, he understood everything'.

20

Before he left Melikhovo for the Crimea in September, he had a discharge of blood from the lungs, and this time it was his family that insisted on his going to Yalta. It was noticed by Michael that after his return from France he no longer joked as before, that he often looked sad and pensive, and that he was more reticent than ever. He went on tending his roses and pruning the bushes in the orchard, and the only thing that still aroused his former enthusiasm was fishing and mushroom-gathering. The site of the Melikhovo school was consecrated on August 29th. This is Chekhov's entry in his father's diary (Pavel had gone to visit Ivan in Moscow for a fortnight) for that day: 'M. +5°. Rain, cold, near the village pubs muddy. Melikhovo school consecrated. The priest dined with us. Stoves heated. A. +8°. (Evening) We had a literary evening. Ladyzhensky read his poems in presence of several women holiday-makers.' Menshikov had paid him a short visit a little earlier and told him that Tolstoy and his family had invited him to Yasnaya Polyana and would be offended if he did not go, but, he wrote to Suvorin, 'it got cold and damp and I started coughing again. . . . and I did not feel like going there, though I ought to have gone for a day or two.'

He left Melikhovo on September 9th, having previously warned Nemirovich-Danchenko, who had been urging him to go to some of the rehearsals of *The Seagull*, of his coming. He went to the theatre on the same day and again two days later and saw a few scenes from his play without scenery or costumes. He was also present at one of the rehearsals of Count Alexey Tolstoy's historical play, *Czar Fyodor Ioannovich*, with which the Moscow Art Theatre opened its first season. There can be no doubt that Chekhov was greatly interested in the new theatrical venture of Stanislavsky and Nemirovich-Danchenko and that he was impressed with what he had seen of it. 'I did not want to leave Moscow,' he wrote to Leeka Mizinov from Yalta on September 21st, 'but I had to because I am still carrying on an illicit affair with my bacilli and the stories that I have put on weight and even grown fat are mere inventions. Nemirovich and Stanislavsky', he went on, 'have a very interesting theatre. Lovely actresses. If I had stayed another week, I should have lost my head, for the older I grow, the faster and stronger does the pulse of life beat in me.'

But while admiring the new theatre, Chekhov was far from en-thusiastic about what he had seen of the production of *The Seagull*. When discussing the different realistic touches introduced by Stani-slavsky, such as the croaking of frogs, the chirring of grasshoppers and the barking of dogs, Chekhov said: 'Realistic? But the stage is art. Kramskoy has a picture on which the faces are painted beautifully. What would happen if one cut out the nose of one of the faces and substituted a real one for it? The nose would be realistic but the picture would be ruined.' And when an actor told him that at the end of Act III Stanislavsky, who was rather famous for his crowd scenes, wanted to bring on a woman with a crying baby among the servants who were taking leave of Arkadina, he said: 'That is quite unnecessary. It is as if the top of the piano came down with a crash while you were playing a pianissimo passage.' In reply to the retort that in real life a forte unexpectedly drowned a pianissimo, he said: 'Quite true, but the stage demands a certain amount of convention. You have no fourth wall, for instance. Besides, the stage is art; the stage reflects the quintessence of life. Nothing superfluous should be introduced on the stage.'

Chekhov spent about five days in Moscow, during which he saw Sardou's play *Thermidor* and went to the circus with Suvorin.

In Yalta Chekhov's health improved at first. 'The sea is calm,' he wrote to his brother Ivan on September 19th, 'the weather is charming, warm and quiet as in June. Everything is all right. I have two rooms, one of them very good, and a garden.' He wrote in the same vein to Mary. He found the Crimean shore more picturesque than the Riviera, but, he complained to Suvorin, 'there is no culture here'. He had been to Sebastopol. 'On a moonlight night', he wrote to Mary, 'I drove to the Georgiev monastery and looked down on the sea from the top of a mountain; there was a cemetery with white crosses on the mountain. It was a fantastic sight. And near the cells a woman was sobbing bitterly and saying in an imploring voice to a monk, "If you love me, you'd better go away."'

He wrote to his father about the trees he had ordered for the Melikhovo orchard and park, and asked to be sent stamps from the village post office he had taken so much trouble to get opened, for it depended on the amount of business it was transacting whether it was to be kept open or not. During his first few weeks in Yalta he became acquainted with Shalyapin, who was giving a concert there, and had dinner with the famous singer. He also received a copy of 'Fantasy for an Orchestra' from its composer, Sergey Rakhmaninov, who wrote on the score that the work owed its origin to Chekhov's story *On the Road*. He had already a circle of close friends there: Dr. Leonid Sredin, a consumptive like himself, who was interested in art and literature; Barbara Kharkeyevich, the founder and headmistress of the Yalta School for Girls, who made him an 'honorary inspector' of her school; and Isaac Sinani, the genial owner of a book and tobacco shop which writers, artists and actors in Yalta used as their club.

It was during his first weeks in Yalta that Chekhov was advised by his doctors to get himself a permanent home there. But while looking for what he still hoped to be only a temporary residence with his friend Sinani, he came across a small cottage standing in three acres of ground in a very picturesque spot near the village of Kuchukoye, twenty miles from Yalta, and he decided to buy it. He also found a site for his Yalta house which appealed to him strongly because it not only afforded a beautiful view of Yalta and the sea, but also had a cemetery next to it, and cemeteries always fascinated him. In *Ionych*, for instance, he gives a beautiful description of a cemetery bathed in moonlight, 'where there is no life, but where in every dark poplar and in every grave one feels the presence of a mystery which holds out the promise of a quiet, beautiful and everlasting life'.

For the time being Chekhov decided to wait with the purchase of the site for his Yalta house. A decision, however, was forced upon him by the sudden death of his father. Pavel had tried to lift a heavy box with books and ruptured himself. He was rushed to Moscow, but died on the operating table of a strangulated hernia. 'I am sorry for father,' Chekhov wrote to Mary; 'I am sorry for all of you. The consciousness of what you had to go through in Moscow while I was living quietly here preys on my mind all the time. . . . It seems to me', he added, 'that after father's death life in Melikhovo will never be the same, as though with his diary everything has come to an end.'

Nemirovich-Danchenko sent him a telegram of condolences on the death of his father and in his reply Chekhov congratulated him on the brilliant success of *Czar Fyodor Ioannovich*, the play with which the Moscow Art Theatre had opened its first season on October 14th: 'This success of yours', he wrote on October 21st, 'is merely another proof that both the playgoing public and the actors want a cultured theatre. But', he asked anxiously, 'why is there no mention in the papers of Irina-Knipper? Has something gone wrong? I did not like Fyodor, but Irina was quite exceptionally good; but now they talk more of Fyodor than of Irina.'

By the time Mary had arrived in Yalta on October 27th Chekhov had bought the Autka plot of land adjoining the Tartar cemetery (he bought the little estate of Kuchukoye in December).

'In Yalta', Mary writes in her reminiscences, 'Chekhov met me with the words, "You know, I've bought that plot of land. Let's go and inspect it tomorrow." Next day I went with my brother to have a look at the site. We walked a long time. I felt vexed that he should have bought the land so far from the sea. When we came there, I could hardly believe my eyes. An old gnarled vine surrounded by a wattle-fence. Not a tree, not a bush, and no building of any kind. Near the fence—a Tartar cemetery and, as though on purpose, there was a funeral there. I could not conceal my first disagreeable impression, and my brother noticed it and looked upset. It is true, the view from the site was beautiful: the whole of Yalta could be clearly seen as well as the sea. At that time one could still see the mole from there and the ships in the harbour. I admired the view of the mountains.

'I felt annoyed with myself for not concealing my disappointment from my brother and for having upset him. When we returned to his flat, I decided to make amends for my mistake and, pretending to be interested in the plot of land, spread out a sheet of paper and began to draw a sketch of it. We marked a spot where the house was to be built and where the paths in the garden were to be laid out, talked about grottoes and fountains, and got so carried away that we forgot that the plot of land was entirely unsuitable and that we had no money to carry out our plans.'

All the money Chekhov could raise for the moment was an advance of five thousand roubles from Suvorin on the royalties of his books. Of that, as he wrote to Mary, he had given a deposit of one thousand for the plot of land, which cost four thousand, another thousand as an advance to the builder, two thousand for the Kuchukoye estate, five hundred for the title deeds and the rest as an advance to the architect. He had no money at all left for the building of the house, which cost ten thousand roubles, seven thousand of which he could raise on a mortgage from the bank. He had to get three thousand roubles, and Levitan again came to his rescue by offering to ask Morozov for a loan. This time Chekhov would have been glad to get the loan from 'the millionaire', but, remembering the slight he had received in Nice, Morozov demanded a written request from Chekhov. 'The whole thing', Chekhov wrote to Mary, 'is rather unfortunate. Please, don't say anything to Levitan about it I shall, of course, not accept any money either from him or from Morozov, and I hope he won't make me any more friendly offers. I shall find some way of raising the money myself and I hope to pay up all my debts, except those I owe to the bank, before the dawn of the twentieth century.'

He paid off all his debts much sooner than he thought, but for the time being he went on with the building of his house, more in anticipation of the money for the four stories he had written in Yalta—*A Doctor's Visit, The Darling, The New Country House, On Official Duty*—than of the money he hoped to get from the publication of a collected edition of his works which he was negotiating with Suvorin. He received gifts of rose trees and cypresses for his future garden, and when the building of the house had sufficiently advanced he set about planting it. 'Chekhov's whole attention', Mary writes, 'was concentrated on the garden. I can still see the two Turks in red fezes uprooting the old vine, levelling the ground and digging holes for the trees. Chekhov, like a child, ran from one hole to another with little trees looking like twigs and planted them. Preference was given to deciduous trees and not to evergreens which he did not like because their leaves, as he expressed it, looked as though they had been cut out of tin, but he made an exception for cypresses. His main preoccupation, however, was rose-trees of which we always had masses afterwards.'

For the time being Chekhov agreed with Mary not to dispose of his Melikhovo estate. But he knew perfectly well that his illness was too far advanced for him to be able to live in Melikhovo even in summer. Besides, his mother could not be left alone there during the winter months. Mary was very concerned about her. She was fretting and even the barking of dogs and the noise made by the *samovar* upset her. 'Tell mother', Chekhov wrote, 'that, however badly the dogs and the *samovars* behave, winter will always follow spring, old age will follow youth, unhappiness will follow happiness, and vice versa; a man cannot be in good health and cheerful all his life; he must always expect bereavements; he cannot protect himself against death were he Alexander of Macedon himself; and he must always be prepared for everything and regard everything as necessary and unavoidable, however melancholy that may be. He must only do his duty, as much as it lies within his powers to do so—and nothing more.'

It is passages like these, written under the stress of circumstance, that have given rise to the notion that Chekhov was a fatalist. There has always been a tendency to exaggerate Chekhov's remarks in his correspondence without paying due regard to the occasion that gave rise to them. But such passages as the above must never be read out of their context. Chekhov's attitude to life was never that of a fatalist. In his story *Gooseberries* he dismissed with contempt Tolstoy's often quoted phrase that all a man needed was six feet of ground. 'Man', he wrote, 'needs not six feet of ground, but the whole globe, all nature, where he can freely display all the qualities and arts of his freedom-loving spirit.' And in another famous passage from the same story, Chekhov wrote: 'Look at this life of ours: the powerful are arrogant and idle, the weak are ignorant and live like cattle, all around us—incredible poverty, overcrowding, degeneration, drunkenness, hypocrisy, lying. . . . And yet not a sound is to be heard in all the houses and all the streets; not one man among the fifty thousand inhabitants of our town utters a cry or expresses his indignation in a loud voice. We see those who go to the market to buy food, who eat in the day and sleep at night, who go on uttering their stupid sentiments, who get married and grow old, who complacently carry their dead to the cemetery; but we do not see those who suffer, and the things that are so terrible in life seem to take place somewhere behind the scenes. Everything is so quiet and calm; mute statistics alone protest: so many have gone mad, so many quarts of vodka have been drunk, so many children have died of undernourishment. . . . And it would seem that such an order of things is necessary; it would seem as if a happy man felt so well because the unhappy ones carried their burdens in silence and that without that silence happiness would be impossible. This is nothing but a state of general hypnosis. A man with a hammer ought to stand behind the door of every satisfied man and by knocking on it remind him constantly that there are people who are unhappy and that, however happy he may be now, sooner or later he, too, will feel life's sharp claws and that when misfortune overtakes him—illness, poverty, bereavements—no one will see or hear him, as he does not see or hear others. But there is no man with a hammer, and the happy man, only slightly stirred, like the wind touching the aspen, by the small troubles of life, goes on living unconcernedly—and everything is all right.'

The man with a hammer in his hand knocking at the conscience of mankind—that was what Chekhov conceived the role of the creative writer to be, and that was what he conceived his own role as a writer to be, which is the very opposite of a fatalistic acceptance of things as they are. But his contemporaries were so fascinated by his art of showing 'life as it is' that they overlooked the profounder aspect of his work. The best example of that was provided by the Moscow production of *The Seagull*, which, though it was a great success, he later repudiated. Mary naturally feared the effect another failure of his play would have on his health. At the end of October a notice appeared in *Moscow News* about a serious deterioration in his health, which Chekhov immediately denied. But a month later he had a discharge of blood from the lungs which lasted five days. 'Please, don't tell anyone about it,' he wrote to Suvorin on November 29th. 'I am not coughing at all, my temperature is normal, and the blood frightens others more than myself, and that is why I am trying to keep it a secret from my family.' But Mary got to know about it, and before the first night of *The Seagull* on December 17th she went to Nemirovich-Danchenko and asked him to postpone the performance, as another failure of the play might have a most unfortunate effect on Chekhov's health, a request the two producers could not possibly accede to.

Chekhov took a great interest in the casting of his play, but Nemirovich-Danchenko quite rightly considered it better not to worry him with the last-minute changes that were thought necessary. On the day of the first performance of the play Chekhov wrote to Mary: 'While I am writing these lines, *The Seagull* is being performed in Moscow. It is a pity you did not go to the first night.' But Chekhov was not left long in doubt about the great success of the play. He got two excited telegrams from Nemirovich-Danchenko on the following day announcing not only the 'triumph' of the play, but also the unanimous enthusiasm of the press notices. Chekhov wired in reply: 'Tell everybody that I am infinitely grateful. I am confined to Yalta like Dreyfus on Devil's Island. I am sorry I am not with you. Your telegram has made me happy and well.'

'Oh, if only you knew how awful I felt not to have been able to be at the performance of *The Seagull* and to see you all,' Chekhov wrote to Vishnevsky[1] on December 19th. 'The telegrams from Moscow have completely bowled me over.' And after receiving a circumstantial account from Nemirovich-Danchenko of the reception of the play, he again wrote to Vishnevsky: 'I could not understand anything from the papers, but my brother Ivan arrived in Yalta and I received a letter from Nemirovich and I realised how well you must all have played, how wonderful it all is, and how absurd it is that I am not in Moscow. Where and when will I see *The Seagull*?' He was upset by a postponement of the performances owing to the indisposition of Olga Knipper, who played Arkadina. 'I am receiving letters from Moscow about the great success of *The Seagull*,' he wrote to Helen Shavrov, 'but as I have always had bad luck in the theatre, one of the actresses has fallen ill and my *Seagull* is not being performed. I have such bad luck in the theatre', he added, 'that if I were to marry an actress she would probably give birth to an orang-utang or a porcupine.'

But, at the same time, looking back on his work for the theatre, which began while he was still at school in Taganrog, he could not help wondering at the strange way in which fame on the stage had come to him at last. 'Who could have thought', he wrote to Sergeyenko on January 1st, 1900, about their schoolfellow Vishnevsky, 'that Vishnevsky, who never got a good mark at school and who never had a decent meal, would one day act in a play at the Moscow Art Theatre written by one of his schoolfellows who never had a good mark or a decent meal, either?'

21

It was Sergeyenko who negotiated the publication of Chekhov's collected works with Fyodor Marx, one of the biggest publishers in Russia, who eventually bought them for seventy-five thousand roubles. It seems that Tolstoy, whose novel *Resurrection* was being serialised in Marx's weekly *Neeva* in 1899, discussed the publication of Chekhov's works with Marx and told Sergeyenko about it. 'Tolstoy', Sergeyenko wrote to Chekhov on January 18th, 1899, 'told me that he envied me the trouble I was taking in conducting these negotiations. He takes a most warm interest in you. He spent a whole evening discussing the conditions and asked me to tell Marx that he had no hesitation in advising him to issue your works as soon as possible, for they were much more interesting than the artificial things of Turgenev

---

[1] Alexander Vishnevsky (1863–1943), actor of the Moscow Art Theatre, a native of Taganrog and a schoolfellow of Chekhov's.

or Goncharov. He had meant to write to you more than once and he asked me to tell you all this.'

Chekhov had, as a matter of fact, already for some time been discussing with Suvorin the publication of his works in a collected edition. In August 1898 he wrote to Suvorin that sooner or later he would have to publish his stories in consecutive volumes and proposed to set to work editing them immediately. 'I'd rather edit and publish them myself', he declared, 'than leave it to my heirs.' He realised very well, he wrote to Suvorin again in October, that a collected edition of his works might, if he were to sell it outright, mean a considerable financial loss to him in the end, but it was useless to probe into the future, which, for all he knew, might hold other disagreeable surprises for him. A month later he suggested that they should start publishing his works in separate consecutive volumes without bothering about a collected edition. The first volume had actually been published by Suvorin at the time Sergeyenko approached Chekhov with Marx's proposal. Chekhov immediately informed Suvorin about it, but, as he wrote to Michael on January 29th, 1900, 'when I asked him whether he was willing to make me an offer, he replied that he had no money, that his children would not allow him to buy my works and that, anyway, he would not have offered me more than Marx'. Suvorin apparently offered him an advance of twenty thousand roubles, but Chekhov could not accept such an offer, as he feared that he would never be able to repay the money. 'When my negotiations with Marx were concluded', Chekhov told Michael, 'Suvorin wrote to me that he was very glad, as his conscience was constantly troubling him about publishing my works so badly.'

So far as Suvorin was concerned, Chekhov's conscience was clear, and on receiving Marx's offer, he wrote to Sergeyenko that he would be very glad to sell him his works, but not the royalties from his plays. There was a great deal of bargaining before an agreement was finally reached, Marx offering only fifty thousand, Sergeyenko demanding eighty thousand, and Chekhov holding out for his original seventy-five thousand, which he got in the end. The money Marx undertook to pay in four instalments: twenty thousand roubles immediately on the receipt of a written assurance from Chekhov that he had not entered into any previous agreement for the publication of any of his works, ten thousand roubles in December 1899, twenty thousand roubles in January 1900, ten thousand roubles in December 1900, and the remaining fifteen thousand roubles in January 1901.

Chekhov reserved the right to publish any new work of his in a periodical or newspaper prior to its publication by Marx, who had to pay him for it at the rate of two hundred and fifty roubles for twenty-five thousand words during the next five years, rising to four hundred and fifty, six hundred and fifty and eight hundred and fifty roubles during the three subsequent periods of five years respectively. As for the royalties from his plays, Marx would at first only concede him the right to draw them during his lifetime, but Chekhov would not budge from his original offer, and in the end Marx had to give in, a clause to the effect that all the royalties from the plays belonged to Chekhov and his heirs being added to the agreement on February 6th.

Chekhov realised very well that the sale of his works to Marx was a bad mistake, but he wanted money too badly to be able to hold out for better terms. Besides, all his life he had had to be satisfied with such small advances that the sum of seventy-five thousand roubles appeared a fortune to him. 'I know myself', he wrote to Suvorin a few days before he signed his agreement with Marx, 'that I ought not to be in such a hurry, but to get twenty thousand roubles all at once is too tempting.' As soon as Mary got to know about his negotiations with Marx, she asked him not to sell his works, but it was too late. 'The sale of my works to Marx', Chekhov wrote to her from Yalta on January 27th, 'may seem inadvisable and indeed will most certainly appear to be so in the future, but it appeals to me greatly because now I shall have nothing to do with publishers any more to the end of my days'. He wrote to the same effect to Sergeyenko on February 1st: "I am telling you frankly that what is so important to me is not so much the seventy-five thousand roubles as that my works will be published decently, that I shall have no longer to worry about finding a different title for every new book of mine, choose its format, and reconcile myself to bad paper or to the rumours that "free" copies of my books were being sold at the flea-market and in the provinces at reduced prices. I have a feeling as though the Holy Synod had granted me a divorce after a long period of weary waiting.' He was even more explicit with Suvorin. 'I think', he wrote a fortnight after the signing of the agreement with Marx, 'that the sale will be profitable if I live less than five or at most ten years and unprofitable if I live longer.' But his real reason he only revealed in a letter to Olga Knipper in January 1903. He had concluded the agreement with Marx, he wrote, because 'I was getting ready to die and I wanted to bring my affairs into some kind of order'.

At the beginning of 1899 Suvorin was again involved in a political row which turned public opinion against him and made his relations with Chekhov particularly difficult. On February 8th the Petersburg students celebrated the anniversary of the foundation of their university and, as they gathered outside the university building, they were dispersed by the police. This unprovoked attack led to a strike of students all over Russia, followed by more represssive measures, culminating in the threat that many students would be pressed into the army. Suvorin not only defended the action of the authorities in one of his 'Little Letters' in *New Times*, but went out of his way to condemn the strike of the students and stress the 'generosity and mercy' of the Czar in appointing a special commission to investigate the causes of the strike. The students thereupon declared a boycott of *New Times*, which spread all over Russia, so that even the Yalta Club, as Chekhov wrote to a correspondent, decided to stop its subscription to the paper. 'I am receiving letters from the old man,' Chekhov wrote to Alexander, 'and their tone reminds me of a penitent's confession. It looks as though he were going through a very bad time.' And to Lydia Avilov, who had asked him if he was sorry for Suvorin, he wrote: 'Of course I am sorry for him. He has to pay dearly for his mistakes. But I am not at all sorry for those who surround him.'

The upshot of the matter was that Suvorin was summoned to appear before a 'court of honour' by the Self-aid Committee of Russian Writers. Suvorin refused to appear before this 'court', and Chekhov, to whom he had sent a copy of his correspondence with the Writers' Committee, supported him in his decision. 'A court of honour set up by writers', Chekhov wrote to Suvorin on April 24th, 'is an absurdity; in an Asiatic country, where freedom of the press and freedom of conscience do not exist, where the Government and nine-tenths of society look upon a journalist as an enemy, where life is crowded and miserable and where there is no hope of better times, such amusements as pouring slops on one another, courts of honour, etc., put writers in the ridiculous and wretched position of little animals which, finding themselves in a cage, start biting off each other's tails.' To try Suvorin for having expressed his opinion (whatever it may have been) in public was, Chekhov thought, a very risky business, since it was an attempt on the freedom of the press and might make the position of any journalist intolerable. At the same time, however, Chekhov considered it only right to point out to Suvorin that public opinion had turned violently against him and his paper. 'The conviction has gained ground', he wrote in the same letter, 'that *New Times* is receiving a subsidy from the Government and from the French General Staff. And *New Times* does its utmost to justify this undeserved reputation and it is difficult to understand why it is doing so. . . . You have gained the reputation of a man who has powerful friends in the Government and people think you are cruel and merciless—and again *New Times* is doing its utmost to keep up this opinion of you.'

Earlier Chekhov had warned Suvorin of the consequences of his reactionary policies. 'Drive nature out of the door', he wrote, 'and she'll fly in by the window. When people are deprived of their right to express their opinions freely, they will express them with passion and irritation and often, from the point of view of the Government, in an ugly and shocking manner. Give us freedom of the press and freedom of conscience and the peace and calm everybody is hoping for will come, and though, it is true, it may not last long, it will last our lifetime.'

At the end of March Chekhov received a letter from Mrs. Suvorin, who accused him of acting treacherously towards her husband from whom he had received so many favours by not coming to his defence at a time when he needed it so badly. Chekhov thought Mrs. Suvorin a charming woman, but, as he wrote to Michael, a very cunning one, too. 'I believe she is well disposed towards me,' he told Michael, 'but when I talk to her I never for a moment forget that she is a cunning woman and that her husband is a very kindly man who owns *New Times*.' In his reply to her Chekhov was therefore very careful to point out that the feeling against Suvorin and *New Times* had not arisen all of a sudden, but had been growing up in the course of many years. 'What people are saying now', he wrote, 'they have been saying for a long time everywhere and you and your husband did not know the truth, as kings do not know the truth.' All the comfort he could offer her was that *New Times* was and would remain a power in Russia and that after a short time the agitation against it would die down and 'everything will be as it has been'.

But it was not. It is true that Chekhov still continued to correspond with Suvorin, but the occasional letters they exchanged, compared with their former voluminous correspondence, merely emphasised the great gulf that had opened up between them and that was growing wider and wider. In December 1899 he could already write to Mary: 'I have long since stopped corresponding with Suvorin (the Dreyfus Case)', a statement he repeated to Nemirovich-Danchenko. And when a month later Michael, who, like Alexander, was trying to exploit Chekhov's friendship with Suvorin in order to get a job on *New Times*, raised the question of a reconciliation between him and Suvorin, Chekhov wrote back dryly: 'There can be no question of any reconciliation, because

Suvorin and I have never quarrelled and we are exchanging letters again as if nothing had happened.'

Chekhov's break with Suvorin coincided with the beginning of his close friendship with Maxim Gorky. It was in October 1898 that Chekhov received a book and a modestly worded letter from a man he had never heard of before and in whom he at once recognised a man of genius. For years he had been receiving letters from aspiring authors, but this was the first time he knew that he was dealing, as he wrote to Gorky in a long letter on November 16th, with 'an artist'. There were two characteristics of Gorky's writings which Chekhov singled out as the true qualities of a creative writer: his fine sensibility and what he called his 'plasticity', or, in other words, his ability to 'see' the thing he described and to 'feel' it as if with his hands. But at the same time Chekhov also put his finger on one of Gorky's chief faults as a writer. 'In my opinion', Chekhov wrote, 'you lack restraint. You are like a spectator at a play who expresses his enthusiasm so unrestrainedly that he cannot hear what the actors are saying and does not let others hear it. This lack of restraint is particularly felt in the descriptive passages with which you interrupt your dialogue; reading them, one cannot help wishing that they were more compact and shorter by two or three lines. . . . The same lack of restraint is also felt in your descriptions of women and love scenes. . . . In your description of educated people', Chekhov went on, 'one feels a certain tension, a sort of over-carefulness; that is not because you have not observed them enough; you know them all right, but you don't seem to be sure from what direction to approach them.' And in his next letter Chekhov again dwelt on a number of shortcomings of Gorky's style, such as his use of foreign words, which would not have mattered with any other writer. Gorky's prose, however, was so musical that the slightest roughness was immediately perceived. Again Chekhov stressed the importance of restraint, and there was also, he thought, a certain lack of grace in Gorky's style. 'When a man spends the least possible number of movements on a certain definite action,' he explained, 'that is grace.' Referring once more to Gorky's descriptive passages, Chekhov, himself a great master in the art of painting in words, warned Gorky against 'frequent anthropomorphism, such as the sea breathes, the sky looks down, the steppe luxuriates, nature whispers, speaks, looks sad, etc., which,' he pointed out, 'makes descriptions somewhat monotonous, sometimes too sugary and sometimes too obscure; vividness and expressiveness in descriptions of nature,' he emphasised, 'are achieved only by simplicity, by such simple phrases as "the sun sets", "it grows dark", "it began to rain", etc., and this simplicity is natural to you more than to any other writer I know of'.

There was no doubt at all in Chekhov's mind that in Gorky he had discovered, as he wrote to a correspondent, 'a great talent, crude and rudimentary, but great all the same'.

He met Gorky for the first time on March 18th, 1899, and for the next three weeks they saw each other almost daily. 'Gorky looks like a tramp,' Chekhov wrote to Lydia Avilov, 'but inside he is a refined man—and I am very glad. I want to introduce him to women, and I think it will be useful to him, but he jibs at it.' To the critic Rozanov he described Gorky as 'a simple man, a tramp, who began reading books only after he had grown up, and every day reads avidly everything that is published, uncritically, with enthusiasm'. And to Mary he put it more succinctly: 'Gorky is here. A nice fellow.'

22

Chekhov left Yalta for Moscow on April 12th. During the last three months the weather had been wretched and he had had to stay indoors most of the time. His health, too, was steadily deteriorating. 'My doctors don't permit me to go to Moscow or Petersburg,' he wrote to Vladimir Tikhonov, 'and yet I want to go there badly. I am bored here, I have become a philistine and seem to have reached the point of marrying a pockmarked peasant woman who will beat me on weekdays and pity me on Sundays.' He was dreaming of Moscow, of the Moscow newspapers and the Moscow churchbells whose peals he liked so much. And there was also, of course, Olga Knipper there. 'Knipper', he wrote to Mary at the beginning of February, 'is very sweet and I think I'm a fool not to live in Moscow.' To accustom himself to the vagaries of the weather in Moscow he took long walks in the evenings and on cold, rainy days. His only entertainment was provided by the laying out of the garden of his Yalta house. He hired a Turk called Mustafa to help him with it. 'Mustafa has a kind face,' he wrote to Mary. 'He is as strong as a horse, poor, sober, and full of noble principles. I bought him a spade, a pickaxe and an axe. We shall dig up the garden and plant trees.' On January 17th, his thirty-ninth birthday, or rather name-day, he gave a party and received presents: a cake, a cushion, an azalea plant and four pots of mignonette.

After the conclusion of his agreement with Marx he wrote to several of his friends in Moscow and Petersburg to ask them to arrange for the

YEVGENIA CHEKHOV, ANTON CHEKHOV,
MARY CHEKHOV AND OLGA KNIPPER IN YALTA

copying out of his old and long-forgotten stories published in different weeklies and dailies in the 'eighties. He also wrote to Lydia Avilov on February 8th, asking her to engage someone to copy out his stories from her brother-in-law's *Petersburg Gazette*. 'I am terribly sorry to trouble you,' he declared, 'but after giving it a great deal of thought I decided that there is no one else I could approach. I want those stories; I must send them to Marx, with whom I have just concluded an agreement, and what is much worse, I shall have to edit them and, as Pushkin says, "read over my life with disgust".'

Chekhov certainly felt sorry that they should not have parted friends. 'At least write to me that you are not angry,' he begged her. And he finished his letter with a pun: 'Now I shall be published not by Suvorin but by Marx. I am a "marxist" now.'

Lydia was only too willing to help him and he was very grateful to her. 'You are very good,' he wrote; 'I've said so a thousand times before and I repeat it again.' There followed a sort of soft afterglow of their former love, a period which lasted two months and during which he wrote her eight letters. 'You write that I seem to know how to make the best of my life,' he wrote on February 28th, 'but what is the use of that if I have to be away all the time, as though I lived in exile?' A week later he scolded her for writing so little. 'Take an example from the English lady novelists,' he wrote. 'How marvellously industrious they are! But', he added hurriedly, 'I seem to be indulging in criticism again and I fear that you will write something edifying in reply.' Ten days later he wrote to her again. He gave her instructions how he wanted his stories to be copied and advised her how to get on with the peasants on the estate her husband had just then bought in the province of Tula. 'Well, how shall I thank you?' he concluded. 'How? Tell me, please.' And in his next letter on March 23rd: 'You don't want me to thank you, but, my dear child, let me at least pay due tribute to your goodness and efficiency. Everything is excellent—couldn't be better.' And referring to something Lydia had written about Tolstoy, he gave this significant description of his attitude to the sage of Yasnaya Polyana: 'I think I know Tolstoy. I know him very well and I understand every movement of his eyebrows, but I am fond of him all the same.'

It was in this letter that Chekhov told Lydia of his plan to buy a small house in Moscow for his mother and sister and asked her advice how to go about it. 'I want to go to Moscow, but my doctors won't let me,' he wrote. 'My money flies away from me like a wild fledgling, and in two years' time I shall have to become a philosopher.' But already in his next letter to her, shortly before his departure from Yalta, he expressed his regret that he would not be able to afford a house in Moscow. 'If I buy a house', he wrote, 'I shall be left with nothing—neither works, nor money. I shall have to get a job as a tax assessor.'

Before he left Yalta the weather had improved. 'In Yalta', he wrote to Mary, 'the trees are in bloom. Every day I go out for a drive in a cab. I have decided to spend three hundred roubles on cab drives, but so far I have not spent even twenty. I am usually accompanied on my drives by the wife of our local priest—there is a great deal of talk about it and I understand that the priest has been making inquiries about what sort of man I am. Last night I was at a party. I have gastric catarrh again, and I have grown a little thinner; Napoleon suffered from the same kind of catarrh, and during battles he listened to the reports of his aide-de-camps and issued his orders in a highly undignified pose' Three weeks later he wrote to Suvorin: 'I am quite well, except that today and yesterday I had a temperature—I don't know why. I am reading *Figaro* and *Temps* every day, planting trees, going out for walks, and I can't help feeling that my idleness and the spring have been going on for sixty years and that it is high time I went north. The life of a man who does not live but vegetates in order "to recover his health" is very boring. I walk about in the harbour and the streets like a retired priest.'

Already before his arrival in Moscow Chekhov disposed of *Uncle Vanya* to the Maly Theatre. Nemirovich-Danchenko had repeatedly asked him for the play, and he repeated his request at the end of January after the great success of *The Seagull*. 'I am not writing to you anything about *Uncle Vanya*,' Chekhov replied on February 8th, 'because I don't know what to say. I have promised it verbally to the Maly Theatre and it would look as though I were trying to snub them.' On February 19th, however, he wrote to Mary: 'I have just received a letter from the Maly Theatre: they are asking for *Uncle Vanya*. I shall, of course, tell them that they can have it. And if Nemirovich should be offended, I'll write another play [for the Moscow Art Theatre].' Next day he wrote to the producer of the Maly Theatre placing the play at his disposal. Chekhov, therefore, offered the play to the Maly Theatre *after* Nemirovich-Danchenko had asked him for it. It seems at first sight a rather inexplicable decision in view of the great success of *The Seagull*. But Chekhov had been receiving reports about the acting of the central parts of Trigorin by Stanislavsky and Nina by Roxanova which must have made him doubt whether his play had been rightly interpreted by the Moscow Art Theatre. On February 4th he wrote to

Mary: 'I have read in the *Courier* that Stanislavsky acts Trigorin as a sort of weakling. What idiotic nonsense is this? Trigorin appeals to women, he is captivating and charming, in short, only a third-rate and unthinking actor could act him as a flabby weakling.' His old mistrust of Stanislavsky was certainly awakened by these reports, and that is confirmed by Stanislavsky's own account of their first meeting in Moscow in April 1899. 'Do not imagine', Stanislavsky writes, 'that after the success of *The Seagull* and his absence from Moscow our meeting was in any way cordial. Chekhov's handshake seemed to be a little firmer than usual and he smiled charmingly at me—that was all. ... I tried to appear bigger and more intelligent than God has created me and therefore chose my words carefully, tried to talk of important things and gave the impression of a neurotic female in the presence of her idol. Chekhov noticed it and looked embarrassed. And', Stanislavsky adds, 'for many years afterwards I found it very hard to establish friendly relations with him.' There was something else that made their meeting more painful than usual. 'Besides,' Stanislavsky writes, 'at this interview I could not conceal my feeling of shock at the fatal change that had taken place in him. His illness was doing its own fell work. The look on my face must have frightened Chekhov, for we found it very painful to be aione in the room.' Fortunately, Nemirovich-Danchenko soon arrived. The visit of the two directors of the Moscow Art Theatre was in connexion with *Uncle Vanya*. They came to demand the play Chekhov had already given to the Maly Theatre. After one or two evasive answers Chekhov told them bluntly that he still had his doubts about their theatre. 'I don't know your theatre,' he said. 'I must first see how you play.'

It was only then that it was arranged to give a private performance of *The Seagull* specially for Chekhov's benefit.

In Moscow Chekhov stayed at Mary's small flat. His study was sparsely furnished: a plain table with heaps of thin note-books (the early stories he was revising for Marx's edition of his works), a few chairs, a sofa, and a trunkful of books. In the next room a *samovar* was always on the boil and round the tea-table a large number of his friends—Levitan, Ivan Bunin, Nemirovich-Danchenko, Vishnevsky, Sullerzhitsky[1] and others—carried on an animated conversation. There were usually one or two people in the room nobody seemed to know who would sit for hours without uttering a word. Those were either some childhood friend Chekhov scarcely remembered, or some

[1] Chekhov made the acquaintance of Leopold Sullerzhitsky, one of Tolstoy's most ardent disciples and a future producer of the Moscow Art Theatre, during his Moscow visit in April 1899.

country neighbour, or some woman admirer. To escape from these unbidden guests Chekhov would suddenly disappear, and it was then that his suppressed coughing and measured steps could be heard in his study. Very often, too, Mary had to get rid of some author who would bring his manuscript for Chekhov to read. The moment the doorbell rang, everybody stopped talking and Chekhov would sit down quickly on the sofa and try not to cough. There would be a long discussion in the hall, till the author, deceived by the dead silence in the flat, would retire, leaving his dog-eared manuscript behind.

Chekhov's uninvited guests were not always unwelcome. On April 22nd Tolstoy himself turned up at his flat, but unfortunately it was, as usual, crowded with visitors, so that Chekhov could not have a proper talk with him. Next day he returned Tolstoy's visit and stayed to dinner. They discussed Suvorin's troubles in connexion with the student disturbances. 'Tolstoy', Chekhov wrote to Suvorin, 'spoke very warmly of you and told me that he liked your review of *Resurrection*.' They also discussed Gorky. 'Tolstoy', Chekhov wrote to Gorky on April 25th, 'praised you very much. He said that you were a remarkable writer. He also said,' Chekhov added with a twinkle: ' "A writer can invent anything he likes, but he must never invent his own psychology, and in Gorky it is just psychological inventions that you find; he describes what he does not feel." So there you are. I told him that when you come to Moscow we shall both pay him a call.'

23

The private performance of *The Seagull* took place on Saturday, May 1st. Lydia Avilov was that day passing through Moscow with her children and their governess on the way to her new country estate, and Chekhov asked her to meet him. 'I must see you, he wrote to her on April 27th, 'to tell you how infinitely grateful I am to you and, besides, I really want to see you. Won't you come and have coffee with me in the morning? If your children are with you, bring them along. Coffee with rolls and cream; I'll have some ham for you, too.' But Lydia had to change trains and, as she had only two hours to spare, she found it 'inconvenient' to call on Chekhov. But though it was a cold, frosty morning, he went to the station himself, brought sweets for her children, and saw her off on the train. He asked her to accompany him to the performance of *The Seagull*, but again she refused. It was their last meeting and everything seemed to go wrong. Even as he took leave of her in the railway carriage, she remembered the parting scene in Chekhov's short story *About Love* and was suddenly overcome with panic lest Chekhov, like the hero of his story, should kiss her. In *Chekhov in my Life* Lydia tells of a terrible dream she had while travelling to Petersburg after her meeting with Chekhov at the Moscow clinic. In her dream the two of them were walking on the seashore and he wanted to throw a little boy, who had blood on his mouth and who was running towards them, into the sea. And it seems pretty certain that she dreaded being kissed by him and that the cause of her sudden panic in the corridor of the train did not escape him. He shook her hand and left the compartment quickly. As the train moved out of the station, he did not even turn round to look back at her. It was certainly an inauspicious beginning of a day which held an even greater disappointment for him.

The performance of *The Seagull* was given on the bare stage of the Paradise Theatre where Stanislavsky used often to act as an amateur. The actors played without costume or make-up. That, it is suggested, was largely responsible for Chekhov's disappointment with the production of his play. But, as a matter of fact, it merely helped to emphasise its complete misinterpretation by the two producers. 'I saw a performance of *The Seagull* without scenery,' Chekhov wrote to Gorky, 'and I cannot say that I am able to pass an impartial judgment on it because the Seagull herself acted abominably, sobbing all the time, and Trigorin (the novelist) walked about on the stage and talked as though he were paralysed; he has "no will of his own", so the actor interpreted it in such a way that it made me sick to look at him.' And as late as December he wrote to Nemirovich-Danchenko: 'The thought of Alexeyev's acting fills me with so much gloom that I can't shake it off, and I just can't believe that he acts well in *Uncle Vanya*, though everybody writes to me that he is not only good but very good.'

That Chekhov should have objected so strongly to Nina's sobbing 'all the time' is particularly significant, for that alone destroyed the fundamental conception of the play in which Nina (especially in the fourth act) emerges as a strong character, as a woman who knows what she is after, who, in the words Chekhov put into Konstantin Treplyov's mouth, 'has an aim in life' and who is determined to achieve it. It was this complete distortion of the ruling idea of the play that made Chekhov, as Olga Knipper relates, walk on to the stage, looking grave and pale, and declare 'in a very determined voice' that his play should end with the third act as the fourth act was not his at all. And it was that that made him criticise Nina's performance, as Stanislavsky records, 'so severely and almost brutally that it was difficult to imagine a man of such exceptional gentleness capable of such brutality'. Stanislavsky was mistaken about Chekhov's gentleness, which was not, as is so widely believed, natural to him at all, but which he had achieved after a long and exacting course of rigorous self-discipline. 'Chekhov', Stanislavsky writes, 'demanded that the actress should be deprived of her part immediately. He would not listen to any excuses and threatened to forbid us to perform the play again.' Neither Nemirovich-Danchenko nor Stanislavsky, however, took the slightest notice of Chekhov's request, and indeed they could hardly have blamed Roxanova, whom Nemirovich-Danchenko had recommended to Chekhov as 'a little Duse', for something for which they themselves were responsible, for in those days they never allowed their actors any latitude and demanded that their own interpretation of the parts should be faithfully copied.

But however much Chekhov might have been disappointed with the performance of *The Seagull*, he never lost sight of the fact that the Moscow Art Theatre was one of the most go-ahead and promising theatrical ventures in Russia, and that was brought home to him very forcibly by an interview he had with one of the officials of the Maly Theatre to discuss certain alterations in *Uncle Vanya*. The play, though passed by the censor, had still to be approved by the repertoire commission of the Maly Theatre, which included several professors of Moscow University, among them Professor Storozhenko. The interview, according to Stanislavsky's version of it, began rather strangely.

'What are you doing at present?' asked the official.

'I am writing,' Chekhov, taken aback by the question, replied curtly.

'Yes, I know,' said the official. 'I mean, what are you writing at present?'

Chekhov reached for his hat, and the official hastened to explain the reason for the summons. The members of the repertoire committee of the Maly Theatre, he said, objected very strongly to the scene at the end of Act III, in which Uncle Vanya fires at the professor, on the ground that it was quite inadmissible that a university professor should be fired at on the stage. They therefore asked Chekhov to write a different version for the end of the third act. Chekhov listened quietly to this extraordinary demand and then asked that a copy of the committee's decision should be sent to him. Having received it, he showed it ('with ill-concealed indignation,' Stanislavsky observes) to

the two directors of the Moscow Art Theatre. On May 9th he informed
the producer of the Maly Theatre that he had decided to give *Uncle
Vanya* to the Moscow Art Theatre for production during their 1899–
1900 season.

Before he left for Melikhovo on May 8th, Chekhov had himself
photographed with the cast of *The Seagull* and its two producers. His
interest in Olga Knipper, who was ten years younger than he, was
reciprocated, and both felt themselves drawn to each other. Olga
Knipper spent three days in Melikhovo, where, as she declares in her
short memoir of Chekhov written on the thirtieth anniversary of his
death, 'everything charmed me: the hospitality, the affectionateness and
the conversations, full of humour and wit'. She soon left for the
Caucasus to spend her summer holidays with her brother, and it was
while she was there that her correspondence with Chekhov began.
She was a native of Alsace and had been brought to Russia as a child.
Her father was an engineer who emigrated to Moscow, where he got a
job at a vinegar factory. Her mother was a talented musician, and after
the death of her husband she became a teacher at the Moscow Philharmonic Society. Having failed to pass her entrance examination at
the dramatic school of the Maly Theatre, Olga Knipper joined the
dramatic school of the Philharmonic Society which was under the
direction of Nemirovich-Danchenko, and when the Moscow Art
Theatre was founded she became a member of the company. Nemirovich-Danchenko wrote to Chekhov that she was the only one
of his women students who had finished her course with the highest
distinction.

In Melikhovo Chekhov proceeded with the building of his third
village school. 'I live in Melikhovo now,' he wrote to Gorky on May
9th. 'It is hot, the rooks are cawing, the peasants come to see me. For
the time being life is not dull. I have bought myself a watch, a gold one
but banal.' He sent Gorky a present of a watch and a copy of Strindberg's play *Miss Julie*, translated by Helen Shavrov. 'Strindberg', he
wrote to Shavrov, 'is a remarkable writer. He possesses a talent which
is far from ordinary.' A week later he wrote: 'I am almost well. I am
reading proofs, revising my old stories, and have already sent about
two hundred stories to Marx. I am building a school. The weather is
not too good. It is cold, frosts at night, no rain. In a word, nothing to
boast about.' And to complete the description of his life in Melikhovo
during the last spring he was to spend there, to Kharkeyevich, the
headmistress of the Yalta girls' school, he wrote: 'I am writing this
letter to you in my little cottage. The weather here is more often bad

341

than good, the sky is lowering, and recently we had three nights of frost; carpenters, bricklayers and caulkers are constantly coming to see me, and I have to spend hours haggling with them, explaining things to them, going to the school I am building here—and on the whole my life is neither particularly gay nor particularly dull, but just fair to middling. I am feeling quite well, even better than I felt in Yalta. My financial position is absolutely brilliant: I spent three thousand roubles in one month in Moscow, just as if I had lost them at roulette, and I am counting on spending as much again before I leave for the Crimea, so that there is every hope that soon there will remain only a pleasant memory of the money I received for my works.'

At the beginning of June Chekhov left for Petersburg to see Marx, but the weather was so bad that, on reaching Moscow, he decided to return home. His failing health and financial difficulties convinced him that he would have to sell Melikhovo which, after his *Peasants*; he wrote to Suvorin, had lost its value for him even from a literary point of view. On June 9th he left for Petersburg again. He arrived there on Friday, June 11th, and went back to Melikhovo on the same day because of the cold. He had had no news from Olga Knipper and he was worried by her silence. Had she got married in the Caucasus? Had she decided to leave the stage? On June 16th he wrote his first letter to her: 'The author has been forgotten—oh, how dreadful, how cruel, how disloyal!' She replied at once, telling him that she was so delighted to receive his letter that she burst out laughing for joy. She promised to meet him in the Crimea on her way back to Moscow at the end of July, and by the end of June he was becoming so impatient that he left for Moscow, where he spent three weeks, interviewing prospective buyers of his Melikhovo estate (he sold it the same year) and amusing himself by going to see the acrobats at the Aquarium (a Moscow music hall) and talking to 'fallen women'. He also visited his father's grave in the Novo-Devichy cemetery and, finding it overgrown with weeds, decided to place a tombstone on it. On July 1st he wrote to Olga Knipper again and arranged to meet her in Batum and then leave with her for Yalta, 'provided', he wrote, 'you promise not to turn my head'. On July 8th he wrote to her again to tell her of a sudden change of plans and arranging to meet her in Novorossisk instead of Batum. 'It is impossible to live worse or more disgustingly than the Muscovites live in summer,' he wrote. 'The only amusements are provided by the Aquarium and the farces, and in the streets everybody is suffocated by the smoke from the asphalt. They are boiling asphalt under my very window and the smoke is stifling me.' The prospect of having to settle in Yalta appalled him. Already in February he had complained to Mary about the constant squabbling among his Yalta friends, whose only occupation seemed to be telling scandalous stories about each other. He therefore decided to go to Taganrog and see whether he could not make his home there. He arrived in Taganrog on July 15th and spent three days there, looking up old friends, paying a visit to the town library, and discussing the erection of the memorial to Peter the Great with Iordanov. On July 17th he had himself examined by a Taganrog doctor, a school friend of his, who came to the conclusion that, in view of the advanced stage of his illness, the Taganrog climate did not suit him and that he would have to live in Yalta. He then went off to Novorossisk, where he met Olga Knipper and travelled with her to Yalta, where she lived at Dr. Sredin's while he stayed at a hotel in the harbour. 'Our Yalta house', Chekhov wrote to Mary on July 21st, 'is very nice. We don't want a better one. The rooms are small, but you don't notice it very much. The view from your room is so lovely that I am beginning to feel sorry we did not have this house before. The wing of the house is finished. It is cosy and charming. All the trees I planted have taken root. . . . Knipper is in Yalta,' he added. 'She is depressed. Yesterday she paid me a visit and had tea; she just sits without uttering a word.' And next day: 'Knipper is here, she is very charming, but she feels depressed.'

There was a good reason for Olga Knipper's depression: she was worried about Chekhov's health. 'Every day', she writes, 'Chekhov used to go to see how the building of his house in Autka was progressing. He did not have regular meals, as he never thought of food, he got tired, and however much Sredin and I tried to persuade him to have dinner with us so as to make sure that he had at least one decent meal a day, we were seldom successful, as he disliked going out for dinner and preferred to have it at his hotel.' They saw each other every day, Knipper often accompanying him to Autka, went for walks together, and amused themselves by watching the performing fleas at one of the side-shows in the harbour.

At the beginning of August Chekhov and Olga Knipper left together for Moscow, where Chekhov wanted to be present at the rehearsals of *Uncle Vanya*. They travelled by coach to Bakhchisarai across the Ai Petri mountain range. 'It was nice travelling in a well-sprung carriage,' Olga Knipper writes, 'breathing the air laden with the fragrance of the pine-trees, chattering in the charming, jocular Chekhov tone and dozing in the broiling heat of the southern sun. . . .' There were other memories of that Crimean journey which Olga Knipper only hints at in her letters to Chekhov. By that time their friendship had grown closer, and when three weeks later Chekhov, who fell ill in Moscow and could not go to the rehearsals of his play after all, went back to Yalta, he wrote to her that he could not reconcile himself to the thought that he would not see her again till spring. Olga Knipper had written to him on August 29th (three days after Chekhov had left Moscow): 'As soon as you left I felt so awful that but for Vishnevsky, who saw me home, I should have howled all the way. . . . Are you having dinner every day?' she asked him anxiously. 'See that you eat a lot.' In his reply Chekhov told her that he was living in his own house, guarded by the faithful Mustafa, but that he did not have dinner every day, as it was too far to walk to Yalta and he did not feel like cooking it on his paraffin stove, as that would 'undermine the prestige of the Moscow Art Theatre'. In the evening he ate cheese. The weather was lovely, but for the last two days it had been raining and venomous centipedes were crawling on the damp walls of his unfinished house and in the garden toads and crocodiles were hopping about. The cactus plant she had sent him and which he had nicknamed 'the green reptile' had arrived safely and was just then sitting under a tree in the garden and basking in the sun. A naval squadron had arrived in the harbour and he was watching it through binoculars. There was an operetta at the Yalta theatre. The performing fleas continued to serve the cause of sacred art. He had no money but plenty of visitors and he was bored, bored, excruciatingly bored, and missed his 'charming, rare actress' terribly.

He was expecting his mother and sister to arrive on September 5th and only hoped that their rooms would be ready by that time. They arrived on the 9th, he wrote to Knipper, acknowledging the bottle of scent and the sweets she had sent him, and they were settling down comfortably. His telephone was already installed and he was ringing up his friends every hour. 'Don't forget your author,' he concluded; 'don't forget him, or I shall drown myself or marry a centipede.' He resumed his regular correspondence. He received a telegram from the Alexandrinsky Theatre asking for *Uncle Vanya* and was already writing to Karpov about the casting of the play to the great dismay of Nemirovich-Danchenko, who was planning to take the Moscow Art Theatre to Petersburg the next year and who in the end succeeded in persuading Chekhov not to give his play to the Petersburg Imperial Theatre. Gorky had written for permission to dedicate his novel *Foma Gorgeyev* to him. Chekhov gave his permission provided all Gorky wrote was 'dedicated to ——' He then proceeded to give Gorky a very characteristic piece of advice. 'You are by nature a lyrical writer,' he wrote. 'To be coarse and noisy, to hurt and expose fiercely is not characteristic of your genius. You will therefore understand when I advise you to cut out in your proofs the sons-of-bitches, curs, etc., which are scattered here and there on the pages of *Life* [the organ of the "legal marxists" published in Petersburg].'

24

On the eve of the opening of the second season of the Moscow Art Theatre on October 1st Chekhov received a telegram of good wishes from its company. He wired them the following reply: 'Infinitely grateful. Accept congratulations and good wishes. Let us work conscientiously, cheerfully, indefatigably, harmoniously so that your fine beginning will be a guarantee of more conquests and the life of your theatre will pass as a bright page into the history of Russian art and the life of every one of us. Believe in the sincerity of my friendship. Chekhov.'

He was again hard up ('I have spent all I had,' he wrote to Menshikov, 'and am now waiting impatiently for December, when Marx will send me money'), and very ill. He spent most of his time in his small study (its large square window had a semicircular top of stained glass), sitting at his desk and writing *The Lady with a Dog*, that remarkable story of a great love arising out of the pick-up of a young unhappily married woman by an old roué, revising his stories, reading his proofs, or writing letters. Occasionally he would lie down for a rest on the divan behind his desk in the small recess with its tiny skylight. On the night of September 29th there was a fire in the neighbourhood and he got out of bed and watched it from the terrace. He felt terribly lonely and, he wrote to Olga Knipper, envied the rat that lived under the floor of her theatre.

The first night of *Uncle Vanya* was on October 26th and from the telegrams he received the next day he divined that the play had had only a moderately successful reception. The telegrams were read to him over the telephone, and every time the telephone rang he woke up, ran barefoot to answer it, went back to bed, but the moment he fell asleep the telephone rang again. Next day he got ready his slippers and dressing gown, but there were no more telegrams. 'I am receiving letters

345

from the performers of *Uncle Vanya*, who are in despair,' he wrote to his friend Dr. Kurkin, who had prepared the map Dr. Astrov is supposed to be drawing in the play and who had spent about a fortnight at his Yalta house in September. 'They expected to have a sensational success and, having got only a moderate one, they are worried. I have been writing for twenty-one years and I know that a moderate success is the best kind of success for a writer and actor. After a great success', he added, recalling no doubt the resounding success of *Ivanov* at the Alexandrinsky Theatre so many years before, 'there always comes a reaction which takes the form of raised expectations followed by disappointment and a cooling off—a reaction which can be easily explained physiologically.'

It was getting cold. The mountains were covered with snow. To live in the Crimea just when the theatrical season in Moscow was at its height, Chekhov felt, was perfectly absurd. 'How awful it is', he wrote to Mary on November 11th, 'to go to bed at nine o'clock, feeling that there is nowhere to go to, no one to talk to, nothing to work for since you won't see or hear your work anyway. The piano and I', he. declared bitterly, 'are the only two objects in our house that drag on a mute existence, wondering why we have been put in a place where there is no one to play us.'

He knew that there could be no question of his going to Moscow before the end of the theatrical season and he appealed to Vishnevsky to ask Nemirovich-Danchenko and Stanislavsky to take the theatre to the Crimea in the spring. Chekhov himself had not written to Nemirovich-Danchenko since June, and on November 24th he asked him not to be angry with him for his long silence: he had been busy writing his stories, reading proofs for Marx, and more recently trying to found a sanatorium for poor consumptives who were constantly pestering him to help them, 'Of course,' he wrote, 'I find life here desperately dull. In the daytime I work, and towards evening I begin to ask myself what I should do or where I ought to go to—and at the time when the curtain goes up on the second act in your theatre I am already in bed. I get up when it is still dark, the wind howls, the rain patters against the windows. . . . I am not writing any plays,' he added. 'I have a subject— three sisters—but before I finish the short stories which have been lying on my conscience so long I shall not sit down to write it. There will be no play of mine during the next season—that's final.'

Chekhov never mentioned his wish to see the Moscow Art Theatre in Yalta to Nemirovich-Danchenko, except indirectly by the implied threat not to give the theatre a new play for the coming season; but that, he knew, would be quite sufficient to bring them down to the Crimea—eventually. He was right. A few days later he received a letter from Nemirovich-Danchenko, who wrote that they would simply have to have a play for the new season. 'I'll do my best, of course,' Chekhov replied. 'However, we'll discuss it when, if I am to believe Vishnevsky and the papers, your theatre comes to Yalta.'

At the beginning of November there was 'a ministerial crisis', as Chekhov called it, in his Yalta house. Mustafa the Turk had given notice, and Chekhov engaged a mild, sober-looking, literate Russian, Arseny, as his gardener and man about the house. Arseny was to become one of the institutions of Chekhov's Yalta establishment. When Chekhov introduced a crane into his garden, the bird followed Arseny about like a shadow, hopping about, flapping its clipped wings, and performing the characteristic crane dance which always used to amuse Chekhov. It was also towards the end of 1899 that two more inmates joined Chekhov's household, though without being at first particularly welcome there. On November 14th Chekhov wrote to Mary: 'More trouble: a mongrel puppy has attached itself to our yard, looking wretched and stupid. Every time I drive it out, it barks at me. Another dog, a big and terrifying one, has taken to spending the night in the cellar.' And ten days later: 'The dog has finally taken up its quarters under the olive tree. We have decided not to drive it away— let it live there. But cats we shall shoot.'

Chekhov's decision was not surprising, considering how fond he was of dogs and that he had not any in Yalta, his two dachshunds and huskies having died in Melikhovo. One of the mongrels was called Tuzik and the other Kashtan (Chestnut). Kashtan was a fat, clumsy dog with a smooth coat of light-brown colour and two foolish yellow eyes. It always followed Tuzik's lead in barking at strangers, but the moment it was spoken to it would start wriggling on the ground with its legs in the air. Chekhov would push it away gently with his walking-stick when it got too friendly, saying with feigned severity, 'Go away, sir! Go away, you fool! Don't pester me!' Then turning to one of his visitors, he would add irritably, though with a twinkle in his eyes: 'Would you like me to make you a present of this dog? You can't imagine what a stupid creature it is!'

In November Chekhov began his long story of village life, *In the Ravine*, which he had promised Gorky to contribute to the Petersburg Marxist periodical *Life*. 'In this story', Chekhov told a friend, 'I am describing life in our central provinces. The merchants Khrymins actually exist, though in reality they are much worse. Their children start drinking vodka at the age of eight and lead a depraved life; they have infected their whole district with syphilis. I am not mentioning this in my story because it is considered inartistic.' Together with his *Peasants* this story throws a sombre light on village life in Chekhov's day, and like his earlier story it is full of pity for the common people and paints the heroism of their daily lives with severe detachment. *In the Ravine* completes Chekhov's last productive year as a short-story writer. He wrote three stories in that year: *The Lady with the Dog* and *In the Ravine*, both of some considerable length, and the short story *At Christmas Time*, which he wrote at the special request of Khudekov for the Christmas number of the *Petersburg Gazette*. He was to write only two more stories before he died: *The Bishop*, published in March 1901, and *The Betrothed*, published in December 1903.

The year 1899 closed for Chekhov with no glimmer of hope of a happier future. 'We live in Yalta,' he wrote on December 3rd to Michael, from whom he had become estranged lately. 'We have built a house. The house is small but comfortable. We get our provisions on credit from the shops and our caretaker goes to market every morning. All day long the telephone rings, and I am plagued with visitors. We don't go out anywhere and I am always waiting for the time when I shall be able to leave for Moscow or run away somewhere abroad. My financial position is far from satisfactory and I have to economise. I am no longer getting any royalties from my books. According to our agreement, Marx will not pay me the rest of my money for a long time, and what I received from him I have already spent. But though I economise, my affairs are not improving, and it is as if there were a tall factory chimney over my head and my prosperity went up that chimney. I spend very little on myself and the house does not cost me much to run, but my literary position, my literary (I don't know what to call it) habits eat away three-fourths of the money I earn. I am working now. If my working mood persists till March, I shall earn about three thousand, otherwise I shall have to spend the money I am expecting to get from Marx.'

To relieve the tedium of his life Chekhov invented a new sport, 'the only sport', he wrote to Mary, 'open to me at the present time': he bought a mouse-trap and caught mice, which (as he used to do in Melikhovo) he released next day some distance from the house. He asked Mary to invite Olga Knipper to spend the summer at his house.

'I am bored without her,' he wrote, 'and I shall pay her a salary.' Olga Knipper replied: 'I am willing to spend the summer at your house if you really will pay me a salary and provide my board.' To his inquiry whether the Moscow Art Theatre would come to the Crimea in the spring, she replied that she could not say. 'You know', she wrote, 'how mysterious our directors are.'

At Christmas Chekhov had a visit from Levitan. The artist, who had only a few more months to live, seemed to be in good spirits and drank a lot of wine. It was during this visit that Levitan painted the moonlight landscape with haystacks and a distant wood on the panel above Chekhov's fireplace.

25

In May 1899 the Russian Academy of Science celebrated the centenary of Pushkin's death by the foundation of a special literary section, and on January 8th, 1900, Chekhov was among the first writers to be elected a member of it with the title of 'honorary academician'. He was ill at the time and the news of his election to the Russian Academy merely made him wonder, he wrote to Goltsev, whether he would not after all cheat those who had placed him among the 'immortals'. Telegrams and letters of congratulations poured into Yalta, and though he dreaded the necessity of having to answer them all, he sat down to do it with a will, 'as otherwise', he wrote to Dr. Kurkin, 'posterity will accuse me of bad manners.'

Chekhov's illness in January lasted a fortnight. His doctor diagnosed an improvement in the condition of his right lung, but a steady deterioration of his left lung. His gastric catarrh, which he did not take as seriously as he should have done since even his doctors did not connect it at the time with the tubercular condition of his bowels, was also troubling him and gradually sapping his strength. On top of that there was his old haemorrhoidal trouble, which he had neglected in the old days for fear that a medical examination might disclose that he was consumptive. But what worried him even more than his own illness was the report that Tolstoy was ill. 'Tolstoy's illness', he wrote to Menshikov, 'alarmed me. I dread Tolstoy's death, which would leave a gap in my life. To begin with, I never loved any man as I love him; I am an unbeliever, but of all existing religions his appeals to me most. Secondly, while there is a Tolstoy in literature it is pleasant and agreeable to be a writer; even to realise that you have not done, and are not

349

doing, anything of importance is not so terrible, because Tolstoy does enough for everybody. His activity serves as a justification of those hopes and expectations which one reposes in literature. Thirdly, Tolstoy's position is as firm as a rock, his authority is immense, and while he is alive, bad taste in literature, every kind of vulgarity, and every kind of malicious and spiteful vanity will remain hidden in the dark shadows. His moral authority alone is capable of keeping the so-called literary moods and movements at a certain level. Without him we should have been a shepherdless flock and everything would have been in a state of hopeless confusion.'

But Chekhov's high opinion of Tolstoy's position as a writer never blinded him to his shortcomings as a man. 'I have just read *Resurrection*,' he wrote to Gorky in February. 'Everything in it, with the exception of the rather obscure and artificial relations between Nekhlyudov and Katya, struck me by its richness and strength and breadth of conception as well as', he added, 'by the insincerity of a man who is afraid of death but does not want to admit it and clutches desperately at the texts from the holy writ.'

In February the weather, which had been stormy most of the time, had improved sufficiently for Chekhov to do some gardening (when he got old, he once told Iordanov, he would apply to the Taganrog municipality for a job as a gardener, and on February 20th he wrote to Menshikov that if he had not been a writer he would like to have been a gardener). As soon as the first signs of spring appeared he was planting palms, putting up wooden seats which he painted green, and tending his roses. He had been thinking of going to the Paris World Exhibition in the summer, but gave up the idea on getting a letter from Olga Knipper. 'Yesterday Mary told me that you were going to spend the whole summer abroad,' she wrote. 'You can't do that! Do you hear? Write to me at once that it isn't true and that we shall spend the summer together.'

At the end of February it was still uncertain whether the Moscow Art Theatre would visit Yalta, but in March the decision to take the entire theatre to the Crimea in April was finally taken, and at the beginning of March Vishnevsky (who took the title part in *Uncle Vanya*) was sent on to make the necessary arrangements. He spent four days with Chekhov. 'All the time', Chekhov wrote to Mary, 'he sat at my desk and composed letters to his superiors or told me how wonderfully he had acted in my play. He read his part from *Uncle Vanya*, thrust the play into my hands, asked me to give him his cues: screamed, shook, clutched his head, and I looked and listened with despair in my heart, but could not go out as it was snowing—and so it went on for four days!'

Olga Knipper, who arrived a week before the Moscow Art Theatre company, found Chekhov's new house warm and cosy. He showed her round the garden, where he spent all his mornings with his two mongrel dogs and the two cranes with clipped wings he had recently acquired. Gorky, who was also in Yalta, came to see them often, and they would all sit in Chekhov's study, listening to the stories of his adventurous life.

On the Saturday before Easter (the first of the four performances of the Moscow Art Theatre in Sebastopol was on Easter Monday), Olga Knipper left for Sebastopol. She brought the news that Chekhov was very ill (he had had another serious haemorrhage) and might not be able to come. 'On Sunday', Stanislavsky records, 'we waited impatiently for the boat from Yalta on which Chekhov was to arrive. At last we saw him. He was the last to leave his cabin and he looked very pale and haggard. He had a bad cough. His eyes looked sad. They were the eyes of a sick man. But he tried his best to smile at us. I felt like crying. Our amateur photographers snapped him as he was coming down the gangway and he put in that scene in the play [*The Three Sisters*] he was just then planning to write. The actors rather tactlessly asked him how he was. "I'm all right," he replied. "Never felt better." Soon he went away to his hotel and we did not worry him till the next day. He stayed at a different hotel from us. He was probably afraid to be near the sea.' During the performance (they were giving *Uncle Vanya* on the first night) he sat unobtrusively behind Nemirovich-Danchenko and his wife and it was only with great reluctance that he consented to take a call after the final curtain. He liked the performance of his play very much and his attitude towards Stanislavsky became more cordial after that. He spent most of the time on the terrace in front of the theatre, talking to the actors and actresses, or discussing sound effects with the stage carpenter. He was interested in the smallest detail of play production. Hauptmann's play *The Lonely* made a great impression on him, but during the performance of *Hedda Gabler* he was mostly to be found in the dressing-rooms. Asked why he was not watching the play, he replied that he did not regard Ibsen as a dramatist. According to Olga Knipper, he disliked Ibsen because he did not think him simple enough. Ibsen, he often said, did not know life. He left Sebastopol before the performance of *The Seagull*, remarking dryly that he had already seen it once.

In Yalta, where the Moscow Art Theatre gave eight performances, the entire company spent their free time at Chekhov's house. 'Chekhov', Stanislavsky records, 'looked quite a different man. He was transfigured. He reminded me—and I remember that impression very well—of a house which had stood shuttered and locked all winter suddenly opened up in spring so that all its rooms were filled with sunshine.'

The Yalta visit of the Moscow Art Theatre was wound up on Saturday, April 22nd, with a 'literary evening' in aid of Chekhov's fund for the poor T.B. patients in Yalta. Next day one of the rich admirers of the theatre gave a luncheon party on the big, flat roof of her house. 'I remember', Stanislavsky writes, 'a hot day, a gay awning, and the sparkling sea in the distance. The whole company was there and the entire literary world, with Chekhov and Gorky at the head. . . . I remember the enthusiastic speeches full of confidence in the brilliant future of our theatre. With this wonderful open-air entertainment our visit to Yalta came to an end.'

26

It was Chekhov's great tragedy that he should have met the only woman he wanted to marry at a time when he knew that he had not long to live. There were two conditions he considered necessary before he made up his mind to marry. He could not put up with the sort of happiness, he confessed to Suvorin, that went on from one morning to another. He wanted, in fact, that the woman he married should have interests and work of her own. The other was that he should be in love with her. 'I am not against marriage,' he wrote to Michael in October 1898, 'but I shall only marry for love. To marry a girl only because she is nice is like buying yourself something you don't want only because it is nice. The most important thing in family life is love, sexual desire, one flesh; everything else is unimportant and boring, however clever your calculations might be. So, you see, it is not a question of finding a nice girl, but one with whom I should fall in love —just a little thing like that.' But two years later he had found the 'little thing' that made marriage possible so far as he was concerned, and yet the obstacles to his marriage to Olga Knipper seemed almost insurmountable. Could he, a dying man, agree to bring sorrow into the life of a woman who loved him? Besides, there was his family to be considered. How would his marriage affect them? It did not take him long to find that out.

Olga Knipper had left Yalta with the Moscow Art Theatre as the rehearsals of the new season's plays were due to start on their return to Moscow. 'I don't want to go to Moscow,' she wrote to Chekhov in the train. 'I don't want to! ! ! ! Yalta is like a dream.' And on her arrival in Moscow she wrote to him: 'I can't forget how happy I was at your house. Write me a nice letter and don't use all sorts of meaningless phrases as you are so fond of doing.' Instead of writing to her, he went to Moscow himself early in May, but the cold weather forced him to return to Yalta after a fortnight.

It was only when Olga Knipper wrote to ask him why he had looked so upset when he left that he told her that he had been very ill on the way to Yalta and that he had had very bad headaches in Moscow which he concealed from her. She soon left for the Caucasus with her mother, and at the end of May, Chekhov, too, went for a short trip to the Caucasus with Gorky and a few friends. He was to have met Olga Knipper in Batum, but they only met by accident for a few hours in the train between Batum and Tiflis. In July Olga Knipper came to stay with Chekhov in Yalta and it was during that visit that they became lovers. Already in January Chekhov had bought a small strip of coast near Gurzuf with a little cottage and a solitary olive tree. It was there that he and Olga Knipper spent most of their time together. At the beginning of August Olga Knipper had to return to Moscow to resume rehearsals and Chekhov saw her off to Sebastopol. He did not feel like going back to Yalta, where his mother was already suspecting something, and, in Olga Knipper's words, feared that the shameless Moscow actress would carry off her Antosha by main force and make him un-happy. He knew perfectly well what his mother thought of his love affair and he could not face her. He did not want another scene with her, not immediately after Olga Knipper's departure. He therefore went to Balaclava, but there he was recognised by a whole troop of female admirers and had to flee to an hotel, where he stayed till next morning, when he left for Yalta by sea.

At home he found a letter from Olga Knipper already waiting for him. Their letters now assumed quite a different tone. They were full of expressions of the most ardent love. His letters, in particular, were of a kind he had never written to any woman before. It was as if the floodgates of his deepest feelings had burst open and he was at last able to give full vent to the great store of tenderness that he had kept locked in his heart all his life. The affection of a woman which, as Alexander had told him, he had missed so badly, was his now, and though it came too late to leave any mark on his writings, it did bring

353

happiness to the last four years of his life. And yet the fact remained that she was a complete stranger with whom he could not, and in fact did not, discuss anything that concerned his literary work, or, in other words, the things that mattered most to him. Even the random hints he gave her about his plays in which she acted came only in answer to the questions she herself raised. He admired her as an actress and he often found (to his surprise!) that she was also a woman of uncommon intelligence, but he never in his voluminous correspondence with her (and they wrote almost daily to one another during the long periods of their enforced separations) discussed a single literary problem that interested him. It was as if by throwing open his heart to her he had at the same time locked and bolted the door to his mind. She made many attempts to force an entrance, but every time was met with complete and devastating silence. In Melikhovo Chekhov used to seal his letters with a seal bearing the inscription: 'To the lonely the world is a desert.' He no longer did so now, for Olga Knipper had peopled the desert for him, but his loneliness of spirit remained. It was true he had already worked out the proper technique for meeting an awkward situation: he either joked or talked about the most ordinary things in so charming a manner that people seemed to forget that he was completely ignoring the things that mattered to them most. It took Olga Knipper some time to discover this peculiarity of his, but, as her remark about his fondness for using meaningless phrases shows, she did discover it in the end. She therefore decided to force the issue of their marriage immediately on her return to Moscow.

Already on August 10th she dropped the first hint. 'How is your study?' she wrote. 'Is it being dusted? Do they brush your coat and polish your brown boots? Are the cranes all right? I'm not given a moment's rest in Moscow: many people are convinced that we are married. I've spoken so little to you about it, and now everything is so vague—don't you find it so?' And a fortnight later: 'Vishnevsky keeps on calling me "The Poor Bride"[1] and every time bursts out laughing significantly. Sanin[2] lets me pay less for subscriptions because "the poor girl needs a lot of money now"—do you understand what they are driving at?' Or: 'How primly you wrote to Mary: "Give my best regards to Miss Knipper"—we had a good laugh over it. Oh, what a big baby you are!' Or: 'I feel terribly hurt that you are not frank with me. . . . Please come to Moscow, or can't you bear the thought that you don't want to join your life with mine?' Chekhov wrote back:

[1] The title of an Ostrovsky play.
[2] A. A. Schoenberg (Sanin), an actor and assistant producer in the Moscow Art Theatre who shortly afterwards married Leeka Mizinov.

'Yesterday and the day before I went to Gurzuf, and now I am again sitting in my Yalta prison. . . . There is a terrible wind outside, but no rain, everything has dried up; in a word, everything has gone wrong since you left. Without you I shall hang myself. . . . My brown shoes have not been polished since the day I saw you off. No one brushes my clothes, and I am walking about covered in dust, fluff and feathers. . . . One of my cranes has flown away.' In another letter he complained of being exasperated and bored. He was spending so much money that he would be bankrupt soon. There was a gale blowing outside and the trees were withering. 'How I should have loved to have a brisk run in a field beside a wood, or a stream, or a herd of cattle. Isn't it silly that for two years I have not seen any grass?' On September 14th he wrote that he had been confined to his house for seven days with a high temperature and a cough and was feeling very weak and went as near as he possibly could to hinting at the reason for his reluctance to discuss the question of marriage. 'It seems', he wrote, 'that I shall not be able to come to Moscow, so I suppose you will forget what I am like during the winter and I will fall in love with someone else, if I meet someone else like you—and everything will be as before.' The Yalta theatre, he told her a week later, had burnt down. His mother was leaving for Moscow, and it was quite likely that he, too, would be there soon. But was there any sense in his going to Moscow just to see her and then leave again? No. He would rather go to Paris, then to Nice and Africa, for he had to do something to live through that winter. 'I miss you, my dear,' he concluded. 'Goodbye, keep well and cheerful. Think of me more often. You are not writing to me as frequently as you used to. I suppose you must be tired of me and other men are after you. Well, why not? Good luck, darling!' And at last a few days later: 'You seem to expect some kind of explanation, some kind of long talk with serious faces and serious consequences; but I don't know what to say to you except what I have already told you a hundred thousand times and will probably go on telling you a long time, that is, that I love you—and nothing more.' Olga Knipper's reply shows that she realised that she was being a little too hasty in pressing her suit. 'Don't be afraid, I don't want any talk with serious faces and serious consequences,' she wrote. 'I shan't pester you any more, I shan't torment you, but only love you. I shall be good and tender and interesting to you—do you want me to?'

The question of their marriage was shelved for the time being.

From August to October Chekhov was busy writing *The Three Sisters*. Stanislavsky had visited him twice in Yalta to impress on him the urgency of having it ready for the coming season. But his work was continually interrupted by his illness and his visitors. Besides, this play in which he brought his new technique of playwriting to the highest point of perfection demanded a tremendous amount of mental concentration, and in his present state of health he found such an exertion of all his mental faculties very fatiguing. He finished it by the middle of October, and, instead of sending it on, took it to Moscow himself. But already at the first reading of the play he realised how completely it was misunderstood both by the two producers and the actors, and, after a furious scene with Stanislavsky at his hotel, he no longer even attempted to put them right. When Nemirovich-Danchenko met him in Nice several weeks later (he left Moscow on December 10th owing to his steadily deterioriating health), he wrote to Olga Knipper that he could not help feeling that the play would be a failure and that he would never again write for the Moscow Art Theatre. His second visit to Nice did not do him much good. He was ill and he felt, he wrote to Olga Knipper, 'as though there were rust on my soul'. He was wondering whether such a love as theirs would last fifteen years. It would with him, he told her, but not with her.

The news of his ill-health had reached Moscow and Olga Knipper was getting very worried. 'Tell me what was the matter with you,' she wrote to him in January. 'Don't conceal anything from me. I am not a doll, and I find such an attitude as yours insulting. . . . I want you to be happy with me, I want us to have our own little slice of life and I don't want anyone to interfere with it. . . . Your laughter', she added, 'is ringing in my ears just now; my heart beats fast every time I think of our next meeting.' And three days later: 'I think of our future life as bright and beautiful. Don't you? Are you coming back in April? We shall have a quiet wedding and we shall live together. Do you agree?'

Chekhov did not commit himself. He told her that he was thinking of going to Spitsbergen or the Solovetsky Islands next summer and he hoped she would go with him.[1] His work on *The Three Sisters* had exhausted him and he thought it would be a good thing if he did not write for another five years, but spent all his time travelling and sat down to work on his return. In the meantime he went to Italy at the end of January in the company of Professor Kovalevsky and another Russian professor, but the weather had turned cold and he cancelled his proposed visit to Naples where a telegram from the Moscow Art

[1] According to Olga Knipper, Chekhov was thinking of writing a play about a scientist who is crossed in love and goes off on an arctic expedition. One of the acts of the play was to have taken place in the polar regions.

Theatre was waiting for him with news of the first night of *The Three Sisters* on January 31st, 1901.

He arrived in Yalta on February 16th. From the way people avoided talking to him about his play, and perhaps even more from the way Mary had put it on in her letters about its great success, Chekhov came to the conclusion that it was a failure. He was also annoyed by the publication of *The Three Sisters* in *Russian Thought* before he had time to read the proofs, and, as usual, threatened never again to write anything for the theatre. He was very ill again and his cough got worse. But in spite of his illness, he still got up early and was usually in his study, neatly dressed, before nine o'clock. He went on reading the proofs of his stories for Marx and started writing a new story—*The Bishop*—which he had kept putting off for many months. When the weather was good he pottered about in the garden or sat on a bench in the most secluded part of the courtyard at the back of the house beside the oleander tubs along the white wall. He would sit there for an hour or more, gazing in silence at the sea, his hands folded on his lap. In the afternoon his visitors began to arrive; and behind the iron railings, which separated his small plot of land from the road, girls in white straw hats with wide brims hung about for hours in the hope of catching a glimpse of him. The Moscow Art Theatre was in Petersburg just then, and one day Chekhov received a most extraordinary letter from Olga Knipper about a rumour she had heard that he was already married. 'I was told', she wrote, 'that you were married in the province of Yekaterinoslav to a girl you had only known for four days. Why did you never mention it to me?' But he was used to the incredible stories they invented about him in Petersburg. He wrote back: 'When I get my divorce from the Yekaterinoslav province I shall marry again. May I propose to you then?'

Olga Knipper was getting really worried about the uncertainty of her position. Chekhov's reticence filled her with apprehension and doubt—was he falling out of love with her? And every moment she seemed to stumble on some alarming fact from his past everybody·but she seemed to know about. She received a letter from Lydia Avilov, who wanted to see her. 'You know her, don't you?' she wrote to Chekhov. 'She seems anxious to renew your acquaintance, but I suspect what she really wants is a free ticket for *The Three Sisters*. I wrote back a very polite letter regretting I could get no ticket for her.' To Chekhov such treatment of Lydia Avilov seemed a little high-handed and he inquired anxiously whether she had seen Mrs. Avilov. But Olga Knipper refused to see Lydia, who is never again mentioned in their letters.

Chekhov wanted Olga Knipper to go to Yalta after the Petersburg season of the Moscow Art Theatre. 'If you won't come', he wrote, 'I shall be deeply hurt and you will poison my existence.' But Olga Knipper was determined to regularise her relations with Chekhov. 'Please understand', she wrote to him at the beginning of March, 'that I can't possibly come to Yalta now. What will be my position there? Shall I have to conceal my relationship to you again? Shall I have to watch your mother's suffering again? I can't go through with it any more. Please, believe me. You don't seem to understand this, and I find it hard to talk about it. You remember how difficult it was last summer, how painful. And why do we have to do it? People are much more likely to leave us in peace and to stop talking about us if they realise that it is an accomplished fact. And it will be better for both of us, too. I can't bear these uncertainties. Why make life so difficult? Have you understood me now? Do you agree?'

But all he would say was that, of course, if she did not want to come to Yalta it could not be helped. He was sorry he could not accept her proposal to meet her somewhere else, as he hated the thought of trains and hotels. However, he added, why make such a fuss about it if he would soon be in Moscow himself and see her there? She replied: 'I am sorry I can't come to Yalta, but it would be most inconvenient. I don't think you understand me. Do you?' He understood her all right, and he also knew that in a sparring match with her he would always get the better in the end. All he said, therefore, was that the weather in Yalta was marvellous and that he would have enjoyed it if she were with him. 'I should have come to you,' she wrote back, 'but we can't live just like two good friends now. You understand that, don't you? I am tired of this game of hide and seek. I can't bear the thought of having to watch your mother's suffering again, of having to see Mary's bewildered face again. . . . It's awful! I feel as if I were between two fires at your place. Tell me what you think about it. You never say anything!' She was furious with him when he signed his letters from France 'Academician Toto', so now he signed his letters 'Your Monk Antonius'. The implication of the signature was clear enough, and she must have felt sorry to have led him such a dance, for she wrote back: 'Don't dare to sign yourself monk—I don't like monks.' But she relented. 'Please, don't feel lonely,' she wrote. 'You hurt me when you say that. I'm coming, I'm coming ! ! ! Are you glad? Today a literary lady asked me if I was Chekhov's fiancée in the presence of Savitskaya [another actress of the Moscow Art Theatre]. I blushed, laughed and said nothing in reply. Silly?'

Olga Knipper arrived in Yalta on March 28th and stayed till April 14th, when she left for Moscow with Mary. 'I can't help thinking', she wrote to Chekhov on her return to Moscow, 'that it was silly of me to leave you once I am free. Was it done for the sake of appearances? When I told you that I was leaving with Mary, you never said anything to me about staying or about not wishing to part from me. You said nothing. I decided that you did not want me to stay after Mary had left. *Que dira le monde?* Was that the reason? I don't think so. I have been racking my brains to find the real reason. I realise very well what is going on inside you and that is perhaps why I found it so difficult to say what I wanted to say. You remember how unsociable I was on the last day. You thought I was angry with you. . . . What do you think? Is it better to be silent about what one wants to say or vice versa? I know that you hate "serious" explanations, but I do not want to have it out with you. I only want to talk things over with you as one who is close to me. I don't know why, but the thought of my last visit to you horrifies me. It has left a bitter taste in my mouth—an impression of something vague, something left hanging in the air—I have again been "on a visit" to Yalta and again got back. Write to me what you think— scold me if you must, *only don't be silent*. Come to Moscow at the beginning of May and let us get married and live together. Write to me about everything, and don't always dismiss everything with a joke.' And next day she wrote: 'I can't help feeling that you don't love me any more, that you no longer look on me as one who is near and dear to you. All during my visit you never called me Olya as you do in your letters—why was that?'

This time Chekhov had to give in. 'If you give me your word', he wrote to Olga Knipper on April 19th, 'that not a single soul in Moscow will know of our wedding till it is over, then I shall be ready to marry you on the very first day of my arrival. I don't know why, but I am simply terrified of the wedding ceremony, and the congratu- lations and the glass of champagne you have to hold in your hand at the same time smiling vaguely.' But that was not what had made him hesitate so long. His real reason he hinted at in a short sentence at the end of his letter: 'I have everything in order, everything except one small trifle—my health.' And in fact the first thing Chekhov did on his arrival in Moscow was to have himself examined by a specialist, who found that his condition had deteriorated and ordered him to go im- mediately to a sanatorium in the remote Ufa province which specialised in *kumys* (fermented mare's milk) treatment.

Chekhov's wedding to Olga Knipper took place on Friday, May 25th, 1901, in a small Moscow church in the presence of only four witnesses, two of them Olga Knipper's uncle and brother. None of Chekhov's family was present. His brother Ivan had been to see him a few hours before the wedding, but he did not tell him anything about it. And he made sure that none of his numerous friends turned up at his wedding by arranging with Vishnevsky to invite them all to a special luncheon. While they were all waiting and wondering what the idea of the luncheon was, Chekhov and Olga Knipper got married and, after paying a visit to Olga's mother, took a train for Nizhny-Novgorod, where they went to see Gorky, who was under house arrest at the time. From Nizhny-Novgorod they went by boat to Ufa and from there by coach to the sanatorium at Axenovo, where they spent their honeymoon.

'In Axenovo', Olga Knipper writes, 'Chekhov liked the countryside, the long shadows on the steppe after six o'clock, the snorting of the horses in the droves, the flora, the river Dema to which we drove to fish one day. The sanatorium was in a beautiful oak wood, but everything there was rather primitive and uncomfortable. I even had to go to Ufa for some pillows. At first Chekhov liked the *kumys*, but soon he got tired of it and after six weeks we returned to Yalta.' Chekhov loved to sit on the steps of their Axenovo bungalow and watch the sunset, the distant hills and the wide steppe. 'We were so close to each other there,' Olga Knipper wrote to Chekhov in January 1902. 'And that wonderful view from our bungalow! And do you remember the little priest? And the general's wife who lost her way, and the young people, and the maid who always rushed in with the dishes and dropped them on the floor?'

They returned to Yalta at the beginning of July. Soon Olga Knipper left for Moscow, where the rehearsals at the Moscow Art Theatre were due to begin on August 20th, and Chekhov joined her there on September 16th.

In Moscow Chekhov took a hand in the rehearsals of *The Three Sisters*. 'I have rehearsed the play a little,' he wrote to Dr. Sredin in Yalta, 'and I am told that it is being performed much better than last season.'

He was often at the Moscow Art Theatre, and his chief occupation seems, according to Stanislavsky, to have been watching the actors

ANTON CHEKHOV AND OLGA KNIPPER IN
AXENOVO (1901)

put on their make-up. He would watch an actor with rapt attention, and when a line on the face suddenly changed it in accordance with the requirement of his part, he would suddenly burst out laughing. Then he would fall silent again and resume his concentrated study of the actor's face.

He returned to Yalta on October 26th. The excited, almost frantic letters he began to receive from Olga Knipper show that, having married a famous author, she now expected a new masterpiece from him almost daily. In one of her first letters at the beginning of November she wrote: 'Anton, you must now write something new. There are so many subjects in your head. Don't be lazy, darling. Do make an effort and write.' Four days later: 'Anton, write something. I can hardly wait for the time when I shall read your new story. Write, darling. It will help to while away the time of our separation.' Again three days later: 'I am glad that you are writing, though only reluctantly. Work, darling, work.' A week later: 'Write, Anton, darling. I shall tremble with excitement when I read something new you have written.' A few days later: 'Darling, you will let me know what you are writing, won't you? You will send it to me, won't you?' Five days later: 'Darling, don't you feel any pleasure in being able to write? Doesn't it thrill you? I can't help thinking that it is just when you are going through a dull patch in your life that your only salvation is to devote yourself entirely to your work—to dream, to create, to enjoy it all. Besides, you possess such a rich store of material and observations that all you have to do is to sit down at your desk for a short time and something beautiful is sure to emerge. You are my great genius. You are the Russian Maupassant.' And next day: 'Don't give way to melancholy. Write something more for me and for Russia.' A week later: 'Anton, darling, you must write a comedy. It will create a sensation—there are no Russian comedies.' Five days later: 'Stanislavsky and the rest keep asking me whether you are writing or will be writing a comedy. It would be so nice to get it in spring and open our season with it—I wish that could be so. I am waiting in a frenzy of excitement for something new from Chekhov—what will he produce, I wonder.' And after reminding him twice of his promise to write a comedy for the Moscow Art Theatre (he seems to have outlined the plot of *The Cherry Orchard* to Stanislavsky and others during his last visit to Moscow), she finished her last letter in 1901 with this final admonition: 'Darling Anton, are you going to start work or not? Please, make a little effort. Surely your time will pass more quickly if you are writing. Don't you think so? I know you will write something nice, something

361

elegant—elegant in form, of course. I feel terribly excited about it already.'

In reading these naïve exhortations one is almost driven to the reflection that she had only married Chekhov because he was a famous author and that, having married him, she naturally wanted to have something to show for it. But that would certainly be a totally unfair judgment. To begin with, one can hardly blame an actress, however brilliant, for being ignorant of the creative processes of a writer like Chekhov, who in his last period took such infinite pains with every sentence he wrote. Besides, if she was behaving with a singular lack of understanding in trying to cajole Chekhov into producing new master-pieces at a time when he was so seriously ill, it was to a large extent Chekhov's own fault. For nearly twenty years he had practised the art of concealing from the whole world his serious illness till he had become so adept at it that even when the terrible inroads his illness had made on his health could no longer be hidden he was still able to take in his wife and closest friends—he could apparently deceive everybody about the real state of his health except perhaps his mother, and that was why they quarrelled so often: she would never dare to reveal her anxiety to him, but he saw it all and—resented it. But even when one allows for Olga Knipper's ignorance of the secrets of the literary craft and of the gravity of Chekhov's condition, these continuous remonstrances and exhortations, these urgings of a great writer not to be lazy, to make a *little* effort, and so on, seem a trifle excessive.

Chekhov's reaction to these continuous promptings is very char-acteristic. For a time he ignored them; then, typically, he tried to evade a straight answer by making a joke: 'Today I caught two mice so that nobody can say that I am not doing anything.' Then at the end of November he tried to put the blame on Yalta and the weather: 'I am working, writing, but in Yalta it is impossible to write—it is impossible to write so far from the world; it is not interesting, and, besides, it is cold.' A few days later: 'It is snowing outside and raining. My hands are cold, it is cold and gloomy in my study—my fingers refuse to obey me.' Four days later: 'I am working, but not much. The weather is foul, it is cold in my room, it is far from Moscow, and as a result a mood is created in which writing seems quite an unnecessary occupa-tion.' Two days later: 'In my present mood, in this horrible Yalta, I can't write anything that could, in your opinion, quench anybody's thirst.' Again: 'It is difficult to write when the temperature in my study is only 12 degrees above zero. It merely irritates me, and that is all, though I realise that it is silly.' Four days later: 'I write slowly, without any interest. Don't expect anything special from me at present. But all the same, I shall write a comedy. And there will be a part for you in it.' And just before the serious attack of his illness at the beginning of December: 'If I gave up literature now and became a gardener, it would add ten years to my life.' Then the truth at last: 'All that I have written or begun to write has been wasted so that I shall have to start all over again. I have to write without any interruption, otherwise nothing comes of it.' And to soften the blow, he added: 'Your letters are the best medicine for me and without them I could no longer live.' A week later (on December 18th): 'I am not writing anything at present. I have postponed it till next year, but I am still hoping to write a very amusing comedy in which everybody will be running wild.' On December 23rd: 'After Christmas I shall sit down to write'; and on January 2nd, 1902: 'I am not writing anything—absolutely nothing, but I am reading such a lot that I shall soon be a very clever chap.'

What could anyone who knew nothing about the agonies of creative writing and had no idea how serious Chekhov's illness was—that, in fact, he was a dying man—make of it all? And can Olga Knipper be blamed for treating Chekhov's strange excuses as the caprices of genius? She wanted to share his thoughts, she begged him again and again to tell her exactly what was wrong with him. Was it her fault if, as she wrote to him, the entrance to his spiritual world was barred to her? Or could he be blamed if, knowing how hopeless his condition was, he preferred to treat her, as she reminded him again on December 8th, as a doll? 'Why', she wrote to him, 'are you pushing me further and further away from you? Don't do it, I beg you. Be frank with me. I am not a doll but a human being. You offend me by such an attitude.'

But he never took up her challenge. Her questions remained un-answered, except perhaps indirectly, as when he wrote on December 15th: 'I am alive and, as much as it is possible for a man who is convalescing, feeling well. I am weak and angry with myself for not doing anything. In a word, you have got yourself such a husband that I can only congratulate you.' And when she asked him whether he was not reproaching her for at least not giving up the stage, he replied firmly: 'I have not reproached you once for remaining on the stage, but, on the contrary, I am glad that you have an aim in life and are not wasting your time like your husband.'

But, as a matter of fact, he did write something. He finished *The Bishop*, the story he began in March 1901, on February 20th, 1902, and from then on till he sat down to write his last story, *The Betrothed*, in October, he wrote nothing.

During the six months Chekhov spent in Yalta between November, 1901, and May, 1902, he was often in nearby Gaspra, where Tolstoy was recovering from a serious illness. After he had left for his last visit to Nice, Tolstoy had sent him a message through Sullerzhitsky, which shows that he, at any rate, was aware of the polemic Chekhov was conducting against his teachings in some of his stories. He wanted Chekhov to know, however, that though he sometimes disagreed with him, there was not a single occasion when he could put down a story of his without reading it to the end. Tolstoy's eldest daughter Tatyana had earlier written to Chekhov that her father was delighted with his humorous story *The Darling* and read it aloud to his friends on four consecutive nights. Chekhov could not help noticing that it was just his innocuous stories that Tolstoy seemed to enjoy so much; a story like *Gooseberries*, which was published in the same year as *The Darling*, 'the crafty old man', as Chekhov called Tolstoy, left without comment. All the same, he was very pleased with Tolstoy's message and thanked Olga Knipper for sending it on to him.[1]

Chekhov visited Gaspra for the first time on November 6th, and was on the whole favourably impressed with Tolstoy's condition, though he did look very old and feeble (Tolstoy was seventy-three at the time). Sonia, Tolstoy's wife, left the following note about Chekhov's visit in her diary: 'Chekhov was here and we all liked his simplicity. He seemed to be very near to us in spirit. His terrible illness—consumption—had already left its mark on him, and we felt all the more taken with him.'

To mark the occasion Sonia took a photograph of Chekhov and Tolstoy.

Ten days later Gorky arrived in Yalta and stopped at Chekhov's house. Chekhov liked him more than ever, though he did object strongly to his Russian shirt. 'I can't get used to it,' he wrote to Olga Knipper, 'as I can't get used to a court chamberlain's uniform.' On November 17th Chekhov, Gorky and the symbolist poet Balmont went to see Tolstoy together. Chekhov had been again reading Turgenev recently and their conversation naturally turned on the great Russian novelist Tolstoy had once challenged to a duel.

'Turgenev', Tolstoy said, 'did a great thing by writing his marvellous portraits of women.'

'I find his women rather artificial,' objected Chekhov.

'I grant you', Tolstoy replied, 'that such women never existed before

[1] Tolstoy's essay on *The Darling* is a pitiful attempt to foist on Chekhov his own ideas on the subordinate position of women. It is published in the first volume of Constance Garnett's translation of the *Tales of Chekhov*.

he wrote his novels, but they certainly did afterwards. I myself have observed such Turgenev women in life.'

'Turgenev', Tolstoy went on, 'was a good writer who wrote an honest, straightforward prose, and you, too,' he said, turning to Chekhov, 'know how to write a good, honest prose.'

Balmont recited his poem *The Fragrance of the Sun* to Tolstoy's great amusement. Chekhov did not express any opinion of the poem at the time, but a few days later Gorky was surprised to see him sitting in the garden and apparently trying to catch a sunbeam in his hat and then—quite unsuccessfully—put it on his head. He tried it a few times and then gave it up, rammed his hat on his head and, pushing away his dog Tuzik irritably with his cane, walked towards the house.

'Good morning,' he said to Gorky with a grin. 'I've been thinking of Balmont's poem *The Fragrance of the Sun*. It's silly. In Russia the sun smells of Kazan soap and here it smells of Tartar sweat.'

On December 7th Tolstoy rang him up. 'I feel so happy today', he said, 'that I want you, too, to be happy. You especially. You are such a good man—such a very good man!'

Tolstoy was very fond of Chekhov, but it is doubtful whether he ever really understood him. They never corresponded, and they did not discuss Chekhov's stories. As for his plays, Chekhov did ask Tolstoy one day if he liked them, but Tolstoy replied that he thought they were even worse than Shakespeare's. But perhaps nothing shows Tolstoy's inability to penetrate behind the façade Chekhov presented to the world than the words Gorky one day heard him muttering on the terrace of the Gaspra mansion. 'Oh, what a nice, charming man,' Tolstoy whispered to himself as he watched Chekhov walking in the park. 'So modest and gentle, just like a young girl, and he walks like a young girl, too.' One could hardly imagine anyone who was less like the sweet young thing Tolstoy had in mind than Chekhov.

Unfortunately, Gorky was more interested in recording what Tolstoy rather than what Chekhov said during these literary encounters at Gaspra, and he was even more prone to sentimentalise Chekhov than Tolstoy.

In December 1901 Chekhov received the news that the Russian Academy had elected Gorky an honorary member of its literary section. He immediately conveyed the news to Gorky, who, he noticed, was very pleased. Neither of them suspected at the time that this election (officially confirmed on February 12th) would so soon become one of the political sensations of the day. It was not, indeed, till March 11th that a brief report appeared in the press to the effect that 'in view of certain facts which were not known to the Imperial Russian Academy at the time' the election of Gorky had been declared invalid. The academicians themselves never knew of the annulment of Gorky's election till they read it in the papers. The Government never bothered to consult them about it, having received its orders from the Czar himself, who wrote to the Minister of Education that 'like every other right-thinking Russian' he was profoundly shocked that a politically unreliable person like Gorky should have been elected an honorary academician.

At first Chekhov was not sure what to do. He felt that Gorky's arbitrary dismissal by the authorities was a slight against all the members of the Academy and, besides, he had taken so personal an interest in Gorky's election that he could not possibly disregard it. He decided to talk it over with Tolstoy, who had been elected an honorary member of the Academy at the same time as he, but who had never bothered to acknowledge the letter announcing his election. 'When I mentioned Gorky and the Academy to Tolstoy', Chekhov wrote to Korolenko, another honorary academician, on April 19th, 'he said, "I do not regard myself as an academician," and went on reading his book.' Korolenko agreed that they ought to resign from the Academy and they met at Chekhov's house in Yalta on May 24th to discuss the statement they intended to issue to the press on their resignation.

Korolenko left the following account of his meeting with Chekhov:

'I saw Chekhov for the last time in Yalta when I came specially to discuss a certain public statement we intended to issue. He lived in his own house, which he built (artistically unpractical) near Yalta; his sister and his wife lived with him. As at our first meeting, Chekhov's sister met me downstairs. Soon I saw Chekhov himself coming down the stairs as he did the first time we met. As I recalled our first meeting a pang went through my heart. It was the same Chekhov, but where had his former confident and quiet cheerfulness gone? His features had sharpened and seemed to have become harsher, and only his eyes occasionally beamed gently as before. But there was already in them a frozen expression of sadness. His sister told me that at times he sat for hours staring motionless at one point. During our conversation he picked up a book which Tolstoy had recently recommended.

' "Have you read it?" he asked. "It's a good book. If only I were to write one such book, I'd consider that I'd done enough. I could die then." '

It was not till August 25th that Chekhov issued his statement of resignation from the Academy.

The year 1902 began pleasantly enough for Chekhov. In Moscow his medical colleagues had gathered for their eighth annual conference, and on January 11th the Moscow Art Theatre gave a gala performance of *Uncle Vanya* in their honour. After the performance the doctors sent two telegrams to Chekhov, which moved him deeply. 'During the conference', he wrote to one of the doctors who took part in it, 'I felt like a prince. The telegrams I received raised me to a height I never dreamt of.' And to his friend Dr. Kurkin he wrote: 'I have never expected such an honour and I accept my reward with joy, though I realise that I don't deserve it.' What displeased him was that the doctors should have presented his portrait by Braz to the Moscow Art Theatre. He wished, he wrote to his wife, they had taken that portrait out of the frame and put a large photograph in its place.

At the end of February Olga Knipper spent about a week with Chekhov in Yalta. It was in November that Chekhov had suggested to his wife that they should have a child. 'I dearly wish', he wrote to her, 'we had a little half-German who would divert you and fill your life.' Olga Knipper was as anxious to have a child as he was. 'Oh, how I wish that we could have our little half-German,' she replied, and in December she referred to it again: 'One day we shall have a little creature we shall worship. I am sure we shall. You want it, too, Anton, don't you?' On the way back from Yalta in February, she felt sick in the train and almost fainted. A woman in her compartment suggested that she might be pregnant, but she dismissed the idea, believing that her sickness was caused by some lobster she had eaten at a literary party in Yalta before she left for Moscow. On March 31st she wrote to Chekhov from Petersburg where the Moscow Art Theatre was on tour at the time: 'An extraordinary thing has happened to me: it seems that I left Yalta with the hope of presenting you with a little Pamphilius, but did not realise it. I felt unwell all the time, but I thought it was my stomach, and though I wanted to be pregnant, I did not know that I was. I should have taken greater care of myself if I had known that I was going to have a baby....'

Olga Knipper was taken ill during a performance of Gorky's play *The Philistines* and rushed to hospital, where she underwent an operation. She was on the danger list for several days. Telegrams arrived from Chekhov every day, but his doctors forbade him to go to Petersburg. She arrived in Yalta on April 14th and had a relapse. 'The

dining-room in Chekhov's house', Stanislavsky, who had brought
Olga Knipper back to Yalta, records, 'was converted into a bedroom
for the patient and Chekhov looked after her like a most devoted
nurse. In the evening he sat in the next room correcting the proofs of
his stories. When I reminded him of the play he had promised to give
us, he would take a small piece of paper out of his pocket and say,
"Why, here it is—here!"'

By the end of May Olga Knipper had recovered sufficiently to be
able to travel, and on May 25th, the day after Korolenko's visit, she and
Chekhov left for Moscow, intending to spend the summer somewhere
on the Volga. But in Moscow Olga Knipper had another relapse and
was again very ill. 'Chekhov', Stanislavsky writes, 'did not leave the
bedside of his wife by day or by night. We, too, took turns to watch
not over the patient who was well looked after anyhow, but over
Chekhov, who had grown very thin and weak during his wife's illness. . . . Chekhov's only amusement during that time', Stanislavsky
states, 'was to go and see a very clever juggler at the Aquarium.'

When Olga Knipper was out of danger, Chekhov was persuaded to
accompany Morozov, who was building the Moscow Art Theatre at
the time, to his estate in the remote province of Ufa. He left Moscow
on June 18th and arrived on Morozov's estate after a long and weary
journey by rail and boat on June 23rd.

He met a young student there, with whom he spent most of the
time. The student, Alexander Tikhonov, who was later to become a
writer, left a detailed account of Chekhov's visit. The first thing
Chekhov did was to glance at a little stream at the bottom of a hill and
ask whether there were any pike there. After lunch they went down to
the village, Chekhov walking behind Morozov and the student and
prodding the cracked earth with his stick. The student remembered
Gorky's saying: 'Chekhov walks on the earth like a doctor in a hospital:
there are many patients there, but no medicines, and, besides, the
doctor is not so sure that medicines are any good.' Morozov was
building a school on his estate, but Chekhov did not go in to inspect
it, but sat down on some logs and, rattling a tin of sweets he always
carried in his waistcoat pocket, tried to inveigle some of the village
children to come and talk to him. But the children were too shy and
dared not go near the strange 'uncle'. Next morning Morozov went off
on a tour of his estate, and in the evening Chekhov invited the student
to have tea with him. Knowing that Gorky was a great friend of
Chekhov's, the young man was soon talking excitedly about what a
wonderful writer Gorky was.

'Excuse me,' Chekhov interrupted with what sounded like the rasping civility of a man who had had his favourite corn trodden on, 'but I fail to understand why you and our young men in general are in such raptures over Gorky. He is undoubtedly a man of talent, but what you all seem to like so much is his *Song of the Falcon* and his *Stormy Petrel*. That's not literature. It's only a collection of high-sounding words. I know what you're going to say—politics! But what kind of politics is it? "Forward without fear or doubt!"—that's not politics. If you ask me to go forward, you must show me the way, the aim, the means. Nothing has so far been achieved in politics by "the frenzy of the brave".'

Chekhov kept touching the things on the table with his long fingers: the ash-tray, the saucer, the milk-jug, and immediately pushing them away with a wry look on his face.

'You have just mentioned *Foma Gorgeyev*,' he went on, 'but you're wrong again. It's all along one straight line, it's all constructed round one character, just like *shashlyk* on a spit. To construct a novel one must know the law of symmetry and the equilibrium of masses. A novel is a palace, and the reader must feel free to move about in it. He must not be startled or bored as in a museum. He must be given time to rest occasionally from his author and his chief characters. That's where a landscape comes in useful, or something humorous, or some new twist in the plot, or some new characters. I've told Gorky that a hundred times, but he won't listen. He's proud and not bitter.'[1]

Tikhonov mentioned the Moscow Art Theatre, but there again Chekhov, to his surprise, had very little to say in its favour.

'There's nothing special about it,' he declared emphatically. 'It's a theatre. At least the actors there know their parts. In other theatres you won't find even that. I remember my *Seagull* being performed at the Alexandrinsky Theatre. The actors had to wait for the prompter to give them their cues. What nonsense they talked! Our actors are as a rule still very uncultured, and they don't know how to deport themselves on the stage. While they are young, they all scrape their feet and neigh like foals. When they get old their voices become hoarse from drinking and you can't hear what they're saying.'

Crushed again, the young student said something in praise of the 'decadents', whom he considered 'a new movement in literature'.

'There aren't any decadents and there never were any,' said Chekhov. 'Where did you get them from? Maupassant in France and I in Russia began writing very short stories—there's your new movement in

[1] Gorky means bitter in Russian.

literature. As for the so-called decadents, they're cheats, the lot of them—cheats and not decadents. They're selling inferior goods. Religion, mysticism, and all that sort of thing. The Russian peasant', he went on, repeating the view he had already expressed in his *Peasants*, 'never was religious, and he long ago shoved the devil under the sweating bench in the steam bath. They've invented it all themselves to hoax the public. Don't believe them. And their legs aren't "pale" at all, as one of their poets claims, but hairy like the legs of other men.'

Chekhov was obviously anxious to shock the young idealistic student by his heterodox opinions, but there is plenty of evidence in his letters and in the recorded talks of his friends to show that he had never allowed himself to be deceived by the political tub-thumper and that, though he loathed the reactionary clique that was ruling Russia, his innate scepticism and cool judgment kept him aloof from the more starry-eyed reformers of mankind. His belief in a brighter future was ounded on his faith in the fundamental goodness of the human heart and in the final victory of beauty over the beast in man. He disliked the Russian aristocracy as only a serf could dislike his former masters, and he despised the new capitalist who was emerging in Russia and who to him was only another and more sinister version of the Gavrilovs and the 'Chokhovs' whom he knew so well in his youth. His dislike of Morozov was something he could not help. One day he paid a visit to the surgery on Morozov's estate, and as he was washing his hands on his return Tikhonov overheard him muttering:

'A rich merchant—builds theatres—flirts with the revolution—but there's no iodine at the dispensary and the doctor's assistant has drunk all the alcohol in the bottles and treats rheumatism with castor oil. They're all the same—our Russian Rockefellers!'

A few months earlier he wrote to his wife: 'Why, oh why, does Morozov invite the aristocrats to his house? All they do is to eat his food, and on leaving his house, laugh at him just as they would laugh at a Yakut. I'd have driven the lot out with a stick.'

At the same time, however, Chekhov was appalled by the inert mass of half-savage peasantry and had little faith in the ability of the Russian working class either to organise itself or to lead a revolution. It was only in the last year of his life that he became conscious of the stirring of a mighty force in Russia. 'Don't you see,' he said to a friend excitedly a few months before his death and shortly before the outbreak of the 1905 revolution, 'don't you see that everything is on the move—society and the workers.'

The next few days Chekhov and Tikhonov spent fishing. Chekhov was right: there were plenty of pike in the river.

'Fishing's a wonderful occupation,' Chekhov said, spitting on a worm he was threading on the hook of his line. 'A quiet sort of insanity. Pleasant and harmless. And what is so nice about it is that you haven't got to think. It's wonderful!'

He was an excellent fisherman and caught more fish than the student.

'We're such a bone-lazy people,' Chekhov said, stretching himself blissfully. 'We've even infected nature with our laziness. Look at this stream—it's too lazy to move. And see how it twists and turns, and all because of laziness. All our famous "psychology", all that Dostoevsky stuff, is part of it, too. We're too lazy to work, so we invent things.'

Chekhov dozed off, his head drooping on his long neck, just like a dead duck, Tikhonov thought irreverently. Every time he dozed off, a red-haired mongrel bitch, which materialised out of nowhere, watched the floats for him, and every time there was a bite she would jump up and start barking furiously. As a reward, he fed her on the fish he caught. He watched her greedily swallowing a perch, which beat her across her muzzle with its tail.

'Just like our critics,' he observed dryly.

Chekhov left Morozov's estate suddenly after another haemorrhage. He had been talking to the young student all the evening. It was very close, and he was unusually quiet and pensive. There was no sign of his former nervous irritation. He sat with his head bent in a chair in front of the open french window of the terrace, grasping his bony knees with his long hands and gazing intently at the dark shapes of the trees in the park.

'First of all, my friend,' he said slowly, addressing himself not to the student but to some invisible man in the park, 'we must rid ourselves of lies. Art is so good just because it does not tolerate a lie. You can tell lies in love, politics, medicine—you can deceive men as much as you like and you can deceive even God himself—such cases have been known—but you cannot practise deception in art.'

He paused for a moment, as though expecting an objection from the invisible man outside, and, not receiving any reply, went on:

'I am often reproached—even Tolstoy has reproached me—with writing about trifles. I'm told I have no positive heroes: revolutionaries, Alexanders of Macedon, or even, as in Leskov's stories, honest police inspectors. But where am I to get them from?' He smiled sadly. 'Our life is provincial, our towns are unpaved, our villages are poor, our people are shabby. When we are young, we all chirp rapturously like sparrows on a heap of muck, but at the age of forty', he went on, thinking of a letter he had recently received from Nemirovich-Danchenko, 'we are already old and start thinking of death. . . . What sort of heroes are we?'

Again his head drooped and he gazed unblinkingly into the park. Then he talked of the way Stanislavsky had been misinterpreting his plays. His aim in writing them, he said, was to make people realise how bad and boring their lives were.

'And what about those who have already realised it?' the student asked.

'Those who have realised it', Chekhov replied, 'will find the way without me.' And getting up, he added: 'Let's go to bed. There's going to be a storm.'

Through the thin partition that separated their bedrooms, Tikhonov could hear Chekhov's muffled cough: he had not heard him cough so much or so long before. A few times Chekhov got out of bed, walked about the room, drank something from a glass, started coughing, went back to bed and got up again. In the middle of the night Tikhonov was awakened by a strange sensation of danger. Blinding flashes of lightning lit up the room, followed by deafening claps of thunder. Suddenly he became aware of a long drawn-out groan coming from Chekhov's bedroom. He jumped out of bed, put his ear to the partition, and a moment later the groan was repeated, rising almost to an agonised scream and ending with what sounded like a sob.

Tikhonov thought Chekhov was dying and he rushed barefoot to his bedroom. There was a sudden lull in the storm and through the bedroom door he could distinctly hear the sound of muffled groans and coughing. He opened the door and in the light of a guttering candle burning on the small bedside table he saw Chekhov lying on the bed in a twisted heap with his face over the edge. His whole body shook with coughing, and every time he coughed blood spurted out of his wide-open mouth into an enamelled blue spittoon.

'Anton Pavlovich!' Tikhonov called, but the storm had started again and Chekhov did not hear him. He called him a second time. Chekhov fell back on the pillow.

'I'm sorry, old man, I—I——' Chekhov brought out the words in a strangled voice, wiping the blood off his beard and moustache.

A flash of lightning and a deafening clap of thunder drowned the rest of the sentence. All Tikhonov could see was Chekhov's lips moving soundlessly under his moustache which was sticky with blood.

Next day Morozov arrived and took Chekhov back to the nearest railway station.

29

On his return from Morozov's estate, Chekhov spent about six weeks at Lyubimovka, Stanislavsky's country house near Moscow, where Olga Knipper was convalescing after her illness. He enjoyed his stay there. He fished, he sat on the balcony reading the papers, or in the garden during the church services (Stanislavsky's mother was very pious and there were services almost every day), or he talked to the English governess employed by one of Stanislavsky's cousins, an eccentric girl whom he afterwards used for his model of Charlotte in *The Cherry Orchard*. Then he suddenly left for Yalta, merely telling his wife that he would be back in a few days. The whole thing was very odd, and Olga Knipper, from whom he concealed the real reason for his hasty departure, namely his fear of a recurrence of the dreadful attack he had had at Morozov's country house, could not help being puzzled and dismayed. She assumed that Chekhov had got tired of her. Then she wondered whether it might not be a plot on the part of his mother and sister to take him away from her. This fantastic suspicion grew and grew till it became a certainty in her mind and she wrote a furious letter to Mary, which was, of course, shown to Chekhov (he later claimed that he had picked it up in his mother's room by mistake). The subsequent correspondence that passed between them throws a strange light on a relationship that owed its difficulties and misunderstandings mainly, if not wholly, to Chekhov's morbid reticence, aggravated by the circumstance that intellectually there was (fortunately, perhaps) no point of contact between them. 'If only I could understand your letters,' Olga Knipper wrote to him at the end of August. 'There are so many contradictions in them.' A few days later she accused him of treating her like a stranger. 'You are capable of living with me', she wrote, 'and never uttering a word all the time. And sometimes I feel that you do not want me. I feel that you only want me as a pleasant woman companion and that as a human being I am a stranger to you. You can bear anything in silence. You never feel the need of sharing your thoughts with anyone. You like your own special kind of life and you look on everyday life with complete indifference. . . . I am writing this', she declared in another letter, 'because I am oppressed by my own worthlessness. I terribly want you to be happy and yet I can see that you are not any happier with me. Just now I feel like going down on my knees before you and asking your forgiveness. You are a lucky man. You are always so even-tempered, so imperturbable that sometimes I feel that no separations, no feelings, no changes make any difference to you. That isn't because you are cold or indifferent by nature, but because there is something in you that does not let you regard the phenomena of everyday life as of any consequence.'

What is really amazing, however, is that Chekhov should have failed to realise, or, at any rate, refused to admit, that he was in any way responsible for the misunderstanding that had arisen between him and Olga Knipper. 'What is it you don't understand?' he asked her in one of his first letters from Yalta. 'Am I talking in riddles? Am I deceiving you? No, darling, that is not nice.' And next day he complained of the 'strange' letters he was receiving from her. 'Aren't you my wife?' he asked with genuine surprise. 'I have loved you dearly and I still love you, and you are telling me that you are just a pleasant woman companion to me.' And what is even more extraordinary, he, too, had jumped to the fantastic conclusion that someone had been telling all sorts of tales about him to Olga Knipper with the idea of taking her away from him. 'Don't leave me so soon', he begged her, 'without having lived with me properly and without having presented me with a boy or a girl. When you have given me a child, you can do what you like.' And driven to desperation by her letters, he wrote: 'Darling, be good and don't torture me.'

Already in his first letters from Yalta Chekhov hinted at the real reason why he had to leave Lyubimovka. He told her that he had been coughing up blood and he pretended that in Yalta his condition had improved. But he could not keep up the pretence very long and he soon had to admit that he could not join her in Moscow because 'the moment I arrived in Yalta my barometer began to fall and I began to cough devilishly and completely lost my appetite. I don't feel either like writing or like travelling'. He asked her to send him his blue bottle which he carried about with him constantly now and which he used to spit into. When Olga Knipper suggested that his present illness was due to a cold he had caught while sitting in the bathing pavilion in Lyubimovka during a storm, he told her the truth at last. 'I did not catch a cold in Lyubimovka,' he wrote. 'Please, don't invent things. There was simply an aggravation of the pulmonary process as a result of the heat and the dust in Yalta.' At first he refused to see his doctor (a sure sign that he feared the worst). Dr. Altschuler had to threaten to write to Olga Knipper before he allowed himself to be examined. But by that time his condition had again improved. 'Dr. Altschuler', he wrote to Olga

Knipper on September 22nd, 'came to see me yesterday and he found that there was a definite improvement in my condition and that, to judge by the changes since last spring, my illness was showing signs of getting better. He even gave me permission to go to Moscow—so greatly has my condition improved.' To this obviously too optimistic diagnosis Chekhov thought it necessary, however, to add: 'He said that I couldn't go at once and that I'd have to wait for the first frosts. And his orders are that I shall have to leave Moscow immediately on my arrival. So,' he concluded rather inconsequentially, 'as you see, I am perfectly all right. Make a note of that.'

In spite of his illness, Chekhov's life in Yalta went on as usual. He spent the mornings in his study reading the papers and attending to his correspondence. By lunchtime the floor of the study was strewn with discarded newspapers and the fireplace (which never had a fire, as the burning logs hurt his eyes) was full of torn envelopes. In the afternoon he received his visitors. 'I have come to the conclusion', Olga Knipper observed shrewdly in one of her letters, 'that you really like to have visitors and are merely showing off when you complain that they irritate you.' Among his visitors that autumn were the actress Alla Nazimova, who was to become a Hollywood star many years later, and Suvorin, who spent two days with him and whose talk he still found 'new and interesting'. Kuprin, too, came to see him often.

The news of the death of Zola came as a great shock to him: he never liked him as a writer, he wrote to Olga Knipper, but he admired him greatly as a man.

There could be no question of his even attempting to write the new play for the Moscow Art Theatre in spite of the constant proddings from Nemirovich-Danchenko and Olga Knipper. His illness had weakened him so much that he had neither the strength nor the energy for writing a play. Another thing that worried the directors of the Moscow Art Theatre was his sudden decision to resign as a shareholder of the new company Morozov had formed to run the theatre. But he resigned not, as Stanislavsky had feared, because he wanted to sever his connexion with the Moscow Art Theatre, but because he realised that he would never be able to afford the subscription of ten thousand roubles which in a moment of great optimism he had undertaken to pay.

On October 14th Chekhov was again in Moscow, but he stayed there only for about six weeks. He continued to work on his last story, *The Betrothed*, which he finished about three months later in Yalta. He was also present at a few rehearsals of Gorky's second play, *The*

Lower Depths. After the first night of the play on December 19th, a telegram was sent to Chekhov to tell him of its great success. When Sumbatov asked him what he thought of Gorky's plays, Chekhov wrote on February 2nd, 1903: 'The *Philistines* is, in my opinion, a schoolboy's work, but Gorky's merit as a playwright is not that people like him but that he is the first one in Russia and in the world generally to talk with contempt and disgust of the philistine and that he did so just at a time when society was prepared for it. Both from the Christian, economic or any other point of view, philistinism is an evil; like a dam on a river, it always causes stagnation, and Gorky's tramps, though drunk and not elegant, are, or at any rate appear to be, a most effective remedy against stagnation, and though the dam has not been broken through, it has sprung a dangerous leak. I don't know if I am expressing myself clearly enough. The time will come when Gorky's works will be forgotten, but he will not be forgotten himself in a thousand years. That's what I think of him, but I may be mistaken.'

In Yalta Chekhov's health continued to deteriorate. However much he tried to conceal it from Olga Knipper, the gravity of his condition was obvious to her. She was just then going through a very difficult time. She was beginning to suspect that Chekhov and her doctors had been keeping the truth from her about the grave consequences of her operation, namely that she would never be able to have children. Chekhov did his best to reassure her, but she did not believe him. The strain of having to pretend that there was nothing seriously wrong with Chekhov was also proving too much for her, and she often found herself losing patience with him. She was worried by the thought that she was not looking after him properly and she wondered if she ought not to leave the stage. Chekhov did his best to set her mind at rest. He assured her that during his last visit to Moscow she had become dearer to him than she had ever been and that he loved her more than ever. He denied that there had been any unpleasant moments while he had been with her. If she had lived with him in Yalta all winter, he wrote, her life would be spoilt and for that he would never have forgiven himself. Besides, it was not her fault that she could not live with him. On the contrary, their married life, he maintained, was a success because they did not prevent each other from carrying on with their work. But occasionally he thought it wise to warn her. He was anxious to go to Switzerland in the summer and he was overjoyed when she accepted his proposal. 'We have not got long to live together,' he wrote to her on January 24th. 'Our youth, if we can call it youth, will be gone in two or three years, and we must hurry.' And in March he tried to prepare her for the change for the worse in his condition by telling her that after his long confinement indoors his Yalta friends looked compassionately at him when they met him in the street and said 'all sorts of things'. And when she wrote to him that the new flat she had taken in Moscow was on the third floor, he confessed (shortly before his visit to Moscow in April 1903) that he might find it hard to walk up the stairs, as he was suffering from attacks of breathlessness.

In February Chekhov at last sat down to write his long-promised play. Shortly before, he told Olga Knipper that he wanted badly to write a light comedy and that he thought that one-act comedies of the kind he had been successful in writing would be fashionable again. The worse his health became, the stronger did this urge to write something gay grow on him. That was natural: all his life, from his early childhood, he had laughed off any disagreeable situation in which he happened to find himself; the joke became his most effective weapon in a crisis—he even joked with his wife a few hours before his death. But he found the work on his last play very hard going. He got the paper ready, put it on his desk, wrote the title—*The Cherry Orchard*—at the top of the first page, and only several days later forced himself to sit down to write. 'I am writing four lines a day,' he wrote to a friend, 'and even that gives me unbearable pain.' His work on the play was interrupted by his visit to Moscow, and he did not resume it till his return to Yalta in July.

30

Chekhov arrived in Moscow at the end of April. The money he had received from Marx for the complete edition of his works was all gone by then and he was again in serious financial difficulties. Gorky urged him to break his contract with Marx, promising to raise enough money to repay the seventy-five thousand roubles he had received for his works and guaranteeing him an annual income of twenty-thousand roubles. A number of his friends and admirers, including Shalyapin, Goltsev, Leonid Andreyev, Veresayev, and Ivan Bunin, drafted a letter to Marx in which they urged the publisher to reconsider his contract with Chekhov, quoting as a precedent Zola's publisher who had not only released him from his contract but agreed to conclude a new one. Olga Knipper, too, was prevailed on to write to her husband about it. 'You mustn't forget', Chekhov wrote in reply, 'that when the question of selling my works to Marx arose I hadn't a brass farthing, I owed money to Suvorin and my books were being published in a most disgraceful way.' However, it seems that Chekhov was at last persuaded to take the matter up with Marx, and on May 13th he left Moscow for Petersburg, though, as he wrote to Olga Knipper in the train, 'I do not expect anything good from the German'. His premonition was justified. He spent only one day in Petersburg, and on his return to Moscow he stopped the collection of more signatures to the letter his friends were intending to send to Marx. 'I signed the agreement with Marx of my own free will,' he said, 'and I do not consider it right to go back on it. If I sold my works too cheaply, it was my own fault: I have made a stupid mistake, and Marx cannot be held responsible for my stupidities. I shall be more careful next time.'

That statement sounds almost like a repetition of what Marx must have told him at their interview. That was the end of the matter.[1]

In Moscow Chekhov had himself thoroughly examined by Professor Ostroumov, at whose clinic he spent several weeks in 1897. 'I have news,' he wrote to Dr. Sredin on June 4th. 'I went to see Professor Ostroumov. He found that I had emphysema of the lungs, a very bad right lung, remnants of pleurisy, etc. etc. He forbade me to spend the winter in Yalta, and ordered me to spend it somewhere in the country near Moscow.'

The specialist must have realised that Chekhov's constant journeys from Yalta to Moscow were more harmful to his health than his residence in the country near Moscow could possibly be. Chekhov's Yalta doctor was utterly confounded by Ostroumov's advice and went so far as to say that the professor must have been drunk when he gave it. But, as it happened, Chekhov only availed himself of the permission to live in Moscow in winter a few months before his death. The summer of 1903 was so hot that he gave up the idea of going to Switzerland, feeling too weakened by the heat to undertake a long journey. He drove with his wife to Zvenigorod, where he had spent such a happy time after he had finished his medical studies, and stayed for a few days at the New Jerusalem monastery. Most of June and half of July they lived on an estate at Naro-Fominsk near Moscow. Chekhov disliked his life there intensely. 'Such a hideous, idle, absurd and tasteless life as at the white country house [in Naro-Fominsk]', he wrote to his wife from Yalta in October, 'one can hardly imagine. The people there seem to live exclusively for the sake of the pleasure of entertaining some

---

[1] 'I spent only a few hours in Petersburg,' Chekhov wrote to Suvorin on June 17th. 'I saw Marx. We did not discuss anything in particular. He offered to lend me 5,000 roubles [for his proposed trip to Switzerland], but I refused to accept the money. Then he presented me with a few hundredweights of his publications, which I accepted, and we parted, having decided to meet again in August and think things over in the meantime.' They never met again.

General or having a walk with an Under-Secretary of State. And why doesn't Vishnevsky, who looks on those people as on gods, understand that?'

From time to time Chekhov would go down to Moscow for a day or two, but by the middle of July he and Olga Knipper left for Yalta, where he resumed his work on *The Cherry Orchard*. Olga Knipper left for Moscow on September 19th without the play. Chekhov went on sending his wife optimistic bulletins about his health, but she could hardly take them seriously. 'I simply don't know what to write to you about,' she wrote to him at the beginning of October. 'I know that you are ill and that I am just a nobody who comes, lives with you and goes away. My whole life is such a piece of horrible hypocrisy that I don't know what to do.... And here, too, I walk about as though I had no home of my own. I keep on accusing myself, I feel that it is all my fault. I don't seem to be able to cope with life.... Of course you mustn't think of coming to Moscow.'

Chekhov did his best to cheer her up. He begged her not to be unjust to herself. 'You are at home,' he wrote, 'you have your work which you love, you are in good health, your husband is away, but he will soon be with you. One must be sensible!' And a few days later: 'I shall most certainly come to Moscow. Play conscientiously and well; learn, darling; develop your powers of observation, you are still a young actress; and please don't be depressed.' On October 12th he could already send her the news that his play was finished. 'Oh, how hard it was for me to write this play!' he wrote. He also told her that he was taking great care of himself, and her reply shows how bad a patient Chekhov must have been. 'So at last you are attending to your illness,' she wrote. 'Why do you find it so difficult while I am with you? Why do you torture me and never do anything? But when I go back to Moscow or when you leave me—the medical treatment starts and you begin to eat a lot. Mary seems to be able to do everything for you.'

The reception of *The Cherry Orchard* by the two directors of the Moscow Art Theatre did little to allay Chekhov's fears that his play would again be misinterpreted. Stanislavsky wrote him an excited letter asserting that the play was not at all a gay comedy as he (Chekhov) seemed to believe, but a tragedy, an opinion with which Nemirovich-Danchenko seemed to concur, for he, too, complained that there were too many 'tears' in it. Chekhov knew very well that there was little he could do to make them see how wrong they were: he could not fight what had become a tradition because that tradition was too firmly established by then. He still hoped to be able to change their opinion during the rehearsals, but the weather in Moscow was bad and he had to wait till the beginning of December before he could leave for Moscow. There he soon discovered that neither Stanislavsky nor Nemirovich-Danchenko would accept his interpretation of *The Cherry Orchard*, and after a few stormy meetings with them, he realised that nothing could be done about it. He was too ill and in the end he had to give way.

On December 16th Professor Rossolimo met Chekhov at the funeral of the rector of Moscow University. 'During the service in the university chapel', he writes, 'Chekhov took me by the elbow. I did not know he was there, but I was very glad to see him. He had greatly changed during the past six months; he was very thin and his face was yellow and covered with wrinkles. And yet he still looked as young and as kind as ever. He joined in the singing of the choir in his soft, low voice, his head thrown back, his gaze fixed in the distance, and his lips distended in a dreamy and tender smile.

'Feeling tired at the end of the service, he asked me to take him to my flat for a rest and some food before going to the cemetery, and we took a cab to my place. My wife took a photograph of Chekhov and myself and, while posing, he cracked jokes about which of us would be the first to join the late rector. We had to wait a long time for the coffin to be carried through the gates of the cemetery. Chekhov told me that he loved cemeteries, especially in winter, when, as on that day, the graves could hardly be seen under the deep drifts of snow. And pointing to the students who were carrying the wreaths, he said: "These are the people who are burying the old and bringing fresh flowers and new hopes into the kingdom of death." '

A fortnight later Chekhov and Gorky were present at a New Year's party given by the Moscow Art Theatre, where, as Chekhov put it, they had a most 'interesting cough' with one another. They sat talking at a table at the far end of the foyer, unobserved by the gay throng of dancers, till Stanislavsky, in immaculate evening dress, with a mop of white hair and a black moustache, loomed up behind them and led them away behind the scenes.

31

The first night of *The Cherry Orchard* took place on Chekhov's forty-fourth birthday, or rather name-day, on January 17th, 1904. Already before his arrival in Moscow Chekhov was cautiously sounded about the exact date of the twenty-fifth anniversary of his literary

ANTON CHEKHOV (1904)

activities. He must have smelt a rat (he hated to be involved in public demonstrations of any kind), for he replied that he believed that they would have to wait another year or two before they could celebrate his silver jubilee as a writer. He was, as a matter of fact, quite right since his first story was published in *The Dragonfly* on March 9th, 1880. But in spite of his violent protests and, what was even more important, his failing health, the directors of the Moscow Art Theatre were determined to celebrate it on the opening night of *The Cherry Orchard*. Stanislavsky's defence of what was an unnecessary piece of cruelty perpetrated against a dying man is interesting as showing the utter disregard with which Chekhov's wishes and feelings were treated by those who were sincerely and devotedly attached to him. 'Chekhov', Stanislavsky writes, 'resisted strongly, threatened that he would stay at home and refuse to come to the first night of his play, but the temptation was too great for us and we had our way.'

Chekhov, in fact, refused to go to the first night of *The Cherry Orchard*, but before the end of the third act Vishnevsky was dispatched to his flat and brought him to the theatre almost by main force.

'On the day of the anniversary', Stanislavsky writes, 'Chekhov was not very cheerful. It was as though he felt that he had not long to live. When after the third act he could not suppress his cough as he stood in the middle of the stage while speeches were being delivered in his honour and gifts presented to him, our hearts contracted painfully. Someone in the audience shouted to him to sit down. Chekhov frowned and remained standing throughout the long-drawn-out ceremony over which he so good-humouredly laughed in his stories. But even then he could not resist a smile. When one of the writers began his speech with the words with which Gayev addresses the bookcase in the first act of *The Cherry Orchard*: "My dear and highly honoured ――――" putting in Chekhov's name instead of the word "bookcase", Chekhov looked at me from the corner of his eye and an artful smile passed over his lips.

'The anniversary celebration', Stanislavsky concludes as naïvely as he began, 'was a very impressive affair, but it had a very depressing effect upon me. There was the feeling of a funeral about it.'

A much more factual account of the 'anniversary celebration' was left by the writer Stepan Skitalets, who was present on the first night of *The Cherry Orchard*.

'After the third act', he writes, 'came the public tributes to the author. Chekhov presented a touching and a pitiful figure on the stage: tall, haggard, unable to find a place for his hands, slightly stooping, in a dock-tailed morning coat and rather short trousers, with dishevelled hair and a grey, pointed heard, surrounded on the stage by a semicircle of actors, he reminded me of Don Quixote or Baudelaire's "Albatros" among the jeering sailors.

' "Sit down!" a compassionate voice called from the gallery. But one of our greatest writers was apparently so embarrassed that he did not know what to do. Besides, there was nothing he could sit down on, for nobody had thought of providing a chair, although Chekhov looked so weak and ill. The only thing he would have dearly liked to do would be to leave the stage as quickly as possible and hide himself from the gaze of thousands of curious eyes. But opposite him stood his friend, the man who was responsible for the celebration— Nemiro-vich-Danchenko, holding a huge, unrolled sheet of paper in his hands: that was the address he had to deliver in the name of the company and the entire Moscow Art Theatre, the anniversary address, beginning with the intimate allocution—Anton!'

Chekhov's own feelings are perhaps best summed up in one sentence from his letter to Leontyev on January 18th: 'My play was performed yesterday and therefore I am not in a particularly bright mood today.'[1]

The search for a country cottage near Moscow where Chekhov could spend the winter months proved fruitless, but at least he enjoyed his country drive in a sledge on a sunny February day. 'We went by train to Tsarytsino' (a small town near Moscow), Olga Knipper describes the last winter Chekhov was to spend in the country, 'to inspect a small country house. On our way back we either missed the train or did not want to wait for it, and we decided to drive back to Moscow—a distance of about twenty-five miles. In spite of the rather hard frost, Chekhov immensely enjoyed the view of the white plain gleaming in the sun and the crunch of the runners on the firm, smooth snow. It was as if fate had decided to treat him with particular indulgence and in the last year of his life to grant him the joys he prized most: Moscow, a real Russian winter, and . . . the people he was so fond of. . . .'

Chekhov returned to Yalta for the last time on February 18th because of a sudden thaw in Moscow. Alexander and his family were spending a month in Yalta at the time, and Chekhov was glad to see that his eldest brother had given up drink (for the time being, at any rate) and, generally, as he put it in a letter to Olga Knipper, comforted him by his behaviour. The Russo-Japanese war had started and

[1] Writing to Olga Knipper on March 29th, that is, about three months before his death, Chekhov summed up his opinion of the Moscow Art Theatre's production of *The Cherry Orchard* in one sentence: ' One thing I can say : Stanislavsky has ruined my play for me.'

Chekhov was planning to go to the front as a doctor if he felt sufficiently well in June or July.

In Yalta the usual routine began all over again: the unending stream of visitors, the now regular attacks of ill-health, complicated by abdominal pains which necessitated the resort to opium, and an occasional visit to the theatre, where he saw Ibsen's *Ghosts* ('A trashy play and mediocre acting,' Chekhov wrote to Olga Knipper). During the last weeks of his stay in Moscow he had undertaken to supervise the literary section of *Russian Thought* on condition that only the works of new writers were sent to him, and in Yalta he was busy reading manuscripts for the journal. The war and his illness, however, interfered with his work. He still pretended not to be unduly worried by his illness, which had now reached its final stage, but Olga Knipper was not deceived by the optimistic reports he sent her. 'I feel', she wrote to him, 'a terrible calamity hanging over my head.' Chekhov, however, was still hoping that he might recover some of his strength. 'I am dreaming of the summer,' he wrote to Olga Knipper a week before he left for Moscow. 'I wish I could be left in peace to think and write.' Olga Knipper had asked him his opinion of the meaning of life. 'You ask me what life is?' he wrote to her on April 20th. 'It is like asking what a carrot is. A carrot is a carrot, and nothing more is known.'

32

Chekhov left Yalta on May 1st. He had planned to spend the summer in the country near Moscow, but when he arrived in Moscow he had to take to his bed, where he stayed for three weeks. This time few visitors were admitted to see him. One of them, Professor Rossolimo, saw him a day or two before he left, on the advice of his doctors, to go to the German spa of Badenweiler. 'Chekhov', Rossolimo writes, 'sent me an urgent note to go and see him. I went to see him on a late afternoon of a hot, cloudless day. It was very close. As I entered his study, I found him lying in bed by the wall, with his head turned to the window. His wife sat at the writing desk by the window and, as far as I can remember, was turning over the pages of *Russian Thought* by the light of a lamp with a green shade. The room was in semi-darkness; the pale light of the dying day seemed to be fighting unsuccessfully against the greenish light of the lamp. Chekhov's hand was hot and dry, his cheeks were flushed. He complained of the excruciating pain his indigestion caused him, but at the same time expressed his great pleasure at the marvellous dishes his doctor was so good at inventing. Of his illness he spoke, like other T.B. patients, optimistically. . . .'

But the reason for Chekhov's urgent summons to Professor Rossolimo showed that he was not as optimistic about his illness as he wished to appear, especially in the presence of Olga Knipper. Before leaving for Germany, from where he did not think he would return, Chekhov apparently wanted to hear from Rossolimo about their mutual friends at the university, the students who had been in the same year with them, as though he wished in that way to bid them a last farewell. They discussed them all at great length, those who were alive and those who were already dead, not forgetting Chekhov's Taganrog schoolmate, Vassily Zembulatov, who had died recently. He also asked Rossolimo where he had been lately, and, anxious to distract him, Rossolimo embarked on a long description of his travels in Greece. Chekhov listened to him attentively, although he was all the time tossing feverishly on his bed.

Another description of Chekhov a day before he left for Germany by the writer Nicolai Teleshov leaves no doubt that he knew very well that he would never return to Russia alive.

'Our last meeting', Teleshov writes, 'took place in Moscow on the eve of Chekhov's departure abroad. On a sofa, propped up by cushions, wearing an overcoat or a dressing-gown and with a rug over his legs, sat a very thin and apparently small man, with narrow shoulders and a narrow, bloodless face—so emaciated and unrecognisable had Chekhov become. I should never have thought that a man could change so much.

'He stretched out his weak, waxen hand, which I was afraid to look at, and gazed at me with his gentle but no longer smiling eyes.

' "I'm leaving tomorrow," he said. "I'm going away to die."

'He used a different word, a more cruel word than "to die", which I should not like to repeat now.

' "I'm going away to die," he repeated emphatically. "Say goodbye for me to your friends. . . . Tell them that I remember them and that I am very fond of some of them. Wish them success and happiness from me. We shall never meet again." '

Chekhov and Olga Knipper left Moscow for Badenweiler on June 3rd. They stopped for a few days in Berlin, where Chekhov consulted a specialist, who seemed to be hopeful of an eventual improvement in his health. But he was very ill indeed. Sobolevsky had asked a friend of his, Grigory Iollos, Berlin Correspondent of the *Russian Gazette*, to look up Chekhov at his Berlin hotel. 'All the time I was in Berlin',

Chekhov wrote to Sobolevsky; 'I was conscious of the great care Iollos bestowed on me. Unfortunately, my legs refused to obey me and I was far from well, especially at the beginning, so that I could not place myself at his disposal even for two hours.'

Iollos himself wrote to Sobolevsky: 'Already in Berlin I personally got the impression that Chekhov's days were numbered. He looked a very sick man to me: terribly emaciated, coughing at the slightest movement, gasping for breath, and running a high temperature. In Berlin he found it hard to mount the few steps to the Potsdam station; for a few minutes he had to sit down to recover his breath, looking utterly exhausted.'

In Badenweiler, where Chekhov and Olga Knipper arrived on June 8th, there seemed at first to have been a definite improvement in his condition. 'Badenweiler', he wrote to Kuprin, 'is a pleasant little town, warm, comfortable and cheap, but I expect that in about three days I shall be bored and start thinking of running away somewhere.'

They stopped at one of the most select Badenweiler guest-houses, the Villa Friederike. 'The villa', Chekhov wrote to Mary, 'is a detached house standing in the middle of a lovely garden. We live there and pay for our board and lodging.'

'My health is improving,' he wrote to Sobolevsky. 'It is coming back to me not in ounces but in pounds. My feet have long since stopped aching, just as if they had never ached. I eat a lot and with an appetite; all that is left from my recent illness is shortness of breath and general weakness. I am attended by a very good doctor here, an intelligent and knowledgeable man. It is Dr. Schwoerer, who is married to a Moscow woman.'

And in a letter to Mary on June 16th he wrote: 'My health is improving and when I walk I am no longer conscious of being ill. . . . I am not so much worried now by shortness of breath and I have no pains. But my illness has left me terribly emaciated; my legs, in particular, have grown so thin that I cannot remember ever having had such thin legs. The German doctors have turned my life upside down. At seven o'clock in the morning I have tea in bed, and at half-past a German masseur comes and rubs me down with cold water, which is quite pleasant; after a little rest, I get up at eight o'clock, have a cup of cocoa and consume an enormous quantity of butter; at ten o'clock I have oatmeal porridge, very tasty and excellently flavoured, quite unlike the oatmeal porridge we get in Russia. Then I go out. Fresh air, sun. I read the newspapers. At one o'clock we have lunch. At four o'clock another cup of cocoa. At seven o'clock we have our dinner. Before going to bed I have a cup of wild strawberry tea—that's to make me sleep.'

He hoped to be able to leave Badenweiler 'in about three weeks' and he was planning to go to Italy, 'whither I am drawn irresistibly.'

But already during his second week in Badenweiler he became very restless: he did not like his room, he wanted to go somewhere else. The proprietors of the villa, too, fearing that his death might frighten away some of their guests, wanted them to go, and Olga Knipper found a room for them at the hotel Sommer. It had two beds near the door leading to the corridor, and between the window and the door leading on to a little balcony was a small sofa, covered with velvet. There were also a round table in the room, a wash-stand, a wardrobe and a few chairs. The furniture was new and everything was spotlessly clean, the dark wallpaper enhancing the general feeling of cosiness.

Chekhov used to sit for hours on the balcony, watching the street scene below. He seemed to be fascinated by the incessant comings and goings at the post office opposite the hotel. 'You see what culture means,' he said to Olga Knipper one day. 'They are all coming in and going out, and every one of them writes and receives letters.'

Almost every day Olga Knipper would take him out for a drive in the woods. As they drove through a village, he would draw his wife's attention to the clean houses of the German villagers. 'When will our peasants live like that?' he would say with a sigh.

'There is not an atom of talent in anything here,' he wrote to Mary, 'not an atom of good taste, but plenty of orderliness and honesty. Life in Russia is much more talented, not to speak of life in France or Italy.'

His interest in life never forsook him, even when, according to Iollos, who had followed him to Badenweiler, he gave the impression of a man who was mortally ill. And it was the interest Chekhov showed in everything around him that deceived people into believing that he could not possibly die so soon. When Iollos asked Dr. Schwoerer whether Chekhov's death had taken him by surprise, he replied that he was worried by the condition of his heart, but that he thought that his lungs were good enough for another four or six months, no more.

In his last letter to Mary, a few days before he died, Chekhov told her that he hoped to return to Russia by way of Trieste. He was thinking of spending some time at Lake Como, he wrote, adding: 'Italian lakes are famous for their beauty.' German women, he went on, dressed so badly that their lack of taste made him feel depressed. On the same day he wrote a letter to Professor Rossolimo in which he also spoke of his wish to return to Russia by way of the Mediterranean and the Black Sea.[1]

But in spite of all his optimistic plans, Chekhov certainly expected to die quite soon. A few days before his death he sent a cheque to a Berlin bank and ordered the money to be forwarded on his wife's name. When Olga Knipper asked him why he did that, he replied, 'Oh, you know, just in case. . . .'

He died suddenly on the night of July 2nd (old style).

'A few hours before his death', Olga Knipper writes, 'he made me laugh by inventing a funny story. After three anxious days he felt better towards the evening, and as I had not left him during all that time, he insisted that I should go out for a walk in the park. When I came back, he kept asking me to go down and have my dinner, but I told him that the gong had not sounded yet. As it appeared afterwards, we did not hear the gong, and Chekhov began telling me a story of a fashionable holiday resort which was packed with well-fed, fat bankers and healthy red-cheeked Englishmen and Americans. One evening they all returned to their hotel to find that the cook had run off and that there was no dinner waiting for them. Chekhov went on describing how that blow affected each of these pampered people. I sat huddled up on the sofa and laughed gaily. It never occurred to me that a few hours later I would be standing before Chekhov's dead body.'

Chekhov woke up at half-past twelve in the morning and began to gasp for breath. For the first time he asked Olga Knipper to send for the doctor. There were two Russian students staying at the same hotel and Olga Knipper asked one of them to go and fetch Dr. Schwoerer. She herself went down to chop up some ice to put on Chekhov's heart. When the doctor arrived, Chekhov said to him in German:

'*Tod?*'

'Oh, no,' the doctor replied. 'Please, calm yourself.'

Chekhov was still finding it difficult to breathe and ice was placed on his heart. The doctor sent one of the students for oxygen.

'Don't bother,' Chekhov said. 'I shall be dead before they bring it.'

The doctor then ordered some champagne. Chekhov took the glass, turned to Olga Knipper and said with a smile, 'It's a long time since I drank champagne.' He had a few sips and fell back on the pillows. Soon he began to ramble. 'Has the sailor gone? Which sailor?'

[1] The letter is quoted on pp. 81 and 82.

He was apparently thinking of the Russo-Japanese war. That went on for several minutes. His last words were: 'I'm dying'; then in a very low voice to the doctor in German: '*Ich sterbe.*' His pulse was getting weaker. He sat doubled up on his bed, propped up by pillows. Suddenly, without uttering a sound, he fell sideways. He was dead. His face looked very young, contented and almost happy. The doctor went away. A fresh breeze blew into the room, bringing with it the smell of newly mown hay. The sun was rising slowly from behind the woods. Outside, the birds began to stir and twitter, and in the room the silence was broken by the loud buzzing of a huge black moth, which was whirling round and round the electric light, and by the soft sobbing of Olga Knipper as she leaned with her head against Chekhov's body.

Chekhov died on Friday morning and the same night his body was removed to a chapel. On July 5th it was placed in a zinc coffin and began its journey back to Russia. It arrived in Moscow on July 9th in a goods waggon which bore the inscription in large letters over the doors: 'Fresh oysters.' As it happened, a Russian general, killed in the fighting in the Far East, arrived on another platform at the same time and the two funeral processions, headed by a military band, merged. 'Part of the small crowd which came to pay its last respects to the writer so "dearly beloved" by Moscow', Gorky writes, 'went after the coffin of General Keller who had been brought from Manchuria, and were surprised that Chekhov was being buried with a military band. When the mistake was discovered, people began to grin and laugh. Behind Chekhov's coffin walked about a hundred people, no more; I can still remember two Moscow lawyers, both of whom wore new shoes and coloured ties and looked like bridegrooms. Walking behind, I heard one of them discussing the intelligence of dogs, and the other describing the comforts of his country house and the beautiful views around it. And a woman in a mauve dress, walking under a lace parasol, was saying excitedly to an old man, "Oh, he was such a nice 1 an, so witty!" The old man coughed sceptically a few times.

'It was a very hot and dusty day. In front of the procession a fat police officer rode majestically on a fat white horse. All that and a great deal more was cruelly vulgar and incompatible with the memory of a great and sensitive artist.'

Gorky's bitterness is understandable, but, oddly enough, it was just one of those incongruous spectacles—the pomp and circumstance of a military funeral side by side with the inconspicuous funeral of a great writer—that would have made Chekhov laugh.

Chekhov was buried beside his father's grave in the Novo-Devichy cemetery, which he used to visit so often. Almost thirty years later, on November 16th, 1933, the coffin with his remains was exhumed and reburied in the part of the cemetery assigned to the actors of the Moscow Art Theatre. Olga Knipper and Vishnevsky as well as a few relatives and friends were present at the reburial.

RUSSIAN TRANSLITERATION TABLE

The method used for transliterating Russian letters in this book is explained in the following table. The Russian palatal consonants are indicated by a single inverted comma after each consonant, thus: n'. The letter a is always pronounced like the a in father; the letter g is always hard; the letter i is pronounced like ee in sleep.

А а—A a	П п—P p
Б б—B b	Р р—R r
В в—V v	С с—S s
Г г—G g	Т т—T t
Д д—D d	У у—U u
Е е—E e (e=ye; after ы, e=ie)	Ф ф—F f
Ж ж—Zh zh	Х х—Kh kh
З з—Z z	Ц ц—Ts ts
И и—I i	Ч ч—Ch ch
Й й—I i (the combinations ии =i and ый=y)	III ш—Sh sh
	Щ щ—Shch shch
К к—K k	ы—y
Л л—L l	Э э—E e
М м—M n	Ю ю—Yu yu (after ы, ю=iu)
Н н—N n	Я я—Ya ya (after ы, я=ia)
О о—O o	

BIBLIOGRAPHICAL INDEX

of the Complete Works of Anton Chekhov

This Index contains the title of every play, short story, article, etc., Chekhov wrote between 1880 and 1904. The English title is followed by the original Russian date of publication, the Russian title, the name of the English translator and publisher and the date of the English publication. Any work that has so far remained untranslated is marked by an asterisk.[1]

A Bad Business (1887) *Nedobroye Delo* (Constance Garnett: Chatto & Windus, 1916–50).

A Bibliography (1883) *Bibliografia.*

A Blunder (1886) *Neudacha* (Constance Garnett: Chatto & Windus, 1916–50).

A Boring Story (From the diary of an old man) (1899) *Skuchnaya istoriya (Iz zapisok starovo cheloveka)* (S. Koteliansky and J. M. Murry: Maunsel & Co., 1915; Constance Garnett: Chatto & Windus, 1916–50; Select Tales, 1927, 1949).

*A Businessman (1885) *Delets.*

*A Captain's Uniform (1885) *Kapitanski mundir.*

*A Case of *mania grandiosa* (To the attention of the paper 'Doctor') (1883) *Sluchay mania grandiosa (Vnimaniyu gazety 'Vrach').*

*A Case from a Lawyer's Practice (1883) *Sluchay iz sudebnoy praktiki).*

A Chameleon (1884) *Khameleon* (Constance Garnett: Chatto & Windus, 1916–50).

*A Charitable Publican (1883) *Dobrodetel'ny Kabatchik.*

*A Civil Service Examination (1884) *Ekzamen na chin.*

A Classical Student (1883) *Sluchay s klassikom* (Marian Fell: Duckworth, 1915; Constance Garnett: Chatto & Windus, 1922).

*A Clever Fellow (1883) *Khitrets.*

*A Collection of Children's Stories (1883) *Sbornik dlya detey.*

*A Competition (1886) *Konkurs.*

*A Conversation between a Drunken Man and a Sober Devil (1886) *Beseda p'yanovo s trezvym chortom.*

---

[1] The dates 1916–50 after a Constance Garnett translation refer to the five editions of the thirteen small volumes of the *Tales of Chekhov.*

At the Telephone (1886) *U telefona.*

*At the Zelyonins' (1895–1897) *U Zelyoninykh.*

Bad Weather (1887) *Nenastye* (Constance Garnett: Chatto & Windus, 1916–50).

*Bandakov, V.A., Father (an obituary) (1890).

*Baron, The (1882) *Baron.*

*Battle, The (An Old Soldier's Story), (A poem) (1887) *Bitva (Rasskaz starovo soldata).*

*Baubles (1885) *Fintiflyushki.*

Bear, The (A Joke in One Act) (1888) *Medved' (Shutka v odnom deystvii)* (Hilmar Baukage: Samuel French, 1915; Julius West: Duckworth, 1923, 1939, 1949, 1950; Constance Garnett: Chatto & Windus, 1923, 1928, 1935, 1940, 1946, 1950).

Beauties, The (1888) *Krasavitsy* (Marian Fell: Duckworth, 1915; Constance Garnett: Chatto & Windus, 1916–50; Select Tales, 1927, 1949).

*Beauties, The (From a Doctor's Diary) (1895–1897) *Krasavitsy (Iz sapisok vracha).*

*Before the Eclipse (Extract from a Fairy-Play) (1887) *Pered zatmeniyem (Otryvok iz feyerii).*

*Before the Wedding (1880) *Pered svad'boy.*

Beggar, The (1887) *Nishchy* (Marian Fell: Duckworth, 1914; Constance Garnett: Chatto & Windus, 1916–50).

Belated Blossom *see* Late Flowers.

Bet, The (1888) *Pari* (S. Koteliansky & J. M. Murry: Maunsel & Co., 1915; Constance Garnett: Chatto & Windus, 1916–50; A. E. Chamot: Stanley Paul, 1926).

Betrothed, The (1903) *Nevesta* (Constance Garnett: Chatto & Windus, 1916–50).

*Biggest City, The (1886) *Samy bol'shoy gorod.*

*Biographies of Remarkable Contemporaries. 1. A Letter to the Editor. 2. Alexander Ivanovich Ivanov. Famous inventor of the under-the-saddle-and-hoof, wheel and other grease (1884) *Zhizneopisaniya dostoprimechatel'nykh sovremennikov. 1. Pis'mo v redaktsiyu. 2. Alexandr Ivanovich Ivanov. Znamenity izobretatel podsednokopytnoy, kolesnoy i inykh mazey.*

Bird Market *see* In Moscow in Trubnaya Square.

Bishop, The (1902) *Arkhiyerey* (Marian Fell: Duckworth, 1915; Constance Garnett: Chatto & Windus, 1916–50, Select Tales, 1927, 1949; Penguin Books, 1938).

Black Monk, The (1894) *Chorny monakh* (R. E. C. Long: Duckworth,

1903; Marian Fell: Duckworth, 1914; Constance Garnett: Chatto & Windus, 1916–50; A. E. Chamot: Stanley Paul, 1926).

*Boa-Constrictor and the Rabbit, The (1887) *Udav i krolik.*

*Book of Complaints (1884) *Zhalobnaya kniga.*

Boots, The (1885) *Sapogi* (Constance Garnett: Chatto & Windus, 1916–50).

*Both are better (1885) *Oba lutshe.*

Boys (1887) *Mal'chiki* (Marian Fell: Duckworth, 1915; Constance Garnett: Chatto & Windus, 1916–50).

*Bridegroom and Daddy (Something Modern) (A Sketch) (1885) *Zhenikh i papen'ka (Nechto sovremyonnoye) (Stsenka).*

*Buckwheat Porridge Praises Itself (Something spiritualistic) (1883) *Grechnevaya kasha sama sebya khvalit (nechto spiriticheskoye).*

Burbot, The (1885) *Nalim* (Constance Garnett: Chatto & Windus, 1916–50).

*Cat, The (1883) *Kot.*

Cattle Dealers *see* Cold Blood.

*Champagne (Thoughts after a New Year's Party Hangover) (1886) *Shampanskoye (Mysli s novogodnevo pokhmel'ya).*

Champagne (A Rogue's Story) (1887) *Shampanskoye (Rasskaz prokhodimtsa)* (Marian Fell: Duckworth, 1914; Constance Garnett: Chatto & Windus, 1916–50).

*Chemist's Tax, The (1885) *Aptekarskaya taxa.*

*Chemist's Tax, The, or Help, robbers ! ! ! (A funny treatise on a sad theme) (1885) *Aptekarskaya taxa, ili spasite, grabyat ! ! ! (Shutlivy traktat na plachevnuyu temu).*

Chemist's Wife, The (1886) *Aptekarsha* (Constance Garnett: Chatto & Windus, 1916–50).

Cherry Orchard, The (A comedy in four acts) (1903–1904) *Vishnyovy Sad (Komediya v chetyryokh deystriyakh)* (George Calderon: Grant Richards, 1912, 1924; Julius West: Duckworth, 1912, 1916, 1939, 1949; Constance Garnett: Chatto & Windus, 1923, 1928, 1935, 1940, 1946, 1950; S. Kotelianky: Penguin Books, 1940; Elisaveta Fen: Penguin Classics, 1950; Oliver Sayler, Moscow Art Theatre of Russian Plays, 1923–24; Herbert Butler: Yearbook Press Series of Plays, 1934; Stark Young: French Standard Library Edition, 1947).

Children (1886) *Detvora* (Marian Fell: Duckworth, 1914; Constance Garnett: Chatto & Windus, 1916–50).

Choristers (1884) *Pevchiye* (Constance Garnett: Chatto & Windus, 1916–50).

Chorus Girl, The (1886) *Khoristka* (Marian Fell: Duckworth, 1915; Constance Garnett: Chatto & Windus, 1916–50; Select Tales, 1927, 1949).

*Christmas Tree, The (1884) *Yolka.*

*Clever Caretaker, The (1883) *Umny dvornik.*

Cold Blood (1887) *Kholodnaya krov'* (Constance Garnett: Chatto & Windus, 1916–50).

*Collection, The (1883) *Kollektsiya.*

*Comic Actor, The (1884) *Komik.*

*Comic Advertisements and Announcements (Communicated by Antosha Chekhonte) (1882) *Komicheskiye reklamy i ob'yavleniya* (*Soobshchil* Antosha Chekhonte).

*Conference of Natural Scientists in Philadelphia (A scientific article) (1883) *S'yezd yestestvoispytateley v Filadelfii* (*Stat'ya nauchnovo soderzhaniya*).

*Confession, The (1883) *Ispoved'.*

*Confession, or Olya, Zhenya, Zoya (A Letter) (1882) *Ispoved' ili Olya, Zhenya, Zoya* (*Pis'mo.*).

*Confusion in Rome (1884) *Kavardak v Rime.*

*Conjurers (1891) *Fokusniki.*

*Contract with Mankind of the Year 1884 (1884) *Kontrakt 1884 goda s chelovechestvom.*

*Conversation (1883) *Razgovor.*

*Conversation of a Man with a Dog (1885) *Razgovor cheloveka s sobakoy.*

Cook's Wedding, The (1885) *Kukharka zhenitsya* (Marian Fell: Duckworth, 1915; Constance Garnett: Chatto & Windus, 1916–50).

*Correspondent, The (1882) *Korrespondent.*

Cossack, The (1887) *Kazak* (A. E. Chamot: Stanley Paul, 1926; Constance Garnett: Chatto & Windus, 1916–50).

*Country Pleasures (1884) *Dachnoye udovol'stviye.*

*Country Rules (1884) *Dachnyie pravila.*

*Cripple, The (1900) *Kaleka.*

*Critic, The (1887) *Kritik.*

*Crooked Mirror, The (A Christmas Story) (1883) *Krivoye zerkalo* (*Svyatochny rasskaz*).

*Cross, The (1883) *Krest.*

*Crow, The (1885) *Vorona.*

*Cynic, The (1885) *Tsinik.*

*Daddy (1880) *Papasha.*

In Exile (1892) *V ssylke* (R. E. C. Long: Duckworth, 1903; S. Koteliansky & G. Cannan: C. W. Daniel, 1920; Constance Garnett: Chatto & Windus, 1916–50).

In Moscow (1891) *V Moskve* (Louis S. Friedland: Geoffrey Bles, 1924; S. Koteliansky: George Routledge & Sons, 1927).

In Moscow in Trubnaya Square (1883) *V Moskve na Trubnoy ploshchadi* (Constance Garnett: Chatto & Windus, 1916–50).

*In Our Practical Age when etc. (1883) *V nash praktichesky vek, kogda i t.d.*

In Passion Week (1887) *Na strastnoy nedele* (Marian Fell: Duckworth, 1915; Constance Garnett: Chatto & Windus, 1916–50).

*In Spring (1886) *Vesnoy*.

*In Spring (A Monologue) (1887) *Vesnoy (Stsena monolog)*.

*In the Autumn (1883) *Osenyu*.

In the Cart (1897) *Na podvode* (Marian Fell: Duckworth, 1915; Constance Garnett: Chatto & Windus, 1916–50; Penguin Books, 1938).

In the Coach-house (1887) *V saraye* (Marian Fell: Duckworth, 1915; Constance Garnett: Chatto & Windus, 1916–50).

In the Country (1886) *Na dache* (Constance Garnett: Chatto & Windus, 1916–50).

In the Dark (1886) *V potyomkakh* (Constance Garnett: Chatto & Windus, 1916–50).

*In the Drawing Room (1883) *V gostinoy*.

In the Graveyard (1884) *Na kladbishche* (Constance Garnett: Chatto & Windus, 1916–50; S. Koleliansky: George Routledge & Sons, 1927).

*In the Home for Incurables and the Aged (1884) *V priyute dlya neizlechimo-bol'nykh i prestarelykh*.

*In the Landau (1883) *V lando*.

*In the Railway Compartment (1881) *V vagone*.

*In the Railway Compartment (A Conversational Skirmish) (1885) *V Vagone (Razgovornaya perestrelka)*.

In the Ravine (1900) *V ovrage* (Marian Fell: Duckworth, 1914; Ad. L. Kaye: Heinemann, 1915; A. E. Chamot: Stanley Paul, 1926; Constance Garnett: Chatto & Windus, 1916–50; Select Tales, 1927, 1949).

*In the Steam Bath (1883–1885) *V bane*.

*In the World of Learning (1883) *V uchonom mire* (Captions to six cartoons).

In Trouble (1887) *Beda* (Constance Garnett: Chatto & Windus, 1916–50).

*Incongruous Thoughts (1884) *Nesoobraznyie mysli*.

*Intellectual Publicans (A Letter to the Editor) (1885) *Intelligenty-kabatchiki (Pis'mo v redaktsiyu)*.

*Intrigues (1887) *Intrigi*.

Ionych (1898) *Ionych* (Marian Fell: Duckworth, 1915; Constance Garnett: Chatto & Windus, 1916–50; Select Tales, 1927, 1949).

*Island Sakhalin, The (1891–1894) *Ostrov Sakhalin*.

*It Isn't Fated! (1885) *Nye sud'ba!*

Ivan Matveich (1886) *Ivan Matveich* (Constance Garnett: Chatto & Windus, 1916–50).

Ivanov (A Drama in four Acts) (1887–1889) *Ivanov (Drama v chetyryokh deystviyakh)* (Constance Garnett: Chatto & Windus, 1923, 1928, 1935, 1940, 1946, 1950; Elisaveta Fen: Penguin Classics, 1950; O. M. Sayler: The Moscow Art Theatre Series of Russian Plays, 1923).

Jeune Premier, The (1886) *Pervy lyubovnik* (Constance Garnett: Chatto & Windus, 1916–50).

Joy (1883) *Radost'* (Marian Fell: Duckworth, 1915; Constance Garnett: Chatto & Windus, 1916–50).

*Just Like Grandfather (1883) *Ves' v dedushku*.

*Kalkhas (1886) *Kalkhas*.

Kalkhas (1887) *see* Swan Song.

Kashtanka (A Story) (1887) *Kashtanka (Rasskaz)* (Constance Garnett: Chatto & Windus, 1916–50).

*Kirghizes (A school essay) (1875?) *Kirgizy*.

Kiss, The (1887) *Potseluy* (R. E. C. Long: Duckworth, 1908; Constance Garnett: Chatto & Windus, 1916–50).

*Knights without Fear and without Reproach (1883) *Rytsari bez strakha i upryoka*.

*Korsh's Theatre (1899) *Teatr F. Korsha*.

Ladies (1886) *Damy* (Constance Garnett: Chatto & Windus, 1916–50).

*Lady Holidaymaker, The (1884) *Dachnitsa*.

*Lady Lawyer, The (1883) *Yuristka*.

Lady with a Lapdog, The (1899) *Dama s sobachkoy* (S. Koteliansky & G. Cannan: C. W. Daniel, 1920; S. Koteliansky: Polybooks Todd Publishing Co., 1943; Constance Garnett: Chatto & Windus, 1916–50; Select Tales, 1927, 1949).

*Last Farewell . . . (1883) *Posledneye prosti . . .* (A poem).

*Last Female Mohican, The (1885) *Poslednyaya Mogikansha*.

Late Flowers (1882) *Tsvety zapozdalyie* (A. E. Chamot: The Commodore Press, 1941).

'A Journey to the Moon') *Na lune* (*Stsena, nye popavshaya v feyeriyu Lentovskovo* 'Puteshestviye ya lunu').

*On the Nail (1883) *Na gvozde*.

On the River (Spring scenes) (1886) *Na reke* (*Vesenniye kartinki*) (A. E. Chamot: The Commodore Press, 1941).

On the Road (1886) *Na puti* (R. E. C. Long: Duckworth, 1903; Marian Fell: Duckworth, 1914; Constance Garnett: Chatto & Windus, 1916–50).

Once a Year (1883) *Raz v god* (A. E. Chamot: The Commodore Press, 1941).

*One of Many (1887) *Odin iz mnogikh*.

*One Thousand and One Passions or The Terrible Night (A Novel in one Part with an Epilogue—dedicated to Victor Hugo) (1880) *Tysyacha odna strast'ili strashnaya noch* (*Roman v odnoy chasti s epilogom*). *Posvayashchayu Viktoru Gyugo*.

*Only Remedy, The (Apropos of the trial of the Petersburg Mutual Credit Society) (1883) *Yedinstvennoye Sredstvo* (*A propos protsesa Peter. Obshchestva Vzaimnovo Kredita*).

*Opinions about the Hat Catastrophe (1885) *Mneniya po povodu shlyapnoy katastrofy*.

Orator, The (1886) *Orator* (Marian Fell: Duckworth, 1915; Constance Garnett: Chatto & Windus, 1916–50).

*Order, The (1886) *Zakaz*.

*Our Beggars (1888) *Nashe nishchenstvo*.

Out of Sorts (1884) *Nye v dukhe* (Marian Fell: Duckworth, 1915; Constance Garnett: Chatto & Windus, 1916–50).

Overseasoned (Overdoing it) (1885) *Peresolil* (Marian Fell: Duckworth, 1914; Constance Garnett: Chatto & Windus, 1916–50).

Oysters (1884) *Ustritsy* (R. E. C. Long: Duckworth, 1908; Constance Garnett: Chatto & Windus, 1916–50).

*Pancakes (1886) *Bliny*.

Panic Fears (1886) *Strakhi* (Constance Garnett: Chatto & Windus, 1916–50).

Party, The *see* Name-Day.

*Past Experience (A psychological study) (1882) *Perezhitoye* (*Psikhologichesky etyud*).

*Patriot, The (1883) *Patriot svoevo otechestva*.

*Patronage (1883) *Protektsiya*.

Peasants (1897) *Muzhiki* (R. E. C. Long: Duckworth, 1908; Constance Garnett: Chatto & Windus, 1916–50; A. E. Chamot: Stanley Paul, 1926).

Bibliographical Index

APPENDIX TO THE REPRINT EDITION

Chekhov and Lydia Avilov

In the tenth volume of the complete edition of his works, published in 1935, Ivan Bunin, a close friend of Chekhov and Lydia Avilov, wrote: "Was there at least one great love in Chekhov's life? I don't think there was." In 1953 Bunin underlined these lines in red pencil and wrote "in a firm hand," according to his wife, "Yes, there was. With Lydia Avilov."

"I knew Lydia Avilov very well," Bunin wrote in his unfinished manuscript *About Chekhov*, "and the distinguishing traits of her character were truthfulness, intelligence, talent, modesty, a rare sense of humour even if directed against herself. After reading her reminiscences I got a different idea of Chekhov and I saw him in quite a new light. I never suspected the relationship that existed between them. Yet people still think that Chekhov never experienced a great love. I had thought so myself, but now I can say emphatically: he did experience such a love—for Lydia Avilov.

"I cannot help feeling that some people may ask: can one have absolute trust in her reminiscences? Lydia Avilov was quite exceptionally truthful. She did not conceal even the critical remarks Chekhov made about her writings nor what he had said about her. She never hinted at her love for Chekhov during her lifetime (and I had met her frequently). And yet to think how many years she had concealed it. A rare woman!

"I read the introduction to her reminiscences by a certain Kotov and I was amazed at his stupidity. He writes: 'For all that one cannot conceal the extraordinary subjectivity and onesidedness of the author [Lydia Avilov] in her treatment of the material in connection with Chekhov. One can hardly consider it entirely credible that Chekhov had expressed his feelings for Lydia Avilov in his story *About Love*.* Actually, Chekhov's attitude towards Lydia Avilov is revealed in his interest in her as a writer who could have dealt with the highly relevant subject of a woman's dependent position and the abnormalities of family life.' "

* Professor Simmons repeats this statement almost word for word!

425

Ivan Bunin underlined the last sentence and wrote in the margin in blue pencil: "What an extraordinary * * * to have written that!"

That Bunin never changed his mind about the real relationship between Chekhov and Lydia Avilov is clear from a letter I received from Mrs. Bunin on February 9, 1956. "I know," she wrote," that your opinion (about the love affair of Chekhov with Lydia Avilov) coincided with the opinion of my late husband."

The eloquent asterisks with which Bunin expressed his opinion of Kotov could be quite legitimately applied to Professor Ernest J. Simmons'laborious attempt to discredit Lydia Avilov's reminiscences published under the title *Chekhov in My Life*. A quotation or two should suffice to show how utterly divorced from life the mind of an academic can be. Professor Simmons writes: "Yet it is certainly a curious fact that though Bunin and Lydia Avilov were devoted admirers of Chekhov, not one word about him appears in their letters." Is It so curious? Would not the very fact of their "great love" have precluded Lydia from mentioning Chekhov in her letters or, indeed, as Bunin himself implies, in her talks with Bunin? To quote Professor Simmons again: "That Chekhov's exaggerated sense of duty to his family at that time could have prevented him from confirming a love once conceived is probably true, but it can be just as logically argued that it would have kept him from falling in love at all." A logical or ridiculous argument?

Professor Simmons finally quotes Chekhov's sister Masha to clinch his theory that there was "no tangible evidence" on Chekhov's part that he was in love with Lydia Avilov. Masha, it seems, declared in that characteristically proprietorial way of hers that there was "nothing to it" and that it was all "a fantasy." Does anyone really expect her to have said anything else? Is it not a fact that Chekhov never discussed his intimate life with her? Is it not also a fact that she was dead set against Chekhov's marriage to Olga Knipper?

—DAVID MAGARSHACK
Hamstead, London, 1970

INDEX

Index

Index

Index

Index

Index